MICHAEL SHAMIYEH ‹
and DOM Research Laboratory (Ed.)

CREATING DESIRED FUTURES

How Design Thinking Innovates Business ≪

Birkhäuser
Basel

Editor
Michael Shamiyeh

Copy Editing
Raquel Macho

Design
Reklamebüro Linz/Austria
www.reklamebuero.at

A CIP catalogue record for this book is available from the
Library of Congress, Washington D.C., USA.

Bibliographic information published by the German National
Library. The German National Library lists this publication
in the Deutsche Nationalbibliografie; detailed bibliographic
data are available on the Internet at http://dnb.d-nb.de.

© 2010 Birkhäuser GmbH, Basel
P.O. Box 133, CH-4010 Basel, Switzerland
Printed on acid-free paper produced from
chlorine-free pulp. TCF ∞

Printed in Germany

ISBN 978-3-0346-0368-3

Despite intensive research efforts it was not possible to identify the copyright
holders in all cases. Justifiable claims will be honored within the parameters of
customary agreements.

9 8 7 6 5 4 3 2 1

www.birkhauser-architecture.com

Bundesministerium für
Unterricht, Kunst und Kultur

gmbh

TABLE OF CONTENTS ❮

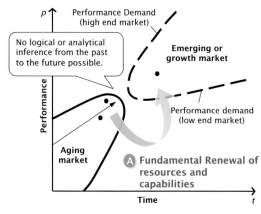

Performance Demand
(high end market)

No logical or analytical
inference from the past
to the future possible.

Emerging or
growth market

Performance demand
(low end market)

Performance

Aging
market

Ⓐ Fundamental Renewal of
resources and
capabilities

Time   t

1< Radical Remaking

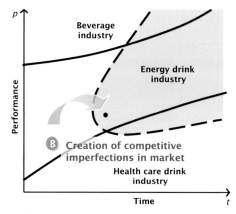

Beverage
industry

Energy drink
industry

Performance

Ⓑ Creation of competitive
imperfections in market

Health care drink
industry

Time   t

3< Opportunity Creation

4

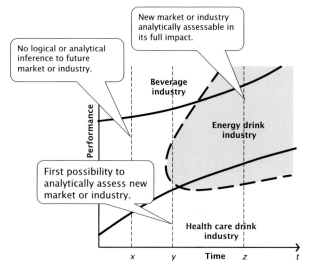

New market or industry
analytically assessable in
its full impact.

No logical or analytical
inference to future
market or industry.

Beverage
industry

Energy drink
industry

Performance

First possibility to
analytically assess new
market or industry.

Health care drink
industry

x   y   Time   z   t

2< Assessing the Future

FOREWORD ❮ Michael Shamiyeh

Mechanisms of Discontent

"Most corporate strategy problems and governmental policy problems are at least as ill structured as problems of architectural or engineering design. The tools now being forged for aiding architectural design will provide a basis for building tools that can aid in formulating, assessing, and monitoring public energy or environmental policies, or in guiding corporate product and investment strategies."
Herbert Simon (1986)

Every economic organization or institution is faced with two basic challenges: Executing its current business objectives in order to survive today's challenges, and adapting those objectives to threats and opportunities to survive the challenges of tomorrow. As Axelrod and Cohen (2000) have shown recently in "Harnessing Complexity," or Drucker (1969) in "The Age of Discontinuity" some decades ago, executing and adapting are the absolute essentials for any design in living systems. In a world that is increasingly driven by faster cycles of change, the risk of eventually destroying a business by merely continuing what one is doing—that is, in failing to adapt to a changing internal or external environment simultaneously—is higher than ever today. In other words, an organization is continuously called upon to identify what it must avoid at all costs to avert self-destruction and to explore strategies for potential moves with respect to current objectives (Beinhocker, 2007; Collins & Porras, 2002; Peters, 1997; Peters & Waterman, 1982).

RECENT HISTORY REVEALS THAT IN A WORLD THAT IS INCREASINGLY DRIVEN BY FASTER CYCLES OF CHANGE, THE NEED TO RADICALLY REMAKE—AS OPPOSED TO JUST MODIFY OR OPTIMIZE—A BUSINESS TO ONGOING ENVIRONMENTAL CHANGES IS HIGHER THAN EVER TODAY.

Take the music industry as an example. The shift from stereo records to compact discs certainly did not demand a fundamental redesign of the very business model of selling music. For people engaged in this business, it was not necessary to substantially alter existing capabilities or to acquire new ones. That is to say, this particular change of the music's medium did not necessitate a deep transformation of the knowledge and skills required to create and replicate capabilities needed by the business such as procedures for ordering new inventory, advertising and accounting among many other activities. Despite the negligible need for some new shelves or record players, existing orders and channels of interaction between consumers, distributors and manufacturers simply remained unchanged for the most part. On the other hand, the transformation towards online music stores necessitated a radical remaking of the business model. It totally changed the means, ends and processes the music industry was accustomed to. Engaging in such a business means acquiring completely new combinations of resources to create value.

Confronted with such disruptive situations, the managerial practice of problem solving—of trying to "fix" something established that is suddenly broken—becomes misleading if not unfeasible. It entices someone to seek something one does not wish to go away rather than to create something one really desires to exist. The distinction between the two is fundamental. In problem solving, in analytically identifying flaws in existing situations, established products, processes or organizational structures are adapted to a changing business environment; in creation, energies are spent in establishing those resources that possibly generate value in light of a vision a business is seen as evolving towards in the future. Hence, whereas the former attempts to modify or optimize prevailing knowledge, skills and capabilities, the latter is forced to ask a new set of questions about how to run the business.

But for other reasons, the managerial practice of problem solving becomes misleading, particularly in the context of organizations facing disruptive situations. Men and women trained in business schools tend to take insights gathered from either directly observable facts or past evidence as a source for successful problem solving. It is assumed that possible futures are to be derived from what has been established. Nevertheless, such an approach is entangled in a series of shortcomings with regard to creating desired futures.

First, though people do not analyze their way into the future (neither on the basis of what has been established, nor on the basis of an analysis of something that does not exist), an inference from an analytic examination of prevailing or past circumstances does not necessarily successfully predicting upcoming futures. By the same token, one cannot expect people to lead organizations towards the creation of something radically new that they do not need now but rather tomorrow (Christensen, 2000). As Apple founder Steve Jobs put it, "People don't know what they want until you show it to them"(Kahney, 2008).

IN OTHER WORDS, PEOPLE CANNOT SERIOUSLY ANSWER QUESTIONS REGARDING AN INTEREST IN FUTURE PRODUCTS OR SERVICES THEY HAVE NEITHER DIRECTLY NOR INDIRECTLY EXPERIENCED.

To give an example: For managers in the beverage industry or its biggest competitor, the health care drink industry, it was not possible to analytically assess the upcoming new energy drink industry with Red Bull at its forefront. Certainly, various trends in society may have indicated the need for drinks that are able to quickly energize people—for example, in light of the growing demands placed on people in all spheres of life, beginning from school to business life. However, indications did not tell industry executives the means by which to energize people. Aside from Dietrich Mateschitz's energy drink, there could have been many answers to this demand, starting from more traditional offerings such as coffee or tea all the way to various kinds of drugs. Even industry experts were unable to predict the success of this sector. When consultants were asked by Red Bull founder Dietrich Mateschitz to give their insights into the drink, their reaction was devastating. The drink was considered to be extremely bad, the sticky-sweet taste horrible, and the argument that the drink energizes body and soul regarded as completely irrelevant. Today the success of this industry is well known;

with growth rates of about 50% a year, it is one of today's fastest growing sectors (Heller, 2007).

Second, a focus on problem solving entices the problem solver to exploit the potential of established situations (rather than those he imagines). Henderson and Clark (1990), among others (Cyert & March, 1992; Nelson & Winter, 1990), have shown that organizations build knowledge and capability around the recurrent tasks they perform. The sort of skills and knowledge an organization accumulates in its history thereby determines the choices about which technological problems it would solve and which it would avoid. For example, in the early days of the automobile industry, there was a great deal of experimentation. Cars were built with gasoline, electric or steam engines, with steering wheels or tillers, and with wooden or metal bodies. Aware of the virtues of the horse-drawn carriage in muddy streets, engineers even tried to place engines on front axles without success because the weight of the engine hampered steering. However, once these phases of experimentation were brought to an end, core design concepts of how major functions are performed and how certain components are integrated became accepted. The established core design concept for the car then encompassed the use of a gasoline engine that was connected to the back wheels through a transmission and a drive train, and was mounted on a frame rather than on the axles. Hence, once core concepts of automobile design had been accepted, engineers did not re-evaluate previous decisions in every subsequent design; rather, initial sets of components were refined and elaborated.

PAST EXPERIENCE IN GRADUAL ELABORATION MOLDED ENGINEERS' INFORMATION FILTERS AND ENTICED THEM TO IMMEDIATELY IDENTIFY WHAT IS MOST CRUCIAL IN THE INFORMATION STREAM.

This led to the situation in which, for about 150 years, the automobile industry ceased investment in imagining alternative configurations of the established set of components—for example, to imagine a front-wheel drive. It

- An organization's communication channels develop around those interactions that are critical to its task.
- Information filters of an organization also embody its core knowledge.
- Information filters and communication channels develop and help engineers to work efficiently.

Tesla Induction motor

Lohner–Porsche Wheel Hub Car, 1900

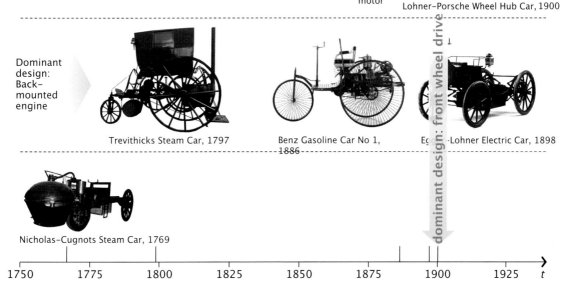

Dominant design: Back-mounted engine

Trevithicks Steam Car, 1797

Benz Gasoline Car No 1, 1886

Egger-Lohner Electric Car, 1898

dominant design: front wheel drive

Nicholas–Cugnots Steam Car, 1769

1750   1775   1800   1825   1850   1875   1900   1925   *t*

4❬ Gradual evolution/revolution of dominant car design

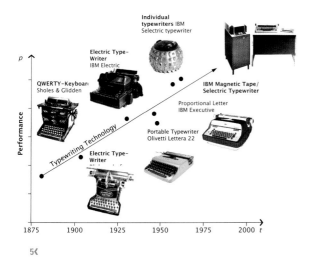

p

Individual typewriters IBM Selectric typewriter

Electric Type-Writer IBM Electric

QWERTY-Keyboard Sholes & Glidden

Performance

IBM Magnetic Tape/ Selectric Typewriter

Proportional Letter IBM Executive

Portable Typewriter Olivetti Lettera 22

Electric Type-Writer

Typewriting Technology

1875   1900   1925   1950   1975   2000 *t*

5❬

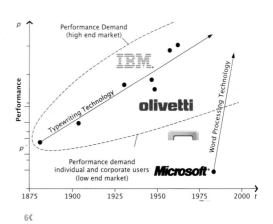

p

Performance Demand (high end market)

IBM

Performance

Typewriting Technology

olivetti

Word Processing Technology

p'

Performance demand individual and corporate users (low end market)

Microsoft

1875   1900   1925   1950   1975   2000 *t*

6❬

The gradual automation of writing and editing, and the refinement (sustaining) of the technology

7

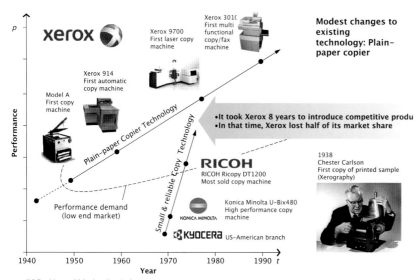

Modest changes to existing technology: Plain-paper copier

xerox

Xerox 301(
First multi functional copy/fax machine

Xerox 9700
First laser copy machine

Xerox 914
First automatic copy machine

Model A
First copy machine

Plain-paper Copier Technology

Small & reliable Copy Technology

•It took Xerox 8 years to introduce competitive produ
•In that time, Xerox lost half of its market share

RICOH
RICOH Ricopy DT1200
Most sold copy machine

Performance demand
(low end market)

Konica Minolta U-Bix480
High performance copy machine

KONICA MINOLTA

KYOCERA US-American branch

1938
Chester Carlson
First copy of printed sample
(Xerography)

p

Performance

1940   1950   1960   1970   1980   1990 *t*

Year

8

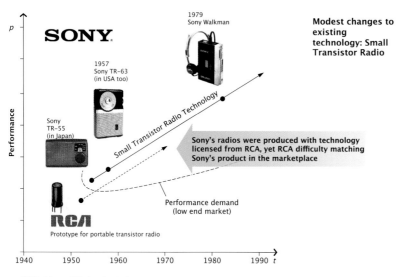

Modest changes to existing technology: Small Transistor Radio

SONY.

1979
Sony Walkman

1957
Sony TR-63
(in USA too)

Sony
TR-55
(in Japan)

Small Transistor Radio Technology

Sony's radios were produced with technology licensed from RCA, yet RCA difficulty matching Sony's product in the marketplace

Performance demand
(low end market)

RCA
Prototype for portable transistor radio

p

Performance

1940   1950   1960   1970   1980   1990 *t*

was up to young entrepreneur Ferdinand Porsche to ignore past experience and to imagine the first front-wheel drive by proposing to attach an induction motor directly to the wheel hubs. By doing so, he not only reduced the transmission's loss of engine power by half but also succeeded in inventing the first four-wheel drive and the world's first hybrid car ("Das Elektormotorautomobil Lohner-Porsche," 1900). A similar case can be made for IBM and Olivetti. Both organizations, whose knowledge, skills and capabilities grew tremendously in the wake of the gradual refinement of typewriting technology, were unable to decipher the emergence of word processing technology. Even a close look at their customers did not provide information necessary for both companies to recognize the emergence of the disruptive technology of word processing. This leads us to the next limitation of common managerial practice.

THIRD, DIRECTLY OBSERVABLE FACTS DO NOT NECESSARILY MAKE SENSE AT THE TIME THEY ARE GATHERED.

The case of Xerox and small tablet copiers, and the case of Sony's transistor radio are two examples. Xerox pioneered the plain-paper copier by inventing the industry's core technologies. In the late 1940s, the company released the first copy machine. By carefully listening to its customers, Xerox gradually improved copier machines over subsequent years by adding features such as automatization, speed enhancement, laser printing technology, colour, or other functions such as fax. However, in the mid-1970s, Xerox was confronted with competitors offering copiers that were much smaller and more reliable than the traditional product. The new product, which required little new scientific or engineering knowledge, obviously did not make sense to Xerox, which always stays close to its customers. Despite the fact that Xerox invented the core technologies and had enormous experience, the competitive products captured half of Xerox's market share. It took Xerox almost eight years to introduce a competitive product (Clark, 1985). The case of Sony is similar. RCA developed a prototype of a portable transistorized radio in the mid-1950s. Since it saw little reason to pursue such an apparently inferior technology, it licensed the technology to Sony, which then was a fairly small company intent on gaining entry to the US market. Even after Sony's success became apparent, RCA had great difficulty matching Sony's product in the marketplace (Clark, 1985). In short, the important managerial impetus to observe and stay in touch with customers to sustain a business may provide misleading facts for handling the future, simply because the pace of progress that markets demand or can absorb may be different from the progress offered by products or services.

In summary, business is in need of new ways to create desired futures. Managerial practice of problem solving on the premises of either observable facts or past experience may be sufficient for sustaining a business; however, at times of disruptive situations, they are certainly insufficient for the long-term sustainability of the business.

THEN, A BUSINESS NEEDS RADICAL REMAKING RATHER THAN INCREMENTAL IMPROVEMENT.

The creative-analytical approach at work in design, on the other hand, takes for granted that the process of finding a solution to a problem will require the invention of new alternatives given certain parameters and constrains. That is, rather than directing someone's attention particularly to the problem space and its likely solution, the design approach favors creating and seizing new opportunities.

It does not exploit established situations but supports paradigm shifts—radical changes of how a business is conceived in regard to existing products, processes or organizational structures. And because its goal is to create a set of actions transforming a situation from its current reality to its desired future, design becomes the very essence in today's strategic business thinking, whose very objective is to bring about those conditions most favorable to a business' future.

This book sets forth a series of contributions on design thinking broaching the issue on several grounds. It starts with a section on the relevance of the design approach for the future of management practice and education, and is followed by a section with detailed insights into its operative nature. Section three demonstrates the virtues of the design approach in the context of sustainability and shows how design is able to create a positive link between business and the environment. A series of cases are presented.

SECTION FOUR FOCUSES ON THE BENEFITS OF DESIGN METHODOLOGY IN BUSINESS STRATEGY FORMATION. THE FINAL SECTION HIGHLIGHTS ORGANIZATIONAL REQUESTS TO SUPPORT DESIGN PROCESSES FOR INNOVATION.

References

Axelrod, R., and Cohen, M. D. 2000. *Harnessing complexity: Organizational implications of a scientific frontier.* New York: Simon & Schuster.

Beinhocker, E. D. 2007. *The origin of wealth: The radical remaking of economics and what it means for business and society.* Cambridge, MA: Harvard Business.

Christensen, C. M. 2000. *The innovator's dilemma.* New York: Harper Collins Business Essentials.

Clark, K. B. 1985. The interaction of design hierarchies and market concepts in technological evolution. *Research Policy,* 14(5), 235–251.

Collins, J. C. and Porras, J. I. 2002. *Built to last. Successful habits of visionary companies (3 ed.).* New York: HarperCollins.

Cyert, R. M. and March, G. J. 1992. *Behavioral theory of the firm (3rd ed.).* London: Blackwell Publishers.

Das Elektormotorautomobil Lohner-Porsche. 1900. *Allgemeine Automobile-Zeitung.* February, 25.

Drucker, P. 1969. *Age of discontinuity: Guidelines to our changing society.* New York: Harper & Row.

Heller, L. 2007. Energy drinks outperform all other beverages, report. http://www.nutraingredients-usa.com/Consumer-Trends/Energy-drinks-outperform-all-other-beverages-report. Accessed on Dec 7, 2009.

Henderson, R. M. and Clark, K. B. 1990. Architectural innovation—the reconfiguration of existing product technologies and the failure of established firms. *Administrative Science Quarterly,* 35(1), 9–30.

Kahney, L. 2008. *Inside Steven's brain.* New York: Penguin Group.

Nelson, R. R. and Winter, G. S. 1990. *An evolutionary theory of economic change (Reprint ed.):* Belknap Press.

Peters, T. 1997. *The circle of innovation: You can't shrink your way to greatness.* London: Hodder & Stoughton.

Peters, T. and Waterman, R. H. 1982. *In search of excellence.* New York: Harper and Row.

Simon, H. A. 1986. *Decision making and problem solving.* Washington, DC: National Academy of Sciences.

11

CONTRIBUTORS ❮

Adam Kahane ❮ Adam Kahane is a partner in Reos Partners, an international organisation dedicated to supporting and building capacity for innovative collective action in complex social systems, and an Associate Fellow of the Institute for Science, Innovation and Society at the University of Oxford's Saïd Business School. Adam is a leading organizer, designer and facilitator of processes through which business, government, and civil society leaders can work together to address their most complex challenges. He is the author of "Solving Tough Problems: An Open Way of Talking, Listening, and Creating New Realities" and "Power and Love: A Theory and Practice of Social Change." During the early 1990s, Adam was head of Social, Political, Economic and Technological Scenarios for Royal Dutch Shell in London. Previously he held strategy and research positions with Pacific Gas and Electric Company (San Francisco), the Organisation for Economic Cooperation and Development (Paris), the International Institute for Applied Systems Analysis (Vienna), the Institute for Energy Economics (Tokyo), and the Universities of Toronto, British Columbia, California, and the Western Cape. Adam has a B.Sc. in Physics (First Class Honors) from McGill University, an M.A. in Energy and Resource Economics from the University of California, and an M.A. in Applied Behavioral Science from Bastyr University.

Albin Kälin ❮ Albin Kälin is CEO of EPEA Switzerland GmbH. In the 90s under his management, the Swiss Rohner Textil AG won 19 international recognitions and design awards. This environmental and economic management approach led him to become a world renowned pioneer. As a result the development of the first Cradle to Cradle® products worldwide: the product lines Climatex®. In 2005 Prof. Dr. Michael Braungart appointed Albin Kälin as CEO of the scientific consultancy EPEA Internationale Umweltforschung GmbH in Hamburg, Germany (www.epea.com). Since 2006 he has supported additional intensive developments of Cradle to Cradle® for the Netherlands and as CEO of EPEA Nederland bv, established in 2008. At the end of 2009, Albin Kälin founded EPEA Switzerland GmbH. As CEO of a management team he implements Cradle to Cradle® projects in all industries in Switzerland and Austria and in accordance with its core expertise in the textile industry—worldwide. Under the slogan "Back to the Roots" Albin Kälin stepped down from his two managing activities with EPEA Hamburg and Netherlands at the end of 2009 to continue to focus on his passion: to successfully implement Cradle to Cradle® projects worldwide thereby encouraging the Cradle to Cradle® breakthrough.

Alejandro Gutierrez ❮ Alejandro Gutierrez is an Associate Director at Arup Urban Design leading a range of urban development projects globally. The projects take place in Dongtan Eco City, Shanghai, Wanzhuang Eco City, Beijing and Port Regeneration Strategy, Copenhagen. Further projects are Dubai Waterfront, Masterplan Sustainability Review, Stratford City, London, Battersea Power Station, London, Wembley Industrial Estates in London, and Urbanya Strategic Plan in Santiago, Chile. He also is an invited lecturer at London School of Economics, Said Business School, Oxford University, UCL Bartlett School of Architecture, Universidad Iberoamericana, Universidad Catolica in Chile, Architectural Association, UK, RIBA. He has also done several interviews for the BBC, The Guardian, Le Monde, Wired Magazine and Monocle, regarding sustainable urban development in the context of China and developing countries. Prior to joining Arup he worked in Chile in a range of practices and projects associated with urban development, urban planning and regeneration.

Andrew Bollinger ❮ Andrew Bollinger graduated from Dartmouth College in the United States in 2002 and worked with Prof. Dr. Michael Braungart at EPEA in Hamburg, Germany from 2003 to 2005. In this context, he performed research on projects relating to the application of Cradle to Cradle Design in various industries, such as textiles and automobiles. After spending a year teaching at a technical university in Hangzhou, China in 2006, Andrew undertook a Master's degree in Industrial Ecology at TU Delft and Leiden University in the Netherlands. For the past year, he has been performing research within the Faculty of Technology, Policy and Management at TU Delft, focusing on combining aspects of Cradle to Cradle and Industrial Ecology. Andrew's current research is premised on the idea that material flows exist in a complex socio-technical environment, and explores the application of simulation modeling approaches to realizing Cradle to Cradle metabolisms within such a context.

Arnab Chatterjee ❮ Dr Arnab Chatterjee graduated with an honours degree in Chemistry from Oriel College, University of Oxford in 2000. Between 2000 and 2004, he worked for Professor John Foord, in the Oxford Centre for Surface Science, developing novel semiconductors for use in electrochemical applications. Having completed his doctorate, Dr Chatterjee set up a science communication company to help explain how the findings of scientists translate into tangible consequences in the "real world". The increasing prominence of questions surrounding sustainable and secure energy led to a position within Shell Global Solutions, Innovation Research in 2005. Between 2005 and 2008, he developed novel chemistries and processes for natural gas production and next generation automotive drivetrains. From 2007 to 2008, he also headed an innovation network whose intent was to capture a whole range of ideas around both the current and future business environments, and demonstrate their preliminary feasibility. From the beginning of 2009, Arnab Chatterjee has been based in Canada, working within the unconventional oil domain. The project demonstrates the difficulties of translating a complex technical solution to operational scale in a challenging metereological, political, and economic environment.

Christian Votava ‹ Christian Votava is an expert in strategy, value-added marketing, and organizational efficiency and is developing new marketing and market research methodologies for saturated markets. He holds a doctorate in chemistry and an MBA. He was active for more than 10 years in leading marketing & sales positions in Europe and USA. He was a consultant at companies like A.T. Kearney or Logika AG. Today he is a Partner at REALISE strategic consultants, www.realise.de, where he empowers financial and consumer goods companies to operate safely and successfully in highly competitive markets. In addition to project work, he assists business managers and boards in their strategic and tactical decisions. Parallel to his business activity, Dr Votava has been lecturing Strategic Management at the University of Borås in Sweden since 2005. Together with Prof. Simonetta Carbonaro he has been co-directing the The Design of Prosperity initiative, a think tank focused on socio-cultural forces influencing new cultural movements, driving societal changes, and fostering new lifestyles.

David Griesbach ‹ David Griesbach is senior consultant at the Strategic Knowledge Group (www.skgroup.ch) in Zurich and writes his dissertation on "Strategic Agility" as research associate of RISE Management Research (www.rise.com) and in cooperation with the Swiss Institute for Small and Middle-Sized Companies of the University of St. Gallen. In the years before, he worked as a consultant at GGK Basel which became the Swiss subsidiary of Lowe Worldwide Advertising Agency where he was in charge of national and international customers of this branch.

Fred Collopy ‹ Fred Collopy received his PhD from the Wharton School of the University of Pennsylvania. He does research on business forecasting, visualization, and the application of design ideas to management. His research has been published in both academic and practitioner journals including Chief Executive and Interfaces. He co-edited the book "Managing as Designing," which was published by Stanford University Press in 2004. He has designed systems for forecasting, desk management, and both abstract and accounting visualization. He is an expert contributor to the Business Week and Fast Company blogs dealing with innovation, design and management. A website detailing his work is available at http://collopy.case.edu.

Fred Dust ‹ Fred Dust is a partner and a practice lead at IDEO. Fred leads Systems at Scale, the group responsible for helping clients with large systemic infrastructural questions from governmental shifts, to behavior change, and beyond.

Gerald Fliegel ❮ Gerald Fliegel graduated in the field Mechanical Engineering in 1984 at the Technical University of Graz. After a two years' engagement at Voest Alpine in Linz, he started working for Siemens as a project manager and consultant for internal software projects, mostly in Munich and Berlin in 1986. In 1995 he moved to Vienna as a project director and later on as product manager, responsible for the Siemens chip card terminals for the nationwide operating "electronic wallet". In 1998 he was assigned head of Innovation Management and began working on the conceptual design and build-up of this department. His main focus was to identify and develop new business opportunities for Siemens Austria. From 2003 to 2007 he was responsible for the newly created department "Intellectual Asset Management" which was created to exploit synergies between the activities of Innovation Management, patent department and the employees' "Suggestion of Improvement" System. Moving to Siemens VAI in Linz in 2007 he was assigned Vice President "Research and Development" and actually holds the function of a Business Administrator for central R&D. From 2004–2008 he lectured "Business Communication" at the Fachhochschule Kuchl and the University of Salzburg.

Greg Van Alstyne ❮ Associate Professor at the Ontario College of Art & Design (OCAD), and Director of Research at Strategic Innovation Lab (sLab), Toronto. Greg is a design educator and consultant with 20 years of experience in communications and creative direction. He holds a Master of Science in Integrated Digital Media from Polytechnic Institute of NYU. Greg's current research centers on causes and effects of innovation stemming from the relationship between design and emergence in complex systems, and he is co-PI on a project to investigate the future of the book. Prior to his OCAD appointment, as inaugural director of the Institute without Boundaries, Greg oversaw the student team that conceived, designed and produced the multi-faceted Massive Change project. His work as creative director with venerable interaction design firm IconNicholson NY includes collaboration with Rem Koolhaas and IDEO on Prada's New York Epicenter Store, and he was formerly the founding head of the Department of New Media at The Museum of Modern Art, New York.

16

Heather Fraser ❮ Heather Fraser is Director and co-founder of Rotman DesignWorks™ at the Rotman School of Management, University of Toronto. She is also an adjunct professor of Business Design at Rotman, which she joined in 2005 after over 25 years in industry. A center for design-based innovation and education at the University of Toronto's Rotman School of Management, DesignWorks develops and delivers leading edge practices in the field of Business Design to students and executives internationally. As director and adjunct professor, Heather leads the research and development of Business Design methodologies, student programs and enterprise training through collaboration with corporations, educational institutions and design practitioners around the world. Through executive training and project consulting, DesignWorks has helped corporations and public sector organizations around the world adopt new practices and create value through the application of Business Design principles and practices. Heather brings over 25 years of business experience in Business Design to DesignWorks (Procter & Gamble, Ogilvy & Mather, TAXI Advertising and Design).

Ilya Prokopoff ❮ Ilya Prokopoff is an IDEO partner and co-leads the firm's Transformation practice, which helps clients use the tools and methods of design to work in new ways, address the challenges of the future, and effect change within their organizations.

Jamshid Gharajedaghi ❮ Jamshid Gharajedaghi, Managing Partner of INTERACT, was formerly the Director of The Busch Center, the research arm of the Social Systems Sciences Department, and Adjunct Professor of Systems Sciences at The Wharton School, University of Pennsylvania (1979–1986). He began his career with IBM's World Trade Corporation where he served as a Senior Systems Engineer (1963–1969). He left IBM to become CEO of the Industrial Management Institute (1969–1979). He has held teaching positions at: Villanova University School of Management (2000–present), Wharton School, University of Pennsylvania (1979–1986), IBM Education Centers (1965–1969), University of California, Berkeley (1961–1963). Jamshid was the project manager for two internationally acclaimed projects: New Economic Order, an United Nations project and Goals for Mankind, a Club of Rome project. Mr. Gharajedaghi has written several books, including "Systems Thinking, Managing Chaos & Complexity, A Platform for Designing Business Architecture," "Prologue to National Development Planning," "Towards a Systems Theory of Organization," and "A Guide to Controlling Your Corporation's Future." He is the author of numerous published articles in various international scientific and management journals.

Jeanne Liedtka ❮ Jeanne Liedtka is a professor at the Darden Graduate School of Business Administration at the University of Virginia. Formerly the Executive Director of the School's Batten Institute, Jeanne has also served as Chief Learning Officer for the United Technologies Corporation (UTC), headquartered in Hartford, Connecticut, and as the Associate Dean of the MBA Program at Darden. Jeanne's current teaching responsibilities focus on design thinking, innovation, and organic growth in the MBA and Executive Education Programs at Darden. Jeanne's current research interests focus on exploring how design thinking can be used to enrich our ability to create inclusive strategic conversations about organizational futures. Her new book, "The Catalyst: How YOU Can Lead Extraordinary Growth," co-authored with R. Rosen and R. Wiltbank was published in March, 2009. Jeanne received her DBA in Management Policy from Boston University and her MBA from the Harvard Business School. She has been involved in the corporate strategy field since beginning her career as a strategy consultant for the Boston Consulting Group.

John Thackara ❮ John Thackara is Director of Doors of Perception (Doors), a sustainability design network active in Europe and India. People participate in Doors who need to imagine sustainable and engaging futures—and take design steps to realize them. Founded as a conference in 1993, Doors now connects together a worldwide network of paradigm-changing designers, artists, technology innovators, and grassroots innovators. John Thackara also helps cities and regions build next-generations institutions. These enable designers, other specialists, and citizens, to learn together in new ways. A former London bus driver, and later a book and magazine editor, John was the first Director (1993–1999) of the Netherlands Design Institute. He was program director in 2007 of Designs of the time (Dott 07) a new biennial in North East England. And in 2008 he was commissioner of City Eco Lab at Cité du Design in St. Etienne, the French desing biennal. John is an associate of the social innovation incubator, The Young Foundation, and is a senior advisor on sustainability to the UK Design Council.

Kamil Michlewski ❮ Dr Kamil Michlewski is a Senior Consultant at The Value Engineers—a strategic brand consultancy based in UK. He is an account manager and works with a number of blue-chip clients on issue ranging from global consumer segmentation to brand strategy. Dr Michlewski, previously worked as a senior strategy lecturer at Newcastle Business School. He was awarded a PhD by the School of Design at Northumbria, having completed a programme supported by University and Oxford's Saïd Business School. In his academic capacity he has published on the role of design and designers in organisational settings; dimensions of tacit knowledge and aesthetics in organisational learning. He has presented at international conferences including the European Academy of Management, European Group for Organisational Studies, Design Management Institute and European Academy of Design.

18

Marco Murillo ❮ Marco began his career in commerce at age seven when he launched his first business Blackberries Inc. Marco has since worked at Nike's World headquarters as a Global Footwear Product Line Manager prior to joining Nike's European Headquarters in The Netherlands. He currently works as a European Footwear Category Manager presiding over a sizable footwear business while continually seeking and translating market and consumer insights into product solutions. Marco consults on product design and concept briefing for Nike and other non-footwear related companies. He regularly participates on behalf of Nike at industry and PR events. He most recently partook in the Fashion v. Sport Symposium organized by the Victoria and Albert Museum in London. Outside of the business world, Marco enjoys restoring vintage road bikes, cooking and collecting antique oddities. Marco holds a BA in International Management from Pepperdine University and currently lives and works in Amsterdam.

Markus Miessen ❰ Markus Miessen (*1978) is an architect, writer and consultant. In 2002, he set up Studio Miessen (www.studiomiessen.com), a collaborative agency for spatial practice and cultural inquiry, and in 2007 was founding partner of the architectural practice nOffice (www.nOffice.eu). In various collaborations, Miessen has published books such as "The Nightmare of Participation" (Sternberg/Merve, 2010), "East Coast Europe" (Sternberg, 2008), "The Violence of Participation" (Sternberg, 2007), "With/Without—Spatial Products, Practices and Politics in the Middle East" (Bidoun, 2007), and "Did Someone Say Participate?" (MIT Press, 2006). His work has been exhibited and published widely, including at the Lyon, Venice, and Shenzhen Biennials. Miessen has taught internationally at institutions such as the AA (London), Berlage Institute (Rotterdam), Columbia and MIT. He has consulted the Slovenian Government, the European Kunsthalle, the Serpentine Gallery and the Swiss think tank WIRE. In 2008, he founded the Winter School Middle East. Miessen is a Harvard fellow, a PhD candidate at Goldsmiths, and a Professor for Architecture at the Hochschule für Gestaltung, Karlsruhe.

Michael Braungart ❰ Michael Braungart is a chemist and founder of EPEA International ecology (1987) and co-founder of McDonough Braungart Design Chemistry (MBDC), in Charlottesville, Virginia. While completing his doctorate at the University of Hannover, he founded the international chemistry division of Greenpeace. Since 1984 he has lectured to businesses, and institutions around the world proposing critical new concepts for ecological chemistry and materials flow management called Cradle to Cradle®. In 2002, he co-authored with William McDonough, the bestseller "Cradle to Cradle: Remaking the Way We Make Things." The documentary film "Waste Equals Food" followed the success of the book. Prof. Dr. Braungart currently concentrates his efforts on collaboration with multinationals like Nike shoes, Aveda Cosmetics, Herman Miller furniture, and Method cleaning products. He has worked on issues of materials assessment, waste and energy balances, life-cycle design, design for reincarnation and designing for disassembly. Prof. Dr. Braungart was instrumental in the creation of the compostable fabric line Climatex Lifecycle, and he continues to expand the range of his consultations with companies such as Heidelberg Cement, Desso carpets, AVR van Gansewinkel, Forbo flooring, Continental Tire, and DSM.

Michael Shamiyeh ❰ Michael Shamiyeh holds degrees from Harvard, AA London and TU Vienna and is head and professor of DOM Research Laboratory as well as CEO of Shamiyeh Associates. He concerns himself with the creation and integration of innovative business ideas in organizations. Since 2008 he investigates this topic also at the Department for Strategic Management at the University of St. Gallen. Michael has published in several international journals and books as well as popular media. He has won several national and international awards including the Innovation Prize (2008) awarded by the Austrian Ministry of Science and Research.

Richard J. Boland, Jr. ❮ Richard J. Boland Jr. is Professor of Information Systems and Professor of Cognitives Science at the Weatherhead School of Management, Case Western Reserve University. Prior to joining the Weatherhead School in 1989, Richard Boland was Professor of Accounting at the University of Illinois at Urbana-Champaign. He has been a visiting Professor at the UCLA Anderson Graduate School of Management, and has held the Malmsten Chair at the Gothenburg School of Economics, University of Gothenburg, Sweden. Currently, he also serves as a Fellow at the Judge Business School. Professor Boland's research emphasizes interpretive studies of how individuals experience the design, implemention and use of information technologies. Some representative publications include "Perspective Making and Perspective Taking in Communities of Knowing," Organization Science (1995), "Knowledge Representation and Knowledge Transfer," Academy of Management Journal (2001), and "Wakes of Innovation in Project Networks" Organization Science (2007) which won an Academy of Management 2008 award for best published paper.

20

Robert Bauer ❮ Robert M. Bauer is professor of Organization and Innovation at Johannes Kepler University, Linz. His research focuses on the management of innovation processes and the enhancement of industrial creativity—including the potential and risk in integrating management with art and design. Dr. Bauer was a visiting professor for several years at the University of Toronto's Rotman School of Management, where he developed curriculum on "Integrative Thinking". His research has appeared in major journals in North America and the German speaking realm. He has been active as a speaker and advisor in Europe and North America and is also a registered psychotherapist coaching senior executives. His writings explore the consequences of different epistemological modes for organizational design and behavior as well as for the philosophy of management and organization.

Simon Grand ❮ Simon Grand is an economist and entrepreneur / founder and academic director of RISE Management Research at the University of St. Gallen (www.rise.ch), researching the strategic entrepreneurship and management of technological innovation and organizational change / founding partner of TATIN Strategy Innovation Zurich GmbH, developing innovative perspectives and robust solutions in the areas of strategy and innovation, change and succession, management and corporate governance, on the level of executives and owners, board of directors and management teams (www.tatin.info) / senior researcher at the Academy of Art and Design, Basel. Simon Grand is engaged in international research, publication, lecture, teaching and consulting activities, with a focus on entrepreneurial strategizing, innovation strategy, strategic change, research and knowledge management, artistic research and design fiction.

Simonetta Carbonaro ❮ Simonetta Carbonaro is an expert in consumer psychology, strategic marketing and design management. Carbonaro has been working as senior strategic advisor for main design, fashion design and branding companies, retailing companies, IT corporations, luxury goods companies, food service brands and investment banks. In 1999 she co-founded REALISE, a business consulting firm based in Germany, where she is actively involved in values branding, strategic design and innovation management. She has been lecturing at the postgraduate design school Domus Academy in Milan and is a partner of the research pool and member of the advisory board of the internationally renowned Swiss Gottlieb Duttweiler Institute for marketing and social studies. Since 2002 she has been a professor in Design Management and Humanistic Marketing at The Swedish School of Textiles at the University of Borås.

 Sonja Zillner ❮ Sonja Zillner studied Mathematics and Psychology, and did her PHD-Studies in computer science specializing in knowledge management. For several years she has been working as project leader for technology and innovation projects at Siemens AG Corporate Technology. She is a consultant at osb Tübingen GmbH specializing in innovation and change and lecturing at University of Vienna.

 Thomas Duschlbauer ❮ Cultural theorist and lecturer at the Johannes Kepler University and University of Applied Sciences Hagenberg. Graduated in Media Science and Politics at the University of Vienna. Cultural Studies at the University of London. Several research stays in the USA and U.K. He participated in several congresses and published in scholarly magazines. Associate member of staff at the Goldsmiths College (Centre for Urban and Community Research), London.

 Ward M. Eagen ❮ Ward M. Eagen is a Senior Researcher in Design and Innovation, Institute of Innovation and Technology Management, Ted Rogers School of Management, Ryerson University. His research focuses on the design process and the morality of design in an increasingly interdependent and global landscape. Ward is interested in Immanent Design as the natural unfolding of the solution space from within the problem space guided by architectures of participation of all those impacted. Ward holds degrees in architecture and philosophy from the University of Toronto and the University of Guelph. Having worked for ten years with the premier design firm of Arthur Erickson Architects, Ward has taught design from a number of perspectives including architecture, film, photography, web design, and new media in North America and Africa.

William McDonough ❮ William McDonough is the founding principal of William McDonough + Partners, an internationally recognized design firm practicing ecologically, socially, and economically intelligent architecture and planning in the U.S. and abroad, principal of MBDC, a product and systems development firm assisting prominent client companies in designing profitable and environmentally intelligent solutions and a Venture Partner at VantagePoint Venture Partners in San Bruno, California. Mr. McDonough is a Consulting Professor of Civil and Environmental Engineering at Stanford University. He is on the Advisory Board of the University of Cambridge Programme for Sustainability Leadership and since January 2010 Chairman Emeritus of the U.S. Board of Councilors. William has written and lectured extensively on his design philosophy and practice. With Michael Braungart he co-authored "Cradle to Cradle: Remaking the Way We Make Things."

Wolfgang Schwaiger ❮ Wolfgang Schwaiger received a doctorate in Business Studies at the Graduate School of Management, University of Dallas, Texas. After completing his doctorate he held a number of management positions in several large industrial companies. He then joined the lare international technology firm (VA TECH) as director of corporate strategy, communication and investor relations. Wolfgang has been a visiting professor at the University of Linz and the Art University Linz. He also lectures in Restructuring and Privatization at the World Bank Economic Development Institute in Washington and Vienna. His main areas of expertise lie in the design and management of complex, long-term change processes, internal communication, innovation management, mergers and aquisitions as well as strategy development and implementation. He is a Project Manager with Königswieser & Network.

DESIGN
NEW FUTURES ❮

MICHAEL SHAMIYEH ❮

Today, in times of manic cycles of disruptive changes that effect almost every aspect of our daily life, common managerial practice of exploiting potentials of existing situations, established products, processes or organizational structures in an attempt to adapt them to a changing environment proves to no longer be a feasible approach to sustaining a business in the long run.

IN STICKING TO WHAT HAS BEEN ESTABLISHED, IT NOT ONLY FORSAKES THE OPPORTUNITY TO EXPEND ENERGY IN CREATING NEW CONDITIONS THAT POSSIBLY GENERATE VALUE IN THE FUTURE;

it first and foremost adheres to the wrong assumption that at all times it is possible to transfer an established solution successfully into an effective prospective one. The design approach, on the other hand, is about creating and seizing new opportunities. It does not exploit established situations but rather directs ones attention towards thinking about the nature of possible futures.

The differences among attitudes in establishing desired futures are at the center of the articles in this section.

Presented perspectives shift alternately between those of design and management practitioners and those of educators. For instance, Michael Shamiyeh addresses the need for new ways of approaching contemporary problems in management practice and the capability of initiating the radical rather than merely modifying changes in prevailing business models. Richard J. Boland Jr. and Fred Collopy explain why design matters for management now and particularly point to the difference between the decision attitude as practiced in management, and the design attitude.
Simonetta Carbonaro highlights the benefits of design as a radical action resulting in social innovation. She shows how design leads to the elaboration of new models for living from which new products, new services or new processes can be derived. Greg Van Alstyne discusses design in its most powerful form as a transformative process of participation supporting strategic foresight and including methods that have evolved specifically to deal with situations of great complexity and uncertainty.
Wolfgang Schwaiger, finally, argues that change processes in complex realities may be developed on the grounds of continuous and iterative learning processes towards an organization's vision of the future rather than managed by progressing on a linear path.

27

The architect's or designer's mode of operation, his/her way of thinking, harbors a strong and even unique potential among, of course, some other powerful competences: Here, I am particularly referring to the architect's creative-analytical approach towards problem solving and decision making that—were architects to utilize it to a greater extent than they have heretofore—would possibly allow them to become much more active in what goes on in society today. The current great outpouring of interest in the specific problem-solving process at work in architecture on the part of corporate executives and major business schools supports the assumption that the architect's approach harbors something valuable.

The article originally appeared in Volume (Archis), Columbia University. USA, No. 14. 2007.

In order to make my point clear, it is necessary to briefly give an account on the virtues of architectural design thinking in relation to strategic business thinking: In contemporary management practice and education it is still common to solve problems by making decisions upon alternatives. That is to say, on the basis of an actual situation—as, e.g., Fink (2003) in reference to famous management consultants explains—the problem solver investigates and evaluates a series of alternatives by the support of scientific or empirical methods for economic analysis as well as by taking his/her personal experience into account, if necessary gathers even more information, to finally come to a decision for further actions. Significantly, such a problem-solving approach entails a problematic limitation. It assumes that the analysis of a prevailing condition equally entails the perfect solution. Moreover, it supposes that in an evolutionary problem-solving process a prevailing condition can be transformed into a perfect one. However, such an approach misses to bring in new ideas foreign to the determined problem space. It is in this sense that men and women running businesses begin to understand, that in face of the increasing diverse forms of complexities of our world the very concept of "problem solving" can be impediment. Rather than initiating a larger process of creating—of designing—what one truly values or wants, it suggests a thinking that proposes to fix something that is broken. It prevents someone asking the more fundamental question of "what desired future do we want to create?" Take the generally known classical inventory control problem as an example:

Management has traditionally faced the inventory control problem by establishing a stock between various parties of a production process, distribution and selling (e.g., Liker, 2004; Dell and Fredman, 1999). For many decades, this solution became the default model. Although education and management practice has worked to optimize this model in respect to lower costs of inventory and to speed up flow and tracking of all parts and materials purchased, products processed, and products stored and prepared for shipment, to question the very necessity of inventories per se was not at stake at all.

Still at the turn to the 21st century Wired-Guru Kevin Kelly (1999:14) praises smart techniques for managing

more elegant and more cost reductive this "default" model that carried within it its own form of closure. For decades management was blind in regard the possibility that inventories could be minimized or eliminated at all by redefining the very problem itself; that is to say, by broadening the initial problem space to be able to rethink the overall organization of production processes, relations with suppliers, workforce and information systems to finally discover the virtues of a lean manufacturing approach towards production. Think of Michael Dell's computer corporation that revolutionized the PC industry by becoming the first in the industry to sell custom-built computers directly to end-users, bypassing the dominant system of using computer resellers to sell mass-produced computers (Dell, 2006): Rather than coming up with new ways of managing more cost effectively inventories for assembling a whole range of different PC models, he broke from the decision attitude in thinking about inventory control and started to see how a just-in-time production process with web-based connections between customers, Dell and its suppliers renders inventories irrelevant.

NOTICE THAT THIS BREAKTHROUGH INNOVATION WAS INTRODUCED FAIRLY RECENTLY, IN 1998!

Beyond being too susceptible to early closure of the problem space, another problem is rooted in the decision attitude—namely, that a decision does not generate ideas that give form to new opportunities, no matter how advanced the analytic capabilities of the decision maker are:

It is commonplace today to note that management as a profession is in a difficult situation. Men and women running businesses begin to understand, that in face of the increasing diverse forms of complexities of our world—in which stakeholders with different agendas and worldviews, organizations, economies and entire societies are extremely interconnected and in which actions affect (or are affected by) others, often literally a world away—the very concept of "problem solving" can be impediment. Rather than initiating a larger process of creating what one truly values or wants, it suggests a thinking that proposes to fix something that is broken. It prevents someone asking the more fundamental question of "what desired future do we want to create?" The case of Cirque du Soleil, one of Canada's largest cultural exports, reveals strikingly this operative limit of a decision attitude towards problem solving in times of emergent realities wherein solutions from the past no longer fit: As known, a circus is most commonly understood as a traveling company of performers that includes artists and trained animals. In a large tent with seating around its edge a series of acts are choreographed to music. Due to alternative forms of entertainment—ranging from various kinds of urban live entertainment to sporting events to home entertainment—the circus industry is suffering from a steadily decreasing audience. Coupled with an increasing sentiment against the use of animals in circus, it is of no surprise that revenues and profits decline. A decision attitude towards solving this problem would ultimately attempt to pinpoint the critical issues—in our case the artists, the animals, and the tent—to subsequently improve them in relation to the overall performance. In case of the most expensive element of a circus, supposedly the animals, this would probably mean to reduce the amount of animals or to select other ones in order to lower costs of training, medical care, housing, insurance, or even transportation. However, in pursuing such an approach one would never end up with concept of a circus that is so different as the one of the Cirque du Soleil. Among many other new features, it did away with all traditional factors (e.g., the animals) and introduced elements completely foreign to the industry, e.g., such as a theme and a story line analog Broadway shows that allows multiple productions and gives people (beyond just children) a reason to come to the circus more frequently.

The case of Cirque du Soleil exemplarily shows that something is missing in management practice, namely the capability to bring in new ideas foreign to the determined problem space. In last few years managers have come to understand that the failings of management are most directly attributed to a famine of good ideas. The problem is rooted in the very concept of "business administration," an activity whose emphasis remains on controlling, integrating, and coordinating. While integration, coordination, and

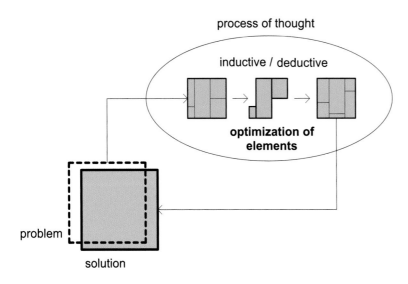

process of thought

inductive / deductive

optimization of elements

problem

solution

‹ Mechanical System Thinking

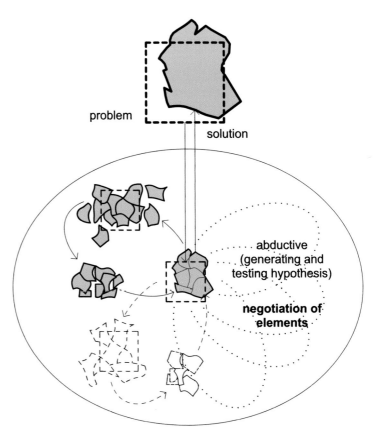

problem

solution

abductive (generating and testing hypothesis)

negotiation of elements

‹ Conjectural (Architectural) Thinking

process of thought

control are all potentially important tasks, a focus on these dramatically underestimates the value and necessity to "design" new futures in a time of change. Apparently, organization must do both, resolve day-to-day problems and generate desired futures. As Peter Senge (2006) notices, there is nothing more elemental to the work of leaders than creation. Significantly, there is a great difference between creating something one truly cares about to exist compared to solving a problem, of making something one does not like to go away. For that reason, management practice and education begin to turn their attention to architects who do not await passively discovery (of some desired future state) but actively invent—create—it and so primarily deal with what does not yet exist.

THEY ARE, AS HERBERT SIMON (1996: 111F.) VIVIDLY REMINDED US, "CONCERNED NOT WITH THE NECESSARY BUT WITH THE CONTINGENT—NOT HOW THINGS ARE BUT HOW THEY MIGHT BE."

Creative architectural thinking, in contrast to traditional managerial thinking, takes for granted that the process of finding a solution to a problem will require the invention, the creation, of new alternatives, given certain parameters and constrains. That is to say, whereas the decision attitude in management usually assumes that the alternatives that are at hand include already the best one, in architecture one is concerned with inventing the "best" one. Hence, whereas the first investigates extant forms to subsequently optimize and respectively perfect them; the latter is interested in initiating novel forms that perfectly meet the problem. Even though architects, of course, are interested in investigating reality, they do so just to the extent of understanding prevailing constraints and their underlying interdependences as much as they are influential to the process of creating desired futures.

Beyond the difference in the emphasis on either existing or future conditions, there is something evident in the architectural approach towards solving problems that is perfectly destined for bringing in new ideas. Rather than

referring to traditional reasoning modes of deduction or induction, the mode of reasoning involved in architectural thinking is essentially abductive: Aside of the two widely known modes of reasoning, deduction and induction, it was Charles Sanders Peirce (1965) who re-introduced the (old) theory of abductive reasoning into the scientific debate at the turn to the 20th Century. In order to point out the differences and similarities between the various modes of reasoning, Peirce preferred to refer to the example of the coffee beans many times: Deductive reasoning is the type of reasoning that proceeds from general principles or premises to derive at particular information. (All coffee beans in this bag are white; in case these beans are from the bag they must be white). Alternative to deductive reasoning is inductive reasoning. Induction or inductive reasoning is the process of reasoning in which the premises of an argument are believed to support the conclusion but do not ensure it. (Those coffee beans are from the bag; they are white, therefore I assume that all beans from this bag are white). Thus, whereas deductive reasoning applies general principles to reach specific conclusions, inductive reasoning examines specific information, perhaps many pieces of specific information, to derive at a general principle. So, deductive reasoning does not provide any new insights as the evidence provided must be a set about which everything is known before the conclusion can be drawn. Differently, inductive reasoning, where the conclusion is likely to follow due to a set of given evidence, does provide the ability to learn new things that are not obvious from the evidence, however, the gained insight is directly linked to—and as such determined by—the supporting premises of the argument.

Both types of reasoning are routinely employed in management practice and education. However, due to their ideal character both modes of reasoning are loosing their relevance in the real world. This holds true particularly in the case of deductive reasoning, as it is simply difficult to know everything before drawing a conclusion. This is where abductive reasoning steps in.

Abduction is a method of reasoning in which one chooses the hypothesis that would, if true, best explain the relevant evidence. Following Peirce (1965: CP 5.171) "deduction proves that something must be; induction shows that something actually is operative; abduction merely suggests that something may be." In other words, abductive reasoning starts from a set of accepted facts and infers to their most likely, or best, explanations. Thus, whereas the other two modes of reasoning reveal a strictly sequential, step-by-step procedure for arriving at specific conclusions—two of three variables are known—abductive reasoning, in which just one of three variables is known, involves an assertion of causation, also known as an "If and Then" statement. E.g., if a particular independent variable changes, then a certain dependent variable also changes. Significantly, in order to arrive at certain conclusions, creativity is required precisely because the creation of a new hypothetical, invented, and untested general rule maintains the starting point for any abduction (Nagl, 1992).

FOR THAT REASON PEIRCE (1965) ARGUED, THAT ABDUCTION IS THE ONLY LOGICAL PROCESS THAT FOSTERS ONE'S OWN INITIATIVE AND THEREBY ACTUALLY CREATES ANYTHING NEW.

Unlike in business, in architectural design the emphasis on systematic procedures, the use of traditional reasoning modes of induction and deduction, as well as the application of prescribed techniques met with immediate criticism for the linearity of their processes and their lack of appreciation for the complexity of given (design) problems. (Refer,e.g., to debates around the 1970s). In reference to Karl Popper, Horst W. Rittel (1972) first called attention to what he described as the "wicked nature" of problems architects are facing in their daily work. Such problems, he asserted, are ill suited for linear techniques. Principles of the scientific method can't be applied to them because wicked problems are characterized by a level of interconnectedness, by the presence of amplifying loops that produce unintended consequences when interfered with, by the presence of tradeoffs and conflicts among stakeholders, and by nature of their constraints. Each formulation of the problem, of which there are many possible, corresponds to different—contestable—solutions. Consequently, when dealing with wicked problems one cannot first define the problem, and

then the solution. Solutions are generated all the time as problems are formulated. For this reason the architect adopts a creative-analytical problem-solving strategy that is based on generating and testing potential solutions and is fundamentally concerned with learning and the search for emergent opportunities. In other words, architectural thinking internalizes a process that begins with generating a series of creative "what if" hypothesis, continues in selecting the most promising one for further inquiry, which then takes the form of a more evaluative "if then" sequence, in which the logical implications of that particular hypothesis are more fully explored and tested. Although the scientific method of induction, with its emphasis on cycles of hypothesis and the acquisition of new information to arrive at new conclusions remains central in architectural thinking, the mode of reasoning is primarily abductive; that is to say, it is hypothesis-driven and uses the logic of conjecture. It conjures an image of a future reality that does not yet exist but may be real. This is the great virtue of the creative-analytical approach in architecture. It is a combination of creative imagination—an initiative that generates and brings in new ideas—and rational analysis, based on known constraints. (see Fig. 2) Take Rem Koolhaas' competition proposal for the Jussieu Library as an example: As Jeff Kippnis (1996) points out, "in his project for the University Libraries at Jussieu, the architect [...] generates a social setting organized less by the program than by the erotic fantasies of the voyeur." The proposed "finite, fluid field of interactions" introduces a theme absolutely foreign to the conventional brief of libraries. Certainly, it is impossible to arrive at such a proposal by applying reasoning modes such as deduction and induction.

In business, complexity and an ongoing change of conditions are at the root of every problem. Confronted with such a situation the very concept of problem solving appears to become misleading and the application of a step by step methodology in "fixing" problems unfeasible. Management too is faced with the "wicked" nature of problems, to cling on Rittel's expression. As such, the possibilities for problem definition and solution are equally unbounded and therefore good hypothesis generation is critical. The opportunities to solve these problems in a strictly sequential process are rare if not null. Thus, business—as probably many other

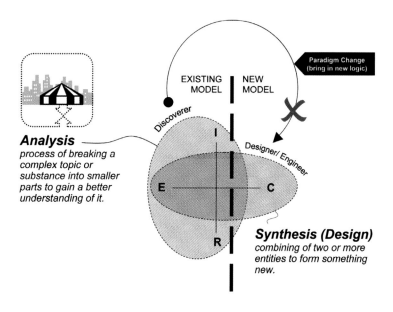

EXISTING MODEL **NEW MODEL**

Paradigm Change
(bring in new logic)

Discoverer

Designer/ Engineer

I

E   C

R

Analysis
process of breaking a
complex topic or
substance into smaller
parts to gain a better
understanding of it.

Synthesis (Design)
combining of two or more
entities to form something
new.

❮ Analysis vs. Design

33

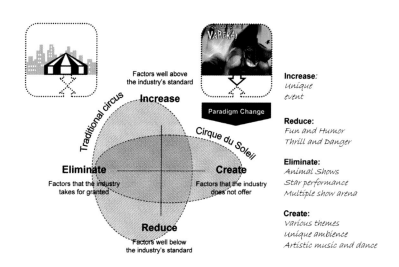

Factors well above
the industry's standard

Paradigm Change

Traditional circus

Cirque du Soleil

Increase

Eliminate
Factors that the industry
takes for granted

Create
Factors that the industry
does not offer

Reduce
Factors well below
the industry's standard

Increase:
unique
event

Reduce:
Fun and Humor
Thrill and Danger

Eliminate:
Animal Shows
Star performance
Multiple show arena

Create:
Various themes
unique ambience
Artistic music and dance

❮ Four Actions Diagram

professions—is in need of new ways for approaching problems respectively for creating desired futures, conditions that they truly want. For that reason the activity of strategic planning, whose very objective is to bring about the conditions most favorable to one's own side, gains more and more importance in business today. Whereas traditional approaches to business assumed that planning creates value primarily through administration—that the power of planning is in the creation of a systematic approach to problem-solving—decomposing a complex problem into sub-problems to be solved and later integrated back into a whole, the value of planning in a time of change and complexity cannot be underestimated.

IT IS IN THIS RESPECT THAT THE PARTICULAR CREATIVE-ANALYTICAL APPROACH AT WORK IN ARCHITECTURE IS OF GREAT VALUE FOR CONTEMPORARY MANAGERIAL PRACTICE.

Architectural thinking opens up a virtual learning laboratory in which a series of assumptions about a set of cause-effect relationships in today's environment are generated and tested with the aim to create a set of actions aimed at transforming a situation from its current reality to its desired future.

The brief discussion on the link between "revolutionary" architectural and "evolutionary" business thinking attempts to reveal that the architect's approach towards solving complex problems respectively generating desired futures may be of great value for current management practice if not for others equally too, due to its incorporation of both creative/artistic and analytical/rational skills. In particular I referred to the role of hypothesis generation and testing and tried to put forward the relevance of such an approach to business practice. Certainly, there is much more valuable potential to be discovered. Paradoxically, since time immemorial the architectural profession has been learning to translate recognized or conceived patterns of relationships (i.e., organizational interdependences or the diffusion of activities) just into a physical, spatial-material form. In other words, the profession's most fundamental and longstanding values induce architects to react with a building—with concrete—instead of examining the extent to which these findings, or their approach to problems in general, would equally be feasible or useful in some other form for society. A glance at current daily affairs would reveal that there is a great demand for people having internalized such a potential. However, a step in such a direction would ultimately imply an ambitious liberation from our traditional disciplinary values.

FOR SURE THIS IS NOT A MODEST STEP, BUT IT WOULD ALLOW THE ARCHITECTURAL PROFESSION TO EXPAND THEIR FIELD OF INTERVENTION EXTRAORDINARILY.

References

Dell, Michael, Catherine Fredman. (1999) Direct from Dell: Strategies that revolutionized an industry. New York, Harper Collins.

Fink, Dietmar. (2003) Die Großen Management Consultants: Ihre Geschichte, ihre Konzepte, ihre Strategien [The famous management consultants: Their history, their concepts, their strategies] München, Vahlen.

Kelly, Kevin. (1999) New rules for the new economy: 10 radical strategies for a connected world. New York, Penguin Books.

Kipnis, Jeffrey. (1996) "Recent Koolhaas". El croquis. No. 79, 29.

Liker, Jeffrey K. (2004) The Toyota way: 4 management principles from the world's greatest manufacturer. New York, McGraw-Hill.

Nagl, Ludwig. (1992) Charles Sanders Peirce. Frankfurt a. Main, 112.

Peirce, C. S. (1965) Collected papers of Charles Sanders Peirce. Volume I (Principles of philosophy) and II (Elements of logic). Hartshorne, Charles, Paul Weiss (Ed.) Cambridge Massachusetts: Harvard University Press.

Peirce, C. S. (1965) Collected papers of Charles Sanders Peirce. Volume III (Exact logic) and IV (The simplest mathematics). Hartshorne, Charles, Paul Weiss (Ed.) Cambridge Massachusetts: Harvard University Press.

Peirce, C. S. (1965) Collected papers of Charles Sanders Peirce. Volume V (Pragmatism & pragmaticism) and VI (Scientific metaphysics). Hartshorne, Charles, Paul Weiss (Ed.) Cambridge Massachusetts: Harvard University Press.

Rittel, Horst W. J. (1972) "On the planning crisis: System analysis of the first and second generations," Bedriftsøkonomen, No. 8. 390–396.

Senge, Peter. (2006) "Creating desired futures in a global economy." in Shamiyeh, Michael (Ed.) Organizing for change. Integrating architectural thinking in other fields. Basel, Birkhäuser.

Simon, Herbert. (1996) The sciences of the artificial. 3rd Edition, Cambridge, MIT Press.

RICHARD J. BOLAND JR. AND
FRED COLLOPY ❮ Design Matters for Management

37

Recently, our faculty had the good fortune to work with the worldrenowned architect Frank O. Gehry and his firm, Gehry Partners, on the design and construction of the Peter B. Lewis Building as a new home for the Weatherhead School of Management. During the four and one half years of working with Gehry Partners on the planning, design, and construction of the Lewis Building, we experienced an approach to problem solving that is quite different from our own, from that of the managers we study, and from what we teach to our students. We refer to this unique mind-set and approach to problem solving as a *design attitude*.

The article originally appeared in Richard J. Boland and Fred Collopy (Eds.), Managing as Designing, Stanford University Press, 2004.

A Design Attitude

We believe that if managers adopted a design attitude, the world of business would be different and better. Managers would approach problems with a sensibility that swept in the broadest array of influences to shape inspiring and energizing designs for products, services, and processes that are both profitable and humanly satisfying. Gehry's approach to problems reflects the entrepreneurial spirit that was at the heart of the industrial and information revolutions. He approaches each new project with a desire to do something differently and better than he has done before and to experiment with materials, technologies, and methods in his quest. Working with him has led us to see how both management practice and education have allowed a limited and narrow vocabulary of decision making to drive an expansive and embracing vocabulary of design out of circulation. In our focus on teaching students advanced analytical techniques for choosing among alternatives, our attention to strengthening their design skills for shaping new alternatives has withered. What is needed in management practice and education today is the development of a design attitude, which goes beyond default solutions in creating new possibilities for the future.

A decision attitude toward problem solving is used extensively in management education. It portrays the manager as facing a set of alternative courses of action from which a choice must be made. The decision attitude assumes it is easy to come up with alternatives to consider, but difficult to choose among them. The design attitude toward problem solving, in contrast, assumes that it is difficult to design a good alternative, but once you have developed a truly great one, the decision about which alternative to select becomes trivial.

THE DESIGN ATTITUDE APPRECIATES THAT THE COST OF NOT CONCEIVING OF A BETTER COURSE OF ACTION THAN THOSE THAT ARE ALREADY BEING CONSIDERED IS OFTEN MUCH HIGHER THAN MAKING THE "WRONG" CHOICE AMONG THEM.

The decision attitude toward problem solving and the many decision-making tools we have developed for supporting it have strengths that make them suitable for certain situations. In a clearly defined and stable situation, when the feasible alternatives are well known, a decision attitude may be the most efficient and effective way to approach problem solving. But when those conditions do not hold, a design attitude is required. The decision attitude and the analytic tools managers have to support it were developed in a simpler time. They are the product of fifty years of concerted effort to strengthen the mathematical and scientific basis of management education. Today's world is much different from that of the 1950s when the movement to expand analytic techniques in management began to flourish. We are suggesting that now is the time to incorporate a better balance of the two approaches to problem solving in management practice and education.

The premise of this paper is that managers are designers as well as decision makers and that although the two are inextricably linked in management action, we have for too long emphasized the decision face of management over the design face.

An Example of the Design Attitude

Toward the end of the design process for the Lewis Building, there was a need to reduce the floor space by about 4,500 square feet. One of us traveled to Gehry's Santa Monica offices and worked with the project architect, Matt Fineout, on the problem. We first identified those miscellaneous spaces that had to be squeezed into the smaller footprint (tea kitchens, closets, rest rooms, storage areas, and spaces for copiers, fax machines, and printers). There were many constraints to be met including proximity to classrooms and offices, "ownership" by various departments and research centers, and circulation patterns in each area. We went through the floor plans, beginning with the lower level and working our way up to the fifth floor. The process took two days.

Working with large sheets of onionskin paper laid on top of floor plans, we would sketch possible arrangements until we had something we all agreed was a good solution. Then we would transfer the arrangement in red pencil onto the plans. Each move of one element affected others and often required backtracking and revising previously located elements. Many times during the two days, we would reach a roadblock where things were just not working out, so we would start with a clean sheet of onionskin and try a different approach. At the end of two days, it was a tremendous sense of accomplishment to have succeeded in locating all the required elements into the reduced floor sizes. We were working at a large table and Matt was leaning far onto it, marking the final changes. As he pushed back from the table, we were joking about how tedious the process had been and how glad we were to have it over. As we joked, Matt gathered all the sheets of onionskin and the marked-up floor plans, stacked them, and then grabbed an edge and tore them in half. Then he crumpled the pieces and threw them in the trash can in the corner of the room. This was a shock! What was he doing? In a matter-of-fact tone, he said, "We proved we could do it, now we can think about how we *want* to do it."

WHAT WAS GOING ON THERE?

A perfectly good solution had been worked out. It responded to all of our requirements and fulfilled the needs of the program. And it was difficult to accomplish. Why tear it up? A very different mind-set for approaching problems was evident here. Was this approach to problem solving an aberration of no consequence, or was it worth figuring out and considering its implications for management generally? The design approach of Frank Gehry and his associates may not mirror the work practices of the vast majority of architects. But he is one of the most successful and highly regarded architects of our day, and we believe there is something in his approach to problem solving that is an important part of his success. Bringing at least the flavor of his design thinking and design attitude to managers stimulated both the workshop and this book. Like the plans that Matt tore up that day, the ideas in this book are not meant to be the end point of managing as designing. They just show that we can do it—we can rethink managing as designing. The question is, how do we as managers want to do our designing?

The Decision Attitude

A DECISION ATTITUDE TOWARD PROBLEM SOLVING IS OVERWHELMINGLY DOMINANT IN MANAGEMENT PRACTICE AND EDUCATION TODAY. IT SOLVES PROBLEMS BY MAKING RATIONAL CHOICES AMONG ALTERNATIVES AND USES TOOLS SUCH AS ECONOMIC ANALYSIS, RISK ASSESSMENT, MULTIPLE CRITERIA DECISION MAKING, SIMULATION, AND THE TIME VALUE OF MONEY.

But for all the power of analytic approaches to problem solving, they share a central weakness in that they take as given the alternative courses of action from which the manager is to choose. The decision attitude is concerned with the various techniques, methods, algorithms, and heuristics that a manager can use in making such choices. In other words, it starts with an assumption that the alternative courses of action are ready at hand—that there is a good set of options already available, or at least readily obtainable. This is a decidedly passive view of the decision maker as a problem solver, and one that makes the untenable assumption that the alternatives that are on the table, or the first ones we will think of, include the best ones. The design attitude, in contrast, is concerned with finding the best answer possible, given the skills, time, and resources of the team, and takes for granted that it will require the invention of new alternatives. So, the decision attitude is In the unrealistic position of assuming that good design work has already taken place, even though that is not usually the case. It is, therefore, doomed to mediocrity in its organizational outcomes.

Take the classic inventory control problem as an example. A decision attitude toward that problem has traditionally modeled the inventory process as a buffer between varying demands placed on different sections of the production, distribution, and consumption chain. That image became the default approach for thirty years, while research and teaching on inventory control worked to perfect that model and enable the best possible decision making about the timing, quantity, and location of inventory acquisitions. As a result, we have developed elegant and powerful techniques for calculating reorder points, economic lot sizes, and risks of stock outs, as well as for minimizing holding costs. But we also became more deeply enmeshed in a default model of the inventory process that carried with it its own form of closure. We were blinded for decades to the possibility that inventories could be minimized by different means, such as by rethinking how we design our production processes, our relations with suppliers, our workforce, and our information systems. Only when we broke from the decision attitude in thinking about inventory control and engaged in a design attitude, did we start to see how it was possible to take the elimination of inventory, rather than its management, as our goal in a lean manufacturing approach to production. The design attitude toward problem solving was a higher order approach that allowed us to step back from the decision-making techniques we had developed and ask the more fundamental question "what are we trying to do?"

THE DECISION ATTITUDE IS TOO SUSCEPTIBLE TO EARLY CLOSURE OF THE PROBLEM SOLVING SPACE, JUST AS THE DESIGN APPROACH IS TOO SUSCEPTIBLE TO KEEPING THE SEARCH GOING LONG AFTER IT IS BENEFICIAL.

There is a time for openness and a time for closure in our project-based episodes of problem solving, and managers need to develop strength in both the decision and design attitudes.

Why Design Matters for Management Now

It is commonplace today to note that management as a profession is in a difficult situation. The last few years have been a continuing tale of misdeeds, failures, and embarrassments. Both the fantasies of a "new economy" and the exuberance of the dot com bubble are things that the entire managerial establishment participated in creating. From government policy to investment banking to venture capitalists, to auditors, to educators, to stock analysts, the scope of complicity is almost universal. Where do we look for an explanation of failure on such a mass scale? Is it the complexity, uncertainty, and chaos of modern times that brought about the dot com bubble, or Enron, or Global Crossing, or First Capital, or the telecom collapse? Or is it something more fundamental? We argue that our everyday image of what a manager is, along with a specialized language of management education that has been developing for more than fifty years, has very much to do with it. The problem is rooted in the training of managers as decision makers and in the vocabulary of choice that is imbedded in our increasingly monoclonal MBA programs and their Executive Education arms.

The recent failings of management have been attributed to moral lapses or lack of adequate regulatory oversight, but that seems an unlikely or at best only partial cause. Over time, we will no doubt see additional regulation and a call for more ethics courses in management schools, but we do not believe that either of those attempts at remedies will be successful. That is because the failings of management are most directly attributed to a famine of good ideas. To take one highly visible example, Enron's management failed to make the earnings and cash flows it had promised and resorted to creating revenues and hiding debt through complex transactions because they didn't have sufficiently good ideas to make sales and profits in real ways. Off-balance-sheet financial manipulation was the best idea they had, and no matter how bad that idea was, they were not able to generate a better alternative.

Exotic methods of financial analysis do not create value. Only inventing and delivering new products, processes, and services that serve human needs can do that. But managers are not trained for that type of life. Instead, they are trained and rewarded for being decision makers—to have alternatives presented to them from which they make choices by computing net present values, optimizing underassumed co straints, and trading off risks for returns. There is something tragically missing from management practice and education today, and missing even from our managerial icons. That missing element is an image of the manager as an idea generator who gives form to new possibilities with a well-developed vocabulary of design. Managers as form-givers care deeply about the world that is being shaped by a business and refuse to accept

the default alternatives. They understand that the design of better products, processes, and services is their core responsibility.

THE DESIGN ATTITUDE IS THE SOURCE OF THOSE INVENTIONS.

A decision does not generate inventions, no matter how advanced its analytic capabilities.
Management school faculty members should also consider how our own role as educators has played a part in bringing about the conditions and mindsets underlying recent events. Like it or not, management education is involved in the current problems of the corporate world and will also be involved in any reforms that help lead to a recovery of management's leadership role in society. More of the same does not seem to be a viable formula for the future of management education.

Precedents for a Design Attitude in Management Thinking

Herbert Simon, Nobel laureate in economics, wrote
The Sciences of the Artificial, which is one of the finest
examples we have of a well-developed theory of the design
attitude for managers. Simon called for a new curriculum
for management education based on design. He saw
management as a profession whose training should follow
that of engineering or architecture as an applied science,
not that of the natural sciences. The manager's professional
responsibility is not to discover the laws of the universe,
but to act responsibly in the world to transform existing
situations into more preferred ones. Simon held that, like the
engineer or the architect, the manager is a form-giver who
shapes organizations and economic processes. As he states
in the preface to the second edition (1996, p. xii):

ENGINEERING, MEDICINE, BUSINESS, ARCHITECTURE, AND PAINTING ARE CONCERNED NOT WITH THE NECESSARY BUT WITH THE CONTINGENT— NOT HOW THINGS ARE BUT HOW THEY MIGHT BE—IN SHORT, WITH DESIGN.

To summarize Simon's argument very briefly, humans have a
limited cognitive capacity for reasoning when searching for
a solution within a problem space. Given the relatively small
size of our brain's working memory, we can only consider
a few aspects of any situation and can only analyze them
in a few ways. This is also true of computers, although
the constraints are less obvious. The problem space that
a manager deals with in their mind or in their computer
is dependent on the way they represent the situation that
they face. The first step in any problem-solving episode
is representing the problem, and to a large extent, that
representation has the solution hidden within it. A decision
attitude carries with it a default representation of the
problem being faced, whereas a design attitude begins by
questioning the way the problem is represented. To use
Donald Schon's classic example, if we refer to an urban
neighborhood as a blight it evokes a particular problem

space where certain types of design intervention are seen as most appropriate (cutting out the blight, bringing in a fresh form of life). We have seen the results in town planning that flattened whole sections of a city and replaced them with more "healthy" elements. If we label the same area a folk community, we can marvel at the resilience of its social support networks and approach it with designs for strengthening its existing social infrastructure.
Simon concludes by asking us to strive for a kind of design that has no final goals beyond that of leaving more possibilities open to future generations than we ourselves inherited. He also asks us to avoid designs that create irreversible commitments for future generations and to strive to open ourselves to the largest number of diverse experiences possible, in order to allow us to draw from an ever-wider variety of idea sources in order to make our designs humanly satisfying as well as economically viable.

Basic Elements of a Design Attitude

By *design attitude*, we refer to the expectations and orientations one brings to a design project. A design attitude views each project as an opportunity for invention that includes a questioning of basic assumptions and a resolve to leave the world a better place than we found it. Designers relish the lack of predetermined outcomes. As Frank Gehry said several times during the workshop, "If I knew how a project was going to turn out, I wouldn't do it." Each project is an opportunity to ask oneself anew what is the real problem being faced and what is a best solution?
In the design of the Peter B. Lewis Building, Gehry Partners started with some disarmingly simple questions: "What is teaching?" "What is learning?" "What is an office?" "What is a faculty?" Design is often an opportunity to go back to those assumptions that have become invisible and unnoticed, yet are the real reasons we are working on the project. A designer looks for the real thing we are trying to accomplish, unvarnished by the residue of years of organizational habit. The single overriding commonality in all design projects, as Simon puts it, is the urge to "change an existing state of affairs into a more preferred one." Each project is an opportunity for better-ment over existing products, services, or processes. Obviously, we don't start with a clean slate and must take into account the current state of technology, human skills,

environmental forces, and so on. Even given that, each project is a chance to ask what we are really trying to accomplish in our organization and how the piece that we are working on now can help make the experience of our workers, customers, suppliers, and public a better and more rewarding one. A good design solution is one that is more satisfying in more ways than any available, feasible alternative.

A GOOD DESIGN SOLUTION SOLVES MANY PROBLEMS, OFTEN ONES THAT WERE NOT ENVISIONED IN ITS DEVELOPMENT.

The importance of the design attitude was attested to by Frank Gehry several times during the workshop, especially when he pointed out that wherever we look in the world, we are surrounded by mediocrity. Why is that? And more importantly, why do we continue to create a mediocre world for ourselves? One often hears the argument that it is "economics" or "costs" or "limited budgets" that are to blame. If only we had more money, more time, more staff, more of something, we would be able to do things better. It is time we rejected such defeatist, shortsighted views. It is time we faced up to the fact that the decision attitude toward problem solving that dominates management education, practice, and research favors default alternatives and locks us into a selfperpetuating cycle of mediocrity.
A design attitude to problem solving does not have to cost more—and is the best alternative we have for breaking out of the path-dependent replication of familiar patterns of management. A design attitude can bring us path-creating ideas about new ways to use technology, new materials, and new work processes that can change the definitions of cost and efficiency, making better solutions attainable at less cost. What attitude toward problem solving should guide us in our work? A decision attitude that chooses from among the alternatives that are already at hand or a design attitude that strives to construct a more satisfying solution than what has so far been proposed? A design attitude fosters an acceptance of and a comfort with a problem-solving process that remains liquid and open, celebrating new alternatives as it strives to develop a best design solution.

Frank Gehry's Design Attitude

Frank Gehry's approach to design is distinctive in that he constantly works from multiple perspectives. He works with multiple models on multiple scales and works with both sketches and physical models simultaneously. Finally, he brings software into the process only at a late stage, working first with hands and materials to shape his design ideas.

Like most architects, he starts with rounds of interviews—in our case, with faculty, staff, and students. He also asked us to write a short statement about our image for the learning environment we desired. From those, a program for the building was developed, showing the various functional needs and the amount of space dedicated to each, such as faculty offices, PhD areas, student study and lounge areas, classrooms, seminar rooms, communal gathering areas, and staff areas. The relative sizes of these required spaces were then translated into sets of wooden blocks of various sizes colored by function. Combinations of blocks were used to play with the massing of the building and to give an overall sense of how the functional areas might be distributed in the building. As a project's design progresses, the number of models grows into the hundreds. Some models are at the grandest scale, filling up one or more eight-foot-by-four-foot pieces of plywood base, and some are of much smaller scale, perhaps modeling just one window or a corner element of the building. For our project, we had dozens of models for faculty offices and many separate models for each classroom.

The Gehry design approach works from both the inside out, as in the massing-models, and from the outside in based on freehand sketches of the building by Frank Gehry, such as that shown in Figure 1.1. These are meant to be spontaneous and evocative of both form and emotion. A constant problem he recognizes is how to keep the feelings of the initial sketches as the architects proceed through the design. An important strategy in that process of trying to keep the feelings alive is to work with their hands, making models of the exterior and interior elements out of paper, metal, plastic, waxed cloth, or whatever material gives them both the form and feeling that they are seeking. There is an important lesson here for management. As Edwin Hutchins demonstrates in *Cognition in the Wild*, thinking is not something done exclusively inside the head, but is often accomplished in interaction with other people with our tools. Spreadsheets are one example of how managers use tools for thinking, and tactile, material models are another, relatively unexplored possibility. The more ways of thinking we have available to us, the better our problem-solving outcomes can be.

Both the interior spaces of the building and the exterior form have a logical as well as an emotional ideal that is being sought. In looking for inspiration on these dual faces of the building, Gehry draws on paintings, sculpture, music, and nature for inspiration. For the exterior of our building, he was working with an image of water flowing over rocks, as well as an image of metal and brick melting into one another. At the same time as the work on our building is proceeding, he is working on other projects, and one can see in his studio how there is a family resemblance among them. As he says, "You cannot escape your vocabulary." But he puts significant effort into trying to do just that, by looking outside of architecture for inspiration and guiding concepts.

THE SENSE OF DISCOVERY IS PALPABLE IN THEIR STUDIO.

The three-dimensional software they use to refine the design and work out the details of how the structure is to be built only comes into play after they have arrived at a model they are satisfied with as their "final" design. But realizing that it is final only in a tentative way, always subject to change as they continue to find better solutions to the many layers of problem solving reflected in the design. Once at this stage of the physical modeling, they digitize the model, both interior and exterior, and begin working with the software system to add the specifications and details that will make it buildable. Many technology advocates will see this practice as anachronistic, noting that you can sketch free form and also model in three dimensions with a computer interface that can essentially replicate whatever medium you prefer to work in. Gehry Partners thinks this is a mistake and that the use of the software as a design tool too early in the thinking process works against their commitment to openness in their search for best solutions. The software will inevitably favor some ways

of approaching the design problem over others and some
ways of working with the tools over others, both of which
are to the detriment of the design process. They believe that
keeping the connection between the initial sketches and the
physical models as close as possible, with both being an
intimate, tactile form of work in which mind, hand, heart, and
materials are a closely integrated instrument of cognition
and creativity, is the best way to maintain the desired feeling
in their work from start to finish.

This illustrates another way in which managers can begin
learning from the work practices of successful designers
to reorient their own thinking. When exactly should an
organizational process be embedded in computers and
information systems? What parts of the process are better
handled outside those systems, relying upon the kinetic and
holistic interaction of participants with materials and with
one another?

THESE ARE QUESTIONS WE DO NOT ASK OURSELVES OFTEN ENOUGH.

The Use of Models in Decision and Design

When the Peter B. Lewis Building project began, we thought we understood what the process would be like. The Lewis Building project was broken into stages running from an initial feasibility study, to a detailed definition of the program requirements, to the conceptual design, to the detailed design, to the construction drawings, to bidding, and finally to construction. Each phase had a clear objective and led to a well-specified outcome and set of deliverable documents.

AND THE PROJECT DID FOLLOW THAT STRUCTURE—BUT THE ARCHITECTS' DESIGN ATTITUDE BROUGHT THE PROCESS TO LIFE IN A UNIQUE WAY.

After the school's requirements were identified and while the architects were in the initial design phase, Frank Gehry visited us with a model to show what he was thinking and get reactions. We were under the impression that his first model was a rough version of the finished project—that it would be refined and perfected over time and eventually become the final design. But that's not what happened. We had anticipated that the essentially favorable reaction that the faculty had to the initial model that Frank Gehry presented, coupled with various suggestions the faculty had made, would lead the architects in a process of refining that initial model to perfect the original idea that was latent in it. So we could not understand the architects' reluctance to take the initial model as seriously as we did. Frank Gehry and his senior partner, Jim Glymph, would say things like, "this is just a place to start," or "it's the beginning and it will change." And of course we thought we knew what they meant by saying it would change, but in hindsight we realize that we didn't. The next model we saw was very different from that first one, and this process continued through several rounds before you could say the underlying form had stabilized and we were working with models that were indeed becoming refined with each iteration.

It struck us that he was using models in a very different way than what we were used to. He sees a model as a kind of three-dimensional sketch to stimulate thinking and explore ideas about possible ways that the project could go. We, in contrast, tend to use the concept of model as a theory of a situation and its solution. When we model, it is much more serious and stable—meant from the beginning to be a kind of truth that captures a situation in an abstract, compressed way.

For Gehry Partners, the model was a physical tool for thinking, not a representation of the building they were designing. Frank Gehry would often point to the model, saying, "This isn't what we are doing—it's not the building."

AND IT TOOK A VERY LONG TIME FOR US TO BEGIN TO REALIZE WHAT HE REALLY MEANT. FACULTY APPROACHED THE MODEL ASSUMING IT WAS THE ABSTRACT ESSENCE OF WHAT THE COMPLETED BUILDING WOULD BE LIKE.

We expected that the work to be done with the model was to improve it against all the many criteria that had been established, in light of the aesthetic statement that the architect intended for it. It was this expectation of our decision attitude that Frank Gehry was saying no to. His model was not the building because his search for a solution was still ongoing in a fundamental sense. The model did not contain an essence of the building, and we as faculty were not prepared to understand that.

The two examples of their design practice that we have seen, and the one that opened the article in particular, show us something that is central to Frank Gehry's design attitude, which is his relentless search for openness. His commitment to openness is evident in his attempts to bring in influences from many other domains during a design project and also in his determination to not allow a problem to be closed prematurely.

Call for a Design Vocabulary

Simon argues that how we describe what a manager is and how a manager should think, what a problem is and how it should be approached, and what a good and true course of action is and how it is to be achieved, are all dependent upon our vocabulary. Good designers show an awareness of their own vocabulary and what it does to their work. Part of engaging in good design is choosing a vocabulary or language to use in defining the design task, generating alternatives, and making judgments of balance, fit, and scale. The awareness of one's own vocabulary and its impact on one's design work makes design an ideal vehicle for creating dialogue across specialized professions. It enables diverse professionals to engage in discussions about the qualities of their vocabularies, the creative experience of designing, and the criteria for making design judgments.

One thing that struck us in the project with Gehry Partners was the frequency with which they used the word *vocabulary*. They meant it in a broadly embracing way to include not just the words they were using, but also the strategies of problem solving they were drawing upon, the kinds of imagery they were being inspired by, and the materials, shapes, and textures of the design elements that formed a kind of language for the project. It was a language unique to that project, and the vocabulary of the project was a distinctive one with its own feelings, tensions, and inner logic. Any new element in the design entered into the context of that vocabulary and was judged not in its own terms, but in light of how it fitted with, resonated with, contrasted with, or clashed with that vocabulary. This awareness of their language and their work practices as a vocabulary is a very important difference between the design and the decision attitudes toward problem solving. An awareness of one's own vocabulary is the first step to questioning it with a design attitude and exploring how different vocabularies yield more creative problem representations and enable the development of better designs.

WE SHOULD MAKE IT CLEAR IN THIS DISCUSSION THAT WE ARE NOT JUST TALKING ABOUT CREATIVITY.

Creativity is certainly a good thing, and creativity is necessary for improvement in all our human endeavors. But creativity is not sufficient for a design attitude to problem solving, just as it is not sufficient for a decision attitude.

The questions really should be: Creativity in what problem space? And creativity toward what end? Consider, for example, the inventory decisionmaking process discussed above. Much creativity has gone into the refinement and elaboration of the decision models for inventory control. Creativity itself is not going to bring us to the organizational, product, or process innovations we require. Creativity needs the guiding energy of a design attitude in order to focus our efforts on results that will be truly innovative and produce long-lasting organizational betterments. Design is in that sense larger than creativity. Design provides a context for creativity by channeling it toward humanly satisfying purposes, and that is why we cannot allow calls for increased creativity and techniques for enhancing creativity to take the place of increased attention to a design attitude in management practice and education.

At the Weatherhead School, we are rethinking the familiar vocabulary, images, and frameworks of management education and reviewing its evolution over the last fifty years. In doing so, we see that the late 1950s were a challenging time in management education, but of a different sort than the difficulties we face today. At that time, advances in the physical and behavioral sciences were showing the power of quantitative analysis and analytic thought processes in those domains, and management education was definitely behind the accomplishments of other academic disciplines. The Carnegie Commission and the Ford Foundation had undertaken major studies of management education and both had concluded that it was in dramatic need of increasing the amount and rigor of quantitative analysis and analytic techniques in the curricula. The Ford Foundation established a number of PhD fellowships to encourage training of new faculty in the application of quantitative and analytic approaches from economics and behavioral sciences to research on management issues. Similarly, the Carnegie Commission outlined a program for strengthening the study of statistics and mathematical techniques in management schools. So, the late 1950s and early 1960s proved a turning point in management education, marked by a recognition that the pendulum of teaching and research had swung too far away from the quantitative and analytic approaches of the sciences and too far toward the detailed practices of management.

TODAY THE PENDULUM HAS ONCE AGAIN SWUNG TOO FAR AND IS IN NEED OF CORRECTION.

An emphasis on quantitative methods and analytic techniques is fine, as long as you are already dealing with your best ideas about the situation you face and the alternatives open to you. But the more turbulent and chaotic the environment of business becomes, the less likely that is to be true. In those conditions, something else is needed—something that will help put better ideas and alternatives on the table for analytic consideration and quantitative assessment. We propose that a design attitude toward problem solving can do that.

Even seemingly nonquantitative frameworks that are central to our curricula today, such as Porter's strategy model or Kaplan's balanced scorecard model, share some of the characteristics of the most advanced analytic techniques. They enable managers to take extremely complex, ambiguous, and multifaceted situations and bring them under a conceptual apparatus that breaks them down into component pieces in order to apply logical operations for thinking through difficult decisions. This seems eminently sensible, but it springs from a mind-set and approach to management problems that is, in part, to blame for the sad record of management performance. They are the latest default alternatives for thinking through complex situations. The ideas and alternatives for action to be considered in a decision are to a large extent already embedded in those frameworks. They do enable the surfacing of the ideas inherent in them, but they are a constraint to generating new and different ideas. This is, of course, even truer for more highly quantitative and analytic techniques.

A Workshop on Managing as Designing

As a first step in encouraging management to take a more balanced approach between the decision attitude and the design attitude, a workshop on managing as designing was the inaugural event in the Peter B. Lewis Building, sponsored by the National Science Foundation and the S. Rose Corporation.

The workshop began with a keynote presentation by Frank Gehry in which he discussed his design process and his approach to managing his own firm, Gehry Partners. That presentation, along with the question-and-answer sessions that followed, seeded the vocabulary and issues for discussion over the next two days.

On the second day, Karl Weick gave a keynote that brilliantly applied Frank Gehry's process of architectural design to the problems of organization design facing managers today. Participants had written and circulated short provocations before the workshop and developed them into the chapters that follow. These capture central themes of the workshop discussion and emphasize that architecture and other design professions have much to offer managers who are looking to increase both the logic and beauty of the organizations that they create through their day-to-day problem solving. Among the themes explored in this volume are:

- Managers, as designers, are thrown into situations that are not of their own making yet for which they are responsible to produce a desirable outcome. They operate in a problem space that has no firm basis for judging one problem-solving move as superior to another, yet they must proceed.
- Design thinking is evident in the history of management methods and organization structures and processes, especially as they relate to ensuring control of an organization. Design thinking is also at the core of effective strategy development, organizational change, and constraint-sensitive problem solving.
- Managing as designing is a collaborative process, not the work of a single, heroic maestro. Innovative methods of collaborating across disciplinary, functional, and organizational boundaries are essential to the design of successful new products and processes. Good dialogue and persuasive argumentation, along with the physical handling of artifacts, contribute to the quality of design ideas.
- Better organizational environments for successful, value-creating designs can be achieved both at the organizational and the societal level. And better approaches to the education of managers in design thinking can also be achieved. These remain as unmet challenges for the next decades on a global scale.

- We are always trapped by our vocabulary. The familiar vocabulary of management brings premature closure to problem solving by, for instance, shifting focus to discounted cash flows and calculations of cost and profit, almost before a design process has started. This can turn a design process that is best kept in a liquid state into a crystallized one and closes design inquiry.
- Using multiple models of a design problem and the working ideas for its solution can bring out different aspects of the design problem, different difficulties to be overcome, and a different sense of what a good solution might be—all of which contribute to a higher quality solution.
- Sketching, mapping, and storytelling are potential complements to models, both physical and analytic, in keeping an evolving understanding of a design problem in a more liquid state.
- Beware of falling in love with your ideas. In a difficult situation, the pressure is intense to find a solution, and the first good idea you encounter will hold great attraction. It is hard not to fall in love with an attractive idea, especially if it is your own, but a good design solution requires that you remain open to letting it go as alternatives arise.
- Seek functional solutions that meet the widest possible meaning of *functional*.
- A design solution is only truly functional if it meets the design criteria of all who are affected by it, including customers, employees, neighbors, public, and future generations. This turns the criteria of functionality into an endless search because all the competing demands can never be met, and helps keep our approach to a problem in a liquid state.
- Above all, try! Try to break from the default solution. Try to solve each design problem in a better way than before. Try to expand the advantageous, innovative use of technologies, including those that are emerging, as well as those that are forgotten. Try improvising with available technologies and ideas as a form of innovation. Try to strengthen the range and power of your design vocabulary, including the metaphorical imagery and narratives you draw on to inspire your thinking. Try to set the highest standards for design excellence and refuse to settle for unnecessary compromises.

References

Simon, H. A. 1996. *The sciences of the artificial*, 3rd ed. Cambridge, MA: MIT Press.

50

‹ Bansky

SIMONETTA CARBONARO AND
CHRISTIAN VOTAVA ❮ Form Follows Sense. New Innovation and Design Strategies for Crisis-Ridden Times

While leaders of countries all around the world are at work wrapping up one of the largest economic stimulus packages since the Great Depression and Roosevelt's New Deal 75 years ago, we cannot simply go on our merry way as if nothing had happened when we talk about innovation and design. If we go about differentiating between what triggered the current economic crisis and its root causes, then we come to realize that what we are going through now is not simply the recession phase of a normal business cycle. We rather find ourselves in the midst of an upheaval shaking the very foundations of our affluent, consumption-oriented Western societies. This cataclysm began gradually about 30 years ago and flared up with growing intensity with each successive crisis—beginning with the two oil shocks of the 1970s, to the bursting of the dot-com bubble and 9/11, and on to our current global economic debacle.

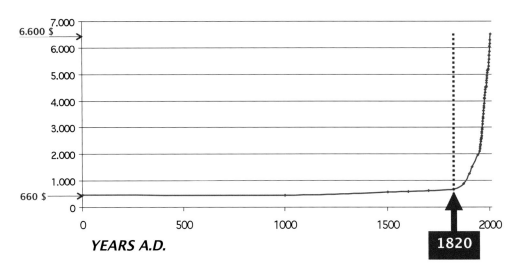

‹ World GDP per CAPITA (in 1990 international $)
Source: Angus Maddison / OECD / IMF

Despite the many signs and omens, we are somehow overcome by surprise as we behold a major shift in the course of our Western developmental model based on non-stop material growth. And nobody really knows for sure in which direction this journey is headed or even where it might ultimately be taking us. Because what we are so desperately lacking nowadays is the design of a future, the design of a new conception of prosperity that can give us hope again in these crisis-ridden times and the strength to effectuate change.

When I speak of the design of prosperity, I use the term "design" in its English-language sense, which does not refer strictly to the configuration of objects as is the case in German. What I mean by design is, first and foremost, the elaboration of new models for living from which, in a second step, real innovations in the form of new products, new services or new processes can be derived. In contrast to inventions, most of which are carried out from a purely technical or technological perspective, these innovations address people, strike a chord, and, with their inherent powers of persuasion, launch social and cultural transformations.

DESIGN IS THUS A MIGHTY CULTURAL INSTRUMENT AND ONE OF THE MOST IMPORTANT ONES IN TIMES OF CRISIS.

In order to design social innovations, one must first of all come to terms with the forces driving change. We have to closely scrutinize the prevailing social paradigm—the patterns of thinking and behavior of our affluent, consumption-oriented society—to understand the reasons for change that could bring about a paradigm shift.

Modernity's Impetus to Growth

When we trace the development of mankind's economic achievements, we notice that not much happened over millions of years. It was not until the beginning of the 19th century that the world's gross domestic product (GDP) truly began to take off—from an estimated $600 per capita to today's figure of approximately $6,600 per capita. This enormous spurt in growth was made possible by a new type of human being, the successor to *homo habilis, homo erectus,* and *homo sapiens* that our Western Civilization has brought forth over the course of successive stages of cultural development: *homo modernicus.*

This *homo modernicus* is a rational being upon whom Enlightenment philosophy made a powerful impact. He is a free and democratic Man who displays solidarity with others and is still guided by the values of the French Revolution. He is the ingenious being who planned and carried out the Industrial Revolution. He is a pragmatic person who thinks in economic terms, the one who created capitalism and the social market economy. But this *homo modernicus* is also

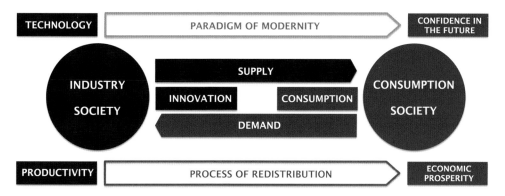

- → LABOUR MARKET
- → SOCIAL PARTNERS
- → WELFARE STATE

an exuberant Man, who threw himself with all his youthful
enthusiasm into hyperconsumerism and the globalization
project in order to be able to keep up with the exponential
trend of economic growth at compound annual growth rates.
And ultimately, he is also a creature that tends to get carried
away, one who, ever since the 1980s, has gone beyond his
goal of harvesting and correctly managing the profit of the
real economy and launched himself into the hazard of the
speculative financial markets.

The Rise and Fall of Consumer Society

According to general economic insights, this economic
growth that has been going on for more than two centuries
now is based upon self-perpetuating processes. On the
supply side, growth makes it possible to invest in research
and development, which brings forth technological
innovations. They lead to new products or more efficient
production processes, which assure further growth as
long as, on the demand side, consumption also steadily
increases. And this, in turn, is possible when growth
contributes to increasing people's material prosperity so
that they can also play the role of consumers and users that
has been assigned to them.

Technological progress as the driving force behind
growth could successfully rebut many of the scenarios of
catastrophe that have been conjured up—for instance,

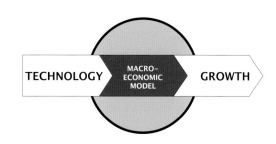

the problem of world hunger, which has been solved (at least on paper) by increases in agricultural productivity. Nevertheless, the ongoing industrialization of our production and manufacturing processes leads to increased stress on the environment and produces the next generation of problems.

Our Consumer Society as the other driving force behind growth has, with its wide array of wares, provided all of us with a certain degree of well-being and enjoyment of life. The fabulous luxuries now offered by our mass markets were available only to the ruling classes of ancient Egypt, the Roman Empire or feudal Europe.

But by the late 1970s, French philosopher Jean-François Lyotard was already pointing out that Western Civilizations would be unable to cope with globalization and the IT Revolution. He showed how the new challenges were beginning to dissolve the modern world's internal integrity based on cohesion, coherence and conformism.

AS A LOGICAL CONSEQUENCE, LYOTARD ANNOUNCED THE BEGINNING OF A NEW AGE: THE POSTMODERN.

This was said to be characterized by the explosion of individuality, the end of the rational attitude towards the world, and the emergence of a fragile and fragmented *Weltanschauung* that, like a patchwork, was comprised of a hodgepodge of deconstructed fragments of the Western past. This postmodern attitude led to a fundamental rethinking in the field of marketing as well. In the Modern Age, standardized mass-produced wares could still appeal to consumers and satisfy their needs, but for the insecure and fragmented ego of the postmodern customer, hyper-reality and fiction were more attractive and more convincing than what is real. This is why marketing people increasingly ceased taking consumers' needs as the point of departure of an enterprise's activities and instead concentrated more intensely on consumers' wishes and desires.

With this change of perspective, Western economies developed away from economies of needs into economies of added values in which more importance was placed on the symbolic and immaterial values of products than on their material and functional qualities. In the dream factory

that materialized as a result, design became an increasingly important marketing instrument for creating factors of differentiation and competitive advantages. To live up to the demands of this new role, designers liberated themselves from the dictates of modernism, and the motto "form follows function" morphed into one better suited to the *Zeitgeist*: "form follows fiction." Since dreams, by their very nature, vanish in the blink of an eye, the marketing model based on wishes instead of needs drives a vicious circle of pressure to innovate and ever-shorter product lifecycles, and floods already saturated markets with regular waves of hyper-differentiated products.

Today, an average person living in a developed country possesses more than 10,000 objects. And the more things that occupy the space in which we spend our everyday lives, the more superficial our relationship to them is and the faster they sink into oblivion. We live amidst material overabundance that makes us bored and weary.

AND LIKE EVERY FORM OF WEARINESS, OUR "EXCESSIVILIZATION" POLARIZES MORE AND MORE PEOPLE'S BEHAVIOR AS CONSUMERS.

They swing back and forth between buying-bulimia and shopping-anorexia, between fleeting, senseless consumption on one hand and resolutely swearing off new purchases on the other, and end up feeling increasingly forlorn and unsatisfied amidst the markets of our Consumer Society that, in the meantime, have become utterly saturated.

The Costs of Doing Nothing

I need not underscore the fact that the ability of our Consumer Society to move forward depends on equilibrium between, on one hand, economic growth and, on the other, material prosperity, general well-being and confidence in the future. Indeed, there are serious doubts as to whether this equilibrium can really be maintained in this day and age. Various indicators such as the Index of Sustainable Economic Welfare that attempt to define and quantify prosperity show that the growth trend of the economy has

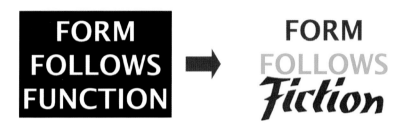

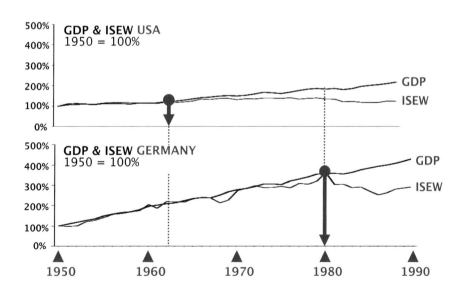

increasingly uncoupled from that of prosperity. Economists agree in principle that an ever-growing proportion of GDP consists of repair and maintenance expenditures by our society for economic growth. Accordingly, this portion of growth makes absolutely no contribution to prosperity and private consumption!

British government advisor Sir Nicholas Stern powerfully expressed the impact of this idle output on the economy in statistical terms with respect to environmental pollution and degradation. His report, which came out in 2006 and was subsequently confirmed in late January 2009 by a McKinsey world climate study, put the costs of climate change at up to 20% of worldwide GDP if we fail to implement countermeasures immediately.

ON THE OTHER HAND, THE COSTS OF A NECESSARY REDUCTION OF GREENHOUSE GASES WERE CALCULATED TO BE APPROXIMATELY 1% OF WORLDWIDE GDP!

In most countries, a much higher percentage of the budget is appropriated for measures to boost economic growth! Nevertheless, many experts have serious doubts about whether these stimulus packages can get us out of the crisis. And these experts have no patent remedies of their own. Macroeconomics today is neither able to describe the effects the many different national economic policy measures have on complex, networked systems like our global economy, nor can it make accurate statements about how long it takes for such systems to react to various types of stimuli. Thus we must realize that not only did we get mixed up in an adventure of deregulation, liberalization and globalization three decades ago that set off with a proclamation of faith though without a tiller to steer our course, but also that we and our economic stimulus programs are still navigating without a map to this day!

Societies' Momentum

Thus, it will take quite a while until macroeconomics can keep pace with real-world economic challenges. Societies, on the other hand, develop in response to the reality of everyday life. A society does indeed adapt to politicians' decisions—be they right or wrong—but it also always develops a momentum of its own that propels it forward and enables it to continuously organize itself in such a way that the actions of individual human beings make sense. On the other side of our world, people live in the hope of attaining prosperity and living a Western lifestyle—a hope

that is, however, threatening to vanish due to the global economic crisis. The inhabitants of our side of the planet, on the other hand, are bidding farewell to what is now seen as an impossible dream: constantly growing material prosperity and climbing the social ladder. This was the dream of John and Jane Doe, who even quite recently were still identifying themselves as members of the middle class. These people aren't all that concerned about which index is used to measure prosperity, nor do they completely understand the logic behind the measures implemented to rescue our economic system. They only notice that the bursting of the speculative bubbles has also left deep holes in their own pockets, that planet Earth has in the meantime become as small as their own flat, and, suddenly, everything from the price of bread and electricity to the yield they're getting on their retirement savings is somehow interconnected. They have understood that the so-called BRIC countries have awakened and are hoovering up energy, raw materials and jobs in order to manufacture cheap products not only for their own domestic consumption but for worldwide export. Of course, as they have gone about their daily shopping trips, they have also come to the realization that these very same cheap products are precisely what has until recently enabled them to more or less maintain their standard of living despite declining real income. Nevertheless, their employer's "headcount reduction measures" have made crystal clear to them the tremendous extent to which competition from emerging countries is belaboring domestic industries and how even their own jobs have come to be strongly dependent on the new markets that are threatening to break away due to the crisis. They have the feeling that they as individuals as well as their political leaders are completely impotent and helpless in the face of these global interlinkages.
The lives of John and Jane Doe have thus suddenly and unexpectedly changed. In addition to worries about their standard of living, their job and their pension, there are their private crises triggered by the demise of the traditional family model and conventional gender roles.

New Forms of Consumer Behavior

In view of the economic, social and environmental turbulence we've experienced of late, the lifestyle we've been enjoying—one oriented on material consumption, ephemeral hedonism and carefree fun—can no longer provide the security we so desperately need today.

WHAT WAS SO SELF-EVIDENT UNTIL RECENTLY NOW SEEMS REMARKABLY UNREASONABLE. NO MORE EXTRAVAGANCES!

aesthetics of ethics

The excesses and exaggerations of an approach to design that, as handmaiden of marketing, dealt in transient fantasies and dream-worlds instead of real innovations belong to the Postmodern Age that is now coming to an end. Consumers are fed up with incessantly running like hamsters on a "hedonistic treadmill" and are beginning to discover "down-to-earth happiness", a kind of "happy frugality", as the new lifestyle of choice. They have developed a profound longing for that which is authentic and what can be termed real quality, since what they aim to achieve with the act of consumption is no longer just satisfying individual needs but also expressing their own personal value system and their social orientation. Of course, consumption still remains connected to the act of acquiring objects of desire; nevertheless, our research results clearly show that consumers can no longer be motivated using the same ways and means in which consumption manifests itself at present.

THEY HAVE COME TO PREFER PRUDENCE AND MODERATION TO HUCKSTERING AND BALLYHOO, AND FIND THE AESTHETICS OF ETHICS INCREASINGLY APPEALING.

‹ Fragile

57

This new consumer behavior—some aspects of which were associated with politicized niche groups espousing extreme austerity-glorifying ideals in the past—is now reemerging among mainstream consumers active in our supersaturated markets. It pervades all social strata and cuts across generational lines. Consumers perceive the plethora of designed products, stylized retail outlets and extravagant messages competing for their attention as mere pretexts to separate them from more of their money. It appears as though they are now pleading for a respite in the wake of all the turmoil and aberrations that have marked this time of "overconsumerism." Nevertheless, many consumer products manufacturers and retailers are steadfastly clinging to their magic formulas of push marketing and lifestyle designs. They are still banking on design of the image, and continue to gaily sprinkle stardust as a glamorous glaze applied to people's everyday lives.

So it's no wonder that consumers have become more shopping reluctant. They are harder to impress with advertising messages, and are paying closer attention to items' price-quality ratio. This is why they prefer discount stores, factory outlets of all sorts or private label retailers like IKEA, Habitat and H&M that are able to offer premium quality and even designer products at discount prices. The only luxuries they are willing to splurge on are a good meal or a very individualized gift, something small that has a big

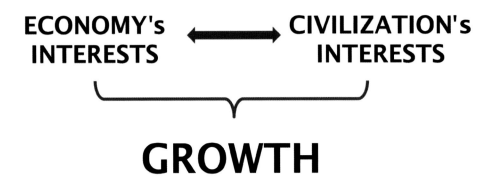

ECONOMY's INTERESTS ⟷ **CIVILIZATION's INTERESTS**

GROWTH

and highly personal meaning because it can succinctly tell a whole story about itself and its new owner. It is one of a kind—that is, not just a "designed" object but very probably one that is handmade as well.

Consuming Critically and Responsibly

For over 10 years now, we have known that consumers are becoming more mature, better informed and more demanding. But we also have to consider that they have suddenly become much more critical too. They are no longer satisfied with the added value of immaterial benefits that have been offered to them up to now. They also want to have a look behind the scenes in order to confront and evaluate the world of consumerism. This critical attitude on the part of the consumer is not directed against consumption per se; instead, it's an expression of the consumer's new need to scrutinize the values an enterprise embodies and espouses, and to be able to get actively involved in the design and value creation process. We ought not interpret this as an "ethification" of consumption, but rather as a concrete manifestation of personal values via the act of consuming. It is the logical consequence of a new sense of social and ecological responsibility on the part of more and more consumers.

The principle of responsibility rings in a new era in the history of consumption. Indeed, if one regards society not as an abstract entity upon which the individual can have hardly any effect but rather as a community that defines

itself in terms of the interplay of individuals' actions, then even the most common everyday activity like shopping takes on social relevance. In this sense, consumption is an active, self-determined and thoroughly political act that is capable not only of endowing our own life with meaning but also of establishing a relationship to all the other people in our society and throughout the world. Thus, consumption today is no longer connected solely with the longing for pleasure and fun—with American-style pursuit of happiness. Now, consumption also expresses a sense of responsibility for society, the environment and our future. Only this synthesis of the interests of our economy and those of our civilization will be able to generate growth in the future.

There is a growing number of websites on which consumers can exchange information about particular brands, goods and services, and form buying co-ops as a means of obtaining genuine, original, natural, organic, traditional or regional products. In Italy, there are consumers who only buy products labeled as containing "Vitamin L," whereby "L" stands for legality and designates products from Sicilian co-ops such as Terra Libera that have taken a stand against organized crime and grow crops on fields confiscated from the Mafia. Others believe that the "0 KM" seal constitutes a guarantee for local production because it stands for products—like the fashion brand "cdsb," for instance—that were manufactured in prisons. It is probably Italy's only fashion brand that provides consumers with absolute assurance that the particular article truly was 100% Made in Italy.

SOCIETY

RESPONSIBILITY **ENVIRONMENT**

FUTURE

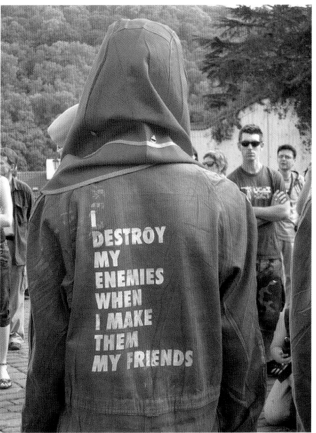

I DESTROY MY ENEMIES WHEN I MAKE THEM MY FRIENDS

‹ Luca Orta

❮ Christien Meindertsma

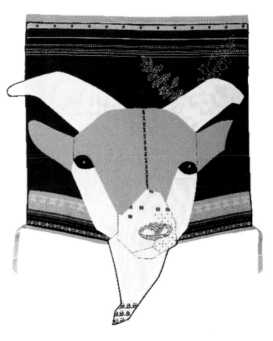

❮ Hella Jongerius for IKEA PS collection 2009

‹ www.do-knit-yourself.com / N. Branzi

‹ JR-ART

And then there are those who have, to some extent or other, gone the do-it-yourself route. They join together to form peaceful armies outfitted with hoes and seed in order to use tiny urban parcels or acreage leased from farmers to cultivate their own fruit and vegetables. Or, equipped with needles and wool, they convene in so-called knitting cafes that have been proliferating in big cities of late. Those attending these get togethers are not just partaking of serene harmony as a setting in which to knit socks and sweaters to augment their own wardrobe; they have also been known to gather into what amounts to street gangs to endow the cityscape with emotionally expressive accents in the form of their "self-knitted graffiti." In the same spirit, DIYers and hobby craftsmen are forming social networks based on mutual assistance and shared experience, and their output can often stand up to comparison with the work of professionals. Just check out some of the elaborate DIY websites to get an idea of the extensive knowledge and information available online.

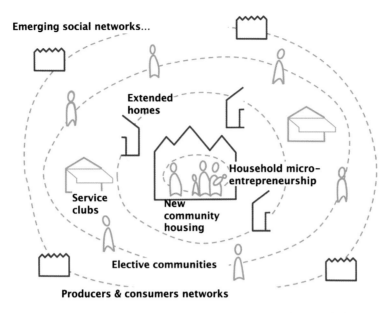

Emerging social networks...

Extended homes

Household micro-entrepreneurship

Service clubs

New community housing

Elective communities

Producers & consumers networks

❮ Creative communities. People inventing sustainable ways of living. Milano. PoliDesign.

As we can see, people have started taking matters into their own hands. They've even begun to develop into designers of new communitarian ways of life. Anyone who plays trend scout and opens his/her eyes to what's happening in the world now will discover countless social innovations of this sort.

The most sensible and most promising social innovations seem to be the so-called co-housing projects in which people from a wide variety of backgrounds band together into new residential, housing or settlement communities. They do not do so for purely economic reasons, but rather first and foremost as a way to escape the alienation of the postmodern way of life and to be able to enjoy a better and more sustainable existence. These usually multigenerational communities define themselves as everyday social networks. Accordingly, in most instances, household chores and a portion of the shopping are accomplished jointly via division of labor or as a group, and the members provide mutual support to a much greater extent than would generally be the case among people who are simply neighbors. Needless to say, each individual household unit—single, family, single parent with kids—has its own living space and a private sphere all of its own.

Designing Social Innovation

Generally speaking, the design of a co-housing project is also done communally. After all, this is not simply a matter of moving into or constructing one or more buildings, but rather of designing a new model for living and thus a

highly existential process for everyone involved. Designers and architects are assigned the task of channeling the creative flow. They interpret and organize the collective creativity, orchestrate it into a new system and, with the concepts they thus develop, give a concrete form to the community's future coexistence. Doing so entails proceeding step-by-step to create a consensus for the final design. Designers and architects such as John Thackara have reinvented social engineering with their strategic design management approach. They serve as consultants to government agencies and NGOs, and are commissioned by municipalities to work together with local residents on new service concepts.

Other designers like Ezio Manzini's group at the Politecnico di Milano use their insights into social innovations as stimuli to come up with highly innovative business models. One example is the concept of the service club that interlinks various thematically related services and, by integrating local users, vendors and infrastructure, makes these services available to citydwellers in a way that is economical and sustainable. For instance, there's a laundromat with an attached restaurant in which people can enjoy a glass of wine, good food and pleasant company while their clothes are in the machine, or even use what would otherwise be their leisure time to do the laundry. Or how about an atelier for the redesign of old clothes? Here, expert supervision can help users transform, perhaps, some worn-out men's shirts into a new evening dress. A service club can also be a website on which you can order your favorite dish from the gourmet granny down the block!

❮ Creative communities. People inventing sustainable ways of living. Milano. PoliDesign. / Emude

But designers don't just plan and implement social innovations and new business models nowadays. There are also those who have broken through the boundary separating conception and production—as entrepreneurs, they're implementing their own projects in small factories or worldshop-like operations. They've gotten into producing specific articles for niche markets and thus constitute a countervailing trend to classical industrial design, a field largely dominated by star designers and top-name consulting firms.

It would be a mistake, though, to conceive of the production facilities of these new design-oriented niche vendors as low-tech crafts and trades workshops. Quite the contrary. These new design entrepreneurs also consider their handicraft as an artform, whereby they have truly mastered the art of deploying and implementing small, flexible, high-tech machinery that is now available to virtually anyone. And like any good artist, they're also good at selling. They establish relationships with local shops or even department stores, which are beginning to open up their shelf space to niche products because smart retailers have come to understand the strategic significance of excellence within the overall assortment of merchandise they purvey. Nevertheless, their preferred channel of distribution and above all communication is the internet with its viral properties. They master the art of word-of-mouth advertising via blogs—and, most recently, video blogs—and see to it that their products, principles and production methods are talked up in particular forums. Just as Chris Anderson brought out in his book "The Long Tail," the internet is an integral part of the business strategy of niche vendors because it turns a mass of markets into a virtual mass market for products that are either truly innovative, one-of-a-kind or of superb quality.

It would be wrong to consider these niche vendors as a direct threat to the industrial mass market because they will never be able to replace it. That would be a regressive development that only a few proponents of neo-pauperism would perhaps advocate. Nevertheless, the creativity of a new generation of young, wild and incredibly talented designers constitutes a supplement and a constant challenge to industrial merchandise offerings, and this can lead to interesting new consumption scenarios and fascinating forms of the symbiosis of Class and Mass.

From a macroeconomic perspective, these niche vendors will develop into an important source of new jobs in our postindustrial society precisely because their business model is not oriented on exploiting economies of scale.

From Materials to Meaning

Understanding the significance of social innovations and socio-cultural currents is not only a very rich source of new business ideas; it's also the point of departure for the design of our material world. Only when we begin to shift our perspective away from material facts and circumstances—whereby material also subsumes clients' wishes, since they are, after all, mostly just projections of the world as it is—and focus on what subliminally motivates and moves people are we able to make really innovative quantum leaps. Otherwise, design remains an exercise in re-styling that continues going round and round in Buy Society's vicious circle.

This shift of perspective from the material onto the social and cultural level is also of particular importance for technological innovations. Let's not lose sight of the fact that technology in the form of inventions only brings forth new technology that does not yet make sense in the lives of actual human users (and thus for the market too). Cultural innovations are what generate new needs and thereby determine which technological innovations people perceive as an enhancement of their quality of life. Thus, a designer who understands how to shape cultural innovations with technological inventions—for example, Steve Jobs with the iPod—is one who ultimately creates technological innovations.

In going about this nowadays, the subject of sustainability assumes particular importance because people are especially concerned about ecological issues like climate change and the depletion of fossil fuel reserves. For the design of the material world, this means a mandatory orientation on the guiding principles of the "cradle-to-cradle" approach that is based on cyclical reusability of all material inputs and regards end products like waste as resources for use in new products. In this way, technology can at least help us take a step in the direction of resolving the contradiction between economy and ecology.

But even assuming—purely theoretically—that we could immediately create a sustainable world with the help of

technology, consumer behavior would change only minimally. As mentioned at the outset, our Western civilization is desperately in search of an ecology of the spirit because the people of this civilization no longer see the sense of material consumption as it now takes place. According to the findings of Nobel Prize-winning psychologist Daniel Kahneman, we are currently in transition from an economy of material wealth to an "economy of happiness." In such an economy, a higher value is assigned to those goods that have significance only in communities and cannot be exchanged, reproduced or substituted—for example, security, peace, friendship, forthrightness, culture, knowledge, or simply time. We are thus moving away from a consumer culture of "possessing" that is oriented on material objects and towards a consumer culture of "being." In this new consumption model, what counts is that which is of substance, our convictions and values. Thus, today there is more validity than ever in Max Weber's insight that consumption is a process of endowing life with meaning that supports people as they go about getting in touch with themselves. Such a paradigm shift requires a profound cultural and social transformation like other such upheavals that have marked the course of human history: the propagation of Christianity, the Renaissance, the Enlightenment. Who else but artists and designers could accompany and impel this cultural transformation taking place today? However, to fulfill this role, designers must escape the clutches of marketing execs and develop a new conception of self oriented on the motto "form follows sense."

Design as Radical Action

Allow me to present a few examples of how design can be a very sensitive seismograph of sociocultural currents and can initiate cultural transformations. In the 1970s, I had the good fortune of working at Olivetti together with Ettore Sottsass, a masterful designer and, by the way, as a South Tyrolean, also a bit of an Austrian. For him, industrial design was a form of discussion, a way to talk about life, society or even the erotic. The possibilities afforded by technology weren't the centerpiece of his nonconformist designs; the focus was always on human beings and their dreams. He understood design as a means of creating a better society via objects employed in everyday life. And he used design to bring humanistic approaches to bear amidst

65

the Modern Age's prevailing corporate culture of "scientific management" that was chiefly characterized at the time by standardization and uniformity.

Back then, fashion designers too were attempting to break out of the rigidity and conformism of the Modern Age. Consider if you will how Vivienne Westwood created a rebellious line of clothing that took a high-profile stand against the traditionalism of the British bourgeoisie. Her unscrupulous creations were an expression of the cry for freedom of an entire generation and of its members' need to break away from bourgeois morality. The *grande dame* of British fashion designers continues to display the courage of her convictions in the campaigns she's still launching to this day. And more than 30 years ago, Armani didn't just invent *prêt-à-porter* fashion and democratize luxury; he broke with the role model of woman as housewife and mother, and created a new type of woman who, with boldly formed shoulders, strode ambitiously, confidently and proudly into a working world dominated by men and pervaded by masculinity. By putting women into slacks without depriving them of a tailored waistline, he perfectly captured the spirit of the times. And then there's Katharine Hamnett, an English fashion designer who, back in the 1980s, was already anticipating elements of the cultural transformation going on today. With her concept of so-called "wearable politics," she was one of the first to address the sustainability problems of our hyperconsumerist society; her famous T-shirts called attention to ecological and social issues inherent in textile production and took an in-your-face stance against Thatcher's neo-liberalism.

Even if these designers didn't change the course of history, they made history and triggered cultural changes. Today, the process of cultural transformation to a new conception of prosperity is in the hands of a new generation of designers. They have the numbers, they have the courage, and they've already gotten busy on the job of re-designing design. They demonstrate that innovations can entail recycling used elements and that it can emerge from the dialog between tradition and the spirit of the age. They show us that technology doesn't necessarily call for muscles; a light and elegant look can work too. They show us that our greatest cultural wealth is our cultural diversity and that this is a source for generating new wealth. Finally, they show us that this new generation of designers is ready to face the new challenge: namely, the design of change.

The Modern Age's conception of values was shaped by the belief in technological progress that was supported by strong social pressure to conform. Globalization and the IT Revolution characterized the transition to the new Postmodern Age distinguished by the explosion of individualism and the emergence of Me, Inc.—one believed only in oneself, and was open to being swept away by

hedonistic seductions of all sorts. Consumers' longings for significance and responsibility is what is driving a new upheaval thrusting our Western Civilization in the direction of a "We Society" based on a wide array of different forms of new collective conceptions of values. This upheaval is being powered by a cultural transformation that will also make an impact on our economy. The transition will be from a mass market arrested in the logic of economies of scale to an economy composed of masses of different markets.

This need for significance and responsibility is closely connected to another one of humankind's fundamental needs: the need to grow and to continuously reinvent oneself. But only that which grows out of our relationship to others is important to us, expands our horizons and spurs us on to transcend our previous limits. Following the economy of material needs and the economy of immaterial wishes, the economy of significance and responsibility rings in Consumer Society's next and probably final growth phase, since it's the only economy that is sustainable while simultaneously allowing for unlimited growth.

66

‹ Ilvio Gallo

References

Anderson, C. 2007. The Long tail. How endless choice is creating unlimited demand. London: Random House Business Books.

Bateson, G. 1973. Steps to an ecology of mind. Collected essays in anthropology, psychiatry, evolution and epistemology. London: Granada.

Baudrillard, J. 2005. The consumer society. Myths and structures. London: Sage.

Braungart, M. 2003. Cradle to cradle. Remarking the way we make things. New York: Rodale Press.

Carbonaro, S. and Votava, C. 2008. The significance of growth. IRT Conference key-note paper, Sept. 2008, Gottlieb Duttweiler Institut.

Daly, E. 1991. Steady-state economics. Washington, DC: Island Press.

Deitch, J. 2001. Form follows fiction: Forma e finzione nell'arte de oggi. Milano: Charta.

Diamond, J. 2004. Collapse: How societies choose to fail or succeed. New York: Viking Adult.

ECP (European Cultural Parliament) Research Group. 2006. Culture, the heart of a knowledge-based economy—the strategic use of culture in the European project. Paper from the 5th Session in the Åbo Akademi University, Turku, Finland, 15–17 Sept. 2006. Tuscany: ECP.

Florida, R. 2002. The rise of the creative class and how it's transforming work, leisure, community and everyday life. New York: Basic Books.

Kahneman, D., Diener, E. and Schwarz, N. (eds.) 2003. Well-being. Foundations of hedonic psychology. New York: Russell Sage Foundation.

Keynes, J. M. 1933. National self-sufficiency. The Yale Review. Vol. 22(4): 755–769.

Lovelock, J. 2009. The face of Gaia. Enjoy it while you can. London: Penguin.

Maddison, A. 2001. The world economy. A millennial perspective. Paris: OECD.

Meroni, A. (ed.) 2007. Creative communities. People inventing sustainable ways of living. Milano: PoliDesign.

Morin, E. 1999. Seven complex lessons in education for the future. Paris: UNESCO.

Ruffolo, G. 2008. Il capitalismo ha i secoli contati. Turin: Einaudi.

Sollow, R. 2007. The last 50 years in growth theory and the next 10. Oxford Review of Economic Policy. Vol. 23(1): 3–14.

Sullivan, L. 1896. The tall office building artistically considered. Lippincott's Magazine. March.

The Design of Prosperity Initiative: www.thedesignofprosperity.se

Virilio, P. 2008. Open sky. London: Verso.

Weber, M. 1922. Wirtschaft und Gesellschaft. Tübingen: Mohr. Later edition: Weber, M. 1978. Economy and Society. Berkeley: Univ. of California Press.

GREG VAN ALSTYNE ❮

How We Learned to Pluralize the Future: Foresight Scenarios as Design Thinking

What is the role of design in addressing complex problems? I make the case that one of the most powerful forms of design thinking is the approach known as strategic foresight, including scenario methods that have evolved specifically to deal with situations of great complexity and uncertainty. Tracing a path from the rise of visualization capabilities in early humans, to the birth of scenarios following World War II, to the foresight and design research of Strategic Innovation Lab (sLab) in present-day Toronto, Canada, the paper develops unexpected connections between the unthinkable terror of nuclear armageddon and our current quest for a better, more sustainable world.

"TO BE FULLY AWARE OF THE SHAPE OF REALITY IS NECESSARILY TO GLANCE BEYOND ITS BOUNDARIES ON ALL SIDES." (HERMAN KAHN, 1963)

One evening, long after business hours, in the middle of the twentieth century, a sociologist, novelist, and screenwriter named Leo Rosten was walking the corridors of a military-funded think tank in Los Angeles known as RAND Corporation, named for its principal activity: "R and D." At the time RAND was playing an increasingly influential role in an emerging US network at the nexus of science, society, strategy and policy. Less than a decade earlier, American technological might had helped to bring closure to the war by obliterating the Japanese towns of Hiroshima and Nagasaki. Now an entirely different set of problems known as the Cold War was keeping a new generation of intellectuals up late, and on that particular night, Rosten was suddenly beckoned into a room by a group of physicists. The scientists needed a name for alternative, hypothetical descriptions for how a satellite might behave, and Rosten, who was moonlighting at RAND, drew on his cinematic experience. "Call them 'scenarios'," he said. The leader of the group, the infamous futurist Herman Kahn, loved the term for its literary, playful, even mythic overtones—and a powerful form of long-range planning was born. (Kleiner, 1996: 150)

The question taken up in this paper concerns the role and relevance of design in solving complex problems and creating desired futures. I wish to interrogate this idea of "futures," in the plural, and ask: how did we learn to think this way? When we think about what could or should happen in years to come, we can think about "*the future*" as a singular term, or we can exercise our deep human capacity to imagine multiple, interrelated possibilities: possible futures. In this brief paper I will tell the story of how we learned to multiply thought and imagination in this

way, to *pluralize the future*. I will argue and advocate for this skill as an indispensable facet and form of design thinking in a world of increasing turbulence and velocity. The story unfolds across three periods of time. To begin to explain these periods and their significance, let me first say what I mean by "we" in the phrase "how we learned to pluralize the future":

- By "we" I mean the human species. Early humans evolved the unique ability to imagine alternative futures roughly 40,000 years ago, near the close of the geological epoch known as the Pleistocene, popularly known as Earth's last Great Ice Age.
- By "we" I mean Western research and managerial culture, in the decades following World War II. Through a brief history of foresight, I will outline the story of how military and civilian researchers and managers invented modern techniques for pluralizing the future, in particular through the methodology known as Scenario Planning or Scenario Learning.
- By "we" I mean my research institute in Toronto, Canada—Strategic Innovation Lab (sLab). sLab is a centre for design research, innovation and strategic foresight at the Ontario College of Art and Design. My colleagues and I are working to develop, refine and apply strategic foresight and innovation theory, methodology, and practice. Scenario learning is a critical technique in which we're investing.

What are Foresight Scenarios?

"UNCERTAINTY TODAY IS NOT JUST AN OCCASIONAL, TEMPORARY DEVIATION FROM A REASONABLE PREDICTABILITY; IT IS A BASIC STRUCTURAL FEATURE OF THE BUSINESS ENVIRONMENT." (PIERRE WACK, 1985)

The aim of this paper is to see what we can learn by viewing foresight scenarios as a form of design thinking. This focus covers the professional discipline known as "strategic foresight," and in particular the methodology known as "scenario planning," sometimes called "scenario learning" or just "scenarios." While I intend to deal with history and theory, my purpose is ultimately practical in several respects: first, design is itself ultimately practical; it seeks to reorganize and improve real aspects of the world and human experience in highly tangible ways. And second, I'm part of an ambitious project to build a research institute and graduate program dedicated to foresight and innovation, whose ultimate goal is to catalyze real, positive change in the world. I have more than two decades experience in communication and experience design, including an ambitious, three-year project on the future of global design entitled *Massive Change*. Following that experience it seemed that my lifelong interest in future possibilities may in fact be a calling, which led me toward my current appointment in higher education and research. Against this backdrop I've undertaken a critical investigation of histories, theories and practical techniques of foresight in the context of design and innovation research.

For those not acquainted with it, strategic foresight is a collaborative, facilitated planning activity that involves thinking about, debating, envisioning, and actively shaping the future. It requires researching, understanding and making choices while anticipating and navigating change, recognizing and making sense of emerging signals from science and technology, the socio-cultural domain, the marketplace, the legal and political environments. Building foresight requires clarity of vision, an honest appraisal of organizational capability, and effective communication, so that insights can be converted into opportunities for innovation and success. Strategic foresight draws from, but differs from, an array of related disciplines including futures studies, forecasting, technology assessment, and science fiction.

AND AS WE WILL SEE, FORESIGHT SHARES DEEP ROOTS WITH THE IMPULSES AND ACTIVITIES THAT UNDERLIE DESIGN PRACTICE AND DESIGN THINKING.

With this definition of foresight in mind, I will briefly outline scenarios and allow further discussion below to fill in between the lines. Scenarios are perhaps best understood as *stories of alternative futures*, that are analytically, synthetically and collaboratively woven together from emerging signals of change. Scenarios are neither predictions, nor forecasts, in that they make no explicit claim to represent a single most likely path or destination. Rather they are developed as a set of multiple divergent stories extending outward from a specific, framing research question in order to help planners foresee *possible* futures. In this way scenarios, and the rigorous yet imaginative, participatory process of envisioning them, provide the sponsoring organization or team with a high quality, multifaceted, shared mental model, such that subsequent strategies and initiatives may be built in ways that are more attentive to change and resilient in the face of uncertainty.

Foresight work uses a highly varied array of research methods. Rafael Popper developed a diamond-shaped array of foresight methods (Figure 1) to help characterize and contrast each according to its salient emphasis and orientation: creativity, interaction, expertise, or evidence. We see from the diamond that Popper positions scenarios as a highly creative, qualitative method that combines elements of both expertise and interaction. Many foresight professionals will precede scenarios work with "scanning" which can be thought of as a form of contextual observation and signal gathering, in order to inform the creative effort with large volumes of evidence. Scenarios method is a well-documented and widely utilized foresight technique. In a recent study reported by Popper (2008), scenarios were used by nearly half of all respondents. The popularity of scenarios leads to some pressing questions. How did this technique arise, what lies behind the method's increasing popularity, and why is it seemingly so relevant today?

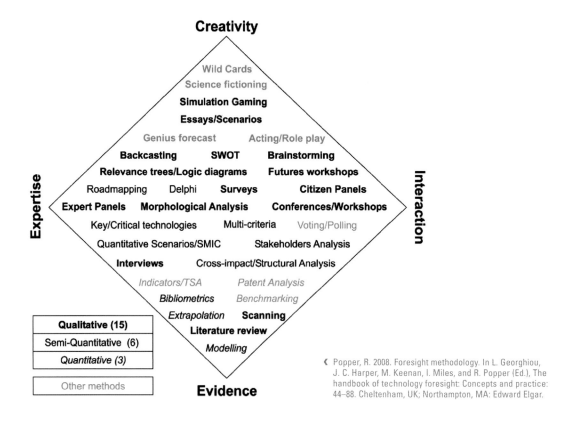

Creativity

Wild Cards
Science fictioning
Simulation Gaming
Essays/Scenarios
Genius forecast   Acting/Role play
Backcasting   SWOT   Brainstorming
Relevance trees/Logic diagrams   Futures workshops
Roadmapping   Delphi   **Surveys   Citizen Panels**
Expert Panels   Morphological Analysis   Conferences/Workshops
Key/Critical technologies   Multi-criteria   Voting/Polling
Quantitative Scenarios/SMIC   Stakeholders Analysis
Interviews   Cross-impact/Structural Analysis
Indicators/TSA   Patent Analysis
Bibliometrics   *Benchmarking*
Extrapolation   **Scanning**
Literature review
Modelling

Expertise

Interaction

Evidence

| **Qualitative (15)** |
| Semi-Quantitative (6) |
| *Quantitative (3)* |

| Other methods |

72

‹ Popper, R. 2008. Foresight methodology. In L. Georghiou, J. C. Harper, M. Keenan, I. Miles, and R. Popper (Ed.), The handbook of technology foresight: Concepts and practice: 44–88. Cheltenham, UK; Northampton, MA: Edward Elgar.

73

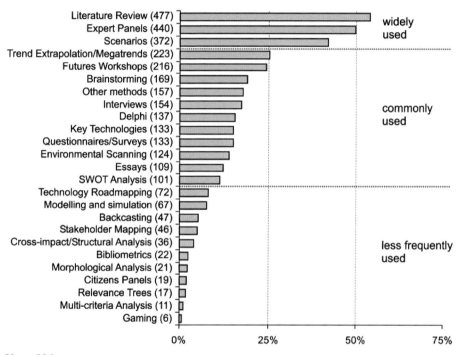

Literature Review (477) — widely used
Expert Panels (440)
Scenarios (372)
Trend Extrapolation/Megatrends (223)
Futures Workshops (216)
Brainstorming (169) — commonly used
Other methods (157)
Interviews (154)
Delphi (137)
Key Technologies (133)
Questionnaires/Surveys (133)
Environmental Scanning (124)
Essays (109)
SWOT Analysis (101)
Technology Roadmapping (72)
Modelling and simulation (67)
Backcasting (47) — less frequently used
Stakeholder Mapping (46)
Cross-impact/Structural Analysis (36)
Bibliometrics (22)
Morphological Analysis (21)
Citizens Panels (19)
Relevance Trees (17)
Multi-criteria Analysis (11)
Gaming (6)

0%   25%   50%   75%

Note: 886 cases

❮ EFMN and SELF-RULE (2008)

A point about business history may be instructive. When Frederick Winslow Taylor developed his principles of scientific management in the 1880s and 90s with the goal of improving industrial efficiency, he became one of the first "management consultants." The advent and rise of Taylorism firmly established "the numbers" as the dominant method of improving business results. Since that time, quantitative, evidence-based techniques have been seen to provide the most authoritative and reliable path to develop strategy for organizations. Yet within this preference lies a trap. For the increasing pace and volatility of change means that past performance is less and less helpful for informing decisions about future results. In contrast, through scenario learning, organizations are equipped with tools that help them make sense of complex situations, imagine unexpected possibilities, and broaden perspectives to support self-possessed and circumspect decision-making. We are enabled to do this collective, participatory sense-making because we can tap into deep-seated human capacities for imagining alternative futures, cognitive survival strategies that arose as an integral facet of our arrival as a species. But how far back do we need to look to understand the birth of our capacity to create and understand scenarios? When did we first recognize this gift?

Scenario Visualization in Early Humans

As humans developed the capacity to pluralize the future it became nothing less than one of our key defining traits, and a competitive advantage that ensured the evolutionary success of *Homo sapiens*. The first place that we learned how to pluralize the future was in the environment of the Pleistocene epoch, roughly 40,000 years ago, during the most recent glacial and interglacial period. A detailed and scholarly account of this development can be found in Robert Arp's 2008 work, *Scenario Visualization: An Evolutionary Account of Creative Problem Solving*, which leverages recent findings in biology, evolutionary psychology, and cognitive science. Arp argues that the advanced forms of toolmaking evidenced by our ancestors require a particular kind of cognitive processing which Arp (2008: 113) calls "scenario visualization":

"Scenario visualization is a conscious process that entails selecting pieces of visual information from a wide range of possibilities, forming a coherent and organized visual cognition, and then projecting that visual cognition into some suitably imagined scenario for the purpose of solving some problem posed by the environment in which one inhabits."

Arp stresses *visual* cognition, which helps support the position that is implicit throughout this paper, that the creative visual disciplines of art and design are not merely helpful but integral to the work of "pluralizing the future." Other scholars place emphasis on the birth and role of human *language*, including Dr. Robert K. Logan, Chief Scientist of Strategic Innovation Lab. In his 2007 book The Extended Mind: *The Emergence of Language, the Human Mind, and Culture*, Logan (2007: 42) states:

"Our earliest human ancestors … emerged in the savannas of Africa, where they were an easy target for various predators. To defend themselves from this threat, as well as to increase their food supply, they acquired the new skills of toolmaking, the control of fire, group foraging, and coordinated hunting. These activities resulted in a more complex form of social organization, which also increased the complexity of their lives. [A]t some point … [i]n the information overload and chaos that ensued, a new abstract level of order emerged in the form of verbal language and conceptual thinking."

What is common to these accounts is that the human gift for storytelling evolved precisely in order to make sense of complex, separate but interrelated events, engaging our cognitive faculties not only in understanding the past and present but in planning future action. Scientists working at the intersection of evolutionary biology, psychology, cognition, and creativity are beginning to articulate the early emergence of language and visual information processing in understanding our species' unique gifts. And central to this inquiry is the evolution of our human, cognitive capacity for working with scenarios.

Scenario Planning in Post-War Research:
A Brief History of the Future

"HIRE THE BRIGHTEST PEOPLE AND LEAVE THEM ALONE." (JOHN WILLIAMS, RAND'S FIRST HIRE).

In the second major period of learning to pluralize the future, Western research and managerial culture developed a new form of futures research and collaborative learning known as "scenario planning." The key discoveries and inventions of this era unfold in an array of post-World War II settings, beginning with RAND Corporation, and including Stanford Research Institute (SRI), Jay Forrester's work in System Dynamics at MIT, Herman Kahn's Hudson Institute, the multinational oil company Royal Dutch/Shell, followed by a small number of digital-era consulting organizations including Global Business Network (GBN). At the beginning of this paper we discussed the birth of the scenarios technique at RAND, the source of its cinematic overtones, and its origins in the realm of defense. RAND was founded in 1946 as a leading think tank for the United States' military, working under exclusive contract to the Air Force. SRI, founded in 1947, was a university-based institute offering consulting services initially to the oil industry and later to business, the military and scientific organizations. After leaving RAND in 1961 Kahn founded The Hudson Institute, a conservative policy think tank. It is perhaps no coincidence that the arc traced by the development of scenario planning parallels that of the Internet, in which a potent, military-funded R and D innovation gradually acquires critical mass within a mixed academic and military setting, then develops rapidly in sophistication and impact once it is taken up by the private sector. But why did scenarios arise in this period?

‹ Nuclear weapon test by the United States military at Bikini Atoll, Micronesia, on 25 July 1946. Photo: United States Department of Defense.

Thinking About the Unthinkable: On the Virtue of Implausibility

Scenarios method arose in the post-World War II period in response to the utter lack of combat experience around nuclear weapons. Military planners at the time found themselves suddenly unequipped to foresee how enemy behavior and events might unfold as their quantitative methods of operations research, geared toward conventional systems, was rendered obsolete by the unwritten rules of new and vastly more powerful technology. As pointed out by Fred Turner in his close study of the work of GBN co-founder Stewart Brand, *From Counterculture to Cyberculture*, "Under conditions of nuclear uncertainty, analysts had to imagine the data.... In short, they had to simulate the future" (2006: 186). This development is a watershed in the formation of today's economies of information, knowledge and imagination, and in many important respects it may be said to mark the early emergence of our contemporary condition.

Research projects in labs like RAND's brought together scientists, analysts and creative intellectuals with remarkable results that were unprecedented at the time, but set the stage for today's public-private, problem-solving, design-thinking, interdisciplinary teams. The profile of the data-wrangling, techno-savvy, imaginative risk taker that we well know today has its roots in this world. In 1960, RAND futurist Herman Kahn published the weighty volume *On Thermonuclear War* in which he made the highly controversial argument that nuclear war was not only feasible but winnable. This kind of provocative perspective—which ran contrary to the prevailing doctrine of MAD or Mutually Assured Destruction—was routine for Kahn, who is remembered for advocating the necessity of "thinking about the unthinkable." While Kahn was not a nihilist, he was apparently fearless. In another example from this text, he asks the question, "Will the survivors envy the dead" and answers unequivocally "No." I suggest that this quality of fearlessness must lie at the heart of today's restlessly creative design thinking, scenario thinking, and disruptive innovation initiatives.

WHAT FORESIGHT DEMANDS ON THE PART OF ITS FACILITATORS AND PARTICIPANTS IS AN UNFLINCHING DESIRE TO STARE INTO THE FACE OF "UNTHINKABLE THOUGHTS."

As evidence that this is a difficult but highly prized goal within the foresight profession, many foresight practitioners consider their highest achievement to have occurred when they succeed not in achieving any specific outcome, but simply in decisively changing the minds and mental models of their client, in any direction. As we have seen, in comparing those qualities most prized in a scenarios exercise, or foresight professional practice, with their counterparts in the world of design, we find many parallels. Another such quality is a state of dynamic tension between rationality and imagination or emotion. If there is any figure in whom the opposing tendencies of hot, creative imagination and cool rationality are embodied, it is Kahn, whose work at RAND in the late 1940s and 50s pioneered the scenarios method as a strategic tool.

Most futurists including Kahn espouse the concept of "plausibility" as a criterion in assessing scenarios. The most important path to achieving plausibility is developed through "internal self-consistency" in the story, an indispensable quality. But plausibility can become a limit to free thought if and when it begins to restrict something more valuable: imagination and surprise. In fact there is a school of thought among foresight practitioners including Herman Kahn, Pierre Wack, Jim Dator, Joseph Coates, and Wendy Schultz who openly state that plausibility must never come at the expense of surprise. Dator once famously said, "Any useful statement about the future should appear to be ridiculous." Or, as Kahn (1968: 264) once put it:
"Since plausibility is a great virtue in a scenario, one should, subject to other considerations, try to achieve it. But it is important not to limit oneself to the most plausible, conventional, or probable situations and behavior.... Future events may not be drawn from the restricted list of those we have learned are possible; we should expect to go on being surprised."

Designers too face the tension between plausibility and imagination that we have seen in foresight. For design the struggle is frequently expressed as a perennial struggle to balance function, utility or usability with beauty, emotion or surprise.

Kahn described himself as a "free-thinking intellectual ... [bearing] a desire to do policy-oriented studies with practical applications ... pragmatic, eclectic, and synthetic in thinking". Imaginative, pragmatic, eclectic, synthetic, rigorous: does this describe a design thinker? I believe it does. "Is there a danger of bringing too much imagination to these problems? Do we risk losing ourselves in a maze of bizarre improbabilities? ... It has usually been the lack of imagination, rather than the excess of it, that has caused unfortunate decisions and missed opportunities." (Hudson Institute and Kahn, 1963: 3, quoted in Ghamari-Tabrizi, 2005: 146)
For these ideas, Kahn was immensely controversial. Famously he is said to have been the role model for the character of Dr. Strangelove in Stanley Kubrick's 1964 film of the same name.

Scenarios Spin Off: Military to Commercial

The popularization of scenario planning in the corporate context has been primarily attributed, through numerous books and articles, to the Group Planning office at multinational oil behemoth Royal Dutch/Shell. This corporate use of scenario planning is said to have begun with Shell's Ted Newland who approached Herman Kahn at his Hudson Institute in the 1960s. In the late 1950s Shell had adopted a radically decentralized and matrixed "group" structure on the advice of McKinsey & Company. Art Kleiner provides an extremely valuable account of these factors in *The Age of Heretics*, a fascinating study that reads as a history of corporate social responsibility (or "CSR"). Kleiner (1996: 148) wrote: "Thanks to this structure, anyone like Ted Newland, with an idea that the future might change, could never simply convince one top boss or another to adopt the appropriate policies. Anyone who wanted Shell to change would have to find a way to make the future clearly visible, so a wide range of people within the company could see it coming."

❮ Atomic bomb test, Yucca Flats, NV, 1953. © Time & Life Pictures.

❮ Herman Kahn, 1965. Photo: U.S. News & World Report

THIS IDEA HELPS TO EXPLAIN THE RELEVANCE OF SCENARIO PLANNING TODAY.

Our near ubiquitous, networked communication technologies increasingly distribute agency and decision support to more and more players and levels in organizations and society. Communication technologies may provide the conduit, or level playing field, but methods such as scenarios are needed as a creative, interpretative process to bring new coherence to the potential chaos. We are enabled and even compelled to draw on diversity, yes, but more critically we must also find ways of making sense of these disparate human experiences. When conditions are right such methods enable the emergence of the Learning Organization, as described by business author Peter Senge in his highly regarded *The Fifth Discipline* (1990), and by former Shell executive, Arie de Geus, in *The Living Company* (1997). While there is a need for more critical case studies of success and failure in scenario planning, anecdotal evidence is abundant. In a widely published example, it is suggested that Shell's use of foresight scenarios helped the oil giant to anticipate the energy crisis of the early 1970s— and thereby rise from seventh to first in sector profitability.

FOR ALL ITS REPORTED EFFECTIVENESS, SCENARIOS METHOD IS PERHAPS BEST UNDERSTOOD NOT SO MUCH IN TERMS OF SHEER *POWER* BUT MORE IN TERMS OF ALTERED *PERCEPTION*.

For Pierre Wack, former leader of Shell's Group Planning Office in London, scenario work involves "the gentle art of reperceiving." Writing in Harvard Business Review, Wack (1985: 73) stated: "The future is no longer stable; it has become a moving target. No single 'right' projection can be deduced from past behavior. The better approach, I believe, is to accept uncertainty, try to understand it, and make it part of our reasoning."
In another unexpected irony, then, further differentiating foresight from forecasting and prediction, scenarios are

used not to try and *dispel* uncertainty but to *incorporate* it in the planning process. And so, if the purpose of scenarios is not to *predict* the future but to *pluralize* it, what benefit arises from this effort? As Wack idiosyncratically put it, "Good scenarios change the microcosms of management." Unpacking this term, Peter Senge describes "microcosms" as the unstated mental models that an organization's people use to orient their perception of the world. Ultimately the purpose is to develop a distributed and sensitive capacity for learning across the organization. This interpretation is driven home by a number of laudable initiatives including Senge's Society for Organizational Learning (SOL), and an anthology of scenario methodologies, "Learning from the Future," in which editors Liam Fahey and Robert M. Randall advocate for the term "scenario learning" over the more well known "scenario planning." Following the guidance of a succession of champions—including Newland, Wack, de Geus, Kees van der Heijden, Joseph Jaworski, and Adam Kahane—Shell continues to evolve its use of scenarios. Having thus reviewed foresight scenarios, let's look more closely at the relationship with design thinking.

Scenarios and Design Thinking

Like scenarios, design thinking has been articulated by a series of theorists and practitioners from the 1960s to the present. In one early and significant work, *Sciences of the Artificial*, polymath intellectual Herbert Simon offered an early articulation of design thinking in the context of "prospective artificial objects having desired properties" (Simon, 1969: 4–5). Drawing parallels between engineering and design, Simon (ibid.) goes on to state,
"The engineer, and more generally the designer, is concerned with how things ought to be—how they ought to be in order to attain goals, and to function."
In the same text (ibid., 55), Simon outlines the design thinking process through seven stages:
* Define
* Research
* Ideate
* Prototype
* Choose
* Implement
* Learn

Simon's description of design process is neither the earliest nor the most definitive, but his steps and their sequence are characteristic of those portrayed by countless design consultants and scholars. A broader overview of the creative process may be found in the form of a poster prepared by Dubberly Design Office (2009) as a project of the Institute for the Creative Process at the Alberta College of Art+Design. By comparing the broad features of the design process as outlined by Simon and others with the sequence of steps used in "Scenario Thinking" as described by Global Business Network in their corporate web site (GBN Scenario Thinking Process), we discover a clear parallel:

- Orient
- Explore
- Synthesize
- Act
- Monitor

As in all design thinking, we must bring unbridled creativity, openness to lateral thinking, drawing on diversity, in order to develop myriad, divergent solutions.

While the source of design's *breadth* is creative divergence, its *depth* comes from rigorous convergence. This approach is well documented in design research.

Let's dive more deeply into our core question: How is scenario learning a form of design thinking? Another parallel is found in the term "scenario" which designers use in a sense that differs from but is related to that of long range scenario planning. When a design professional uses the term "scenario" this term generally indicates a "user scenario," sometimes referred to as a "user experience scenario." Generally in a design context a user scenario is developed as a form of brief story that focuses not on long-range change in environmental conditions over years or decades, but on the moment-to-moment subjective experience of a user of a proposed product, service or system. Clearly the timeframe is not even remotely similar. But are the intentions and results so different? Speaking about user experience scenarios, interaction designer Dan Saffer calls them "prototypes built with words" (2007: 101). In the sense in which scenario planning helps us to mentally "prototype" the feelings and cognitive patterns that arise within alternative futures, this description may also be fruitfully applied to foresight scenarios.

DESIGNERS ARE REVERED FOR BEING ABLE TO OPTIMISTICALLY AND CREATIVELY WORK WITHIN—EVEN TAKE INSPIRATION FROM—*CONSTRAINTS*.

Constraints are those various barriers and limits, imposed and discovered through research, that the successful design solution must somehow negotiate, such as weight or battery life in a mobile device, or budgetary limitations within virtually every design context. In scenario planning a parallel might be the concept of "predetermined elements," or features and trends in the landscape of change that we can reasonably assume are fixed or can be reliably tracked or extrapolated. An example might be an indivertible demographic trend, such as the baby boom, which we can further grasp through a series of visual representations such as population pyramids showing the bulge moving through sequential decades. In a complementary sense, design also builds and takes advantage of *affordances*. The closet analogy in building scenarios is to look for "driving forces"—enabling trends and signals of change—and build strategies that seek to take advantage of these prevailing or emerging currents.

We have seen that the development and structure of scenarios work bears striking similarities to that of design process. As well I hope I have shown that the skills, traits and strengths of an excellent scenario workshop process are not unlike those of a well-run design process. With that we will bring our history of the future to the present day, where a diverse group is bringing foresight theory and methodology to life under the roof of Canada's largest University of art and design.

Scenario Learning at Strategic Innovation Lab

In light of these insights, together with a group of like-minded design colleagues at the Ontario College of Art and Design (OCAD) in Toronto, Canada, I have been part of an undertaking to try and address the complex dilemmas and opportunities presented by contemporary social and economic life. That undertaking is a research centre known as Strategic Innovation Lab (sLab), for which I am a cofounder and the inaugural Director of Research.

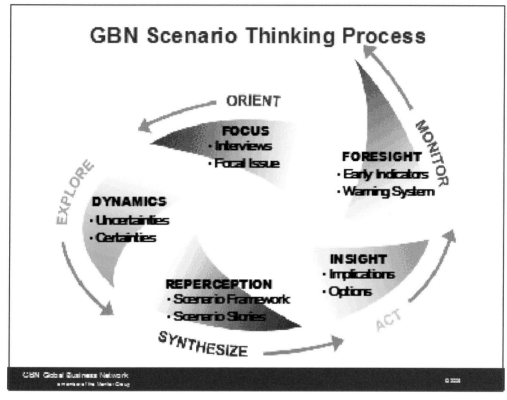

83

❮ Scenario Thinking Process (Global Business Network) http://www.gbn.com/about/scenario_planning.php © Global Business Network

The Scenario Process

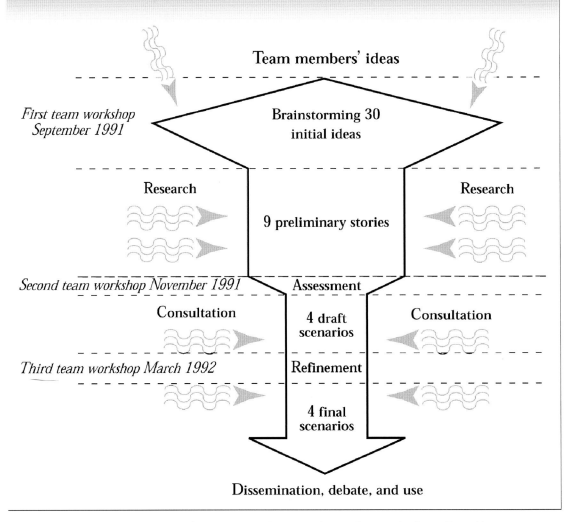

Team members' ideas

First team workshop
September 1991

Brainstorming 30
initial ideas

Research

9 preliminary stories

Research

Second team workshop November 1991

Assessment

Consultation

4 draft
scenarios

Consultation

Third team workshop March 1992

Refinement

4 final
scenarios

Dissemination, debate, and use

❮ Scenarios Process (Mont Fleur Scenarios, 1991). Kahane, A., and le Roux, P. 1992. The mont fleur scenarios. Deeper News, 7(1).

What differentiates sLab from business- and technology-centred innovation efforts is our approach which is rooted in a heritage of design thinking, placing human needs and desires, behavior and culture at the centre of problem finding, problem framing and problem solving. sLab's model addresses complex business problems through design thinking but in going further, we add futures thinking and, in order to help integrate the whole, systems thinking and visual thinking. Located in Will Alsop's landmark "tabletop" building, sLab operates on a model that integrates academic research, professional engagement, education and skills development for the private, public, and not-for-profit sectors. We are a growing community of researchers and practitioners, design and business professionals, teachers and students, who are passionate about envisioning possible futures. Our work investigates the intersections of human behavior, new technologies and organizational capacities.

WE COMBINE EXPERIENCE IN IMAGINATIVE AND VISUAL THINKING WITH SKILLS IN INTERDISCIPLINARY COLLABORATION, BUSINESS ANALYSIS AND STRATEGIC PLANNING.

sLab develops and applies strategic foresight, design research, visualization and prototyping methodologies in order to clarify and feed the front end of the innovation process. Strategic Innovation Lab's work complements the work of management consultants because our imaginative speculations and informed propositions tap into insights and areas that technology tracking, quantitative and rearview mirror analyses cannot reach. We develop and implement action plans that drive toward specific objectives for medium-term and long-term future horizons.

DIVERGENT THINKING
- DISCOVERY & OBSERVATIONS
- FORECASTING POV
- IDENTIFY OPPORTUNITIES

- PRIORITIZE OPPORTUNITIES
- MODEL THE BENEFITS
- GENERATE CONCEPTS
- CREATE MODELS
- REFINE CONCEPTS
- BUILD PROTOTYPES

CONVERGENT THINKING

❮ Innovation Process (Darrel Rhea). Rhea, D. 2003. Bringing clarity to the "Fuzzy front end". In B. Laurel (ed.), Design research: Methods and perspectives: 145–154. Cambridge, MA: MIT Press.

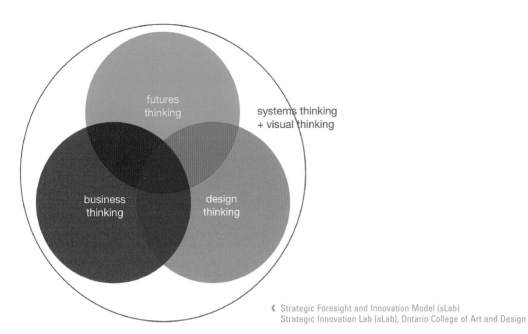

futures
thinking

systems thinking
+ visual thinking

business
thinking

design
thinking

❮ Strategic Foresight and Innovation Model (sLab)
Strategic Innovation Lab (sLab), Ontario College of Art and Design

Scenarios as Transformative Process of Participation

It should be evident by now that the term scenarios applies to both a *product*—a set of highly structured stories about possible futures—and the *process* of creating those stories. At this point I wish to argue that the process of creating scenarios is more important than the product. This is not to deny the value of the stories, which after all can be widely shared with extremely significant effects. But it is critical to emphasize the greater depth of change that is possible within the immersive, co-creative experience of assembling and synthesizing scenario material and insights in what is typically a large workshop context. Experienced and truly effective foresight professionals do not present themselves as magicians or geniuses bringing answers from outside the situation but as facilitators who serve to orient and guide a process of drawing out collective intelligence from the assembly. Shell's Wack espoused this self-effacing approach as follows: "I continue to tell the companies for which I work, 'Do not believe me. I have no particular prophetic gift.' Rather instead, 'Here are elements for your thinking, to exercise your judgment.'" (Kleiner, 1989: 9) The effectiveness of the process comes from precisely its dynamic an interactive, immersive, collaborative *conversation*. At its best, the scenarios conversation has the effect of significantly and productively stretching and transforming the awareness and mindset of each fully engaged participant. Underscoring this interpretation that

the heart of scenarios is dialogic, author and former Shell executive Kees Van der Heijden entitled his recent text on the subject, *Scenarios: The Art of Strategic Conversation (1996).*

ARISING FROM THE SAME HISTORICAL THREADS IN PARALLEL WITH SCENARIO PLANNING IS A RELATED APPROACH WHICH SLAB SENIOR FELLOW PETER H.

Jones refers to as "Dialogic Design." Jones, and colleague Greg Judelman of Bruce Mau Design, carry out a monthly workshop at Strategic Innovation Lab called Design with Dialogue that discovers, examines, compares and teaches a variety of methods for designing strategic conversations. Dialogic Design proceeds from the broad field known as Interactive Management (or IM), developed by Alexander Christakis, co-founder of the Club of Rome, and John Warfield, the founder of Generic Design Science. The Club of Rome rose to prominence in the world of Futures Studies with its 1972 report *The Limits to Growth*, which became one of the most widely read and influential future studies ever published. As in scenario planning, the goal of Dialogic Design is to develop and maintain structured, discursive problem finding and problem framing within diverse groups

❮ Ontario College of Art and Design, Toronto, Canada

of stakeholders, in order to understand complex situations and resolve the dilemmas that develop within and around them. Dialogic Design goes further in that its purpose is to gain concensus from a diverse group of stakeholders on the deep influences in a problem situation, with the typical goal to empower that group to take action on their consensus design scenario.

What Sort of Designing is This? Designing for Emergence

And so, as we have seen, scenario learning is a form of designing. At the same time it is unlike the sort of design many of us have been trained to do in the industrial context—the methods, inputs, and outcomes are not what we are used to dealing with throughout the last century and a half of machine-age design praxis. Like Dialogic Design, in scenario work the primary medium is human opinion, insight, interaction, perception, and participation. Clearly in this case we have seen the design canvas transform and grow, from the classical activity of specifying visual and formal properties of an object or environment, as in graphic design, industrial design or architecture, beyond even the subjective experience of an individual user, as in the more recently articulated practices of interaction design or experience design. Rather what we are seeing when we view scenario learning as a design medium, is a form of what I refer to as "designing for emergence." In a recent paper on this subject with co-author Robert K. Logan (2007: 129), we define emergence as follows: "Emergence is a term used in the study of complex systems, including physical, biological, social, and economic systems. Emergence refers to the process by which a higher level of organization arises through the aggregation and interaction of lower level components, revealing new behaviors or properties not associated with the lower level components."
The occasion and case for attending to emergence in futures work arises through at least two critical conditions. The first is *uncertainty*. As we have been discussing, the future is uncertain, so we must maintain awareness and openness to seeing and understanding the arrival of unprecedented and unanticipated behaviors, properties and forms, that is to say, we must be open to emergence. The second condition is *participation*, and what is increasingly becoming known as "co-creation" or "co-design." As I have

noted earlier, aided by new technologies, more people are acquiring increasing degrees of freedom, agency and decision support. These changes are having an effect on larger numbers of players and levels within many socio-technical systems, including markets, companies, associations, social networks, and governments. What we might be witnessing is a positive feedback loop in which higher presence of both uncertainty and participation with the system feed each other. Against this backdrop we are witnessing the rise of emergence as a property or threshold of ever increasing significance.

At this point it may be most illuminating to depart from my current path. Instead of finding further similarities between foresight and design I now need to emphasize a point of contrast. While foresight and futures work have always been inherently concerned with uncertainty and participation, I wish to argue that design is only just beginning to come to terms with these dynamics. As I put it in "Designing for Emergence": "The training received by most designers is obsessed with control. The new design is about relinquishing control and understanding new spaces of participation and co-creation." (ibid.: 129)
After decades of top-down, Modernist training in which variables have been something that must be pinned down, design is gradually and somewhat reluctantly learning to shed its obsessions with specificity. A diverse array of commentators, including author and former executive editor of *Wired* magazine Kevin Kelly (1994) and *Biomimicry* author Janine Benyus (2002), describe this as a shift from a mechanistic paradigm to one based in biology and ecology. Design is evolving with the rapid and broad uptake of numerous phenomena, largely centred on the Internet, including Web 2.0, social media, crowdsourcing, user generated content, wikinomics, and similar such developments.

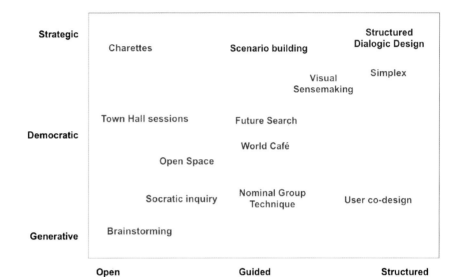

	Open	Guided	Structured

Strategic — Charettes, Scenario building, Structured Dialogic Design, Visual Sensemaking, Simplex

Democratic — Town Hall sessions, Future Search, World Café, Open Space

Socratic inquiry, Nominal Group Technique, User co-design

Generative — Brainstorming

❮ The Space of Dialogic Design (Peter H. Jones)

❮ World Without Oil (worldwithoutoil.org). Center for Public Broadcasting

The Shape of Play to Come: Alternate Reality Games (ARGs)

Having examined some underlying conditions in the space where design thinking and foresight intersect, and having touched on a few of the digitally mediated phenomena that are making this intersection visible, I'd like to conclude this discussion by highlighting a young and intriguing form. The simultaneous presence of designing for emergence and participatory foresight nowhere is more clearly evident than in a type of educational entertainment known as an "Alternate Reality Game" (ARG). Like MMORPGs or massively multiplayer online role-playing games, ARGs generally use the Internet, along with other channels, to support many players at once. A key distinction is that ARGs are not based in fantasy but take the real world as a "platform," and extend it by expecting players to observe their own surroundings and elaborate on them within a broadly narrative, interactive structure.

WHILE A NUMBER OF ARGS CHOOSE TO DEPART FROM THE PRETEXT OF A COMMERCIAL ENTERTAINMENT PROPERTY, THE EXAMPLES MOST PERTINENT TO OUR INTERESTS ARE BETTER UNDERSTOOD AS "SERIOUS GAMES" THAT PROMISE INSIGHT AND FORESIGHT ON REAL WORLD ISSUES.

One of the most prolific developers of serious Alternate Reality Games is also the oldest established research centre for future studies, Silicon Valley-based Institute for the Future (IFTF), where the lead ARG developer is Jane McGonigal. In one engaging 2007 game for which McGonigal played the role of Participation Architect, "A World without Oil," funded by the Center for Public Broadcasting (worldwithoutoil.org), the design team built a multi-channel, Web-supported environment where players could imagine, enact, and share their thoughts and feelings on how things might fall apart, and begin to reassemble, in a near-future peak-oil scenario. By viewing, reading, uploading and downloading, emailing, messaging, participants immersed themselves in a fictional—but plausible—America wracked

by four dollar-per-gallon gas prices, mass chaos, and inventive necessity-driven redesign.

In a related endeavor inspired by McGonigal's work, the veteran futures institute Hawaii Research Center for Futures Studies, established by Jim Dator in 1971, ran an immersive, "playable scenario" in May 2009 called "Coral Cross" (coralcross.org), predicated on the efforts of a grass-roots organization to aid the island community as it braces for a pandemic crisis. Coral Cross was produced for the Hawaii Department of Health (DOH) and funded by the federal Centers for Disease Control and Prevention (CDC) based in Atlanta, GA. Though it was based on its own hypothetical pandemic scenario, in which one day in the scenario equals one month in the real world, the planning and launch of Coral Cross eerily coincided with the rise of H1N1 "swine flu" across the global healthcare and media agenda.

It is hard to imagine a more bracing "coincidence."

THE PACE OF CHANGE WILL CONTINUE TO BRING UNEXPECTED SURPRISES TO OUR DOORSTEP. FOR THOSE DEDICATED TO "CREATING DESIRED FUTURES," IT SEEMS THERE WILL BE NO SHORTAGE OF DEMAND FOR IMAGINATIVE, INVENTIVE, PARTICIPATORY AND TECHNOLOGICALLY ASSISTED FRAMEWORKS FOR DEVELOPING ANTICIPATORY FORESIGHT.

We learned to pluralize the future in the aftermath of global war and fear. The question we must ask today is, what might we be capable of co-creating within a global culture of human-centred inquiry and understanding?

I'd like to thank Michael Shamiyeh and his team for organizing the DOM conference opportunity that lead me to develop this paper. I extend my gratitude also to colleagues at Ontario College of Art and Design and Strategic Innovation Lab (sLab) for supporting this research, including Lenore Richards, Robert K. Logan, Michael Owen, the sLab community, faculty and students of OCAD's Master of Design program in Strategic Foresight and Innovation.

References

Arp, R. 2008. Scenario visualization: An evolutionary account of creative problem solving. Cambridge, MA: MIT Press.

Benyus, J. M. 2002. Biomimicry: Innovation inspired by nature. New York: Perennial.

de Geus, A. 1997. The living company. Boston, MA: Harvard Business School Press.

Dubberly Design Office, Chung, J., Evenson, S., and Pangaro, P. The creative process. http://www.dubberly.com/concept-maps/creative-process.html.

Fahey, L., and Randall, R. M. 1998. Learning from the future: Competitive foresight scenarios. New York: Wiley.

Ghamari-Tabrizi, S. 2005. The worlds of Herman Kahn: The intuitive science of thermonuclear war. Cambridge, MA: Harvard University Press.

Global Business Network. Why scenarios? http://www.gbn.com/about/scenario_planning.php 15 Dec. 2009.

Jana, R. 2008. Jane McGonigal's brave new worlds.

Kahane, A., and le Roux, P. 1992. The mont fleur scenarios. Deeper News, 7(1).

Kahn, H. 1961. On thermonuclear war (2d ed.). Princeton: University Press.

Kelly, K. 1994. Out of control: The new biology of machines, social systems and the economic world. New York: Basic Books.

Kleiner, A. Consequential heresies: How "thinking the unthinkable" changed royal Dutch/Shell. http://www.well.com/user/art/PDF%20Files/gbnshelloil.pdf 15 Dec. 2009.

Kleiner, A. 1996. The age of heretics: Heroes, outlaws, and the forerunners of corporate change (1st ed.). New York: Currency Doubleday.

Logan, R. K. 2007. The extended mind: The emergence of language, the human mind and culture. Toronto: University of Toronto Press.

Popper, R. 2008. Foresight methodology. In L. Georghiou, J. C. Harper, M. Keenan, I. Miles, and R. Popper (Ed.), The handbook of technology foresight: Concepts and practice: 44–88. Cheltenham, UK; Northampton, MA: Edward Elgar.

Rhea, D. 2003. Bringing clarity to the "Fuzzy front end". In B. Laurel (Ed.), Design research: Methods and perspectives: 145–154. Cambridge, MA: MIT Press.

Saffer, D. 2007. Designing for interaction: Creating smart applications and clever devices. Berkeley CA: New Riders: Published in association with AIGA Design Press.

Schwartz, P. 1996; 1991. The art of the long view: Planning for the future in an uncertain world. New York: Currency Doubleday.

Senge, P. M. 1990. The fifth discipline: The art and practice of the learning organization. New York: Doubleday/Currency.

Simon, H. A. 1996. The sciences of the artificial. Cambridge, MA: MIT Press.

Turner, F. 2006. From counterculture to cyberculture: Stewart Brand, the whole earth network, and the rise of digital utopianism. Chicago: University of Chicago Press.

Van Alstyne, G., and Logan, R. K. 2007. Designing for emergence and innovation: Redesigning design. Artifact, 1(2): 120–129.

Van der Heijden, K. 2005. Scenarios: The art of strategic conversation (2nd ed.). Hoboken, NJ: John Wiley & Sons.

Wack, P. 1985. Scenarios: Uncharted waters ahead. Harvard Business Review, 63(5): 73–89.

93

When we look at todays managers we see them face
various dillemata, which affect them in their organization
and also in their private lives. The systemic approach of seeing
the world and organizations may provide a fresh look at these
dilemmata and help developing "new" solutions to "old" problems.

When we look at today's managers we see them face various dillemata, which affect them in their organization and also in their private lives. These are:

- *Instantaneousness:* Having to cope with several, sometimes many, things at the same time, immediately
- *Conflicting Expectations:* The stakeholder approach, requiring top management to cater for the needs of varying interest groups, such as shareholders, customers, suppliers, employees, the media and the general public brings about pressures arising from often conflicting goals and role models of these groups
- *Power/Helplessness:* The CEO of a company often has been compared to a bus driver, he is responsible to take his /her passengers safely to their destinations, however he has no choice but has to follow a predetermined route to get there—thereby obeying all sorts of rules and regulations.
- *Chances/Threats:* The modern manager is expected to act, thereby realizing (all) chances and avoiding threats and risks—but how do you know whether a project is an opportunity or a risk before you start it?
- *Greed/Fear:* When we look at manager bonification schemes, stock option programs and the behavior of quite a few capital market players, we see them swing back and forth between greed to realize the maximum return on their investment and fear to end up with a stranded investment and cynical statements from the media.
- *Life Balance Business/Family:* with the staggering increase in communication and information tools together with globalization, the "need" for 24/7 operations and managerial accessibility around the clock, it gets increasingly difficult to fulfill all these requirements and at the same time be a caring father or mother or spouse with time and nerves to devote quality time to yourself and your family
- *Short-term/Long-term:* We all praise sustainable, long-term thinking and managing, at the same time we have to cater for the short-term, sometimes quickly changing expectations of customers, shareholders and business partners demanding success and growth quarter by quarter.
- *Capital Market Requirements/Corporate Social Responsibility:* despite all the talk about long-term investing, capital market participants often have quite short-term expectations solely confined to financial success, whereas increasingly networked and globalized businesses should live up to their role as good citizens in every country they are operating.
- *Dynamics/Stability:* Employees ask for stability, investors for predictability of earnings while business cycles, new markets, products and technologies bring about unprecedented dynamics to our corporate lives.
- *Purpose:* At the end of the day managers and employees are also human beings who seek sense and purpose in what they are doing, a thing that is ever harder to provide in a world of fast takeovers, ever riskier business models and the ultimate credo in ever more profitable growth.

The systemic approach of seeing the world and organizations may provide a fresh look at these dilemmata and help developing "new" solutions to "old" problems. For a comparison of the traditional "Mechanistic view" and the "Systemic View" see the table below.

Mechanistic view	Systemic view
Objectivity, 1 truth, unchangeable laws	Construction of reality, many „truths", hypotheses
Right-wrong, guilty- innocent	Dependence on context, usefulness, connectivity
External control	Self control, self organization
Linear causal chains	Multiple causes and effects, feedback loops
Measurable difference	Differentiating, changing
Linear progress, change	Development, changing and maintaining, de- blocking
Formal logic, no contradictions, exclusion	Integration of contradictions, inclusion
Hard facts, rational relations	Integration of hard and soft factors (emotions, intuition, communication processes)
Roles: doer, leader and lead ones, manipulation	Roles: impulse provider, gardener, enabler, development worker, coach
Methods: instruction, order, learning by trial and error	Methods: listening, questioning, dialogue, discussion, reflexion, learning how to learn

❬ Mechanistic and systemic view of the world

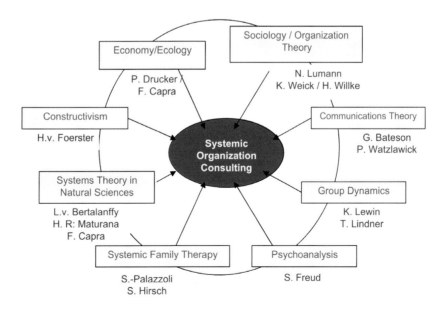

❬ Influences on systemic organization consulting

Thus the systemic approach represents a balance of attitudes between opposite poles, such as:

- Reflecting and learning from feedback *and* being spontaneous and intuitive;
- Being self-confident *and* modest;
- Learning, experimenting, discovering, being curious and open *and* respecting clear norms, distinctions, knowledge and position at the process level;
- Being affected *and* getting involved and maintaining distance and composure;
- Combining a sense of responsibility *and* a playful approach;
- Giving security *and* providing constructive irritation;
- Including both hard *and* soft facts;
- Changing *and* conserving;
- Slowing things down *and* increasing efficiency.

In fact, systemic consulting and organization development has its roots in a variety of sciences and theories, which are combined in ever changing modes as required by the task and the environment. These are (with some prominent authors on the subject in parentheses): Sociology/ Organization Theory (N. Lumann, K. Weick, H. Willke), Communications Theory (G. Bateson, P. Watzlawick), Group Dynamics (K. Lewin, T. Lindner), Psychoanalysis (S. Freud), Systemic Family Therapy (S. Palalozzi, S. Hirsch), Natural Systems Theory (L. V. Bertalanffy, H. R. Maturana, F. Capra), Constructivism (H. V. Foerster), Economy/Ecology (P. Drucker, F. Capra).

ONE OF THE KEY TOOLS OF THE SYSTEMIC APPROACH AND IN MANY SITUATIONS A REAL "EYE AND DOOR OPENER" IS THE "ICEBERG MODEL,"

which visualizes that our manifest behavior is only seemingly (totally) influenced by facts and "real" contents, but to a much larger degree by latent attitudes expressed in patterns, logics, taboos, relations, emotions, all ultimately based on our underlying values and norms.

Values and Norms

‹ Iceberg Model

The chart on "Complementary Consulting" developed by Königswieser & Network sees the development of an organization towards the corporate vision as a fixed star as a triangle of strategy, structure and culture with a process that can be described as "muddling through", rather than progressing on a linear path. Strategy is seen in this context primarily as a means for activating change energy.

This change process may be "facilitated" rather than "managed" in a systemic world-view using the elements
- Architecture
- Design
- Tools

as key elements—each representing an intervention in itself, when applied in organization development.

THE INTERVENTION LEVEL "ARCHITECTURE" ESSENTIALLY IS PLANNING THE SET-UP OF WORK. IT ESTABLISHES THAT SOMETHING IS TO TAKE PLACE AND DETERMINES WHAT THAT SOMETHING WILL BE.

It provides the headings, the cornerstones, the rough planning. Its elements create the framework for further interventions. A good architecture facilitates change in attitudes, allows multiple perspectives and new observations, introduces new differences, provides feedback and reflection possibilities, facilitates a breakdown of entrenched patterns of thought and action, promotes learning to learn, and thus encourages self-governance. Major elements of architecture are:
- Clear project roles of the sponsor and the project leader;
- A system diagnosis with interviews, issues, hypotheses, conclusion;
- Mirroring workshops reflecting on the results of the system diagnosis;
- A steering group leading the development process, typically composed of "the powerful", "the experts" and "the affected";
- Sub-projects to implement the decisions of the steering group;

- A sounding board to check the effectiveness of the process in the organization;
- Large group events;
- Management board counseling.

The intervention level "*design*" means the shaping and structuring of a specific step in the process, an individual architectural element. Basically there are five intervention dimensions:
- Factual dimension: selecting the factual issues, defining the manifest and the latent goals, emphasize actual experiences, make use of "analogue" information transfer methods involving some form of interaction, bringing delicate issues out from the beginning, making regular closing reflections and feedback sessions.
- Time dimension: using delaying tactics like individual exercises according to the rule "less is often more", defining a clear direction and planning the start carefully, while defining the remainder of the process as a set of alternatives thus subsequently adapting the design. In such a context breaks are seen as "unstructured" working time, where people reflect on what is going on, evening sessions are particularly effective for discussing emotional, delicate or even personal issues.
- Social dimension: using a variety of working methods, such as plenary sessions, sub-groups, small groups, one-to-one discussions, individual exercises. Plenary events clearly have the highest potential energy, but also the highest risk. Small groups should be diverse enough to produce good quality results.
- Spatial dimension: it plays a major role in the design— e.g. the room set-up (such as circles of inwardly facing chairs without tables), seating arrangements (e.g. in a circle, theatre style), office furniture (pin boards, podium, etc.) including decisions to use one or more rooms, or the outdoor.
- Symbolic dimension: for example who to select to open an event or kick-off meeting signalizes ownership, starting core group meetings with an update session "What has happened since our last meeting?", organizing special events to mark the completion of a project or acknowledge a milestone as a strong symbol of respect, solidarity and recognition. Large group events are particularly rich in symbolism, highly charged with energy.

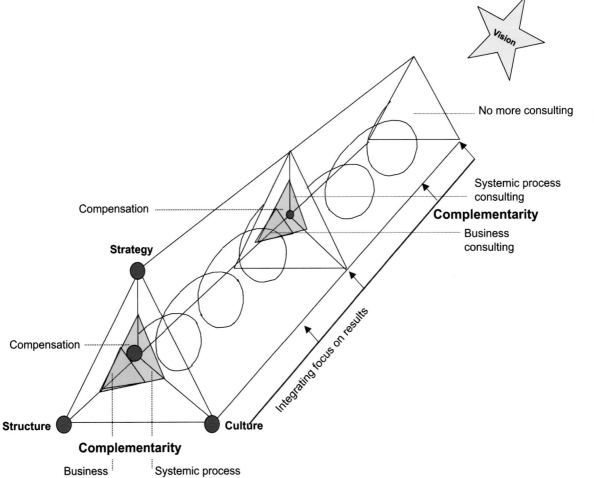

Vision

No more consulting

Systemic process
consulting

Complementarity

Business
consulting

Compensation

Strategy

Compensation

Integrating focus on results

Structure

Culture

Complementarity

Business
consulting

Systemic process
consulting

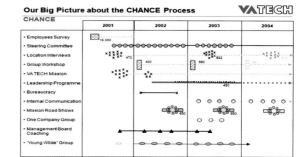

The intervention level "*tools*" basically sees every action as an intervention. The change process in this context is compared to a tree with the roots being the client/consultant relationship supplying power and energy, the trunk being the architecture and design elements providing the basis for the development of tools and techniques, like the tree's leaves and fruit.

Typical systemic tools are circular questions like "How do your employees see you as a manager?" reflecting teams of consultants, who e.g. discuss their impression of the last meeting openly in front of the participants right after the meeting, reframing views and sometimes carefully nurtured patterns of behavior into a positive view, or a paradox intervention, where a tired father after having spent lots of time on tutoring his children for exams with no success, "paradoxically" discourages them from studying, thus possibly provoking and changing attitudes and habits for the better.

FOR A PRACTICAL EXAMPLE OF THE ARCHITECTURE OF A SUCCESSFUL, COMPLEX, MULTI-YEAR CHANGE PROCESS ("CHANCE") AT A MAJOR INTERNATIONAL PLANT BUILDING AND ENGINEERING COMPANY (VA TECHNOLOGIE AG/VA TECH) SEE THE TABLE BELOW.

From the Systemic to the Complementary Approach

Where do we go from here? Is the systemic approach the ultimate answer to organization development? In the last years Königswieser & Network, one of the leading consulting companies that has pioneered the systemic approach, has taken another step forward towards "complementary consulting". The approach starts acknowledging that also the systemic approach is not free of prejudices and calls for a mix of "technical/factual" expertise and process expertise of the consultant with the systemic attitude and values described above still remaining the fundamental basis for the work. In this context technical and process know how serve as two pillars of an umbrella for an integrated approach, in which neither one or the other way alone is followed, but a third way is outlined oscillating between traditional technical/factual consulting and systemic process consulting, as the situation requires. Complementary consulting intervenes along the organization development function Vision/Strategy—Structure—Culture. It clearly distinguishes between the system categories individual, partial and entire system. In the various phases of the process it makes use of the appropriate process dimensions of architecture, design and tools/methods.

IN DOING SO IT APPLIES THE PRINCIPLE OF COMPLEMENTING THE KNOW-HOW IN THE CLIENT SYSTEM AND REFLECTS ON ITS EFFECTS IN VIEW OF THE RESULTS TO BE ACHIEVED.

The complementary approach to organization development thus integrates strategic, structural and cultural elements thereby blending technical/factual expertise and systemic process know how, as appropriate by the client needs and within the situational context. It tailors resources made-to-measure rather than being trapped in a deficit orientation. It promotes a company's ability to self-steering. Partnership between clients and external consultants, i.e. jointly planning and reflecting on the project work is a cornerstone to success.

Finally, "the way is the goal" with a focus on implementation from the very start, accompanying the process by continuous reflection.

WAYS OF BRINGING IT ABOUT 〈

MICHAEL SHAMIYEH ❮

IN THIS SECTION, WE LEARN HOW ARCHITECTS AND DESIGNERS CREATE DESIRED FUTURES, AND THEN EXAMINE SOME OF THE FUTURE EDUCATIONAL AND DEVELOPMENTAL OPPORTUNITIES FOR THOSE IN THE BUSINESS PROFESSIONS.

Jamshid Gharajedaghi starts with a brief introduction to the evolution of design thinking as the final stage of systems methodology, highlights the major operating principles of design thinking and explains why designers construct rather than predict the future.

Michael Shamiyeh gives a detailed account of the "designerly" way of knowing and underlines its differences from the classical-analytical notion of knowing as suggested by leading management consultancies. A series of diagrams and cases are cited to underscore the arguments presented. In a subsequent article, Michael brings forth arguments in favor of abductive reasoning—different from inferring analytically on the premises of either directly observable facts (inductive reasoning) or past evidence (deductive reasoning)—that is immanent to design and might be applied to conjecturing possible futures in business strategy formation. He shows that the process of abductive reasoning, which suggests that something may be, strongly supports the creation of the new, and that it does not, as is generally assumed, lack any kind of logical structure.

Adam Kahane's brief excerpt on his thorough insights into the three dimensions of possible problem complexity illuminates the need for participation and openness in iterative learning and creation processes. Thus, Kahane highlights one of the most important aspects of design processes (although they are not referred to as such).

Robert M. Bauer and Ward M. Eagen propose a conceptualization of a designers' approach to creating a desirable new user experience that comprises three elements: a generic design process, a decentered design agent who relies on individuals preserving a design attitude, and occurrences of "indeterminacy in motion."

Kamil Michlewski empirically explores what constitutes a design attitude. Interview data from senior designers and managers from four internationally recognized, design-led organizations (IDEO, Nissan Design, Philips Design and Wolff Olins) are collected in order to characterize the likely shape of a work-based attitude promoted by designers themselves.

Arnab Chatterjee traces a few examples of innovation and implementation from the Shell stable and explains how the thought process behind solving an ostensibly small (though complex) problem can be applied on a larger scale. The particular method of innovation organization Arnab describes has been successful within the technology wing of Shell. This, by default, encapsulates many of the ideas behind design thinking.

David Griesbach concludes this section by critically reflecting on the current conceptualization of design thinking by suggesting an alternative viewpoint.

MARCO MURILLO ‹

Anecdote by a Nike Product Manager

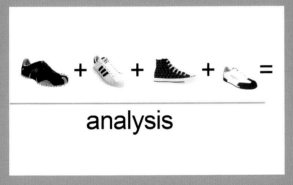

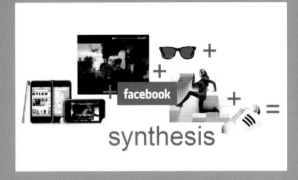

The real world is an abstract landscape with many immeasurable influences, and shifting and rising cultural tides. These shifts in cultural tides influence consumer values and these shifts have overarching consequences across businesses, product types and borders.

AS PRODUCT MANAGERS AT AN INNOVATIVE CONSUMER GOODS COMPANY, IT IS CRUCIAL THAT WE USE SYNTHESIS IN OUR APPROACH. I FIND IT UNIMAGINABLE TO APPROACH ANY DESIGN/ MARKETING BUSINESS TODAY THROUGH THE CONSTRAINING LENS OF ANALYSIS.

If we go back a decade or so, the type of analysis presented below would have been typical when looking for a market opportunity in the footwear market. The approach is linear and looks specifically at the competitive landscape when considering new opportunities.
In this day and age, what are seemingly unrelated spheres need to be acknowledged and accounted for when creating

a new product. In the recent past, analysis of a particular market as well as its competitive landscape and price was enough. Today, that approach is outdated and unreliable. A synthesis or design approach (illustrated below) is a more abstract system that takes these seemingly unrelated products/factors into play when looking to create a new product in a particular market.

The total sum of knowledge is doubling faster than ever before. New platforms of communication and social networking have created a new web of borderless instant information. In the corporate world, synthesis is necessary. Without new systems and models to unveil opportunities and to account for social movements and cultural influences, ones ideas risk being obsolete/irrelevant before going through the creation process. Today, consumer choice is at its highest, and this setting demands new product creation models and innovative products. In the product creation business, it appears that synthesis is the most appropriate approach for the development of new products. Businesses and consumers benefit when we abandon outdated models of analysis. I would venture to say that synthesis breeds innovation into the way we work and the resulting products.

JAMSHID GHARAJEDAGHI ❮
From Operation Research to Cybernetics and Finally to Design Thinking

This paper addresses the evolution of systems methodology from Operation Research to Cybernetics and finally to Design thinking. It also highlights the operating principles of design thinking and explain why designers seek to choose rather than predict the future.

During the sixties, I had the privilege of being an IBMer, a period when the company was probably experiencing some of its best and most exciting time. One of my notable assignments was to learn Operations Research (OR) to help our clients interested in its application. Operation Research was the first attempt at creating an operational systems methodology. It uses mathematical modeling to find optimal solutions in the face of complex set of interdependent variables. The initial version of OR was developed and used by the military during World War II. In the fifties, Russell Ackoff and West Churchman created the first academic OR program at the Case Institute of Technology. By the mid sixties, Case had become a Mecca for Operation Researchers and the profession had advanced to such a level that most well known universities had incorporated an OR program in one form or another.

My fascination with OR only lasted for a few years. After implementing a few projects with a group of clients, I learned that decision makers (despite their willingness to pay handsomely for the work) were not really interested in its optimum solution. They were only interested in confirming the choices they had already made. This is when I came to realize that:

THE WORLD IS NOT RUN BY THOSE WHO ARE RIGHT, IT IS RUN BY THOSE WHO CAN CONVINCE OTHERS THAT THEY ARE RIGHT.

Ironically, around the same period, Professor Ackoff published an article in which he declared: "Future of Operation Research is Past" on the grounds that OR does not appreciate the vital implications of choice.

After this experience, I became preoccupied with the notion of choice and the question of *why people do what they do*. Subsequently, I concluded that there are three dimensions to choice: rational, emotional, and cultural. Much to my surprise, I learned that rational choice does not necessarily mean the "right choice," it only reflects the perceived self-interest of the decision maker. While the emotional choice deals with excitement and the imperative of "I like it," it is the cultural dimension that, I realized, presents the most challenge. Culture not only defines the context but it also acts as an "Operating System" and provides default values for the decision process. This was for me the beginning of a long journey to get a handle on socio-cultural systems.

Meanwhile, Living Systems paradigm, or biological thinking, was gradually replacing the machine mode of organization. Cybernetics, as the second generation of systems methodology, became extremely effective in explaining and handling the dynamic behavior of "self-maintaining" and "goal-seeking" systems. But unfortunately, even the ultimate in this mode of thinking, Stafford Beer's *Brain of the Firm* (1967), despite its elegance, in my experience, is unable to deal with the complexities of "purposeful" systems where parts display choice and behave independently. Members of societies that have outgrown the secure, unifying web of paternalistic culture display real choice. This would be the equivalent of a thermostat developing a mind of its own and thus undermining the essential functionality of communication and control system.

DESPITE THE OVERWHELMING EVIDENCE THAT UNDERSTANDING CHOICE IS A REQUISITE TO UNDERSTANDING HUMAN SYSTEMS, THE DOMINANT ANALYTICAL CULTURE WITH A SCIENTIFIC TAG HAS NO INTEREST TO DISTURB ITS WELL-GROOMED ANALYTICAL APPROACH TO INCLUDE THE MESSY NOTION OF CHOICE.

Self-Organization

The assertion of Quantum theory that the universe is an open system, continuously expanding and moving toward increasing order and complexity, combined with the observation that socio-cultural systems are open living systems exhibiting a tendency toward a predefined order,

lead to the postulation that to be self-organizing and to move toward a predefined order, a system must possess some means of knowing, an internal image of what it wants to be.

Whereas DNA is the source of this image for biological systems, culture serves as the blueprint and must be the source of the desired future for socio-cultural systems. So much so that, despite all kind of obstructions, Socio-cultural systems seem to pursue a predefined order with tenacity. The triumphant resurgence of old patterns of behavior, despite the concerted efforts of change agents, is a constant source of frustration. What seems to make this stubborn insurgency so overpowering is the fact that the set of organizing principles (cultural codes) that make the system behave the way it does, are implicit and in most cases considered sacred.

The notion of self-reference adds to this complexity. Self-reference maintains that with open systems changes do not occur randomly. They are always consistent with what has gone on before, the history and the identity of the system. This means that as long as organizing principles of a dominant culture remain unchallenged, behavior of all social-units originating from this culture will remain unchanged. Thus the baggage of the past tragedies and unpleasant collective memories become a heavy burden for traditional cultures to overcome. Unfortunately, it seems that the "coin" has a memory.

This presented a huge challenge and dilemma. The critical question was how the notion of choice enters in this equation. How one would effectively deals with interdependency, self-organizing tendencies, choice and the process of change. Ironically it was Russell Ackoff himself who came to my rescue. When we met in 1974, I had already read his herculean work, *On Purposeful Systems* (1972). After a whole day of intense discussions he gave me the clue and insight that, for the last 35 years, has become the centerpiece of my professional life. He taught me why Design is the vehicle through which choice is manifested. Design thinking helped me to discover holistic thinking and how to use design to effectively deal with the three concerns of interdependency, self-organizing tendencies and choice all at the same time.

Design Thinking, as the Systems Methodology

In his classic work, *The Sciences of the Artificial* (1996), H.A. Simon makes two profound statements. The first is the observation that: "The natural sciences are concerned with how things are, design on the other hand, is concerned with how things ought to be." The second is the assertion that design thinking has a unique characteristic that makes it possible for it to be "universalized."

THIS MEANS DESIGN COULD BE USED AS A VEHICLE TO COMMUNICATE ACROSS DISCIPLINES.

Any professional whose task is to dissolve problems, to choose, to synthesize and to create is involved with design thinking. Many beautiful designs have been produced in variety of fields ranging from physical environments and artifacts to music (composition), philosophy (design of inquiring systems), and political and economic arrangements. Some great thinkers have even taken whole societies as systems to be redesigned.

Nigel Cross, in his beautiful book entitled *Designerly Way of Knowing*, makes the following indisputable observation: "Everything we have around us has been designed."

Design ability is, in fact, one of the three fundamental dimensions of human intelligence. Design, Science, and Art form an "AND" not an "OR" relationship to create the incredible human cognitive ability:

- Science: finding similarities among things that are different;
- Art: finding differences among things that are similar;
- Design: creating feasible wholes from infeasible parts.

The distinct advantage of design thinking is to produce new alternatives. It goes beyond default solutions, looking for new exciting possibilities. It is not about selecting the "best" from the existing set of alternative. The choices in the existing set usually share one or more properties based on an explicit or implicit set of assumptions or constraints produced by the actors' previous experiences with similar situations. The conventional practice to use advanced analytical tools to help select the best alternative will only result in a revision of the probabilities of choice. But underlying assumptions governing the generation of alternatives remain unchallenged. Design thinking, on the other hand, involves the challenging assumptions. It represents a qualitative change that includes the notion of beauty and desirability. Thus resulting in the re-identification of the available set of alternatives and objectives, looking for new and more desirable possibilities for the future. Einstein put it so beautifully when he said, "We cannot solve our problems with the same thinking we used when we created them."

Design thinking is about real choice, about selecting a desired future and inventing the ways to bring it about. It is about the ability to deal with the real world, its "messy" or "wicked" problems. Designers must develop the confidence to define, redefine and change the problem in light of the situation that emerges as the design activity evolves. Facing the right problem is the most critical phase of this process.

ACCORDING TO ACKOFF, "WE FAIL MORE OFTEN NOT BECAUSE WE FAIL TO SOLVE THE PROBLEM WE FACE BUT BECAUSE WE FAIL TO FACE THE RIGHT PROBLEM."

An iterative process of "holistic thinking" is at the core of the design process. Contrary to widely held belief, the popular notion of a multi-discipline approach is not a systems approach. In fact the ability to synthesize separate findings into a cohesive whole is far more critical than the ability to generate information from different perspective. Without a well-defined synthesizing method, the process of discovery using a multi-discipline approach would be an experience as frustrating as that of blind men trying to identify an elephant.
Despite their success, three well known inquiring systems (analytical thinking, synthetic thinking and dynamic thinking) have concentrated only in one of the three dimensions of the holistic thinking.

Analytical thinking has been the essence of classical science. The scientific method assumes that the whole is nothing but the sum of its parts, and thus understanding the structure is both necessary and sufficient to understanding the whole.

Synthetic thinking has been the main instrument of the functional approach. By defining a system by its outcome, synthesis puts the subject in the context of the larger system of which it is a part, and then studies the effects it produces in its environment.

Dynamic thinking, on the other hand, has long been focus on the Process. It looks to the *how* question, for the necessary answer to define the whole.

However, I believe that seeing the whole requires understanding structure, function, and process at the same time.

THEY REPRESENT THREE ASPECTS OF THE SAME THING AND WITH THE CONTAINING ENVIRONMENT, FORM A COMPLEMENTARY SET.

Therefore, structure, function, and process within a context, define the whole or make the understanding of the whole possible. Structure defines components and their relationships; function defines the outcomes or results produced; process explicitly defines the sequence of activities and the know-how required to produce the outcome; context defines the transactional environment in which the system is situated. Together, these four perspectives form an interdependent set of mutually exclusive and collectively exhaustive variables that define the whole. A set of interdependent variables forms a circular relationship. Each variable co-produces other variables and, in turn, is co-produced by them. Which one comes first is irrelevant because none can exist without the others. They have to happen all at the same time. To fail to see the significance of these interdependencies is to ignore the essential characteristic of the holistic process. Therefore, to handle them holistically requires the understanding of each variable in relation to the others in the set at the same time. This is an *iterative design process.*

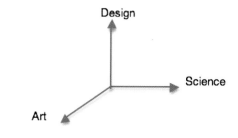

Iterative Process of Inquiry

Design, Process of Change, and Creating Desired Futures

Image building and abstraction are among the most significant characteristic of human beings. We are not only capable of creating images of real things but are also capable of forming and creating images of things that do not exist. This unique ability to create images is what design thinking is all about. To relate to our environment, we have been forced to synthesize scattered findings into a meaningful, unified mental image.

ONCE A MENTAL IMAGE IS FORMED, IT ACTS AS A FILTER.

Significant parts of this image or mental model of our universe is shared with others who live in the same social setting. This "shared image" constitutes the principal bond among members of a community. It is this shared image that we refer to as the culture of a people. It incorporates their experiences, beliefs and ideals. It is the ultimate product and reflection of their history and manifestation of their identity. The shared image, itself a complex design, stands at the center of the process of change. So much so that success of any action invariably depends on the degree it penetrates and modifies this shared image.
Ackoff's systems methodology aims at the core of this conception. In INTEACT, we have used interactive design process to redesign the distorted shared image and to produce a lasting change in the behavioral pattern of social systems.

We believe:
- Self-organizing, purposeful, socio-cultural systems are self-evolving.
- Guided by an implicit shared image, they tend to reproduce a familiar pattern of existence.
- To change this pattern, the shared image (the organizing attractor) needs to be changed.
- This can only be done by the *participation of relevant actors in a design process*.
- People are more likely to accept a change if they have a hand in shaping it.
- The best way to understand and learn a system is to design it.

- Designers are to replace the existing order by operationalizing their most exciting vision of the future, the design of the next generation of the system.
- An explicit and exciting design/vision of the future is a powerful instrument of change.
- The desired future is then realized by successive approximation. (Inventing the ways to close the gap between actual and desired states.)

Donella Meadow's insightful observation that: "The future can't be predicted, but it can be envisioned and brought into being. Social systems cannot be controlled but can be designed and redesigned," is a welcome confirmation of the above operating principles.

I found Interactive Design, the centerpiece of Ackoff's systems methodology, to be a perfect platform to integrate Holistic Thinking, Operational Thinking, and Socio-Cultural Thinking, into a comprehensive systems methodology. The depth and the richness of Interactive Design, the beauty and magic of Holistic Thinking when combined with the dynamic power of Operational Thinking, create a competent and exciting methodology that goes a long way in dealing with the emerging challenges of seemingly complex and chaotic socio-cultural systems.

FINALLY, I WOULD LIKE TO END WITH THE FOLLOWING HUMBLE OBSERVATION: SOCIAL SYSTEMS ARE DYNAMIC AND SURVIVING SYSTEMS, "ALWAYS ON THE GO."

They produce numerous deviations along their path. Independent and insignificant deviations are dampened and fade-away with little or no consequence. But reinforcing feedback loops among highly interdependent deviations get amplified to produce significant events with high impact, where large-scale, catastrophes become highly probable outcomes. Unfortunately, the blind pursuit of efficiency at any cost has resulted in reduced buffers and elimination of much needed redundancies. As a result, we have successfully converted our reasonably flexible and independent sub-systems to highly interdependent chaotic ones. This is why our well-regarded risk models, developed on the assumptions of independency, are failing to protect us against re-occurring events that have long been considered improbable. In this environment, restoring stability and achieving an order of magnitude improvement in our quality of life requires a redesign from a clean slate.

111

References

Ackoff, R.L. 1974. Redesigning the future. New York: John Wiley & Son.

Ackoff, R.L. and Emery, F. 1972. On purposeful systems. Aldine-Atherton Chicago.

Beer, S. 1967. Brain of the firm. Penguin Press.

Cross, N. 2007. Designerly ways of knowing. Board of international research in design. Basel, Boston, Berlin: Birkhäuser.

Gharajedaghi, J. 2006. Systems thinking. Managing chaos & complexity: A platform for designing business architecture. Second Edition, Elsevier.

Meadows, D. 2008. Thinking in systems. Sustainability Institute.

Simon, H.A. 1996. The sciences of the artificial. Third Edition, Cambridge: MIT press.

113

It is commonplace today to note that management as a profession is in a difficult situation. Men and women running businesses are beginning to understand that, in light of the increasingly diverse forms of complexities of our world, the very concept of analytically solving a problem—to take apart that which one seeks to understand—can be an impediment. Rather than initiating a larger process of creating what one truly values or wants, it suggests a way of thinking that proposes to fix something that is broken. It prevents someone from asking the more fundamental question of what desired future do we want to create. Creative design thinking, in contrast to traditional managerial analytical reasoning, takes for granted that the process of finding a solution to a problem will require the envisioning of an ideal solution, which is then worked backwards to where you are. In the following essay, the methodology of idealized design at work will be discussed.

The approach management (among other fields) has opted to apply for understanding and engaging "in the world" is essentially analysis driven by and separated into two distinct and operatively separate entities: framing the problem and finding a solution. Although the limitations of analysis in respect to complex problem-solving tasks are known, it is ironic that the analytical approach still remains intact, particular in three contexts—physical, biological, and social. As Herbert Simon (1968) convincingly put it some 40 years ago, "[e]ngineering schools gradually became schools of physics and mathematics; medical schools became schools of biological sciences; business schools became schools of finite mathematics"—and up to now, nothing has basically changed. It is still generally agreed that by means of analytical thinking, the problematic behaviour of a prevailing condition can be fully grasped. One just has to address the impact that each independent variable has on the overall condition. That is to say, a rigorous fact-based analysis—of course, partly coupled with intuition and experience in the field—still provides the very substance for further decisions in management (Fink, 2003). To quote Tom Peters, a former "McKinsey-ite,": "even the most excellent companies are among the best at getting the numbers, analyzing them, and solving problems with them." For this very reason, one of the most common tools executives (or at least their hired consultants) use for inquiry or to identify and solve problems is analysis.

WITHOUT BEING ABLE TO ANALYTICALLY APPROACH A PROBLEM, ONE WOULD PROBABLY NEVER GET ONES FOOT IN THE DOOR OF A MAJOR MANAGEMENT CONSULTANCY FIRM.

McKinsey's famous analytical approach to solving problems illustrates this point. Structured into separate and distinct phases, the analytical approach starts by taking apart that which one seeks to understand (Rasiel and Friga, 2001; Raisel, 1998). McKinsey calls this step "framing the problem"—that is to say, consultants start by defining the boundaries of the problem. The application of so-called "frameworks" helps to structure and break the problem down into components in order to rapidly come to grips with the main issues. The concept of MECE, an acronym for "mutually exclusive, collectively exhaustive," is a basic theorem at McKinsey to foster such a consistent and logical process of structuring the problem into distinct and non-overlapping issues while assuring that no issue that might be relevant to the problem will

be overlooked. In a subsequent phase, the objective is to get an understanding of the behavior of the identified issues at stake with the aim of aggregating them into an explanation of the whole. Having defined and understood the problem by reducing it to its essential components, the other distinct phase in the analytical approach is to design a solution. Any analytical investigation necessarily brings forth a hypothesis as to a likely solution.

RATHER THAN "BOILING THE OCEAN" BY ANALYSING EVERY POSSIBLE ASPECT OF THE PROBLEM ALL THE WAY DOWN TO ITS FUZZY DETAILS, AN INITIAL HYPOTHESIS PROVIDES A KIND OF ROAD MAP FOR GATHERING FACTS PROVING OR DISPROVING ASSUMPTIONS ABOUT A POSSIBLE SOLUTION.

Significantly, such a problem-solving approach entails a series of problematic limitations. First, the analytical approach can't value in quantitative terms the extra oomph of business endeavours such as Apple's love for the creative, or Disney's and McDonald's fetish for cleanliness. Second, it simply lacks the ability to respond adequately to problems revealing a high degree of interdependency, self-organizational behaviour, or impact of individual choice as evident in contemporary sociocultural systems. The following two current examples illustrate this point. The ongoing debates on possible strategies to effectively reduce greenhouse gas emissions direct public attention to two central issues: energy efficiency and renewable energy. In the building sector—to begin with an example from the realm of architects—photovoltaic has become the world's fastest-growing energy technology to convert solar energy directly into electricity. The high-energy resources that were required for the fabrication of silicon-based solar cells until recently could be diminished in such a way that today's cells produce a surplus of energy within less than four years. For this very reason, analysts regarded photovoltaic as "the" solution for effectively making use of renewable energy by simultaneously reducing CO_2 emissions. Certainly, we may conclude, this holds true today if we look at the system component separately, taking it apart from the context of the larger environment of which it is part of. However, as long as the excess of produced energy can't be fed into a local supply network (which is a fairly recent option and not fully developed in every country) but has to be stored in batteries—so-called stand-alone solutions—the story is a completely different one precisely because the CO_2 emission caused by the production and recycling process of rechargeable batteries, which have a relatively short lifecycle, would surpass possible savings of CO_2 emissions gained by the use of solar cells. Thus, using an analytical approach—taking apart that which one seeks to understand—to deal with these types of problems would be like running on a treadmill. While running faster and faster, one remains at the same place because, in the course of subsequent elaboration, the problem successively transforms its very nature.

The recent euphoric worldwide promotion of biofuel to replace fossil fuels reveals the same striking limitations of classical analysis. There is no doubt that the use of renewable biofuel provides increased independence from fossil fuel and that it tends to be either carbon neutral or even carbon negative. In other words, the carbon released during the use of the fuel—e.g. through burning to power transport or generate electricity—is reabsorbed and balanced by the carbon absorbed by new plant growth. And, without a doubt, analyzed as such, the solution certainly makes sense, though, by the same token, the solution generates a crucial problem on another ground. As we can glean from recent UN statements urging a halt to biofuel investment, millions of people are currently at risk due to food prices that have doubled in the last couple of years due to biofuel production (BBC, 2008).

IT BECOMES OBVIOUS THAT UNDERSTANDING INTERDEPENDENCY REQUIRES AN APPROACH COMPLETELY DIFFERENT FROM ANALYSIS— NAMELY, ONE THAT ADOPTS A HOLISTIC VIEW OF THE WHOLE.

The classical notion of causality embedded in analysis, where cause is both necessary and sufficient for its effect, has proven inadequate because it reduces the scope to a strictly framed environment, ignores possible interdependencies, and important factors may remain external to the analysis. But what is more, thirdly, it assumes that the analysis of a prevailing condition ultimately entails the perfect solution, or, to quote Boland and Collopy (2004:6), "that there is a good set of options already available, or at least readily obtainable." It supposes that in an evolutionary process, a prevailing condition can be transformed into a perfect one. However, such an approach risks a closure of the problem space too early and fails to bring in ideas for new alternatives foreign to the determined problem space.

While analytical thinking essentially retains its widespread role as a way to approach problems throughout our Western world today, system thinking, the holistic approach towards a whole, has gone through several generations of change. Significantly, system thinkers have come to understand that the architectural design approach proves to be a purposeful and twofold operational methodology to understand and define problems and to generate adequate solutions. It is perfectly qualified to deal with interdependency—that is to say, to deal with members of a highly interdependent system such as social organizations or living systems in general (see, e.g., Bertalanffy, 2006; Weinberg, 2001; Gharajedaghi, 1999; Ackhoff, 1974). Design now represents the latest chapter of the evolution of system thinking (Gharajedaghi, 1999).

Previous generations, like Operations Research, either remained mechanical or ignored the vital implications of members actually having a choice (Ackoff, 1974; Churchman, 1971) First and foremost, it was Ackoff and Emery (1972) with their seminal book "On Purposeful Systems" and West C. Churchman (1971) with the book "In the Design of Inquiring Systems" who, in the early 1970s, demonstrated that the design approach provides a perfect means for inquiring into the behavior of complex systems as well as for managing interactions among various members (stakeholders) of a highly interdependent and multi-minded

system. In subsequent years, the idea of considering design as a powerful vehicle for social development, for formulating, assessing and inquiring into public agendas has been further developed by Ackoff (1974), Gharajedaghi (1999) and Simon (1996), just to name a few well-known representatives. Here, it is interesting to observe how architectural design per se was taken as a source of investigation to become acquainted with methods needed to handle problems of corporate strategy and governmental policy, which have been considered as complex and sometimes ill-defined as problems of architectural or engineering design (e.g. Simon, 1986).

The creative-analytical approach at work in design takes for granted that the process of finding a solution to a problem will require the invention or creation of new alternatives, given certain parameters and constrains. Every creative design process usually starts with a broad vision, with a suggestion for a very general "ideal" future state by equally assuming the opportunity to recreate a new model from a clean slate (see e.g. Gharajedaghi, 1999). (Although the vision does not evolve from an existing state, this does not necessarily mean that it is concerned with fiction or a utopia). Rather than directing someone's attention particularly to the problem space and its likely solution, the design approach favors creating and seizing opportunities.

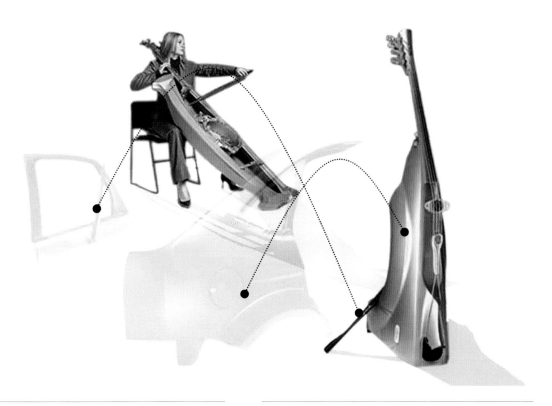

In other words, the design process brings forth new alternatives assuming a replacement of prevailing models and as such enhances paradigm shifts, a change of how we think about existing orders. Thus, the extensive lack of astringency in initial phases of the design approach, the lack of clearly defined objectives or criteria for evaluation, tremendously supports the act of inventing new alternatives and as such is destined to enhance paradigm shifts. The design approach almost "invites" the designer to come up with new alternatives assuming that they will replace existing orders. In other words, in the design process, the option to create the particular context in which to prove or disprove a hypothesis strongly supports the questioning and stretching of the limits of prevailing paradigms—that is, orders, rationales, or sets of shared beliefs about how something ought to be.

THE ANALYTIC APPROACH IN MANAGEMENT, ON THE OTHER HAND, USUALLY ASSUMES THAT THE ALTERNATIVES AT HAND ALREADY INCLUDE THE BEST ONE.

Hence, whereas the analytic approach aims at investigating extant forms to subsequently optimize or perfect them,

the design approach aims at initiating novel forms that in the end—after a series of iterative adaptation processes towards reality—best tackle the problem. The development of Apple's phones very clearly reveals the shortcomings of approaches towards optimization in relation to approaches that intend to create and seize new opportunities.

Consider that by summer 2004, when Apple's iPod business had become more successful but also more vulnerable due to the increasing popularity of phones also operating like a music device, Apple boss Steve Jobs started work on entering the mobile phone industry. In developing the world's first mobile phone with iTunes, a device that was intended to store some 100 songs and play them out randomly like the iPod Shuffle, he approached Motorola, a handset maker known for its perfectly functioning RAZR handset and Cingular, a major US wireless carrier. The collaboration allowed Apple to focus on the implementation of the popular iTunes software on the phone, while Motorola and Cingular could deal with solving the hardware problems. Motorola has been well-known for its high quality standards in pursuing perfection in production processes. In 1986 they developed Six Sigma, an analytic business improvement methodology that enjoys widespread application in industry and primarily focuses an organization on "understanding and managing customer requirements; aligning key business

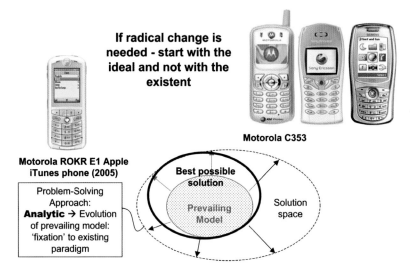

If radical change is needed - start with the ideal and not with the existent

Motorola C353

Motorola ROKR E1 Apple iTunes phone (2005)

Problem-Solving Approach:
Analytic → Evolution of prevailing model: 'fixation' to existing paradigm

Best possible solution

Prevailing Model

Solution space

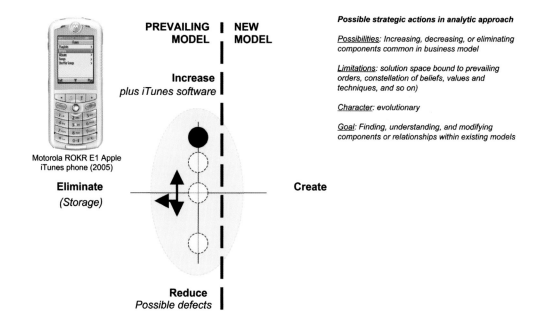

Motorola ROKR E1 Apple iTunes phone (2005)

PREVAILING MODEL | NEW MODEL

Increase
plus iTunes software

Eliminate
(Storage)

Create

Reduce
Possible defects

Possible strategic actions in analytic approach

Possibilities: Increasing, decreasing, or eliminating components common in business model

Limitations: solution space bound to prevailing orders, constellation of beliefs, values and techniques, and so on)

Character: evolutionary

Goal: Finding, understanding, and modifying components or relationships within existing models

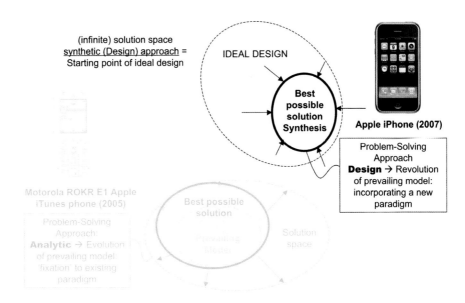

(infinite) solution space
<u>synthetic (Design) approach</u> =
Starting point of ideal design

IDEAL DESIGN

Best possible solution Synthesis

Apple iPhone (2007)

Problem-Solving Approach
Design → Revolution of prevailing model: incorporating a new paradigm

Motorola ROKR E1 Apple iTunes phone (2005)

Problem-Solving Approach:
Analytic → Evolution of prevailing model: 'fixation' to existing paradigm

Best possible solution

Prevailing Model

Solution space

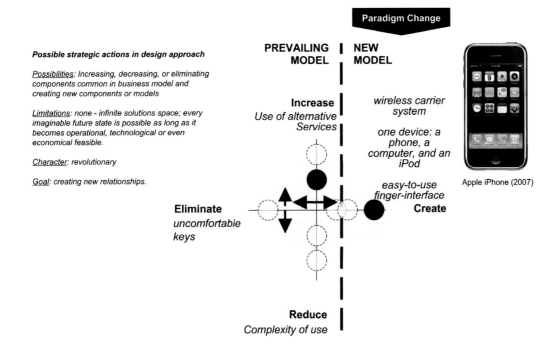

Paradigm Change

Possible strategic actions in design approach

<u>Possibilities</u>: Increasing, decreasing, or eliminating components common in business model and creating new components or models

<u>Limitations</u>: none - infinite solutions space; every imaginable future state is possible as long as it becomes operational, technological or even economical feasible.

<u>Character</u>: revolutionary

<u>Goal</u>: creating new relationships.

PREVAILING MODEL | NEW MODEL

Increase
Use of alternative Services

wireless carrier system

one device: a phone, a computer, and an iPod

easy-to-use finger-interface

Eliminate
uncomfortable keys

Create

Apple iPhone (2007)

Reduce
Complexity of use

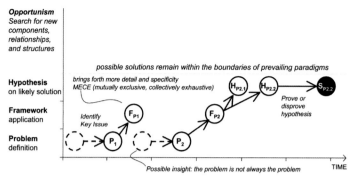

Opportunism
Search for new components, relationships, and structures

possible solutions remain within the boundaries of prevailing paradigms

Hypothesis on likely solution

brings forth more detail and specificity
MECE (mutually exclusive, collectively exhaustive)

$H_{P2.1}$ $H_{P2.2}$ → $S_{P2.2}$

Prove or disprove hypothesis

Framework application

Identify Key Issue

F_{P1} F_{P2}

Problem definition

P_1 P_2

Possible insight: the problem is not always the problem   TIME

Transformation defining boundaries of problem (P_1)   generating hypothesis on likely solution
                    braking it down into its component elements (F_{P1})   prove or disprove hypothesis
                    2nd attempt in defining the boundaries (F_{P2})   Solution

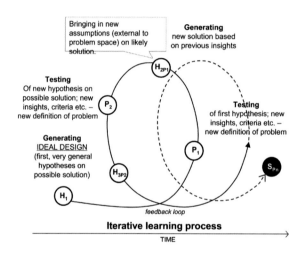

Bringing in new assumptions (external to problem space) on likely solution.

Generating new solution based on previous insights

H_{2P1}

Testing Of new hypothesis on possible solution; new insights, criteria etc. – new definition of problem

P_2

Testing of first hypothesis; new insights, criteria etc. – new definition of problem

Generating IDEAL DESIGN (first, very general hypotheses on possible solution)

P_1

H_{3P2}

S_{Pn}

H_1

feedback loop

Iterative learning process

TIME

120

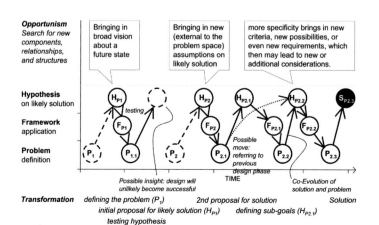

Opportunism
Search for new components, relationships, and structures

Bringing in broad vision about a future state

Bringing in new (external to the problem space) assumptions on likely solution

more specificity brings in new criteria, new possibilities, or even new requirements, which then may lead to new or additional considerations.

Hypothesis on likely solution

H_{P1} H_{P2} $H_{P2.1}$ $H_{P2.2}$ $S_{P2.3}$

testing

Framework application

F_{P1} F_{P2} $F_{P2.1}$ $F_{P2.2}$

Problem definition

P_1 $P_{1.1}$ P_2 $P_{2.1}$ $P_{2.2}$ $P_{2.3}$

Possible move: referring to previous design phase

Possible insight: design will unlikely become successful   TIME

Co-Evolution of solution and problem

Transformation defining the problem (P_1)   2nd proposal for solution   Solution
                    initial proposal for likely solution (H_{P1})   defining sub-goals ($H_{P2.1}$)
                    testing hypothesis

Process Characteristics

Analysis	Synthesis
The process is	
Problem-oriented	Solution-oriented
The focus is on	
Pre-existing structures	New Structures
Potential latitude for action	
Modification (evolutionary)	Creation (revolutionary)
The proposed solution	
Is derived from analysis	Is created parallel to the problem
The solution process is based on	
Pre-existing pradigms	Self-defined paradigms
The validity of the conclusion is thus	
Falsifiable (criteria exist)	Not falsifiable (there is no right or wrong solution)
The solution's success or failure is	
Rationally measurable	Only retroactively measurable
The proposed solution	
Can be rationally communicated	Can be justified (speculation)

Process

Analysis *Pre-existing model*   **Synthesis** *New model*

Understanding the problem
Problem-oriented: Identifying the crux of the problem

Understanding the problem
Solution-oriented: Identifying what you'd like to create

Structuring the problem
Applying a framework
Opening up a solution space

Generating, testing and evaluating hypotheses for solutions
Opportunistic search for a solution

FEEDBACK

NEW CRITERIA

CO-EVOLUTION OF SOLUTION AND PROBLEM

Generating, testing and evaluating hypotheses for solutions

Restructuring and redefining the problem
new considerations to be taken into account

Methods and Techniques

Analysis	Synthesis
Mode of approach	
Framework-driven	Opportunistic
Emphasis is on	
Identifying the crux of the problem	Identifying what you'd like to create
Intention	
Structuring a problem in order to be able to grasp and/or address complex interrelationships	Identifying interrelationships or structures that lead to a convincing solution or partial solution
Actions imply	
Increasing structural clarity about a problem	Permanent paradigm shift and/or restructruing of the problem
Typical form of collaboration	
Emphasis (about 80-95%) on individuals with expertise in analytical process fields (business, natural sciences, law, medicine, social sciences)	Emphasis on individuals with expertise in synthetic process fields and those that operationally deal with "reality". (engineers)

processes to achieve those requirements; utilizing rigorous data analysis to minimize variation in those processes; and, driving rapid and sustainable improvement to business processes" (Motorola, 2008a).

WHEN JOBS UNVEILED THE ROKR IN SEPTEMBER 2005, THE PUBLIC REACTION WAS DEVASTATING.

Instead of becoming the predicted hit of the upcoming holiday season, it garnered severe criticism culminating in WIRED's cover headline of November 2005 disappointingly asking: "You call this the phone of the future?" ROKR revealed a severe lack of any attempt to go beyond prevailing paradigms about how products or services ought to be—that is to say, the device displayed no attempt to bring forth a vision of how phones could look like or what features could be available on them; rather, it merely appeared as an optimized or more perfected version of previous Motorola phones. In addition, the phone's limitation to a maximum of 100 songs appeared even retrogressive in the wake of the plummeting prices of storage cards. Hence, the phone quickly came to represent all that seems to be wrong in contemporary business, the mere presence of a focus on something else in which the consumer is an afterthought. That something else seems to be the over-reliance on analysis, the tool that eliminates risk but also, unfortunately, eliminates creative action.

RATHER THAN TRYING TO DESIGN WHAT ONE TRULY VALUES, IT ADHERED TO WHAT EXISTED.

Pursuing perfection for perfection's sake—remember Motorola's (2008b) Six Sigma strategy to analytically improve business processes to less than 3.4 defects per million parts—probably led to an almost inadvertent obsession with polishing yesterday's paradigm and lack of originality or creative thought that could have brought forth new alternatives. The motive to solve the problem by producing "a world class handset, connected to a world class network, delivering a world class application," as the chief operating officer of Cingular Wireless put it at the phone's public release, just shored up mediocrity and as such symptomatically starved success (Apple, 2005).

The story of the relatively new iPhone is well-known. Even though Apple's iPhone came along with some imperfections, like running on sluggish EDGE networks or being configured with a really poor camera, it scored a tremendous market success by creating something new. The proceedings that led to this highly successful solution are emblematic of the design approach. Rather than taking the existing phone industry as an approach to further optimizing or modifying it, Jobs decided to start from scratch, approximating his initial vision step by step towards the final result. The development history reveals how every part of the phone—beginning with the development of a completely new operating system, antenna design, the assembly of special robot-equipped testing rooms for checking the anticipated lower radio frequency radiation, the incorporation of a touchscreen instead of keys, the rejection of plastic (as commonly used in handsets and Apple's iPod) in favor of glass to minimize scratching—had to be invented from a clean slate (Vogelstein, 2008). What's more, the phone created and seized opportunities going well beyond the problem's initial framework of developing just a music phone coming equipped with an iTunes application.

In an extremely short time, the popular phone reshaped the paradigms of an entire wireless industry and completely redesigned the existing order among consumers, developers and manufacturers. For decades, as Fred Vogelstein (2008), contributing editor of WIRED, notes, US wireless carriers dictated to handset manufacturers using access to their networks what to build and how to build it, treating the hardware basically as a vehicle to get users onto their networks. But the iPhone upsets this balance of power. To begin with the consumers, they got a keyless handset controlled by an easy-to-use finger-interface, uniting in one device all the functionality they had long been requesting—namely a phone, a computer and an iPod (a mp3 music player). As the current "war" for most offered apps (applications running on phones) shows, the device has become even more powerful due to the opening of the product to developers. Application developers are allowed to come up with more alternative services that make use of the iPhone's capabilities and are predicted to provide the wireless world with some of the flexibility and functionality the internet already reveals, such as mobile banking.

And finally, manufacturers have begun to understand their increasing power over carriers by producing a phone that customers will love instead of one that the carriers approve of.

AS MICHAEL OLSON, SECURITIES ANALYST AT PIPER JAFFRAY (CITED IN VOGELSTEIN, 2008:22) PUT IT, "THE IPHONE IS ALREADY CHANGING THE WAY CARRIERS AND MANUFACTURERS BEHAVE."

To sum up, the strength of the design approach derives particularly from the potential to deal holistically with structure, function and process, and their containing environment, which together define the whole—as opposed to classical analysis, which assumes that the whole is nothing but the sum of its parts.

TO HANDLE INTERDEPENDENCY HOLISTICALLY REQUIRES AN UNDERSTANDING OF EACH PART IN RELATION TO OTHERS AND THE WHOLE SET AT THE SAME TIME.

The iterative process of analytical inquiry coupled with a creative process of synthesizing at work in architectural design provides an extremely viable means to learn about as well as to define the behavior of systems holistically. Although design usually starts with an ideal state, an essential factor for its success and operational viability is the capability to iteratively approximate its initial assumptions about given constraints. So, in every stage of the iteration process, the design approach addresses the situation as an integrated whole and brings more detail and specificity into the design until a satisfactory notion of the whole is produced. This iterative process towards more specificity in the course of successive explorations is significantly different from the analytical approach, in which one attempts to detail the problem best at the beginning. The definition of the problem and the generation of the solution evolve then in co-evolution, as opposed to classical analysis in which one attempts to frame and define the problem best at the beginning to subsequently arrive at a solution.

Conclusion

The operational methodology embedded in architectural design practice proves much more viable for understanding and dealing with contemporary complex problems than the analytical approach management practice has adopted from classical science. The iterative design process is a powerful vehicle for operationalizing the most exciting vision of a business' future given the necessity to design a business' model from scratch (which subsequently is approximated to given constraints), rather than modifying a model starting from an existing order (which in many cases is no option anyway). Design has always been about understanding and describing a system, acknowledging the system's vital functions, major elements and their relationships that define the whole (although practitioners of design professions are used to applying their competence just to comprehend it in some kind of physical form). Thus, the design approach provides the operational means to identify the comprehensive set of interdependent variables and to generate a new system in its totality.

Paradoxically, the design approach attracts rather scant attention in business. The diverse backgrounds of people hired by prestigious management consultancies such as McKinsey or Boston Consulting Group reveal that people with an analytic background, being educated in business, natural sciences or social sciences, are most privileged. At McKinsey around 80% of the people hired belong to this group (McKinsey, 2007); at Boston Consulting Group this group accounts for about 88% of the staff (Boston Consulting Group, 2007). Certainly, these figures illustrate the preference towards an analytic approach in solving business problems. However, at the same token, it points to a neglected field of possible intervention. There is no doubt that there is a need for people capable of designing (not finding) futures. Being trained and experienced in the iterative design process, in breaking down "ideal" visions into reality, designers seem to be perfectly qualified to be much more involved in business. Of course, it is not a question of pursing either the analytic or the design approach. Rather, it is question of the synthesis of both— how one can provide great support for the other and vice versa.

But for other related reasons, architects and designers appear to be destined to be involved in business. Creative thinking about a business model that does not yet exist requires a considerable act of faith on the part of the client. Whether one likes it or not, everything in our world that is not well-grounded on a series of hard facts is generally confronted with distrust even though this is not justifiable. Could the Cirque de Soleil or Apple's iPhone have been justified in economic terms before they became real? This is rather implausible, simply because one cannot analyse what does not exist yet and people also do not analyse their actions into the future. Moreover, people cannot answer questions seriously regarding an interest in things they have neither directly nor indirectly experienced.

AS STEVE JOBS PUT IT, "PEOPLE DON'T KNOW WHAT THEY WANT UNTIL YOU SHOW IT TO THEM" (KAHNEY, 2008).

Architects and designers have the powerful capability to think and communicate visually and thus are extremely capable of prototyping conjectures easily comprehensible across the spectrum of clients, the company's decision-makers. A glance at current daily affairs would reveal that there is a great demand for people having internalized such a potential. As Harold Leavitt (1989) put it, business management is not just about decision-making, but equally about path-finding and implementation—though path-finding, the search for new alternatives, appears to be a perfect ground for possible intervention. However, architects and designers have to remain realistic, precisely because such a move requires a paradigm shift, a revolution in both fields, in the field of design as well as in business, to make such a collaborative synthesis come true.

References

Apple. 2005. Apple, Motorola and Cingular launch world's first mobile phone with iTunes: Press release. Sept. 7. http://www.apple.com/pr/library/2005/sep/07rokr.html. Accessed on May 2, 2008.

Ackhoff, R. L. 1974. Redesigning the future: A systems approach to societal problems. New York: John Wiley.

Ackhoff, R. L and Emery, F. E. 1972. On purposeful system: An interdisciplinary analysis of individual and social behavior as a system of purposeful events. New York: Aldine Atherton.

BBC. 2008. BBC News UN urges biofuel investment halt. May, 2. http://news.bbc.co.uk/2/hi/in_depth/7381392.stm. Accessed on May 10, 2008.

Bertalanffy, L. von. 2006. General systems theory. Revised edition. 15th ed. New York: George Braziller.

Boland, R. J. and Collopy, F. 2004. Design matters for management. In R. J. Boland and F. Collopy (Eds.), Managing as designing. Stanford: Stanford University Press.

Boston Consulting Group. 2007. www.bcg.de/karriere/suchen/vielfalt/index.jsp. Accessed on Sept 5, 2007.

Churchman, C. W. 1971. The design of inquiring systems: Basic concepts of systems and organizations. New York and London: Basic Books.

Fink, D. 2003. Die großen Management Consultants: Ihre Geschichte, ihre Konzepte, ihre Strategien [The famous management consultants: Their history, their concepts, their strategies] München: Vahlen.

Gharajedaghi, J. 1999. System thinking: Managing chaos and complexity. Boston: Butterworth Heinemann.

Kahney, L. 2008. Inside Steven's brain. New York: Portfolio.

Leavitt, H. J. 1989. Pathfinding, problem solving and implementing: The management mix. In H. J. Leavitt et al. (Eds.) Readings in managerial psychology. Fourth edition. Chicago: The University of Chicago Press.

McKinsey. 2007. www.mckinsey-karriere.de Accessed on Sept 5, 2007.

Motorola. 2008a. The Inventors of Six Sigma. http://www.motorola.com/content.jsp?globalObjectId=3079 Accessed on May 5, 2008.

Motorola. 2008b. What is Six Sigma. http://www.motorola.com/content.jsp?globalObjectId=3088 Accessed on May 5, 2008.

Peters, T. and Waterman, R.H. Jr. 2006. In search of excellence. Paperback edition. New York: Harper Collins.

Rasiel, E. M. and Friga, P. N. 2001. The McKinsey mind: Understanding and implementing the problem-solving tools and management techniques of the world's top strategic consulting firm. New York: McGraw-Hill.

Rasiel, E. M. 1998. The McKinsey way: Using the techniques of the world's top strategic consultants to help you and your business. New York: McGraw-Hill.

Simon, H. A. 1986. Decision making and problem solving. Research briefings 1986: Report of the research briefing panel on decision making and problem solving. Washington, DC: National Academy Press.

Simon, H. A. 1996. The sciences of the artificial. 3rd edition 1996. Cambridge: MIT Press.

Vogelstein, Fred. 2008. "The demo was not going well. Again." WIRED. No. 16.02.

Weinberg, G. M. 2001. An introduction to general systems thinking. Silver anniversary edition. New York: Dorset House Publishing.

In management practice and education, scant attention is paid to
the notion of abductive reasoning—different from both deductive
and inductive—that might be applied to strategy formation. That
is to say, it is a common practice in business to infer analytically
on the premises of either directly observable facts (inductive
reasoning) or past evidence (deductive reasoning). Abductive
reasoning—which suggests that something may be so—is widely
neglected though this rests upon conjecture and therefore is
mistakenly regarded as speculative and lacking logical determinism.
In the following essay, detailed reasons will be put forward for this
apparent neglect. Moreover, it will be shown that the process of
abductive inference strongly supports the creation of new ideas and
that it does not—as generally assumed—lack any kind of logical
structure. Though in literature the various modes of reasoning are
discussed in the context of scientific work, here too the nature
of abduction will be outlined in relation to the logic of science.
However, given insights on the operative nature of abduction may
be transferred to the field of strategic business thinking; it is also
future-focused and based on the ability to conjure an image of a
future reality that does not yet exist.

Introduction

There has been a long tradition of drawing a sharp distinction between the act of conceiving or inventing an idea or a scientific theory and the process of examining it logically (Schiller, 1917; Popper, 2002 [1]; Peirce, 1965 [2]; Hanson, 1959). Whereas history reveals uncertainty about the existence of any logic embedded in the process of discovery (see, for example, Schiller, 1917, Hanson, 1959, Peirce, 1935/65 CP 6.474), there have been some strong arguments saying that the whole question of how it happens that a new idea or scientific theory comes into being is completely irrelevant for the logic of science (e.g. Popper, 1935/59). In science, in logically analyzing scientific knowledge to justifying knowledge—that is to say, for logically building or testing theories—the two essential methods and criteria to do so are deduction and induction. The dominance of Popper's view, which remained quite accepted until the advent of serious scientific investigation of artificial intelligence (Curd, 1980), may provide a plausible explanation for the reasons for paying so little attention to other notions of reasoning.

On the same ground, research has shown that the accumulative nature of science, which certainly has led to a fascinating extension of our knowledge of reality, equally leads to rigidity in terms of expectations that subsequently fail to produce major novelties, conceptual or phenomenal (Kuhn 1962; 52).

IN OTHER WORDS, SCIENCE FAILS TO FUNCTION PRECISELY AT THE MOMENT THESE EXPECTATIONS ARE VIOLATED.

As Kuhn (1962) convincingly argues, this sort of "crisis" is then not corrigible by the same patterns, methods or "paradigms" scientists have deployed to constitute the body of knowledge but by means of a paradigm change; that is to say, it becomes necessary to introduce a kind of inverted lens allowing the scientist to be acquainted with different legitimizing criteria to perceive the same constellation as before but transformed. Unfortunately, Kuhn did not provide a theory on the nature of this kind of discovery, the process of thinking that leads to this sudden change, despite some merely phenomenological descriptions. However, the main thesis Kuhn put forward makes it clear that it is necessary for a scientist to be able to act in both realms, in scientific discovery (bringing forth new paradigms or theories [3] in times of scientific crisis or at early stages of investigation) and scientific justification (testing and building theories). For this very reason, we may then ask if there is any such thing as logic in discovery and, if so, if it is distinct from the logic of proof. In this paper, I will attempt to show that it is possible to identify logic in discovery by following Charles Sanders Peirce's considerations of abductive reasoning.

The paper illuminates this mode of reasoning along the following lines: First, it will briefly provide background on the logic of scientific discovery, referring thereby to the writings of Popper and Kuhn. Second, abduction will be defined and peculiar characteristics will be put forward in relation to the two other modes of reasoning, namely deduction and induction. In particular, the interplay of the three modes will be discussed in terms of required premises, goals and inferential procedures. Primary source of reference will be Charles Sanders Peirce who re-introduced the (old) theory of abduction into the scientific debate at the turn of the 20th century. In the subsequent section, the modus operandi is given prime focus; that is to say, this part of the paper addresses the question of whether there is a methodology embedded in abduction or not. Finally, the paper proceeds with a reflection on the possible relevance of abductive reasoning for scientific work in general and management research in particular.

Background

Abduction has been neglected in scientific debate. Definitions of deduction and induction are offered in the most widely used textbooks on logic (see, for example, Hurley, 2000) or scientific research (see, for example, Punch, 2005). Deductive thinking proceeds from the general, from the rule to the contention of the particular, the result, via the subsumption of the singular case under the rule. Therefore, following Hurley (2000, 33), a deductive argument is an "argument in which the premises are claimed to support the conclusion in such a way that it is impossible for the premises to be true and the conclusion false." In the case of inductive thinking, one passes from the singular statement, the case, formed on the basis of particular observations or experiments, the result, to a universal statement, theory or rule; this leads to generalizations based on individual instances. Consequently, an inductive argument is "an argument in which the premises are claimed to support the conclusion in such a way that it is improbable that the premises be true and the conclusion false" (Hurley 2000, 33).

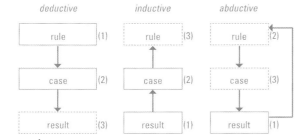

deductive   inductive   abductive

❮ Forms of Inverence.

Abduction is commonly understood as inferring (backwards) from given data to a hypothesis that best explains the data (e.g. Walton, 2004; Harman, 1965). Peirce (CP 2.624 ◀◀) described abduction as a process "where we find some very curious circumstance, which would be explained by the supposition that it was the case of a certain general rule, and thereupon adopt that supposition." In other words, based on an observed phenomenon that is to be explained or understood, in Peirce's terminology a "result" (CP 2.619), an available or newly constructed rule is suggested by means of which the particular case is suppositional.

FOR THE MOMENT, TWO EXAMPLES WILL BRIEFLY ILLUSTRATE WHAT IS MEANT BY ABDUCTIVE INFERENCE AND SHOW THAT IT IS QUITE COMMON IN EVERYDAY REASONING AS WELL AS IN SCIENTIFIC REASONING.

According to Seidel (2004), the way a detective puts together the evidence to arrive at a conclusion can be taken as an adequate instance of inference to the best explanation. Assume that a detective finds a corpse with a bullet wound in the cardiac region and a gun nearby; accordingly, the detective will assume at first that this gun may be the weapon involved. An initial inspection of the gun that reveals fingerprints of the decedent may then quickly lead to the assumption that the person committed suicide. However, if the results of a subsequent autopsy show that the corpse displayed an arsenic concentration 3,000 times higher than normal, the first conclusion most likely will be dismissed; a new hypothesis becomes necessary. In the ideal case, the detective will approximately arrive at the truth—depending on his creativity and that of the murderer.

The second example, "the Fossils Example" by Peirce (CP 2.625), illustrates the use of abduction in science, showing that Peirce was aware of its use in scientific fields: "Fossils are found; say, remains like those of fishes, but far in the interior of the country. To explain the phenomenon, we suppose the sea once washed over this land. This is another hypothesis."
To return to the initial statement of this section, one of the most important reasons for paying less attention to abductive reasoning in sciences rests in the very logic embedded in the process of justification and constitution of scientific knowledge. In his seminal book entitled "The Logic of Scientific Discovery," Popper quite clearly puts forward the task of a scientist: "Whether one is a theorist or experimenter," his/ her task is to put "forward statements, or systems of statements, and test them step by step" (2002: 3). According to a widely accepted view (see, for example, Popper, 2002; Punch, 2005; Carlile et al, 2005), both induction and, more importantly, deduction, thereby constitute the two essential (and exclusive) methods to build or test theories against experience by observation or experiment. Moreover, because inductive inference is not strictly valid—although it attains some degree of reliability or of probability it may lead to conclusions that turn out to be false—in science, preference is more or less given to deduction as most prominently voiced by Popper (2002:8). Ruigrok et al (2008), to cite a recent example in the field of management in regard to this preference, investigated a sample of 159

articles based on cases studies that have been intended to provide a tool for (inductively) generating theory. The research was restricted to articles published in the top 10 leading management journals over a period of six years (1995-2000). The authors' statistical findings reveal that only some six percent of all published articles (159 out of 2,643) are based on case-study research.

Despite the many debates about the virtues of deductive and inductive methods, literature suggests that these are two elements of the same scientific process (Carlile, 2005:5). Every theory-building or testing process must be subjected to those two systematic modes of reasoning, deduction and induction, if it is to be seriously entertained; that is to say, a complete lap around the theory-building process consists of an inductive side and a deductive side.

Nevertheless, there is always a moment in scientific work before one can build up theories inductively or test theories deductively—namely, an initial stage, a discovery stage, in which the act of conceiving or bringing forth a new theory becomes dominant. This holds true for two reasons. Deductive thinking necessitates a theory, a general rule or construct of relationships, because it proceeds from the general to the assertion of the particular. Certainly, theories are not conceived de novo in complete absence of any phenomena but derive consciously or unconsciously on the premises of an inductive source, on observation that leads to the construction of relationships (Carlile, 2005; see footnote 5). On the other hand, a valid induction already presupposes as a hypothesis the general rule that it is supposed to infer in the first place too. This is one of Peirce's insights of greatest relevance to the philosophy of science. For Peirce, inductive inferences must satisfy two conditions in order to be valid: The sample must be a random selection from the underlying totality, and the specific characteristic that is to be examined by means of the sample must have been defined before the sample is drawn, precisely because—as Riemer notes—"if, however, the property to be examined must be defined before the sample is selected, this is only possible on the basis of a conjecture that the property exists in the corresponding totality before the inductive inference is made. How else could the property be known in advance of sample

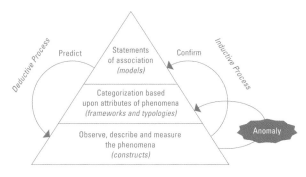

❮ The Process of Building Theory. Source: Carlile, P. R., 2005

selection? Valid induction, therefore, already presupposes as a hypothesis the conclusion that is to be inferred. More precisely, inductive reasoning is based on a given hypothesis [...] and then by means of samples..." (1988: 25f). The conditional premises of induction that the property to be examined must be designated in advance of sample selection raises a question: What leads to thinking up new ideas or scientific theories? In other words, does scientific discovery employ a mode of reasoning and, if so, is it different from deduction or induction, or is it entirely unsystematic and intuitive? Significantly, the history of strictly distinguishing between the act of conceiving or inventing a scientific theory and the process of examining it logically is quiet long and not without controversies. For example, Schiller (1917) argued that scientific discovery has its own logic that differs from deductive logic. Hansen (1959: 85) as well as Peirce (CP 2.96) demonstrated how different the mode of reasoning deployed in scientific discovery is compared to deduction or induction by both stressing the example of Kepler's development of the elliptical orbit theory. (This example will be discussed more in detail later in this paper.) Popper too rigorously distinguished "between the process of conceiving a new idea, and the methods and results of examining it logically" for reasons already cited above (2002: 8).

FOR HIM, IT WAS NOT RELEVANT WHETHER THE ACT OF PUTTING FORTH A THEORY CALLS FOR OR IS SUSCEPTIBLE TO LOGICAL ANALYSIS, THE PREMISES OF SCIENTIFIC KNOWLEDGE;

rather, he regarded the whole question of how it happens that a new theory is put forward as basically "irrelevant to the logical analysis of scientific knowledge," because the latter is purely concerned with questions of justification or validity (Popper, 2002:7). In particular, they entail questions such as: Can a statement be examined logically, or can it be justified and, if so, how? Hence, following Popper's widely accepted argument, it becomes apparent why in empirical sciences attention had been given exclusively to deductive and inductive reasoning. In fact, in so clearly drawing the demarcation line of scientific knowledge by delineating everything related to scientific discovery to the "knowledge of psychology," the possibly applied modes of reasoning are necessarily limited (Popper, 2002: 7).

Regardless of Popper's distinct separation of the logical analysis of scientific knowledge from the act of conceiving or inventing a theory, it was Thomas S. Kuhn in his seminal book entitled "The Structure of Scientific Revolution" who highlighted a decisive paradox inherent in scientific reasoning. In this essay, Kuhn (1962) quite vividly sets out the virtues and limits of the logic embedded in scientific work. Acknowledging science as "a highly cumulative enterprise, eminently successful in its aim, the steady extension of the scope and precision of scientific knowledge," Kuhn outlines how little the models, patterns or "paradigms," the term he coined for them, embedded in science aim to produce major novelties, conceptual or phenomenal (1962: 52). Theories, standards and methods a scientist necessarily acquires, according to Kuhn, simply prove to become constitutive for scientific work itself, providing the "scientist not only with a map but also with some of the directions essential for map-making" (1962: 109). In other words, to desert the paradigm means equally to cease practicing the science it defines. Seen from this point of view, science leads to an immense restriction of the scientist's vision, eliminating from scientific knowledge all non-logical and non-perceptual terms. It is for this very reason that scientific work results in an embodiment of a host of expectations about reality, which, by the same token, begin to fail to function at the moment these expectations are violated. These violations or "anomalies" a body of knowledge is incapable of accounting for appear only against the background provided by the paradigm. The main thesis then, which Kuhn (1962) brings out and which is of particular interest here, is that paradigms are not corrigible by science at all. Anomalies, which lead to scientific crisis, are terminated not by deliberation and interpretation, precisely because the latter presuppose a paradigm that aims to refine, extend and articulate a paradigm that is already in existence (1962: 122). Rather, this paradigm change happens "by a sudden and unstructured event like the gestalt switch" allowing the scientist to be confronted with the same constellation as before but transformed (Kuhn, 1962: 122).

A SIGNIFICANT SHIFT OCCURS IN THE CRITERIA DETERMINING THE LEGITIMACY BOTH OF PROBLEMS AND OF PROPOSED SOLUTIONS.

"Scientists then often speak of the 'scales falling from the eyes' or the 'lighting flash' that 'inundates' a previously obscure puzzle, enabling its components to be seen in a new way that for the first time permits its solution" (Kuhn, 1962: 122). This kind of bringing together something one could not previously perceive as being connected anticipates in an incredible way the concept of abduction Charles Sanders Peirce elaborated in detail and which he claimed to be a logical form of inference preceding the act of logical analysis of scientific knowledge (through deduction and induction): "[The] abductive inference shades into perceptual judgment without any sharp line of demarcation between them; or, in other words, our first premises, the perceptual judgments, are to be regarded as an extreme case of abductive inference, from which they differ in being absolutely beyond criticism. The abductive suggestion comes to us like a flash. It is an act of *insight*, although of extremely fallible insight. It is true that the different elements of the hypothesis were in our mind before; but it is the idea of putting together what we had never before dreamed of putting together with flashes the new suggestion of our contemplation." (CP 5.181; author's italics)

But it is not just the presence of phrases such as "like a flash" or "act of insights" that are identical to Kuhn's associations, but also the view that an impartial approach to questions to be solved—that is to say, dealing with them in a way that is free of any directly related instrumental-rational motives—stands at the forefront of any scientific discovery.

In the following section, I will show how abduction, the inauguration of constructivist thinking, then may be conceived of as a principle that allows us to reconstruct conceptual order through the imposition of a hypothesis. Furthermore, I will show how abductive reasoning, driven by an observation of a particular phenomenon, an anomaly revealing something peculiar about it, can be regarded as a logical procedure for forming an explanatory hypothesis in which a paradigm, a rule or method of measurement is provisionally laid down.

Inferential Procedures

Peirce distinguished among three modes of inference: deduction, induction and abduction, and sketched their different syllogistic forms as well as their peculiar epistemological functions. To Aristotle, it was already known that aside from deduction and induction, a third mode of reasoning exists (Magnani, 2001: 19; Richter, 1995: 50) and as such it was Peirce's merit to investigate this third mode—called "retroductive" reasoning (CP 1.74) or later "abduction" (CP 5.145)—in detail and to make it accessible scientifically. Moreover, it was Peirce who succeeded in demonstrating the fundamental relevance of abduction for the logic of scientific discovery.

Peirce notes that in the first stage of any scientific inquiry "the whole series of mental performances between the notice of the wonderful phenomenon and the acceptance to the hypothesis, [...] the bursting out of the startling conjecture, the remarking of its smooth fitting to the anomaly" is a case of "retroduction" [or "abduction" as mentioned in the footnote] (CP 6.469). And, he continues, that "[e]very inquiry whatsoever takes its rise in the observation [...] of some surprising expectation, or breaks in upon some habit of expectation of the inquisiturus; and each apparent exception to this rule only confirms it" (CP 6.469). To put it differently, in this first stage, the reasoner arrives from a conceived or invented explanatory hypothesis (rule), which has been introduced for the purpose of testing an observed factum (result) that is to be explained and from which speculation has taken its advent, to the insight that the factum is a peculiar case of the tentatively adopted hypothesis (rule).

Accordingly, for Peirce the "play of musement" becomes significant for the success of scientific discovery. "Musement" or pondering, as Peirce often referred to it (CP 6.458), leads to a situation in which one may be capable of seeing that if there existed a certain state of things of whose actual existence the observer knows nothing, that phenomenon would certainly occur, or at any rate, would in all probability occur. Hence, in this circumstance, one wonders if that is not the very state of the case. As Peirce noted, "[t]he inquiry begins with pondering these phenomena in all their aspects, in the search of some point of view whence the wonder shall be resolved. At length a conjecture arises that furnishes a possible explanation, by which I mean a syllogism exhibiting the surprising fact as necessarily consequent upon the circumstances of its occurrence together with the truth of the credible conjecture, as premises.

ON ACCOUNT OF THIS EXPLANATION, THE INQUIRER IS LED TO REGARD HIS CONJECTURE, OR HIS HYPOTHESIS, WITH FAVOUR" (CP 6.469).

In this sense, musement is a kind of procedure for judgment. It begins passively with a broad perception—by "drinking in the impressions" as Peirce puts it—that "soon passes into attentive observation, observation into musing, musing into a lively give and take of communication between self and self. If one's observations and reflections are allowed to specialize themselves too much, the Play will be converted into scientific study" (CP 6.459).

The question that follows is whether this procedure of musement to forming an explanatory hypothesis entails logic or is just intuitive or creative. Before proceeding to this question, a look at the different syllogistic forms of the three modes of inference and their interplay would be beneficial.

Syllogistic Forms of Reasoning and their Potential to Bring Forth New Knowledge

The core task of any logical operation is to classify arguments since all testing clearly depends on classification (Peirce, CP 2.619). The classes defined for logical operations are defined by certain typical forms called syllogisms. In Aristotle's words, "a discourse in which, a certain thing being stated, something other than what is stated follows of necessity from being so" (Cambridge Dictionary, 1995:780).

For example, the syllogism typifying deductive reasoning can be put into the following terms: All men are mortal, the major premises which lays down the rule; Peter is a man, which maintains the minor premises that states the case under the rule; hence, the conclusion is that Peter is mortal, applying the general rule to the particular case. Thus, deduction is

the inference from a given statements (rule) to conclusions (result) by subsumption of the particular case under the rule. If the premises are true, the conclusions must be true too (Cambridge Dictionary, 1995:183; Peirce, CP 5.161). Decisively, for this necessary truth, the information content of the conclusion must be already implicitly contained in the premises. Therefore, deduction is not synthetic (knowledge enlarging). It does not lead to new knowledge but merely is an explanatory statement. Hence, the advantage of deduction, which rests upon its internal stringency necessitating the conclusion, implicitly brings about the disadvantage of abdication of gaining any new knowledge.

Induction is the process of reasoning in which the premises of an argument are believed to support the conclusion but do not entail it (Cambridge Dictionary, 1995; Peirce, CP 5.167). It aims at empirically provable coherence between the premises (case) and experience (result) in order to derive a probable generalization (rule). Its synthesizing nature brings forth new knowledge although it lacks logical admissibility. It is not truth conserving because the inference is only a hypothesis that cannot be proved with ultimate certainty. As Popper brilliantly noted: "How can the examination of some particulars justify the truth of its generalization" (2002; 3).

Abductive reasoning, finally, reveals a syllogistic form of an inverse modus ponens by "reasoning backwards" from a consequent to antecedent—that is to say, it adopts an explanatory hypothesis (rule) for an observed factum (result) that is to be explained as a peculiar case of the tentatively adopted hypothesis. In his Lowell Lectures of 1866, Peirce gave an example of the different syllogistic forms of the three modes of inference by referring to an example involving beans: (Peirce, CP 2.623; for a detailed analysis see, e.g., Richter, 1995: 30f.)

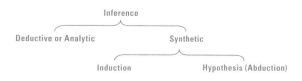

Deduction (a priori)

1. Premises:	Rule	All the beans from this bag are white.
2. Premises:	Case	These beans are from this bag.

Conclusion:	Result	These beans are white.

Induction

1. Premises:	Case	The beans are from this bag.
2. Premises:	Result	These beans are white.

Conclusion:	Rule	All the beans from this bag are white.

Abduction (a posoriori)

1. Premises:	Rule	All the beans from this bag are white.
2. Premises:	Result	These beans are white.

Conclusion:	Case	These beans are from this bag.

Seidel (2004), following Peirce (CP 2.623), notices that abduction corresponds to induction at least in two points: In its synthesizing character leading to new knowledge (as opposed to deduction's analytic and purely explanatory character) and in its reversed syllogistic form to deduction. However, for reasons already discussed above by citing Riemer, a valid induction presupposes as a hypothesis the conclusion that is to be inferred—that is to say, inductive reasoning is only possible on the basis of a conjecture that the property exists in the corresponding totality before the inductive inference is made (Riemer, 1988: 25f). Thus, unless induction builds a hypothesis, a theory that is already known, induction is dependent upon hypotheses which must have been constructed beforehand. And this process of construction is abductive as far as its logical form is concerned. In other words, abduction necessarily precedes induction. For this very reason, to follow Peirce, abduction "is the only logical operation which introduces any new idea; for induction does nothing but determine a value, and deduction merely evolves the necessary consequences of a pure hypothesis. Deduction proves that something must be; Induction shows that something actually is operative; Abduction merely suggests that something may be" (Peirce, CP 5.171).

For Peirce "[t]he object of reasoning was to find out, from the consideration of what we already know, something else we do not know" (CP 5.365). In this sense, abduction can be considered as the only mode of reasoning by which "we ever learn anything or by which we understand phenomena at all [...]. Every single item of scientific theory which stands established today," according to Peirce, "has been due to abduction" (Peirce, CP 5.171)

Syllogistic Forms of Reasoning and Scientific Discovery

Syllogistic forms of reasoning and scientific discovery In Peirce's logic of discovery, the whole notion of abductive reasoning becomes a fundamental aspect in the concept of scientific knowledge. Since "neither deduction nor induction contributes the smallest positive item to the final conclusion of the inquiry, [...] deduction explicates; induction evaluates;" Peirce (CP 6.475) concludes that abduction is the "only kind of reasoning which supplies new ideas" (CP 2.777). Whereas in deduction it is possible to draw a prediction which then can be tested inductively, it must be by abduction that we have the capacity "to learn anything or to understand phenomena at all; [therefore] every single item of scientific theory which stands established today has been due to Abduction" (Peirce, CP 5.172).

Peirce certainly noticed that retroduction (or abduction), the mode of reasoning from consequent to antecedent, does not afford security until the hypothesis is tested. In this sense, he saw the three modes of reasoning as necessary interconnected. "This testing, to be logically valid," Peirce argues, "must honestly start, not as Retroduction starts, with scrutiny of the phenomena, but with the examination of the hypothesis, and a muster of all sorts of conditional experimental consequences which would follow from its truth" (CP 6.470).

Governed by the structural analysis of the various syllogistic forms of the three modes of inference, Peirce (CP 2.96), along with other philosophers (Hanson, 1959), reconstructed Kepler's reasoning in drawing his conclusions about the observed celestial constellation to exemplify their interplay. For purposes of understanding, the example will be recapitulated briefly:

‹ Great Comet of 1577.

‹ Johannes Kepler.

At a certain stage of inquiry into the celestial constellation, Kepler proposed an abductive hypothesis that the observed longitudes of Mars may fit an orbit in the form of an ellipse. He found that the observed longitudes of Mars, which he had long tried in vain to fit into an orbit, were within the possible limits of error of the observations. This was just a suggestion including no certainty at this time. In this sense, Kepler arrived at this abduction introducing a new idea, based on a problem-oriented contemplation, which led to a new construct completely in opposition to the geocentric model of the universe in which the Earth is the center of the universe and other objects go around it.

Kepler did not conclude from this that the orbit really was an ellipse; rather it inclined him to that idea so much as to ascertain whether virtual prediction about the latitudes and parallaxes based on this hypothesis would be verified or not. For this very reason, following Peirce's description, Kepler proceeded to test the hypothesis deductively, meaning he undertook the calculations of the latitudes from his elliptic theory without knowing whether the calculation would agree with the observation or not.

IN OTHER WORDS, HIS THEORETICAL PROPOSITION ALLOWED HIM TO CALCULATE THE EXACT POSITION OF MARS AT ANY GIVEN TIME.

In the third step, Kepler moved on to test inductively his abductively-deductively structured theory whose success he could not know beforehand. What he then found was that the planet was at the time of observation always in the exact position it ought to be according to elliptic theory. To conclude, Kepler's abductively constructed hypothesis of the elliptical orbit of the planet established a new paradigm, a new explanation of a certain phenomenon in the scientific community.

Both theoretical reflection as well as the example of Kepler's development of the new elliptical orbit theory show that there is a strong necessity for interplay of all three modes of reasoning. Furthermore, we can see that if neither induction nor deduction enlarges knowledge, then abduction as the only knowledge-producing mechanism must become the central focus of the epistemological discussion. In the following, section, the logical form of abduction will be discussed.

Logical Form of Abduction

Abductive inference involves two decisive steps: First, a phenomenon—in Peirce's terminology the "result"—to be understood or explained is to be presented; then, in a subsequent step, an available or newly-constructed hypothesis (the rule) is introduced by means of which the case is subpositioned (Walton, 2004; Fischer, 2001). But as Peirce pointed out in regard to "play of musement," as the investigation continues, more and more evidence is typically collected. In a scientific inquiry, the single statement drawn by abduction becomes a hypothesis. And as the inquiry proceeds—remember the example of the detective—that hypothesis may become more and more comprehensive. The conclusion initially drawn may become carefully qualified, and the terms in it may be carefully defined. In other words, the hypothesis will be more refined. At the end, the initial hypothesis may even grow into a scientific theory (Peirce, CP 6.459). In this sense, inference to the best explanation can be regarded as a "dialogue model of explanation" (Walton, 2004) or "reflexive conversation" (Schön, 1983). The procedure of forming an explanatory hypothesis is modeled as a discourse between two agents (whereas it is not necessary that the agents are embodied literally in different persons). One agent is presumed by the other to understand something, and the other asks a question meant to enable him to understand it as well. An explanation is successful if it communicates understanding of a sort needed to enable the questioner to make sense of the thing questioned. Whereas the first dimension of this model involves the generation of initial assumptions on the basis of an inquiry about the observed phenomenon, the second dimension involves a synthesizing process in which initial assumptions are verified and modified and substantially elaborated during further processing. Formulation of new assumptions or understandings suggests new criteria, which may then lead to new or additional considerations. Every discourse sequence then "shapes" the situation and thereby provides continual feedback that brings forth further considerations that may be taken into account (Schön, 1983:77).

THUS, A SEARCH STRATEGY IS ADOPTED THAT IS BASED ON GENERATING AND TESTING POTENTIAL EXPLANATIONS AND IS FUNDAMENTALLY CONCERNED WITH LEARNING.

The process internalizes an activity that begins with generating a series of creative "what if" hypotheses, continues in selecting the most promising one for further

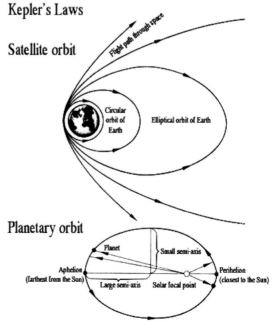

❮ Kepler Laws.

inquiry, which then takes the form of a more evaluative "if then" sequence in which the logical implications of that particular hypothesis are more fully explored and tested. Inference of this kind, therefore, moves forward by examining competing accounts. The model provides a formal structure for the view of explanation articulated by Scriven (2002:49): "Explanation is literally and logically the process of filling in gaps in understanding, and to do this we must start out with some understanding of something." In other words, abduction is a technique narrowing down the number of alternatives by picking out one or a few hypotheses from a much larger number of them that are available.

From a logical point of view, reasoning backwards then seems not to be a valid form of inference since it is conjectural or presumptive thinking aiming at plausibility. Abductive inferences, from this point of view, do indeed violate logical laws and appear to be highly intuitive and creative, but, as Fischer (2001) notices, it "may be interpreted as a creative change of the semantic content of concepts or conceptual systems [...] as is, by the case with all 'paradigm changes'. There is no absolute standard for the rationality of thought and action, but only relational one." Deduction, to give an example, derives its validity only on the premises of "dealing exclusively with pure ideas attaching primarily to symbols and derivatively to other signs of our own creation and the fact that man has a power of explicating his own meaning" (Peirce following Kant, CP 5.474). Scientific reasoning is thought to be objective and impersonal; however, scientific theories, hypotheses and results are supposedly objective. They are propositions that are true or false, and are proved to be so by factual investigations that eliminate the personal element (Walton, 2004:85).

THUS, STANDARDS, LIKE THE LAWS OF LOGIC, ARE NOT TRUE OR FALSE IN THEMSELVES BUT ONLY MORE OR LESS RELATIONAL ACCORDING TO CERTAIN ESTABLISHED PARADIGMS.

Following this line of thought, Peirce considered it possible to claim that abduction does indeed reveal "a perfectly definite logical form." It even can be represented as such precisely because "the operation of adopting an explanatory hypothesis [...] was subject to certain conditions. Namely, the hypothesis cannot be admitted, even as a hypothesis, unless it be supposed that it would account for the facts or some of them" (CP 5.189). The form of inference is therefore: "The surprising fact, C, is observed; But if A were true, C would be a matter of course. Hence, there is reason to suspect that A is true" (CP 5.189).

Thus, if abductively constructed hypotheses are corroborated inductively, then the experience-prior rules, paradigms or logics of a conceptual system are transformed in such a way as is the case with all scientific revolutions. Such abductions must be considered as paradigm shifts of theories, logics, standards and norms of thought more or less fundamentally.

Conclusion

Accepting the two-fold task of a scientist to bring forth new theories as well as to build and test theories, abduction, as the third mode of reasoning in addition to deduction and induction, becomes most usefully applied at the discovery stage—that is to say, before passing on to testing a hypothesis or forming theories by means of inductive or deductive reasoning, the two core tasks of the logical analysis of scientific knowledge. However, the role of abduction in scientific discovery and argumentation has not been appreciated or even recognized in depth (Walton, 2004:252). Scientific discourse often takes the form of citing evidence to prove or disprove a hypothesis or theory. Kathleen Eisenhardt, for example, notices in her article "Building Theories from Case Study Research" that "a priori specification of constructs can help to shape the initial design of theory-building research [a]lthough this type of specification is not common in theory-building studies to date" (2001:536). Punch, to cite another prominent reference, sees induction as central to the investigation of the social world (2005:85): "Concepts are developed inductively from the data and raised to a higher level of abstraction, and their relations are then traced out [...] qualitative data analysis is a series of alternating inductive and deductive steps." No remark is made about abduction. All these assumptions ignore the fact that the relations of the property to be examined must be established in advance of sample selection. Any kind of induction is dependent upon hypotheses which must have been constructed beforehand. And this process of construction is abductive (synthetic) and not analytic to the extent that it concerns its logical form. For this very reason, Peirce's association of abduction with making observations and collecting data does suggest, however, that there is a role for abduction in science. Thus, unless known hypotheses are tested or refined, abduction comes prior to induction and deduction in the process of scientific argumentation. In this sense, it becomes extremely valuable in scientific discovery (but not necessarily in the logical analysis of scientific knowledge) because neither deduction nor induction leads to new discoveries. This condition renders abduction—heretofore neglected in scientific argumentation and discovery—vitally important in scientific methodology.

References

Cambridge dictionary of philosophy. Audi, Robert Ed. Cambridge. Cambridge University Press.

Carlile, P. R. and Christensen, C. M. 2005. The cycles of theory building in management research.

Dew, N. 2007. Abduction: a pre-condition for the intelligent design of strategy. Journal of Business Strategy, vol. 28, no. 4: 38–45.

Fischer, H. R. 2001. Abductive reasoning as a way of worldmaking. In: Foundation of science 6, 361–383. Brussels. Kluwer Academic Publishers.

Fleck, L. 1980. Entstehung und Entwicklung einer wissenschaftlichen Tatsache: Einführung in die Lehre von Denkstil und Denkkollektiv. Frankfurt am Main: Suhrkamp Verlag.

Hanson, Norwood Russel. 1958. Patterns of discovery. Cambridge: Cambridge University.

Hurley, P. J. 2002. Concise introduction to logic. Wadsworth.

Josephson, J. R. and Josephson S. G. (Eds.). 1996. Abductive inference: Computation, philosophy, technology. Cambridge: Cambridge University Press.

Kuhn, T. S. 1962 [1996, third ed.]. The structure of scientific revolutions. Chicago: The University of Chicago Press.

Kuhn, T. S. 1977. The essential tension: Selected studies in scientific tradition and change. Chicago: The University of Chicago Press.

Magnani, L. 2001. Abduction, reason and science: Processes of discovery and explanation. New York: Kluwer Academic/Plenum Publishers.

Nagl, L. 1992. Charles Sanders Peirce. Frankfurt am Main: Campus Verlag.

Nooteboom, B. 1999. Innovation, learning and industrial organisation. Cambridge Journal of Economics, 23: 127–150.

Peirce, C. S. 2002. Das Denken und die Logik des Universums. Frankfurt am Main: Suhrkamp Verlag.

Peirce, C. S. 1965. Collected papers of Charles Sanders Peirce. Volume I (Principles of Philosophy) and II (Elements of Logic). Hartshorne, Charles, Paul Weiss (Ed.) Cambridge Massachusetts: Harvard University Press.

Peirce, C. S. 1965. Collected papers of Charles Sanders Peirce. Volume III (Exact Logic) and IV (The Simplest Mathematics). Hartshorne, Charles, Paul Weiss (Ed.) Cambridge Massachusetts: Harvard University Press.

Peirce, C. S. 1965. Collected papers of Charles Sanders Peirce. Volume V (Pragmatism & Pragmaticism) and VI (Scientific Metaphysics). Hartshorne, Charles, Paul Weiss (Ed.) Cambridge Massachusetts: Harvard University Press.

Peng, Y., and Reggia, J.A. 1990. Abductive inference models for diagnostic problem-solving. New York: Springer Verlag.

Popper, K. 1935 [first English edition published 1959, 2002 paperback]. The logic of scientific discovery. New York: Routledge Classics.

Punch, K. F. 2005. Introduction to social research: Quantitative and qualitative approaches. London: Sage Publications.

Richter, A. 1995. Der Begriff der Abduktion bei Charles Sanders Peirce. Frankfurt am Main: Peter Lang, Europäischer Verlag der Wissenschaften.

Schiller, F. C. S. 1917. Scientific discovery and logical proof. Vol. I of studies in the history and the methods of sciences, 235–89. Oxford: Clarendon Press.

Seidel, J. 2004. Die Theorie der Abduktion bei Charles Sanders Peirce und Umberto Eco. URL: http://seidel.jaiden.de/peirce_eco.php (dl.: 19/10/07).

Schön, D. A. 1983. The reflective practitioner: How professionals think in action. Basic Books.

Schurz, G. 2002. Models of abductive reasoning. Philosophical prepublication series of the chair of theoretical philosophy at the university of Düsseldorf.

Sutton, R. I., and Staw, Barry, M. 1995. What theory is not. Administrative Science Quarterly, 40: 371–384.

Walton, D. 2004. Abductive reasoning. Tuscaloosa: The University of Alabama Press.

Weick, K. E. 1995. What theory is not, Theorizing is. Administrative Science Quarterly, 40: 385–390.

Wirth, Uwe. 1998. What is abductive inference? in Encyclopedia of Semiotics. Bouissac, Paul Ed. Oxford. Oxford University Press.

1❮ Popper's "The Logic of Scientific Discovery" was first published in German language in 1935; the first English version was published in 1959.
2❮ The publication of "Collected Papers of Charles Sanders Peirce, Volume I–VIII" in which Peirce put forward his thoughts on the logic of scientific discovery were first published between 1931 and 1935 by the President and Fellows of Harvard College.
3❮ For Kuhn the terms "paradigm" and "theory" are becoming synonymous in his later essay on the "Logic of Discovery or Psychology of Research?" (1977).
4❮ In literature it has become a common way to cite Peirce philosophical tractate in the following way: CP stands for "Collected Papers;" the first given number left of the period indicates the volume, and the subsequent number the corresponding paragraph as designated by Peirce.

139

Tough problems usually don't get solved peacefully. They either don't get solved at all—they get stuck—or they get solved by force. These frustrating and frightening outcomes occur all the time.

Families replay the same argument over and over, or a parent lays down the law. Organizations keep returning to a familiar crisis, or a boss decrees a new strategy. Communities split over a controversial issue, or a politician dictates the answer. Countries negotiate to a stalemate, or they go to war. Either the people involved in a problem can't agree on what the solution is, or the people with power—authority, money, guns—impose their solution on everyone else.

THERE IS ANOTHER WAY TO SOLVE TOUGH PROBLEMS.

The people involved can talk and listen to each other and thereby work through a solution peacefully. But this way is often too difficult and too slow to produce results, and force therefore becomes the easier, default option.

Problems are tough because they are complex in three ways. They are dynamically complex, which means that cause and effect are far apart in space and time, and so are hard to grasp from first-hand experience. They are generatively complex, which means that they are unfolding in unfamiliar and unpredictable ways. And they are socially complex, which means that the people involved see things very differently, and so the problems become polarized and stuck.

Our talking and listening often fails to solve complex problems because of the way that most of us talk and listen most of the time. Our most common way of talking is telling: asserting the truth about the way things are and must be, not allowing that there might be other truths and possibilities. And our most common way of listening is not listening: listening only to our own talking, not to others. This way of talking and listening works fine for solving simple problems, where an authority or expert can work through the problem piece by piece, applying solutions that have worked in the past. But a complex problem can only be solved peacefully if the people who are part of the problem work together creatively to understand their situation and to improve it.

OUR COMMON WAY OF TALKING AND LISTENING THEREFORE GUARANTEES THAT OUR COMPLEX PROBLEMS WILL EITHER REMAIN STUCK OR WILL GET UNSTUCK ONLY BY FORCE. WE NEED TO LEARN ANOTHER, LESS COMMON, MORE OPEN WAY.

I have reached these conclusions after 25 years of working professionally on tough problems. I started off my career as someone who came up with solutions. First I was a university researcher in physics and economics, and then an expert analyst of government policy and corporate strategy. Then in 1991, inspired by an unexpected and extraordinary experience in South Africa, I began working as a neutral facilitator of problem-solving processes, helping other people come up with their own solutions. I have facilitated leadership teams of companies, governments, and civil society organizations in 50 countries, on every continent, helping them address their organizations' most difficult challenges. And I have also facilitated cross-organizational leadership teams—composed of politicians and guerillas, activists and public servants, clergymen and business people, academics and trade unionists—helping them address some of the most difficult challenges in the world: in South Africa during the struggle to replace apartheid; in Colombia in the midst of the civil war; in Guatemala in the aftermath of the genocide; in Argentina when the society collapsed; and in deeply divided Israel-Palestine, Cyprus, Paraguay, Northern Ireland, and the Basque County.

Commuting back and forth between these different worlds has allowed me to see how tough problems can and cannot be solved. I have been privileged to work with many extraordinary people in many extraordinary projects. From these experiences I have drawn conclusions that apply not only in extraordinary but also in ordinary settings. In the harsh light of life-and-death conflicts, the dynamics of how people create new realities are painted in bright colors, and having seen the dynamics there, I can now recognize them in circumstance where they are painted in muted colors. I have learned what kinds of talking and listening condemn us to stuckness and force, and what kinds enable us to solve peacefully even our most difficult problems.

My favorite movie about getting unstuck is the comedy *Groundhog Day*. Bill Murray plays Phil Connors, a cynical, self-centered television journalist who is filming a story about Groundhog Day in the small town of Punxsutawney, Pennsylvania. He despises the assignment and the town. The next morning, he wakes up to discover, with horror, that it is still Groundhog Day, and that he has to live through these events again. This happens every morning: he is stuck in reliving the same day over and over. He explains this to his producer Rita, but she laughs it off. He tries everything he can in order to break this pattern—getting angry, being nice, killing himself—but nothing works. Eventually he relaxes into appreciating the present, and opens himself up to the town and to Rita. Only then does he wake up to a new day and a better future.

MANY OF US ARE LIKE PHIL CONNORS. WE GET STUCK BY HOLDING ON TIGHTLY TO OUR OPINIONS AND PLANS AND IDENTITIES AND TRUTHS.

But when we relax and are present and open up our minds and hearts and wills, we get unstuck and we unstick the world around us. I have learned that the more open I am—the more attentive I am to the way things are and could be, around me and inside me; the less attached I am to the way things ought to be—the more effective I am in helping to bring forth new realities. And the more I work in this way, the more present and alive I feel. As I have learned to lower my defenses and open myself up, I have become increasingly able to help better futures be born.

The way we talk and listen expresses our relationship with the world. When we fall into the trap of telling and of not listening, we close ourselves off from being changed by the world. We limit ourselves to being able to change the world only by force. But when we talk and listen with an open mind and an open heart and an open spirit, we bring forth our better selves and a better world.

ROBERT M. BAUER AND WARD M. EAGEN [1] ‹

Designing—Innovation at the Crossroads of Structure and Process

145

WE CAN AND CANNOT STEP INTO THE
SAME RIVER TWICE. IT IS US,
AND IT ISN'T. (HERACLITUS)

Promising Designers

In July 1999, ABC News aired "The Deep Dive", a documentary about how industrial designers design, prominently featuring IDEO, the world's largest industrial design firm. In this extremely well received TV broadcast IDEO's CEO David Kelley proclaimed: "The point is that we are not actually experts in any given area. We are experts on the process of how you design stuff. We don't care, if you give us a tooth brush, a toothpaste tube, a tractor, a space shuttle, a chair. It's all the same to us. We want to figure out how to innovate by using our process—applying it."

IT APPEARS IN HINDSIGHT THAT BY INDICATING DESIGNERS POSSESS A GENERIC DESIGN PROCESS, WHICH CAN SERVE AS A TOOL FOR INNOVATION, "THE DEEP DIVE" HAS SET MUCH OF THE TONE FOR TODAY'S BROAD INTEREST IN APPLYING "DESIGN THINKING" TO MANAGEMENT.

Arguably, businesses in technically and economically highly evolved countries face increasing pressure for innovation and the growing significance of "experience" as an economic good. [2] While apparently new for businesses, such conditions are the natural habitat of modern artists, whose products must possess a high degree of originality and serve no function other than enabling the art experience. Hence, artistic intelligence should prove precious for managers who seek to enable continuous streams of new and valuable propositions for customer experience. However, managers have great difficulty learning from artists because artists tend to draw on idiosyncratic creative strategies and are often reluctant to collaborate with businesses as such provision of services could put their autonomy and legitimacy as artists at risk. Designers, on the other hand, act as "creative pragmatists", as service providers with particular expertise in synthesizing economic, technological and aesthetic requirements. Moreover, design firms are following IDEO's example and position themselves as strategic innovation consultancies, advocating that organizational principles of design firms and, in particular, generic design processes can guide innovation management (e.g., Kelly, 2001; Brown, 2009; Esslinger, 2009). As a result, management practitioners, scholars and educators seeking to advance the management of creativity and innovation have turned to designers for inspiration (e.g., Boland and Collopy, 2004; Beckman and Barry, 2006; Utterback et al., 2006; Bauer and Eagen, 2008; Plattner et al., 2009; Verganti, 2009; Martin, 2009; Lockwood, 2010).

The promise implied in David Kelley's statement about IDEO's mastery of a generic design process is indeed intriguing. It invokes the idea of creativity as a general rather than a domain-specific capability—a concept that dominated early psychological research in creativity but has increasingly been supplanted by theories that grant domain-specific skills (i.e., expertise in a specific field) a vital role in human creativity (Amabile, 1996; Csikszentmihalyi, 1999; Sternberg, 2003). Concomitantly, it suggests that one process, repeatedly executed, can yield highly varying results, more specifically, give way to original design solutions. From an innovation management perspective nothing is more desirable than a routine outputting non-routine results: a procedure that routinely generates innovative products or services.

HOWEVER, IT REMAINS TO BE SHOWN HOW A WELL-KNOWN PROCESS CAN POSSIBLY TRANSFORM WELL-KNOWN INPUT INTO OUTPUT BOTH NEW AND VALUABLE (BODEN, 1999; SAWYER, 2006).

Managers' and management scholars' current, elevated interest in how designers design or creatively solve design problems is a young phenomenon. It is probably fair to say it did not exist before IDEO showcased its design process on television and in the associated bestselling business book (Kelly, 2001). By contrast, academic research in "design thinking" (i.e., how designers approach design problems) dates back to the late 1960's [3<] and many stage models of generic design processes have been proposed since. Interestingly however, these models have neither proven satisfactory to practitioners or theorists, nor have attempts at mapping a generic design process been abandoned as

fruitless (Lawson, 2006).

We maintain that the concept of a generic design process is meaningful (or else nothing relevant can be understood and transferred from one creative act to the next) and misleading (because creativity is not based on causation; Brodbeck, 1999). In what follows we interrogate how designers design, in an effort to clarify how, from a managerial perspective, a generic design process is both necessary and impossible.

Designing as Problem Solving: Three Classic Models

Attempts have been made at understanding the process of designing as a sequence of necessary steps leading from the stated design problem to a solution (Lawson, 2006). Such models of design assume that each step builds on the previous ones implying that design processes unfold naturally according to their own internal logic. Not surprisingly, these models bear a great resemblance to models of rational problem solving, specifying basically three major problem-solving steps (which in more fine-grained models are further subdivided): first, the problem is explored; second, various solution alternatives are generated; third, the best solution alternative is identified and chosen for implementation. In retrospect, this depiction of problem-solving appears self-evident: How could one have solved a problem if not through understanding the problem, coming up with potential solutions, and settling for the best one? A good design solution always appears as inevitable and the narrative explaining the process is often believable, yet the narrative is only an explanatory tool, useful after the fact but not in the moment of design.

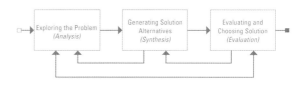

In practice, design processes (including designing) are less clear-cut. Instead of proceeding linearly from one step to the next, designers move back and forth because it is not clear when a step is completed (Lawson, 2006). In addition, steps are often indistinguishable—as designers explore problems *through* solution conjectures (Lawson, 1979; Kolodner and Wills, 1996) or quickly oscillate between developing and evaluating solution alternatives (Schön, 1983). Furthermore, the three-step process is prescriptive rather than descriptive in the sense that it lacks empirical support (Lawson, 2006); yet it remains vague and denies practitioners operable instructions for actually carrying out the steps. To summarize, as a model of how designers move forward towards yet unknown design solutions, this rational view of the design process lacks descriptive and prescriptive qualities. Nevertheless, the rational model, which is generally attributed to Descartes (1736), seems to work well as a structure for building cases that retrospectively justify already-reached design solutions (e.g., to convince stakeholders).

The creative problem-solving literature holds another classic process model, validated by many design experiences, that also relies on essentially three steps (Poincaré, 1908; Wallace, 1926): first, the problem is examined thoroughly but remains unsolved (preparation); second, after a period of time without any (conscious) attempts at solving the problem (incubation), a solution suddenly appears (illumination); third, the solution is verified (evaluation).

HERE, NEITHER THE GENERATION OF VIABLE SOLUTION ALTERNATIVES NOR THE SELECTION OF THE OPTIMAL ALTERNATIVE IS ACCOMPLISHED THROUGH SUCCESSFUL INTENTIONAL ACTION.

Instead, a solution suddenly appears after a time span devoid of intentional problem-solving attempts. Yet, once a solution has appeared, rational thinking is resumed in order to evaluate the solution's quality. More often than not, solutions are not received at once, but instead rely on multiple incubation-based insights into the nature of the problem and its potential solutions (multiple "micro-eurekas"; Sawyer, 2006). In these cases the seemingly linear model becomes cyclical, depicting creative problem-solving as oscillating between intentional, analytical thinking and letting go of the problem, which in turn gives rise to sudden insights that intentional, analytical thinking can only control (evaluate) after the fact. In this view designing appears as more art than technology.

THE RATIONAL PROBLEM-SOLVING MODEL SOLELY RELIES ON ANALYTICAL THINKING—VASTLY OVERESTIMATING THE POWER OF COGNITIVE THOUGHT.

Rational analysis alone cannot cope with the complexity of "wicked" problems for which constraints, solution criteria, and even the problem definitions, change throughout and as a result of, the problem-solving process (Rittel, 1972; Rittel and Webber, 1973). However, the rational model has its prominent place in problem-solving and designing: first, questions such as "What is the actual problem?", "What options do exist?", and "What is the actual goal?" provide vital orientation throughout design processes; second, regardless of how often one moves back and forth between the three stages, the ultimate goal remains, that is, to move from a problem via one or more solution alternatives to a solution. The incubation model acknowledges the importance of analytical thinking but also makes clear that critical steps in the process, in fact the most creative ones, rely on intuition and are therefore not under designers' or problem solvers' immediate voluntary control.

In 1966 Polanyi demonstrated that tacit knowledge— knowledge one implicitly applies but cannot explicate (e.g., riding a bike as compared to providing instructions for how to ride a bike)—plays a crucial role in creativity and intuition. Applying this insight to knowledge creation, Nonaka (1994) suggested "that knowledge is created through a continuous dialogue between tacit and explicit knowledge", thereby echoing the incubation model's proposition that creative problem solving oscillates between intuition and analysis. Nonaka and Takeuchi (1995) using as an example the development of an automatic home bread-making machine, suggest a three-step design process: first, embodying tacit knowledge (e.g., to understand the making of traditional Japanese bread, engineers volunteer to apprentice themselves to a master baker reputed to produce the area's best bread, thereby embodying the master's knowledge through extensive observation, imitation and practice); second, disembodying tacit knowledge through codifying (e.g., the engineers verbalize and formalize the bread-baking process); third, re-embodying explicit knowledge (e.g., engineers build a prototypical home bread-making machine that incorporates their bread-baking knowledge).

As in the previously mentioned models, in practice the three steps are not always fully separable and do not occur in a strictly linear sequence. Yet, this model advances our understanding of the design processes by showing that designing draws on fundamentally different types of knowing.
The above models all have a core of truth and each of them although purporting to describe "the" design process, can be understood as establishing some of the conditions of designing and perhaps the limits to particular design situations.

EACH MODEL HAS INDIVIDUAL TECHNIQUES THAT NEED TO BE INCORPORATED INTO DESIGN PROCESSES AS PARTICULAR CONDITIONS WARRANT.

Moreover, these three classic models suggest minimal criteria for conceptualizing the design process, namely to preserve a central, yet realistic role for analytical thinking; to incorporate intuition and suspended control into the model; and to specify how different types of knowing enable the design process.
In what follows we propose a conceptualization of designing that meets these criteria. Our model of the creativity-specific aspects of how designers create desirable new user experience comprises of three basic elements: first, a general model of the design process; second, a decentered design agent; and third, occurrences of strictly processual experience that necessarily eludes explicit categories (such as words or numbers).

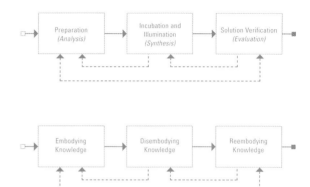

Structuring the Design Process

We use IDEO's showcased design process as a publicly available, stylized case to illustrate our understanding of the design process's structure, showing that IDEO's famous design process is best understood as a three step process, where each step ("movement") is comprised of two sub-steps ("motion"). ◀◀ Most importantly, we maintain that each of the six motions has its distinct epistemic profile—representing a distinct way of knowing and shaping knowledge and thus, a distinct way of relating to the world. While attributing critical importance to tacit knowledge, our argument requires a differentiated perspective that does not lump all epistemic modes (i.e. ways of knowing) other than explicit thought into a single category (namely, "tacit knowledge").

DRAWING ON JUNG (1921) WE SHOW THAT EACH OF THE SIX MOTIONS UNIQUELY COMBINES SENSING, FEELING, THINKING AND INTUITING.

Jungian Epistemic Modes

The Jungian model of psychological base functions provides an early and still outstanding conceptualization of human knowledge rooted in epistemic plurality. Jung (1921) distinguishes four elementary ways of knowing: thinking, feeling, sensing, and intuiting.

Thinking (Cognition): Thinking systematically relates categories of ideas to each other, linking contents of imagining into conceptual relations that enable humans to create possible worlds for risk-free exploration. Thinking ranges from daydreaming to actively manipulating symbols as tokens for ideas along the grammatical structures of natural or formal languages.

Feeling (Emotion): Feeling is an affective, sentimental function that imparts value to content as the basis of likes and dislikes. In essence, feeling positions objects and events, including those of the mind, on a continuum from

embracing through neutral to rejecting, evaluating them in terms of good or bad, pleasant or unpleasant, acceptable or unacceptable. Emotions can strongly fuel or inhibit action. Sensing (Perception and Proprioception): Sensation provides an immediate experience of what is: one thinks and feels about things and events, regardless of their physical presence but one senses them as an object or event only within their immediate physical presence. Sensation is conscious perception that has a certainty based on pure physicality. Sensing is intimately tied to aesthetic categories such as exciting/boring, harmonious/disharmonious, beautiful/ugly, etc.

Intuiting (Intuition): Intuition is a gestalt of unconscious perceptions that possess intrinsic certainty and conviction: Spinoza and Bergson thought of intuition in this sense as the most direct and highest form of knowledge (Jung 1921). Through intuition humans access insights and knowledge without awareness of any trace of the process. Intuition comes with a certainty but no rationale for this certainty, although in hindsight, it may be possible to trace the source of the intuitive knowledge as a specific causal chain. Intuition never directly reflects reality but actively, creatively, insightfully, and imaginatively adds, meaning by reading into the situation things not immediately apparent through sensory data.

Jung points out that the four epistemic modes are incommensurable: insights and knowledge from one cannot be accurately represented in terms of another. Human knowledge is necessarily fragmented and conflicting in nature, permanently struggling, to give a classic example, to resolve the tensions between beauty, truth, and goodness. On the other hand, without this fundamental difference, that is, if one mode could be fully represented in terms of another, one or more epistemic modes would be redundant and consequently could not compliment the others. The fundamentally different modes of knowing may induce struggle and pain but they also stabilize human experience even in situations when one epistemic mode might fail to cope. In addition, if multiple ways of knowing—despite their in-principle difference—align and join to form a coherent experience, they tend to convey an enormous sense of reality or truth.
Source: Bauer and Eagen, 2008.

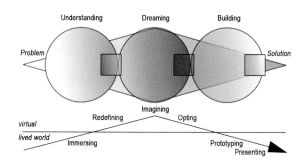

❮ Source: Bauer and Eagen (2008).

What we are indicating as a comprehensive design process that not only incorporates the three classic models we described earlier but also circumscribes the IDEO process is in fact a portmanteau of design steps, dynamically adaptive to the particular design problematic. The process starts in the lived world with the initial problem statement, creatively explores the virtual realm for new, potential solutions and then manifests the solution as real possibility back again in the lived world.

In the first movement, Immersing (into the problem) is a divergent motion, expanding and exploring the problem space from the perspective of the experience of the user, entering the user's world to effectively gather intelligence about the users' needs and desires. Observation (watching, listening, touching, smelling) provides sensory information about user experience in context; empathizing allows the design agent to experience as if they were the user without losing sight of the "as if" condition (Vaihinger 1927). Immersing leads from sensing (engaging physically to absorb through the senses all necessary information) and feeling (empathy as emotionally resonating with users) to thinking and intuiting. Gradually, through repeated (hermeneutic) cycles, Immersing brings forward explicit knowledge of what the user needs (and desires) above and beyond simplistic utility. In addition, true immersing expands the design agent's intuitive understanding as most information presented in experience to the body never becomes conscious (the senses process at least one million times more information than the conscious mind; Maturana and Varela, 1984).

IN THE IDEO CASE WE SPOKE OF ABOVE, A CROSS DISCIPLINARY DESIGN TEAM WAS TASKED WITH REDESIGNING AN ORDINARY SHOPPING CART WITHIN ONE WEEK ON CAMERA.

The team was initially presented with an orientation session that outlined the project and revealed a number of shopping cart "facts". The team then divided into smaller groups to investigate how people use, make, and maintain shopping carts as well as explore peripheral areas such as bike shops and stroller designs. In our understanding objects anchor experience both as vessels for the memory of previous experience and the affording of new experience. In this case the objects produced by the team that climax the first step consisted of a montage of text and visual artifacts to document the variations in, and the scope of, the shopping cart experience.

The second step, the Redefining (of the problem) motion is convergent, gathering the experience of the first motion by compressing resonant data into particular significant trajectories that build on experience gathered, moving forward towards the solution. Immersing oscillates between experiencing (sensing or feeling) and reflecting (thinking), and as field research continues the emphasis shifts towards the thinking: designers require dis-embedded knowledge brought from field to studio, workshop, lab or office as reports, images, etc. The IDEO team however, failed to produce an explicit problem statement as a Redefining step. Dreaming is entirely within the virtual realm as what could be and is composed of a divergent motion, Imagining, expanding the solution space, and a convergent motion, Opting, where choosing alternatives through practical considerations ultimately reduces the area of possible actualization. Imagining, in its quest for new ideas relies on various types of thinking: analytical thinking challenges the presuppositions of extant ideas, destabilizing and shifting them; associative thinking connects ideas in a spontaneous, stochastic fashion; daydreaming playfully combines the powers of conscious and unconscious information processing; and dialogical thinking aloud, e.g., brainstorming, merges and re-combines ideas from different individuals synergistically resulting in something they could not have imagined independently.

Imagining is divergent thinking, a mental activity that proceeds freely from one idea to the next, quickly generating a large set of different ideas, which more often than not includes promising new ones (de Bono, 1967), and rests on two pillars: first, the ability to create or seek out environments that provide plentiful stimuli that can potentially disrupt thinking, and second, a receptive stance that recognizes that humans, in principle, have no control over their next thought (except for a limited capacity for suppressing it; Libet et al., 2004).

This openness and detachment allows one to simply observe

their own thoughts without judging, even those that surprise. Opting, on the other hand, aims at restructuring future options by choosing the optimal possibility and thus relies on factual knowledge and analytical thinking about the realizability and expected utility of the ideas generated. As rational knowledge about future states of the world is necessarily incomplete, intuition bridges the gaps in the rational assessment of extant ideas' future potential. Feeling too has its role in Opting: first, Opting requires trust in the future design process and such trusting is an emotional faculty; second, feeling interferes with thinking, suggesting to choose desired possibilities instead of opting for what remains to appear promising after having been subjected to systematic doubt through analytical thinking.

In the IDEO case, ideas generated were displayed on large pin-up walls where the brainstorming team first evaluated them by voting for the best, most promising ideas. Subsequently, a group of highly experienced designers gathered to interpret the generated ideas identifying four patterns, namely; shopping, safety, checkout, and, finding what you are looking for. By creating four promising areas to move forward with, the experts refocused the team, splitting it into four groups each tasked to develop one specific area as a physical prototype.

The art of Prototyping lies in the creating of physical experiments designed to maximize insight and mitigate risk: to be successful, it requires quick learning based on very short development cycles. Prototyping addresses the motor system, taking a formative, converging stance that translates from abstract to concrete, iteratively refining and integrating multiple ideas into one. The interplay between sensing and thinking in Prototyping is guided by feeling, ensuring that the insights into users' emotional states and dynamics (gained through Immersing) translate into emotional design.

SIMILARLY, DURING PROTOTYPING THE BACKGROUND KNOWLEDGE GAINED THROUGH IMMERSING INCREASES THE LIKELIHOOD OF INTUITIVE SOLUTIONS TO DESIGN PROBLEMS THAT OCCUR.

IDEO spends an amazing amount of energy on Prototyping with professional staff, workshop and tools that can rapidly produce working prototypes and professional quality finished builds in a variety of materials; most firms are without IDEO's prototyping capabilities (budget) and necessarily hint at user experience through lesser models. Prototypes are explored through sensations as well as understood in cognitive and affective modes and are used to test and explore user experience of the design in various levels of working models; and the more effective the prototype, the more it can communicate the actualized experience.

In the end, Presenting must convey just how the user's experience will be made richer through design and requires a very high and focused level of communication. Designing such an experience can be understood as nested cycles that potentially involve all of the above motions where feeling is of crucial importance to presenting, and understood through a design rhetoric intended to convince (sell).

IDEO'S VISUALIZATION SKILLS MATCH THEIR PROFESSIONAL ABILITY TO RAPIDLY PRODUCE QUALITY PROTOTYPES: THEIR GRAPHIC DESIGN, FINISHING OF PROTOTYPES AND EVENT CHOREOGRAPHIES ARE OUTSTANDING.

IDEO's presentation of their shopping cart re-design was masterful in staging and became a landmark in repositioning the firm as a strategic innovation consultancy.

We consider this design process a portmanteau of highly generalizable tools or steps that are unpacked for particular design processes. In-situ design processes are variations, not identical reproductions of a template. Common variations include: long-established design problems (e.g., a fashion designer designing a suit can choose to assume she already knows the user experience and the actual design problem, and thus leap into "building" right from the start); [5] idiosyncratic work styles (e.g., some designers do not start by getting in touch with users' views and experience but instead engage in preliminary "Imagining" to preserve fresh ideas; others move from "Understanding" directly to "Building" but then, at times, inhibit, disengage and shift into

"Dreaming"); intuition-enabled leapfrogging (intuition can bring about ideas typical for earlier or later motions—for instance a guiding vision or a concrete solution concept could appear during Immersing instead of "Dreaming" or "Building", respectively. Usually, if intuition-enabled leapfrogging occurs, fast-forwarded steps are briefly revisited to check if anything important got overlooked; then the design process continues with the subsequent steps necessary to develop the intuitively generated idea further). True, such variations make the design process appear messier than our diagram might seem to suggest, however, our basic structure—namely six motions, each of which is in-principle necessary and has its distinct quality (epistemology)—remains intact. On the other hand our model is limited to problem-driven designing (i.e., a client requiring a design solution for an at least vaguely defined problem); to what extent it can be generalized for problem-finding tasks (e.g., a new technological possibility in search for profitable applications) lies beyond the scope of this paper.

This three movement through six motion model, preserves the rational idea, that exploring the problem, exploring possible solution alternatives and settling for the best such possibility, in roughly that sequence, is a useful approach to solving design problems. "Understanding", "Dreaming" and "Building" bear significant resemblance to the three rational steps: Although various forward-and-backward jumps are expected, the overall movement runs from the problem to the solution, with each step building on the previous ones. Furthermore, our model also captures knowledge transformation in the sense of disembodying and re-embodying knowledge—starting with users' lived (embodied) experience, entering into the virtual realm of ideas and, finally, bringing ideas back into the (embodied) lived world of design artifacts and, eventually, users' experience. Finally, our model conceptualizes designing as interplay between intentionality and openness, between analytical thinking and intuitive creating. Diverging steps enrich designers' options by emphasizing the creation of new possibilities; convergent steps on the other hand analyze and evaluate to separate the wheat from the chaff; oscillation between diverging and converging increases the likelihood of a design solution being new and valuable. Although we have repeatedly hinted at (openness to) intuition, our model of designing reads more like a set of instructions, thus privileging intentionality over openness. After exploring in more detail the characteristics of design agents capable of carrying out the described six motions of designing we return to this issue, demonstrating that in fact this model of the design process is specifically suited for enabling intuition.

A Decentered Design Agent

We have made an effort to describe what it means to design. From this view, what are the implications for the design agent? Leaving domain-specific skills aside, a design agent mastering Understanding, Dreaming and Building should ideally possess capabilities such as anthropologists' professional naïveté and capacity for observation paired with philosophers' and mathematicians' analytical precision, childrens' imagination paired with venture capitalists' merciless determination to select the most promising options, and engineers' ingenuity paired with a bricoleur's playful curiosity, respectively. It is probably fair to assume that most people possess most of these capabilities to some extent, yet it is unlikely for any one individual to master them all.

INDIVIDUALS TEND TO SPECIALIZE IN ONE OR FEW OF THESE WAYS OF DEPLOYING SENSING, FEELING, THINKING AND INTUITING.

Hence, although in principle individuals can execute a design process, such as suggested above, resourceful design agents well equipped for excelling at all six motions are more likely to be teams with members coming from diverse biographical backgrounds and disciplinary trainings, jointly holding a large variety of creativity-relevant and domain-relevant skills. For instance, the team carrying out the shopping cart project at IDEO was comprised of individuals with training in linguistics, marketing, engineering, biology, psychology, or general management (and did not include formally trained industrial designers; ABC News, 1999).
The agent best suited for executing the six design steps is a decentered agent devoid of a stable centre to integrate the agent's heterogeneous competencies into a coherent gestalt. Absent a consolidated knowledge base or consistent set of epistemic styles, such a decentered agent draws on heterogeneous knowledge bundles and epistemic styles (i.e., ways of gathering and transforming knowledge) that constitute a system of loosely coupled perspectives, each of which is, ideally, precise and consistent in itself, and complements or contradicts the others. [6] Hence, such an agent is poised for inner conflict, for knowledge incompatibilities and mental-model clashes.
On an abstract level, the design agent is an assembly of different perspectives (with associated knowledge bundles)—set up for conflict between perspectives that enables the emergence of something new (similar to Hegelian "synthesis" arising from the tension between "thesis" and "anti-thesis"; Hegel, 1807).

PRAGMATICALLY, IN THE LIVED WORLD, PERSPECTIVES ARE VIEWS ADOPTED BY SOMEONE.

Hence, conflicts between perspectives turn out to be intra- or interpersonal conflicts. Consequently, social competence and social structure matter because they influence how conflict is resolved and, in turn, how likely conflicting perspectives lead to resolution through the creation of something new.
With regard to social structure, we suggest that competent design teams are capable of letting different structures govern their interaction. More specifically, competent design agents have the ability to switch between governance structures, thereby ensuring that power relations between (individuals and their) perspectives match the requirements of each design step. Consider as an example the IDEO shopping-cart team: During Imagining, when the team engaged in brainstorming, all team members had equal rights to contribute their ideas and freely—yet within certain brainstorming rules (Sutton and Hargadon, 1996; Kelly, 2001)—use everybody else's ideas. Metaphorically speaking, the brainstorming meeting functioned as an "idea exchange", with the team leader acting as a governing body ensuring that "floor traders" abide by the "trading rules" and, thus, ideas are *exchanged* freely and fairly. This setting guarantees egalitarian relationships among team members who collaborate and compete for quality of ideas, which

eventually translates into reputation (Hargadon and Sutton, 1997). Subsequently, the results of the brainstorming session were evaluated in yet another highly egalitarian fashion: by everyone voting for his or her favorite ideas. However, during Opting the team changed its social structure. A small group of experienced designers including CEO David Kelley (who was not part of the team) took over, interpreted the brainstorming outcome, identifying and integrating the major results, and decided how to move forward into Prototyping. The formation of this in-group, referred to in the television program as the "self-appointed adults", relied on past merits and thus suspended the previously egalitarian order. When the team finally transitioned to Prototyping, the social structure once again shifted, as the team leader divided the team into sub-teams and, in a command-and-control fashion, tasked each sub-team with building a certain prototype. Ouchi (1980) suggested that three types of governance structures—markets, clans and bureaucracies—govern economic transaction. The social structures adopted by the IDEO team bear some resemblance to Ouchi's typology: egalitarian, market-like relationships, meritocratic clan-like relationships and autocratic hierarchy-like relationships. We conclude that the ability to switch between governance structures, thereby re-assigning the weight that each of the potentially colliding perspectives carries, is a critically important characteristic of decentered design agents. With regard to social competence, interpersonal skills are a precondition for a decentered design agent seizing the creative opportunities inherent in colliding perspectives, to the extent that these skills are necessary for constructively resolving conflicts. Specifically, members of design teams need what Scott Fitzgerald considered "the test of a first-rate intelligence, [namely] the ability to hold two opposing ideas in mind at the same time and still retain the ability to function"; and they require the competence to inquire into others' views and empathize with them, paired with the ability to advocate one's own stance and make it intelligible to others (Argyris, 1990). We suggest that a decentered design agent relies on individuals preserving a (shared) design attitude characterized by the ability to not recoil to defensive routines when facing resistance (e.g., constraints or different opinions) or lacking orientation (e.g., ambiguity, uncertainty or even nothingness) but instead react in an open and active fashion—by engaging in search behaviors. Design capability cannot be reduced to personality characteristics. Decades of research seeking to identify the creative personality have, at best, produced mixed results and interest in this type of research has dropped significantly (Sternberg, 2003; Sawyer, 2006). Similarly, studies linking creativity to intrinsic motivation, tolerance for ambiguity, locus of control, optimism, openness and happiness have largely remained inconclusive (Pannells and Claxton, 2008)—with the exception of intrinsic motivation, which appears more consistently tied to creativity (Amabile, 1996).

HOWEVER, WE SUGGEST, THAT ATTITUDE HAS ITS ROLE IN DESIGNING, AS DESIGN AGENTS CANNOT AFFORD TO SHY AWAY FROM THE UNKNOWN.

Instead, in order to create they must find ways of accommodating the experience of difference and, associated with it, the experience of otherness or nothingness—as we will explore in more detail in the following section.

Elements of Designing—At the Crossroads of Structure and Process

To summarize, we have laid out a model of designing that comprises two structural components. The first structure, the *design steps*, concerns epistemology in time. It is derived from decomposing the design process into distinct steps that represent specific perspectives (i.e., specific ways of getting to know a specific aspect of a design problem), which depend on each other sequentially as they follow (from) each other logically and temporally. The second structure, the *decentered design agent*, concerns epistemology in social space. It is derived from decomposing the design agent (i.e., the unit executing the design steps) into different perspectives (i.e., knowledge bundles and corresponding patterns for gaining, developing and applying this knowledge) that are grounded in personal life experience or professional education. These perspectives and the persons adopting them relate to each other according to different governance structures (i.e., schemas for assigning each perspective its relative weight)—with the "design attitude" allowing that the

collision of perspectives becomes a creative process. This model captures the essence of design thinking as it is currently discussed: as an approach for (innovation) management to advance beyond its current overemphasis on analytical thinking. In addition, this model advances the current understanding of design thinking, first, by integrating conceptually the epistemological dimension of designing, more specifically, by showing how a design process can satisfy both logical and epistemological completeness, and second, by indicating how social structure and power governs designing.

Our model is both descriptive and prescriptive in nature. It is highly descriptive of the IDEO design process and is in sync with four decades of empirical design research. On the other hand, for reasons of public availability and because of its role as the paradigmatic example for the relevance of design thinking to management, we chose to focus on the stylized design process showcased by IDEO, which was from the outset meant as a normative suggestion and business proposition for organizations in search of innovation. Our model keeps this prescriptive impetus and, as a consequence, serves as a diagnostic tool for assessing the innovative capacities of organizations, teams and, to a lesser extent, individuals through assessing how well equipped they are to execute each of the six design steps and to what extent they fulfill the requirements of decentered design agents.

However, thus far the model has little explanatory power: Why would a design agent of the described type executing the described design steps have a high likelihood of being creative in the sense of arriving at a new and valuable design solution?

THE DIFFERENCE BETWEEN A STRUCTURAL AND A PROCESSUAL VIEW PROVIDES A CONCEPTUAL BASIS FOR ANSWERING THIS CRUCIAL QUESTION.

Nothing ever repeats itself identically. Heraclitus's famous dictum about the paradoxically simultaneous possibility and impossibility of stepping into the same river twice is prominently echoed by the hermeneutic cycle tying experience and knowledge together into a causal loop—past experience causing current knowledge, current knowledge causing future experience. 7< It is thus meaningful to use the same word repeatedly (or else it wouldn't be meaningful to use it at all), yet its meaning will never stay exactly the same—it constantly evolves, how ever (in)significant the difference may appear. Experience is open for continuity and for change, for experiencing stable recognizable structures as well as for dynamic unknown processes. However, these two views cannot be adopted simultaneously: each excludes the other, or rather each configures the other as ground. Hence, choice is required between prioritizing structure over process or vice versa. The structural view focuses on repetition and sameness: the world appears as a collection of (more or less) constant objects, routine procedures and reoccurring events. This view dominates everyday experience (at least in logocentric cultures); and it is in this view that we have conceptualized designing thus far—by identifying six epistemic patterns (i.e., design steps in the sense of repeatable procedures) and the design agent's internal structure (i.e., stable perspectives held by stable persons relating to each other according to various predefined social structures). The structural view enables us to distill the constants in designing and arrive at a general model capable of informing numerous in situ instantiations of designing. On the other hand, such a model is necessarily incapable of explaining how something new can occur for it relies on fixed categories (routines and objects) that leave no room the unknown.

By contrast, the processual view celebrates the primacy of change, seeking difference rather than essence, uniqueness (i.e., singularity) rather than generality. The simplest example, sitting on the fence between structural and processual view, is the shift from viewing an object as a mere element of a class (e.g., *a* cup, *a* dog, etc.) to viewing an object as a particular member of that class and thus as a unique object (e.g., *the* cup, *the* dog, etc.). However, this view is still concerned with stable objects. Applying the processual view more rigorously means experiencing the "object" (e.g., the cup, the dog, etc.) as a unique event, focusing on what is different in the here and now from what used to be the case at other times and places—in processual view presence trumps memory. Bergson (1903, 1911) developed "philosophical intuition", a method

for experiencing the singular quality of events, including philosophical concepts as events. Interestingly, he noted that in order to capture an event's uniqueness one had to "become" co-extent with this event. Building on Bergson, Deleuze and Guattari (1991) maintain that contemplating something requires becoming it, describing an experience of egolessness, which is associated with the most rigorously applied processual view: Note that experiencing a unique instantiation of something (e.g., the uniqueness of this particular dog or cup in this particular moment) still implies stability and memory, as it still involves comparing current to previous experience (thereby maintaining categories such as "dog", "cup", etc.), which necessitates that one cannot fully experience the here and now of the particular moment. In pure processual view there is no object what so ever, no category at all. Instead, experience becomes flow: undivided, heterogeneous and continuously becoming (Nayak, 2008). With all boundaries dissolving, the difference between the observed and the observer (and his or her ego), between appearing (creation) and disappearing (destruction), between old and new dissolves as well. Experience becomes experiencing singularities, or rather singular experience in constant motion or, in other words, experiencing the world as (in) constant becoming (Deleuze and Guattari, 1980). The processual view provides access to experience as pure creation, but devoid of all (reusable) categories, this experience eludes language.

Traditions of Buddhist meditation such as Vipassana and, to a lesser extent, Zen systematically cultivate the experience of constantly changing experience (Varela et al., 1991; Deleuze and Parnet, 1977).

BY CONTRAST, IN MODERN EVERYDAY LIFE EXPERIENCES OF THE WORLD AS PURE PROCESS IN CONSTANT FLUX, APPEAR TO BE RARE.

Nevertheless, everyday life provides access to some experiential qualities associated with the processual view. Consider for example, re-entering into a familiar situation (e.g., returning home or to a meeting, from which one was briefly called away) and suddenly sensing that something has changed: Something's different! This encounter with difference may not last long, as it immediately sets off search behavior aimed at identifying what caused the difference; but until causes and effects are named and, thus, change is absorbed into the structural view, there is a moment of opportunity for becoming aware of sheer difference as an embodied nameless experience. ⁹ᶜ

Another common exemplary opportunity for experience similar to experiencing the world as process is listening to (instrumental) music. Imagine listening to a classical symphony: the more one becomes absorbed by the music, the more one becomes oblivious of the surroundings and of oneself; experience becomes a continuous (i.e., undivided), constantly changing flow; and all of this occurs in the here and now or, which is essentially the same, beyond time and space—until one returns to adopting the structural view of everyday life.

Given the predominance of the structural view paired with the processual view's tendency to elude language, descriptions of experience grounded in the processual view tend to appear alien. However, process (i.e., becoming) is a logical and epistemological necessity with nothing mysterious or mystical about it. The structural view infers process retrospectively (as change must have occurred, if At ≠ At-1) implicating causation.

THE PROCESSUAL VIEW LENDS ITSELF TO EXPERIENCING PROCESS, UTILIZING FUNDAMENTAL CHARACTERISTICS OF HUMAN ATTENTION.

Humans direct their attention *from* something *to* something and, in particular, *from* stability to change, as the latter presents potential threats or opportunities (Polanyi, 1966; Ornstein, 1972). This implies that the more one pays attention to how one pays attention, one focuses in on one's experience, thereby necessarily zooming in on what changes in the experience. Processual view can be understood as the epitome of reflection, attending from the stable aspects of experience to the changing ones until experience is nothing short of constant change—subject and object become insinuated in process.

The juxtaposition of structural and processual views addresses the root problem of creative design, namely coming up with something both new and valuable—which neither of the two mutually exclusive views can enable. The structural view is entrenched in stable objects but cannot transcend existing boundaries; the processual view, is entrenched in ultimate newness up to the paradoxical extent that there exists neither anything old to contrast the new and nor any (stable) object to which newness could be attributed. Designing something new, thus, requires a combination of structural and processual view, for the former allows stable design solutions, while the latter enables delving into novelty. In what follows, we demonstrate that our conceptualization of design is in fact a model for occupying a middle ground beyond structure and process, by systematically instantiating the experience of structural difference, which in turn provides opportunity windows onto processual experience.

The structural centerpiece in our conceptualization of designing is a set of perspectives: persistent ones that stem from personal life experience or disciplinary training, and temporary ones that design agents adopt for executing particular design steps ("motions"). These perspectives guide and guard design agents' experiencing of the world, effectively blocking out alternative ways of experiencing, thereby, eliminating creativity. Hence, the only place for creativity as the becoming of something new—something not caused and thus not implied in the past—is the betweenness of intersecting perspectives. Every collision between perspectives (e.g., in a brainstorming session a designer pursuing a certain line of thought allows someone who speaks from a different perspective to derail her train of thought and take it in a radically different direction) and every transition between perspectives (e.g., a design agent concluding Immersing and embarking on Redefining) eventuates in an incident of the perspective's experiential straightjackets eradicating each other and thus ceasing to structure the agent's experience—enabling unconstrained flow of experience. In other words, this is how structural difference opens windows of opportunity onto processual experience: the encountering structures cancel each other out; either structure's power to govern experience get's nullified; experience evolves, freely creating itself afresh in every moment.

Our conceptualization of designing can be understood as a structural arrangement that not only uses structure to focus the design agent's experience but also to arrange for numerous collisions and transitions between structural elements (i.e., perspectives), thereby providing opportunities for the design agent to break away from the structural view and adopt a processual view. The multiplicity of perspectives built into the decentered design agent leads to numerous collisions between these perspectives. Analogously, the design steps result in transitions between the steps and, equally important, within each diverging motion. Immersing and Prototyping oscillate between observation and interpretation, and between action and reflection, respectively; Imagining, benefits from ideation techniques that require individuals to sequentially adopt various perspectives (e.g., transitioning between a visionary, a critical and a realist perspective, which is also known as the Walt Disney method, or putting on De Bono's "Six Thinking Hats").

AGAIN, THE MANIFOLD COLLISIONS AND TRANSITIONS BETWEEN PERSPECTIVES ARE MEANT TO FUNCTION AS FRAME-BREAKING CREATIVITY-ENABLING DISCONTINUITIES.

In our view, creative design solutions require designers to frequently transition between the structural and the processual view, thereby increasing the likelihood of bringing something new into the familiar world. Creativity is understood as a stochastic phenomenon that cannot be brought entirely under control because in a processual view experiencing is not causal, and neither is creating. Although our conceptualization places great emphasis on arranging for many such frame-breaking transitions, and empirical research suggests that novelty in design is aided by designers shifting frequently between activities (Akin and Lin, 1995; Cross, 1994; Atman et al., 1999), we do not expect maximizing the number of shifts to be advisable; instead, as getting into a perspective (or activity) needs time and little value lies in breaking frames yet to be established, we propose optimizing the shifts in the sense of finding a rhythm of designing.

The Design Steps

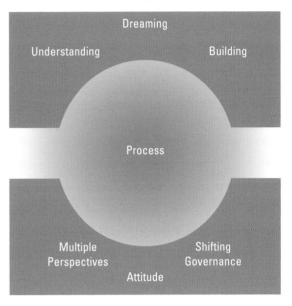

The Design Agent

Finally, attitude matters greatly, as the power of arranged discontinuities depends on individuals' ability to recognize and hold these moments of processual experience. Delving into a world in constant becoming requires the ability to accommodate the experience of otherness and nothingness. In terms of our conceptualization of designing, attitude can be understood as the linking pin that ties the structural component to process.

Implications for Further Research

WE HAVE EXTRACTED FROM THE EXISTING LITERATURE A SET OF MINIMAL CRITERIA FOR CONCEPTUALIZING DESIGNING AND PRESENTED A MODEL THAT SUFFICES THESE CRITERIA.

We have concluded that explaining creativity in design requires a combination of structural and processual view, which translates into the possibility to specify our model's structural components in some detail, while process, the only one processual component, must remain undivided. Further specification of the structural components is required and is left to future research, as this chapter's goal was to introduce the described new framework for understanding designing. In addition, further research is needed to address important questions implied in our model, including: How does the number of frame-breaking discontinuities relate to the length and intensity of experiencing these potential encounters with the world in becoming? How do the number and quality of processual experiences influence design capabilities; to what extent do they influence if solutions are achieved cumulatively rather than in one coherent act; to what extent can they contribute to better understanding the role of individuals, groups and crowds in designing? How can the notion of a "rhythm of designing' help improve design theory and practice? We hope our model contributes to improving the theory and practice of designing, and our ability to understand and manage innovation. We believe this will lead to tighter control over design processes as well as to a growing humility in the face of creativity as a non-causal

phenomenon that poses limits to what humans can bring under their control. As our model illustrates, it is possible and necessary to arrange for encounters with the unknown.

YET, THE UNKNOWN BY DEFINITION ESCAPES HUMAN EFFORTS AND THUS INTUITION WILL CONTINUE TO PLAY A CRITICAL ROLE IN DESIGNING— INCLUDING INTUITION'S CAPACITY TO THWART DESIGNERS' PLANS AT ANY TIME.

1❰ We are indebted to Michael Shamiyeh and Jamie Wallace for stimulating dialogues on designing.

2❰ Trends contributing to increased pressure for innovation include commoditization of (increasingly automated and off-shored) knowledge-intense routine work and accelerated imitation. Factors raising the importance of experience as an economic good include quality plateaus that make products (within a given price range) virtually indistinguishable regarding their basic function—consider as examples cars or cell phones—and increasing fulfillment of customer's basic needs (again shifting emphasis from basic functioning to overall customer experience).

3❰ Pioneering contributions include Simon, 1969; Lawson, 1972, 1979; Darke, 1978; Thomas and Carroll, 1979; Jacques and Powell, 1981; Cross, 1982; Akin, 1986 and Rowe, 1987.

4❰ See Bauer and Eagen (2008) for a detailed account of this attempt at understanding IDEO better than they understand themselves.

5❰ Scholars of "design thinking" have criticized the rational process model based on empirical studies suggesting that experienced designers explore the problem and potential solutions together instead of in sequence. However, these studies use fairly well-structured design problems such as arranging a set of perpendicular building blocks (Lawson, 1979), designing a bathroom (Eastman, 1970) or designing a decontextualized building (Akin, 1986). Participating subjects are not asked or allowed to challenge the nature of the design problem. With our model of the design process in mind, it is thus no surprise that experienced designers deal with these problems through "Building" only. Yet, the question remains open to what extent this approach is generally valid or specifically suitable for well-structured design problems. (In addition, these experiments show that non-designers and inexperienced designers rely more on analytical thinking, while more experienced designers pair cognitive and sensomotor capacities—something they do, too, when exploring problems through "Understanding".)

6❰ De Bono (1971) suggested that brainstorming works best, if all teams members are excellent in their field but only some team members possess problem-specific expertise (i.e., domain-specific skills).

7❰ Consider as an example of the workings of the hermeneutic cycle the meaning of the word "car", which apparently depends on one's prior experience with cars. One's future experience with cars (e.g., how one uses their own car) depends on what one knows about cars and, consequently, associates with "car" (i.e., connotation). As a result, the term "car" or "my car" can never have exactly the same meaning as before. This does not only refer to the fact one's car is never exactly the same (e.g., due to attrition) but also, and more importantly, to the constant change of meaning as a result of life experience. Every single drive adds to how one thinks and feels (i.e., what one knows) about one's car; and so does everything else (e.g., one hears about car accidents, or enjoys a car race, or learns or fantasizes how others think and feel about cars, etc.). True the difference may be small and at times even insignificant; yet the fact remains that "car" means something (slightly) different ever time one uses the word. (This holds too for the fourteen times we have just used "car", even though you may have to make an effort to experience that "car" is now different from what it was before you read this paragraph.)

8❰ Building on Heidegger (1957), Deleuze and Guattari (1980) insist that difference, as opposed to identity, is always difference from itself.

9❰ "Something in the world forces us to think. This something is an object not of recognition but of a fundamental encounter." (Deleuze and Guattari, 1991).

10❰ Polanyi (1966) illustrates his argument by pointing out that a virtuoso pianist moves her fingers not by paying attention to them but instead by listening to the music-in-becoming, thereby connecting movement and music by her attention reaching from the moving fingers to the music-in-becoming. Ornstein (1972) demonstrates that attention is only paid to what is changing. Everything absorbed into the structural view—Ornstein speaks of the mind building a model—is no longer attended, but serves a standard for what to attend, namely whatever departs from the familiar (the model) enough to not being subsumed under the categories in use. For instance, the reader of this text pays no attention to the (constant) surroundings, but instead pushes them into the background and directs his or her attention to the sentences to come—or to whatever significant change occurs in the surroundings, as such change might pose a threat or opportunity.

References

ABC News Productions. 1999. The deep dive. Nightline, 13. July 1999.

Akin, O. 1986. Psychology of architectural design. London: Pion.

Akin, O. and Lin, C. 1995. Design protocol data and novel design decisions. Design Studies, 16(2): 211–236.

Amabile, T. M. 1996. Creativity in context: Update to the social psychology of creativity. Boulder, CO: Westview.

Argyris, C. 1990. Overcoming organizational defenses: Facilitating organizational learning. Needham Heights, MA: Allyn and Bacon.

Atman, C. J., Chimka, J. R., Bursic, K. M., and Nachtmann, H. L. 1999. A comparison of Freshman and senior engineering design processes. Design Studies, 20(2): 131–152.

Bauer, R. M. and Eagen, W. M. 2008. Design thinking— Epistemic Plurality in management and organization. Aesthesis, 2(3): 568–596.

Beckman, S. L. and Barry, M. 2007. Innovation as a learning process. California Management Review, 50(1): 25–56.

Bergson, H. 1903. Introduction à la metaphysique. Revue de Métaphysique et de Morale, 29: 1–36. (An Introduction to Metaphysics. Indianapolis, In: Hackett 1999).

Bergson, H. 1911a. L'Intuition philosophique. Oeuvres. Paris: Presses Universitaires de France, 1959; 1345–1365. (Philosophical Intuition. In: The Creative Mind. New York: Citadel, 107–129.)

Boden, M. A. 1999. Computer models of creativity. In R. J. Sternberg (Ed.), Handbook of Creativity: 351–372. New York et al.: Cambridge University Press.

Boland, R. J. and Collopy, F. (Eds.). 2004. Managing as designing. Stanford, CA: Stanford University Press.

Bono, E. d. 1967. The use of lateral thinking. London: Jonathan Cape.

Bono, E. d. 1971. Lateral thinking for management. New York: McGraw-Hill.

Brodbeck, K.-H. 1999. Entscheidung zur Kreativität. Darmstadt: Primus.

Brown, T. 2009. Change by design. New York: Harper-Collins.

Cross, N. 1982. Designerly ways of knowing. Design Studies, 3(4): 221–227.

Cross, N., Christiaans, H., and Dorst, K. 1994. Design expertise amongst student designers. Journal of Art and Design Education, 13(1): 39–56.

Csikszentmihalyi, M. 1999. Implications of a systems perspective for the study of creativity. In R. J. Sternberg (Ed.), Handbook of Creativity: 313–335. New York et al.: Cambridge University Press.

Darke, J. 1978. The primary generator and the design process. In W. E. Rogers and W. H. Ittelson (Eds.), New directions in environmental design research: Proceedings of EDRA 9: 325–337. Washington: EDRA.

Deleuze, G. and Guattari, F. 1980. Mille Plateaux. Paris: Minuit. (A Thousand Plateaux, Minneapolis: University of Minnesota Press, 1987).

Deleuze, G. and Guattari, F. 1991. Qu'est-ce que la philosophie? Paris: Minuit. (What Is Philosophy? New York: Columbia University Press, 1994).

Deleuze, G. and Parnet, C. 1977. Dialogues. Paris: Flammarion. (Dialogues. London: Athlon, 1987).

Esslinger, H. 2009. A fine line. San Francisco, CA: Jossey-Bass.

Hargadon, A. and Sutton, R. I. 1997. Technology brokering and innovation in a product development firm. Administrative Science Quarterly, 42(4): 716–749.

Hegel, G. W. F. 1807. Phänomenologie des Geistes. Bamberg: Goebhardt. (Phenomenology of Spirit. Oxford et al.: Oxford University Press, 1977.)

Heidegger, M. 1957. Identität und Differenz. Pfullingen: Neske. (Identity and Difference. New York: Harper & Row, 1969).

Jacques, R. and Powell, J. A. (Eds.). 1981. Design: Science: Method. Guildford, UK: Westbury House.

Jung, C. G. 1921. Psychologische Typen. Zürich: Rascher. (Psychological Types; Bollingen Series XX, Volume 6,

Princeton: Princeton University Press, 1971).

Kelly, T. 2001. The art of innovation. New York et al.: Random House.

Kolodner, J. L. and Wills, L. M. 1996. Powers of observation in creative design. Design Studies, 17(4): 385–416.

Lawson, B. 1972. Problem solving in architectural design. University of Aston, Birmingham.

Lawson, B. 1979. Cognitive strategies in architectural design. Ergonomics, 22(1): 59–68.

Lawson, B. 2006. How designers think. 4th Edition. London: Architectural Press.

Libet, B., Freeman, A., and Sutherland, K. (Eds.). 2004. The volitional brain: Toward a neuroscience of free will. Thorverton, UK: Imprint Academic.

Lockwood, T. (Ed.). 2010. Design thinking. New York: Allworth.

Martin, R. L. 2009. The design of business. Boston, MA: Harvard Business School Press.

Maturana, H. R. and Varela, F. J. 1984. El árbol del conocimiento (dt.: Der Baum der Erkenntnis, Bern, München, Wien: Scherz 1987 ed.). Santiago, Chile: Universitaria.

Nayak, A. 2008. On the way to theory: A processual approach. Organization Studies, 29(2): 173–190.

Nonaka, I. 1994. A dynamic theory of organizational knowledge creation. Organization Science, 5(1): 14–37.

Nonaka, I. and Takeuchi, H. 1995. The knowledge-creating company: How japanese companies create the dynamics of innovation. New York: Oxford University Press.

Ornstein, R. 1972. The psychology of consciousness. San Francisco: Freeman.

Ouchi, W. G. 1980. Markets, bureaucracies and clans. Administrative Science Quarterly, 25: 129–141.

Pannells, T. C. and Claxton, A. F. 2008. Happiness, creative ideation and locus of control. Creativity Research Journal, 20(1): 67–71.

Plattner, H., Meinel, C., and Weinberg, U. 2009. Design

thinking. München: Finanzbuchverlag.

Poincaré, J. H. 1908. Science et Méthode. Paris: Flammarion. (Science and Methode. Mineola, N.Y.: Dover, 2003).

Polanyi, M. 1966. The tacit dimension. New York: Doubleday.

Rittel, H. W. J. 1972. On the planning crisis: Systems analysis of the first and second generations. Bedrift Sokonomen, 8: 309–396.

Rittel, H. W. J. and Webber, M. M. 1973. Dilemmas in a General Theory of Planning. Policy Sciences, 4(2): 155–169.

Rowe, P. G. 1987. Design thinking. Cambridge, MA; London, UK: MIT Press.

Sawyer, R. K. 2006. Explaining creativity: the science of human innovation. Oxford et al: Oxford University Press.

Simon, H. A. 1996. The sciences of the artificial. Cambridge, MA: MIT Press.

Sternberg, R. J. 2003. Wisdom, intelligence and creativity sythesized. Cambridge et al.: Cambridge University Press.

Sutton, R. I. and Hargadon, A. 1996. Brainstorming groups in context: Effectiveness in a product design firm. Administrative Science Quarterly, 41(4): 685–718.

Thomas, J. C. and Carroll, J. M. 1979. The psychological study of design. Design Studies, 1: 5–11.

Utterback, J., Vedin, B.-A., Alvarez, E., Ekman, S., Sanderson, S.W., Tether, B., and Verganti, R. 2006. Design-inspired innovation. Hackensack, NJ: World Scientific Publishing.

Vaihinger, H. 1911. Die Philosophie des Als Ob. Berlin: Reuther and Reichardt. (The Philosophy of "As If". London: Routledge, 2000).

Varela, F. J., Thompson, E., and Rosch, E. 1991. The embodied mind. Cambridge, MA: MIT Press.

Verganti, R. 2009. Design driven innovation. Boston, MA: Harvard Business School Press.

Wallas, G. 1926. The art of thought. New York: Harcourt Brace.

165

This paper empirically explores what constitutes design attitude. Previous studies have called on managers to adopt such an attitude in creating products, services and processes that are both profitable and humanly satisfying. However, what a design attitude actually is made of has not been researched. In this study I therefore investigate the nature of this attitude, as displayed by professional designers. Interview data from senior designers and managers from four internationally recognized, design-led organizations (IDEO, Nissan Design, Philips Design and Wolff Olins) are collected in order to characterize the likely shape of a work-based attitude promoted by designers themselves. The five theoretical categories characterizing design attitude that arise from the data are: "Consolidating multidimensional meanings", "Creating, bringing to life", "Embracing discontinuity and open-endedness", "Embracing personal and commercial empathy" and "Engaging polysensorial aesthetics". Finally, the implications of these findings for organization research are discussed.
Keywords: design attitude, design gestalt, professional design culture, design practice, design values.

This article originally appeared in Organization Studies, Vol. 29, No. 3, 373–392 (2008), Sage Publications

"Designers have always had an uneasy working relationship with the management world, and nothing in their education and training makes it easy for them to do so" (Gorb, 1986: 107). This observation is as relevant today as it was over 20 years ago, particularly in the context of the emerging interest in organization studies as a "science of design". Despite the increased interest in design as an alternative mode of engaging in management research (Romme, 2003), very little attention has been devoted to the meaning associated with the design approach, espoused by different professional groups. Recent contributions on "design attitude" (Boland and Collopy, 2004) and "design gestalt" (Yoo et al., 2006) of design professionals suggest that these notions can be an important source of inspiration for management scholars and managers alike.

The revived interest in design has resulted in a steady stream of publications highlighting the links between design and organizations. Researchers have shown, for example, that design should be seen as an important strategic resource and a vehicle for change (Kotler and Rath, 1984; Dumas and Mintzberg, 1989; Peters, 1997; Olson et al., 1998; Marzano, 1999; Myerson, 2001; Johansson and Svengren, 2002; Squires and Byrne 2002; Lojacono and Zaccai, 2004; Ravasi and Lojacono, 2005). In addition, strong links between design, innovativeness and organizational performance have been recognized and evidenced article title (Cooper and Press, 1995; Lester et al., 1998; Bruce and Harun, 2001; Bruce and Bessant, 2002; Broja de Mozota, 2003; Press and Cooper, 2003; Nussbaum, 2004; Rich, 2004).

DESPITE THE FACT THAT RESEARCHERS HAVE SHOWN THE IMPORTANCE OF PROFESSIONAL CULTURES IN ORGANIZATIONAL SETTINGS (BLOOR AND DAWSON, 1994), THERE HAS BEEN NO ATTEMPT TO EMPIRICALLY EXAMINE THE NATURE OF THE DESIGN ATTITUDE ESPOUSED BY PROFESSIONAL DESIGNERS.

Consequently, in the light of the perceived importance of the philosophies, methodologies, tools and techniques associated with and advocated by the design approach, my paper focuses on the question relating to the character of a professional culture shaped by designers. It aims to examine and build upon the design attitude which is being prescribed by Boland and Collopy (2004) as a means of creating products, services and processes that are both "profitable and humanly satisfying" (p.3). Despite the difficulty of extracting a cultural impact of any one group of people on an organizational landscape, the primary objective of this study was to discover and heuristically isolate concepts relating to designers' values and beliefs. My intention was to advance the understanding of design attitude through empirical research. The analysis that follows uses the conceptual framework of a professional/occupational culture (Bloor and Dawson, 1994; Van Maanen and Barley, 1984), and adheres to the spirit and logic of grounded theory approach (Glaser and Strauss, 1967).

The paper first introduces the overall research logic, followed by a description of the research method. Second, the themes representing the culture of designers are empirically examined and illustrated with excerpts from interviews. Finally, I discuss the wider implications of the main empirical findings and outline the associated limitations.

Accessing Design Attitude

Bolland and Collopy define design attitude as "expectations and orientations one brings to a design project" (Boland and Collopy, 2004: 9). The authors provide an example of a learning process that a group of management scholars underwent during an architectural project facilitated by Frank Gehry. Some of their observations, for example, concerned a distinct mindset for problem solving and decision making on the part of the designer/architect. The authors suggested that engaging design attitude might stimulate re-evaluating fundamental assumptions about the way organizations function. Among the aspects which were mentioned was the use of models as sketches to stimulate thinking, an attitude of openness and the creation of an adequate design vocabulary.

These characteristics of design professionals can be observed across a family of design professionals (Press and Cooper, 2003; Ravasi and Lojacono, 2005). This assertion is based on the research into occupational and organizational cultures. In this respect, occupation is not limited to the framework of a given organization or even a given industry or nation, which implies it can be observed beyond those boundaries (Becher, 1981). Van Maanen and Barley (1984) argue that occupations are probably the most distinctive subcultures in organizational life. Once formed, professional groups develop 374 Organization Studies 29(03) not only different knowledge bases, but also different codes for constructing meaningful interpretations of persons, events and objects commonly encountered in their professional world. According to these authors, an occupational community is: "a group of people who consider themselves to be engaged in the same sort of work; who identify (more or less positively) with their work; who share with one another a set of values, norms and perspectives that apply to, but extend beyond, work related matters and whose social relationships merge the realms of work and leisure." (Van Maanen and Barley, 1984: 295)

Bloor and Dawson (1994: 286) add: "Professional subcultures are often stronger than other groupings within an organization in the sense of having extra-organizational associations and peers to aid them in shaping new cultures and codes of conduct, and resisting the imposition of other cultural values and practices."

From the perspective of organizational studies, Martin puts forward the so-called "nexus model" (Martin 1992: 112–114).

A NEXUS IS THE POINT OF INTERACTION OF A VARIETY OF INFLUENCES, THOSE FROM OUTSIDE AS WELL AS FROM THE INSIDE.

The nexus model suggests that what some organizations perceive as unique to their cultures is, in fact, non-unique and often attached to professional cultures which span many organizations (Gregory, 1983; Martin et al., 1983). Building on this logic, I assert that following a group of (design) professionals into companies in which they are clearly present could provide a good basis for sifting out profession-specific cultural themes from organization-specific ones. Consequently, a key assumption in this study is that we can uncover what design attitudein action is through the analysis of the position and nature of professional design culture embedded in successful design-based organizations.

Research Method

To obtain access to the ambiguities and subtleties of design attitude, I adopt a research method that is conducive to inductively uncovering meaning. In this respect, the under-researched nature of design-related professional dispositions requires a direct and situated approach. The exploratory nature of the research presented in this paper is a consequence of the research question as well as the inadequacy of existing theoretical frameworks for studying occupational cultures (Sackmann, 1991; Hofstede, 2001). The approach adopted is congruent with grounded theory development, as advocated by Glaser and Strauss (1967), which concentrates on eliciting meaning from empirical data (Guba and Lincoln, 1994).

THIS STRATEGY AIMS TO SUPPORT RESEARCHERS IN AN ATTEMPT TO "CODIFY AND PUBLISH THEIR OWN METHODS FOR GENERATING THEORY"(GLASER AND STRAUSS, 1967: 8).

The primary intention, in this instance, is to give guidelines that support the highly personal, iterative procedure of conceptualizing and formulating theories. There are currently two variants of grounded theory development (Partington, 2000; Goulding, 2002). In this study, I build on Glaser and Strauss's original spirit of theoretical discovery rather than Strauss and Corbin's highly formulaic method.

Unit of Analysis and Sampling

The choice of companies was deliberately diverse and included organizations specializing in product and services design, innovation training, branding and strategic insight. The precise composition of the sample was informed by the nature of the theoretical sampling procedure. The logic behind this type of sampling pre-scribes to follow cases that are likely to replicate or extend the emergent theory or to fill theoretical categories and provide examples for polar types (Glaser and Strauss, 1967; Eisenhardt, 1989; Goulding, 2002). This type of sampling is primarily concerned with representatives, it seeks information richness and selects the cases purposefully rather than randomly (Gillham, 2000; Meyer, 2001).

Following these guidelines, I have chosen companies using a number of key criteria: (a) their current exceptional reputation among designers and management professionals; (b) the extent to which these companies have been studied and used as exemplars in quality publications in the area of design and management; (c) respectable industry positions; (d) history of successes as measured by the number of design awards and business performance; (e) my perception of the importance placed on designers internally. Subsequently, representatives from four companies took part in this study. These corporations included: IDEO, Philips Design (PD), Nissan Design (ND) and Wolff Olins (WO). Making use of high-level access to these organizations, I carried out a series of semi-structured interviews (Miles and Huberman, 1994; Charmaz, 2003).

IN ORDER TO BUILD A PICTURE OF THE "DESIGN CULTURE" THOSE COMPANIES HAVE IN COMMON, THE UNIT OF ANALYSIS WAS THE INDIVIDUAL INTERVIEWEE.

The participants who agreed to take part in this study included: general managers, senior designers, design managers, consultants and one influential design entrepreneur. Nine of them have been trained and educated in the tradition of either industrial design or interaction design. Three have undertaken management education, one was educated in experimental psychology and computer science, and another was a historian and a self-taught manager-entrepreneur.

Analysis Procedure

In an attempt to extract the essence of the design attitude, I carried out 15 indepth interviews with 14 different people between January 2004 and March 2005. The duration ranged from 40 minutes to two and a half hours. In line with the methodology, I proceeded to assign codes (themes)

in a pyramid-like fashion. First, this involved attaching short statements which summarized fragments of text that referred to the design attitude and values espoused by designers. In total, 643 fragments of interviews were identified and labelled with 74 separate codes (for example of this procedure see Appendix).

SECOND, IN THE AGGREGATION PHASE, THE CODES THAT EMERGED IN THE INITIAL PHASE WERE CROSS-REFERENCED.

The idea here was to reduce the redundancy of concepts and create robust categories which could explain the design attitude. In this process, using "theoretical sensitivity" (Glaser, 1978), I focused on characteristics that were clearly associated with professional designers. Only those concepts that achieved a high level of clarity across all cases were included. Those aspects that appeared to have primarily personal and trait-like nature were discarded. In order to aid the analytical process and the handling of the large quantity of qualitative data, the QSR NUD.IST N6 software package was used.

Table 1. Data Sources

Organization	Profile Data	Sources
IDEO	Design consultancy	3 interviews: general manager (UK branch), senior manager, senior commercial partner
Wolff Olins	Strategic design consultancy	6 interviews: co-founder (twice), 3 senior consultants, junior consultant
Nissan Design	Specialised in-house	2 interviews: general manager (UK), design consultancy senior designer
Philips Design	Product design consultancy	4 interviews: 2 senior directors, 2 senior consultants

169

Table 2. Summary of Empirically Derived Categories Representing the Professional Culture of Designers

Substantive categories	Theoretical categories
Reconciling contradictory commercial objectives Bridging approaches, swinging between synthesising and analysing Consolidating multiple languages and media	Consolidating multidimensional meanings (1)
Creative manifesting Rapid prototyping Working with tangibles	Creating, bringing to life (2)
Allowing oneself not to be "in control" Linear process, detailed planning vs. "let's see how it goes" Freedom to think and behave differently	Embracing discontinuity and open-endedness (3)
Visual discourse, visual thinking, creative dialogue Aesthetics, beauty, taste Intuition, instinct, tacit knowledge	Engaging polysensorial aesthetics (4)
Concentrating on people, human-centredness Transparency of communication	Engaging personal and commercial empathy (5)
Sense of commercial purpose Authenticity, playfulness	

Data Analysis: Exploring the Culture of Designers

This section explains the characteristics of theoretical concepts which are identified as representing the design attitude observed through the culture of designers. Those categories, while attempting to capture the essence on a more abstract level, are not entirely self-sustained and mutually exclusive. Rather, they are conceptual markers that help to map out the milestones on the cultural territory. As the study is based only on a specific group of organizations the results must be assessed through that prism. Where possible, the descriptions are supported by the references from the existing body of knowledge.

The results of the creative-analytical process are represented in the form of descriptive categories (substantive codes) that have been related to each other by abstract concepts (theoretical codes). The core categories were primarily identified following the comparison of existing concepts to other concepts and incidents that emerged from the analysis of transcripts. A list of the main categories is presented in Table 2.

Consolidating Multidimensional Meanings

The interviewees have drawn a great deal of attention to the role of a designer as a person who "consolidates" various meanings and "reconciles" contradicting objectives. The category labelled consolidating multidimensional meanings attempts to capture the essence of what many designers feel they bring with them. They have the ability to "look at a situation from a wide variety of perspectives", bringing together "humanistic standpoint", "deep understanding" and technical limitations (senior commercial partner, IDEO). Their role in the organization is making connections and pulling together different threads:

"Designers themselves are actually managing all the constituent parts, and therefore managing the connection and the connected contribution of all the constituent disciplines in solving any problem or creating a landscape for exploring further problems or further opportunities, further possibilities of growth." (senior director, PD)

The view that the best practice in design is the "art" and "science" of combining all the "technical, financial,

operational and emotional pieces together" is also shared by design management researchers (Lojacono and Zaccai, 2004: 75).

It seems that, contrary to popular belief, where designers are predominantly seen as engaged in "synthesizing" (Bernstein, 1988; Walker, 1990; Sacher, 2002), their strength lies in utilizing both—"putting things together" and "taking them apart" simultaneously:

"...there's only a few things that designers really bring to the party and the first is this kind of way of looking at the world that is at the same time analytical and synthetic". (general manager, IDEO)

"Because what you get is actually... designers bring[ing] the cut-through. If you had just lots and lots of thinkers thinking in one way you'd never get that 'cut-through',that difference. If it's complex on the inside and extremely complex on the outside,they will try and help you simplify everything and actually give it a bit more traction on the market." (senior consultant, WO)

When asked which elements designers "consolidate" in an organization we find "...we are talking about corporate identity, we were talking about the way in which an organization projected an idea of what it was through its buildings, through its environment, through people, through its behavior, through its advertising, literature and everything else" (co-founder WO). When I talked about the role designers played in the development of WO, its co-founder raised two issues—their ability to visualize and their close integration into the culture of WO: "Designers were much more important in WO than you would think, because although WO was very much a strategically based consultancy business, [we] hugely (speaker's emphasis) relied on designers to give... to show, to visualize this stuff and very often [work] was led by designers, not by consultants. You couldn't say who led what. You couldn't say this was a consultancy-led business or design-led business. The thing that most companies don't get right, [which] I think we're trying very hard to get right here, is that there should be no division." (co-founder, WO)

Essentially, the concept of *consolidating multidimensional meanings* emphasizes the designers' role in reconciling different, operational objectives in a company. It points to the ability to operate in an analytical-synthetical loop in order to achieve a balance between internal cohesion and meeting practical constraints. In other words, designers master "...the comprehensive design process [that] is a rich, complex integration of the scientific and the sensual, the intellectual and the intuitive" (Friedman, 2002: 199).

Creating, Bringing to Life

The majority of the interviewees share a real affection for creating things and bringing solutions to life. One of the informers said:

"I like seeing things that are new and different. I get a genuine shock of delight to see something that I've never ever seen before work..." (co-founder, WO)

A senior designer at WO described it in even more profound words:

"Design delights people. Good design is exciting and makes people feel great. You're never going to do that with a PowerPoint presentation or charts or graphs. It can be interesting, it can be intelligent and it can be inspiring in a way that you're projecting into the future, but when you look at something that's just wonderful and it makes you smile or makes you laugh, or just excites you—that transcends that kind of rational thinking. And it's the hardest thing to achieve but it's the most gratifying." (senior designer, WO)

Another way of expressing it is that it is about *creatively manifesting* the ideas that would later shape successful products, services or experiences. The senior director at Philips Design describes it in the following way:

"Designing is about having ideas and creatively manifesting them in the physical or digital realm, things that are made, things that we bring to be. It's like having children, it's about making things and seeing the results of your work and expressing what you've been thinking, converting from an idea in your head through your hands or through someone else's hands." (senior director, PD)

What has been noted across the cases is that "Having something visible and tangible as a result of your work is a very rewarding thing" (senior manager, PD), thereby, stressing the physical dimension of creation process. One of the properties of the creation process is the apparent need for swift execution. It seems that the ability and willingness to quickly bring solutions to life is an important feature of designers' behavior. We find this in the following comments:

"Really important is this bringing things to life, being able to build prototypes, do it fast so that you don't invest a lot of time and money into something that's not what you want it to be." (senior manager, IDEO)

"The beginning of the design process is really about dealing with an enormous amount of intangibles, so it's more about developing understanding, observing, acquiring new knowledge and then the analytical process, applying creativity to it and being able to make rational judgement about those, the various concepts, the various ideas and quickly steer them into the process of product creation. There is this ability to rapidly go from very broad, very kind of subjective project into something that is rational and tangible, something that is discussable and debatable with our clients." (senior consultant, PD)

One of the experienced management consultants now working with designers points to the effects rapid prototyping and visualization have on the business process:

"The first time they see it, they start to get excited by it and actually start to understand how they can actually do it, 'cause before you do that, before you visualize and bring it to life it's just a whole set of facts and presentations of how do you put that whole thing together and they can begin to see and it's more than just bits so you can begin to build this." (senior consultant, WO)

According to a senior figure at IDEO, among the three essential things that designers bring with them is the ability and drive to make "...currently invisible or [inarticulable] or intangible ideas visible" (general manager, IDEO). The category of creating, bringing to life is akin to a key feature of "design gestalt" described by Yoo et al. (2006). The authors explain that focus on form giving, as "putting something remarkable into the world" (p. 227), is central to organization designing. This echoes with the nature of this theme which could be characterized by the following statements: "making things tangible", "seeing the fruits of one's thoughts" or "bringing to fruition".

Embracing Discontinuity and Openendedness

This concept emphasizes designers' willingness to engage in a process that is not predetermined or planned ahead in detail and where outcomes are unknown or uncertain. This attitude is inherently connected with the need to accept higher risk, stipulated by the temporary loss of control over the situation: "It's about people who are willing to be risky and not necessarily comfortable in knowing exactly what the outcome of the project is going to be" (senior manager, IDEO). In this respect, willingness to take risk is not an aim in itself but rather a consequence of accepting a position when one is deeply unsure about the result of a project.

In IDEO the attitude of keeping an open mind is balanced, on a project level, by the generic design process. We know from other sources that this process consists of five distinctive parts: (1) observation: utilizing cognitive psychologists, anthropologists, sociologists in conjunction with the client and designers; (2) brainstorming: a core of the idea-generating activity, drawing on the analysis of data gathered in the observation phase; (3) rapid prototyping: working with models helps everyone visualize and initially verify possible solutions; (4) refining: narrowing options through iterating choices; (5) implementation: creating actual product or service (Nussbaum, 2004: 89). When asked what sorts of people are considered exceptional designers at WO, the senior designer said: "People who are brave, a little bit crazy, not crazy as insane but willing to say, why not? Let's do this! Let's take a chance. That's invaluable. I'd say that's the most important thing" (senior designer, WO).

This is what a senior consultant, previously working for one of the major management consultancies, said about the positive attitude towards discontinuity: "...that's something I initially felt really uncomfortable with because it tends to be quite illogical. If everyone is logical you tend to come up with the same answers but designers help you think illogically almost and jump around and think about things in a completely different way and you get a different result. What you do is see what they need, sort of fill the gap and these sorts of things that are very slow processes, and design can come in and just say 'Why don't we just do this?'." (senior consultant, WO)

According to Lester et al., an "interpretive manager"— one who learns from designers—"embraces ambiguity and improvisation as essential to innovation" and avoids "premature closure" (Lester et al., 1998: 89). Weick talks about designing as a battle between "naming the thing (variable) and losing the dream (overall vision)" (Weick, 2004:48).
There seems to be a danger associated with the attitude of open-endedness. If unchecked by a generic process within a business (such as the one used by IDEO), a culture where *discontinuity and openendedness* are encouraged risks jeopardizing commercial objectives. This might happen in part due to a prolonged search for the "perfect" solution that results in "overdesigning": "Designers fail because they don't know when to stop. The trick in designing is to stop while the design still has life" (Weick, 2004: 43). Discontinuity and constant freezing and unfreezing of solutions could also be compounded by a particularly anarchic behavior of certain members of a design team. Co-founder of WO talks about an extreme case of a designer:

"He didn't respect any discipline—he didn't respect time discipline, he didn't respect business discipline, he didn't respect the boardroom discipline, he didn't respect any dis-cipline, any discipline of any kind. And because of that, in the end he couldn't stay in the company." (co-founder, WO)

The result of keeping an open mind while working on a practically focused solution often brings change. As one senior manager in PD said: "The admirable quality about designers is that they are very capable of embracing change. They actually thrive on it. They actually live on it" (senior manager, PD). This characteristic might have important consequences for the role designers play in supporting change initiatives in organizations.

To sum up, the category labelled *embracing discontinuity and openendedness* reflects designers' need for the freedom to explore and their willingness to improvise, be opportunistic, have an open mind and embrace ambiguity.

Engaging Polysensorial Aesthetics

From a general perspective this concept represents designers' fondness for using their aesthetic sense and judgement while interacting with the environment. We know that one of the most important skills a designer obtains is the ability to visualize and "think through drawing" (Schön, 1983; Cross, 1999). Apart from that there is also a "visual discourse within yourself" (senior designer, WO). As one of the informants notes, engaging the visual has the potential to break the creative deadlock and stimulate dialogue.
A trained management consultant very expressively describes the effect visuals can have on the strategic business process:

"You're blue in the face trying to explain a positioning a strategy, a vision. I mean what is a vision?... You're there, in front of a room trying to explain it and you have used all the analytics. You've analysed, you've talked about customers, competitors and they're nodding as you use words. And then suddenly, you bring visual and the whole room lights up. And that's very special! The ability to get that just right is incredible. So that's what I think designers bring to the process—the ability to capture, not only to create the ideas, but to capture them simply into something visual that people relate to." (senior consultant, WO)

Despite the visual component (which arguably is the most prominent), they also seem to appreciate the importance of other kinds of sensorial stimuli. This preference and ability links to an earlier concept named consolidating multidimensional meanings. In the process of compiling together different constituent elements in order to come up with a solution, designers often conspicuously draw from many disparate sensorial sources.
When we talk about the aesthetical dimensions such as "beautiful" and "ugly" (in the context of designers' preferences), it is important to mention that most of the interviewees actually acknowledged that there is a general perception in society that colloquially "design is about the triumph of form over function". In fact, all of the interviewed designers-by-trade firmly believe that in their commercial practices this is not the case at all: "For me beauty is very important but it's simply the door-opener to something. And I think that really beautiful things that work poorly are no

good. This beautiful tooth brush is a crap toothbrush if it lasts about three brushes. It's no good. I think so much less of this manufacturer because of that. Although it's beautiful, it's crap." (managing director, IDEO)

"When compiling all the different stimuli and meanings to achieve a desirable outcome, designers use not only their rational, technical knowledge but also their implicit, hidden and multifaceted 'sense of knowing'." (Polanyi, 1966)

Complicated arbitrary factors of taste and preference, which need to be addressed in the process of design, are only partially susceptible to scientific or engineering analysis. Therefore, argues Buchanan, they must be responded to through "aesthetics" (Buchanan, 1995: 52).
Engaging with this "immediate and unconscious perception" is how one informant sees his work of integrating a strategic intent into a workable solution: "...we interpret the illogical thought, if you like, to make it real. So if you walk into a building you're not talking about logic, are you? What you talk about is how you feel, and you leave the building with an impression" (co-founder, WO).

Engaging Personal and Commercial Empathy

Designers are often perceived as individual "heroes" whose egos dominate in the relationships with clients and co-workers. While the informants acknowledge that this is generally societies' perception and that indeed "every young designer to a certain extent is somewhat egoistic" (senior manager, PD) they see the reality on the ground to be very different. Time and time again the interviewees stressed that the designers they work with have an exceptional ability and will to empathize and accommodate customers' views:

"Designers are trained by hard work and practice to tune in to how people relate to things around [them], in quite a deep way." (senior commercial partner, IDEO)
"I think designers are much more tuned into people's needs and also market trends, people's lifestyle and socio-cultural trends. Designers are much more tuned to that, certainly within Philips. A lot of Philips business, research and development people come from a technology background that's developing technologies but not necessarily knowing

what they're going to do with those technologies. Designers come almost from the opposite end, which is people. We know about people, you know, what people want, what people need, what kind of quality of life people would like." (senior manager, PD)

"Whatever we're trying to design, we're always doing it from what traditionally you might have referred to as a user-centred, human-centred or customer-centred point of view." (senior consultant, IDEO)

In order to underpin the importance of focusing on the human side of adding value to the future product, service or experience, IDEO have incorporated into their process elements from anthropology, psychology and sociology (Kelley, 2001; Squires and Byrne, 2002). Even though the methods and techniques are not as "in-depth" as their academic versions, they enable IDEO to strengthen their processes in a bid to empathize with the end-users even more.

On top of the personal empathy and deep connection with people, designers in those companies exhibit an attitude that might be described as commercial empathy. That is to say they are sympathetic towards commercially bound reference points of their work. For example, model designers at PD

"... are capable of understanding that they need to work within given constraints, that business environment imposes so many different constraints, not just time constraints. There could be constraints on the design itself in terms of the execution of the design itself, the quality of the materials, components used or many other aspects." (senior manager, PD)

As far as the daily life of a company is concerned, designers appear to have an additional, perhaps more subtle, function of refreshing the atmosphere and reducing tensions: "... what design can do is inject a whole lot of excitement into their everyday experience. What we can offer people is something that is ideas and experiences that revive them, reinvigorate them and inspire them and that's very gratifying. It often requires bravery on their part but if they accept it and they go for it then it can be terrific." (senior designer, WO)

Engaging personal and commercial empathy draws our attention to a rather special, human-centred orientation in designers' professional lives that doesn't fight with but rather complements the commercial requirements. It relates to the deep (aesthetic) listening and dialogue as a means of reaching customers' hidden needs. It encompasses transparency of outcomes and aims to embed emotional reactions into products and services.

Creating Fundamental Value through Exploration

Constant comparison of different categories and statements culminated in the five themes described above. What emerges from the analysis as the central point, the core category, concerns designers' *focus on creating fundamental value through epistemologically unconfined exploration.*

In the process of creating value, designers seem to engage in exploration of new conceptual territories. Where design is *exploratory* (Cross, 1999: 28), designers in the four organizations are seen as cultural explorers. Through the combination of their skills, attitudes and behaviors they often lead to the discovery of novel and uninhibited commercial spaces.

The most important reference point for designers is the future cohesive solution that takes many disparate variables into account (*consolidating multidimensional meanings*): "They [designers] can see things and develop mental steps. They can plot things into the future. Because it's a prepositional and creative discipline, it always sees things in the future and is moving towards them" (senior director, PD). Furthermore, designers, through their *personal and commercial empathizing*, are uniquely positioned to link the emotional and the rational, with social on one hand and commercial on the other. In the process of *consolidating meanings* they create strategic "focal points" in the form of brands which have both internal and external functions and "...translate the business strategy into something 'do-able', understandable and emotional for people" (senior consultant, WO).

What is essential from the epistemological point of view is that designers see the reality as something they create. Their attitude towards creating workable solutions is "assertion-based" and not necessarily "evidence-based". As one informant notes: "Designers don't do it [create knowledge] through writing papers,they don't do it by looking up references. They do it by collecting stimuli and tuning their responses to them and striving to be original in important ways" (senior commercial partner, IDEO).

During a design process, designers are using their analytical skills as well as aesthetic sense (*engaging polysensorial aesthetics*) in an attempt to create something better than what previously existed. The fact that designers are tuned into interaction with the world around them aesthetically also suggests that they might be particularly helpful if a company wants to engage this dimension. There is a strong commitment among designers to make a fundamental difference. A senior consultant from PD notes:

"The thing I love about designers more than anything else is this belief that we can always do better, the belief that we can make a difference, we can make a change. There's this kind of built-in mechanism of designers to accept any form of challenge." (senior consultant, PD)

This somewhat naïve belief drives this group of people towards creating different and often unique propositions. Coupled with their personal and commercial empathy these projections become something that both connects with the customers and is economically viable.

Consequently, designers to a minimal degree rely on predefined, cumulatively created knowledge frameworks. They are stimulated by the challenge of creating solutions in order to bring about fundamental change to the value offered. This attitude at its heart embraces continuous challenge to the organizational status quo and builds in a natural unwillingness to accept the authority of past experiences. This is how a senior designer and a senior manager explain the role of their design-led consultancies:

"What we try to do is help businesses in some way reinvent themselves [clients]. Either reinvent what their offer is,

reinvent their particular position in the market so to redefine the market or create something completely new. So instead of being the best of a kind they are the only of a kind." (senior designer, WO)

This attitude seeks perpetual reconfiguration of the existing rules and boundaries. If translated into the world of strategies this means reconfiguring markets by bringing new, fundamental growth based on insightful and meaningful products, services, systems, brands and experiences. The willingness to *embrace discontinuity* as well as the *openended* character of the design process, in which ambiguity prevails and outcomes are uncertain, are at the centre of designers' attitude to work. The spirit of exploration and challenge is what designers bring to their workplace.

Discussion

There is a growing body of literature that suggests design attitude is an important issue in organization studies (Boland and Collopy, 2004; Dunbar and Starbuck, 2006; Yoo et al., 2006). In this study I examined the culture of professional designers in order to understand the nature of their particular attitude. Despite the fact that the research is in most part exploratory, it describes in some detail espoused values which many managers and scholars alike invoke.

The study points to a number of implications for investigations of the design approach in organization studies. The first is that various professions will have a different appreciation of the notion of "design". According to their enculturation they might either see "design" as a pre-planned, predetermined mode with no space for emergent ideas, as in Mintzberg's "design school" of strategy formulation (Mintzberg, 1998). The meaning of the word "design" in the organization studies literature tends to concentrate on the notion of careful planning, up-front decision making and alignment with predefined criteria (Chandler, 1962; Galbraith, 1973, 1995; Nadler and Tushman, 1997). Within the culture of professional product designers, "design attitude" signifies quite the opposite.

IT UNDERLINES THE FREEDOM TO EXPLORE AND TO FOLLOW UNEXPECTED BUT PROMISING LEADS, WHILE KEEPING THE OVERALL VISION AS A SUBLIMINAL YARDSTICK FOR THE PROJECT'S SUCCESS (WEICK, 2004; YOO ET AL., 2006).

The second implication involves the rhetoric of the discourse on a "science of design", which brings with it the associations of predictability, generalizability, stability of results, and a lexicon of common procedures and methods. As the analysis of (product) designers shows, their definition of design attitude does not necessarily include these characteristics. It is quite common to hear and observe that the very nature of their design attitude is purposefully

a-scientific. Christopher Alexander's well-intentioned but failed "pattern language" (Alexander et al., 1977) is a good case in point. Alexander attempted to create a systematic set of rules for designing architecture, which was simply rejected by the professional architecture community. In this respect, designers take great pride in breaking rules, subverting accepted norms and refusing to align with something that has already been tried and tested. Indeed, their natural tendency is to seek originality and novel forms of operating at any point of the design process. The essence of a truly radical design-based paradigm may, in fact, lie in an attitude and value set that is very different from the dispositions and values espoused by most management scholars.

This study has the following limitations. First, it focused on defining the common attitudes of designers and did not look into their actual behaviors. This implies that the reported values and attitudes might, in fact, be substantially removed from what Argyris and Schön (1978) call the theories-in-action. Second, the paper studied design culture present in companies that predominantly deliver product or brand-based solutions.

EXTENDING THE FINDINGS BEYOND THIS DOMAIN MAY NOT BE POSSIBLE (SEE KRIPPENDORFF 2006).

Finally, some questions remain unanswered. For example: What happens when large sections of the organization adopt the type of design attitude described in this paper? How would this modify the sense-making process in creating new organizational forms and strategies? How does the diffusion of design attitude affect the adoption of a more flexible stance towards disruptive innovations?

Conclusion

Back in 1986, Gorb remarked that cultural inhibitions could constitute the main barrier to appreciating the importance of design (Gorb, 1986). More recently, Buchanan (2004: 55) argued that "properly integrating design into a complex organization is one of the important challenges faced by management". This paper aimed to expose the fabric of the culture of designers, thus providing more detail to those who wish to study the social background of those differences.

This paper draws attention to the following characteristics of this professional group: (a) designers focus on future solutions where they perceive reality and culture as something pliable—their attitude towards workable solutions is "assertion-based rather than evidence-based"; (b) they connect to work on emotional, rational and aesthetic levels, acting on the assumption that they must be coherently consolidated; (c) designers rely only to a limited extent on predetermined, cumulatively created frameworks and prefer proposing novel, original forms that challenge the status quo; (d) designers can potentially stimulate or support change in organizations due to their generally positive attitude towards change itself.

In addition to seeing design as a set of tools, skills or epistemologies for more grounded organizational enquiry (see Romme, 2003; Van Aken, 2004), this paper suggests a no less relevant avenue for researching design, involving the cultural interpretations of design attitude in organizations. Managers and management scholars are trapped not only by our vocabulary (Boland and Collopy, 2004) but also by our professionally bound attitudes and beliefs.

DESIGN ATTITUDES WILL VERY LIKELY DIFFER SIGNIFICANTLY BETWEEN PROFESSIONALS FROM FIELDS SUCH AS PRODUCT DESIGN, ACCOUNTING, OPERATIONS MANAGEMENT, MARKETING, AND SO FORTH.

Each situation and profession will bring its own preferences for variables such as speed of closure, required detail of the organizational brief, level of acceptable ambiguity and fluidity of the assignment, depth of aesthetic appreciation, and many more. Appreciating the differences between the science and design modes of organization research should therefore extend beyond the epistemic and theoretical considerations and include socially constructed thought worlds that inform the creation and implementation of these modes.

Appendix

Sample questions used during semi-structured interviews (Wolff Olins)

Can you tell me what your background is and what your way to WO was? Have you worked in a non-design environment before? If yes, how does it differ? If it's not different, then why design? How do you feel working with designers? What is the nature of your relationship? What do your find particularly interesting, stimulating in design and designers and what are the things that irritate you? What kinds of trajectories, attitudes and principles do they bring with them? Could you describe a situation in which you had to intervene in one way or another amongst designers? What were the circumstances? What is the biggest contribution a designer makes to the team in WO? What is the biggest mistake a designer can make in WO? What kinds of people are considered exemplary designers in WO? Can you describe them to me? What are the benefits of working with WO as perceived by outsiders? What do they find astonishing or amusing? What is the nature of the integration of managers and designers inside WO? What are the difficulties whilst working with them?

Category-Building Snapshot

Informant A (IDEO): [..].	**Informant A (Wolff Olins): [...]**	**Informant B (Philips Design):**
looking for people who are, who have great design skills and so.. but then looking for people who could be really entrepreneurial and do things, kind of be leaders... you know.. have opinions on things not be afraid to voice their opinions, those are the couple of things we're looking for, not all these people have great design skills which is obviously a very important thing but it's also about *people who are willing to be risky, and not necessarily comfortable in knowing exactly what the outcome of the project is going to be.* We get lots of what we call "foggy projects"—where gosh we don't even know... it's not as simple as sitting down and saying—OK here are our plans for doing this but wow, we don't know what the outcome of this would be and being OK with this sort of this kind of foggy world...	really, really imaginative, creative people who were very frequently, very young, they weren't always very young, who were not corporate and who wanted to fulfil themselves creatively. [...] I remember a bloke, a very, very grungy, he'd be working on a supermarket or something, so what are yours thoughts—(mocking a Hackney accent),—"*she like, if you, bend it like* "at, no, is no right, and then, is got that funny shape", and you have to interpret this. *I mean either he's mad or he's completely doped out of his head, or there's something there. About six times out of ten there were something there.* And sometimes, it was absolutely brilliant what he produced, absolutely brilliant. Trying to drag that out of him was not easy. So we had people like that and then we had people who could interpret what he was saying to do that. And you have to be sufficiently tolerant to put up with these loonies.	Well, you need to keep pushing that, you have to say that, a checkmate that's a Friday's timesheet, and I think specifically design organization is a difficult organization to manage because you have to manage that creative tension. And the behavior people show sometimes you wouldn't believe (laughs). So then you have to draw a line, say this is acceptable the other thing is not. But if you stop all the creative process from growing you stop creativity so ... that's why you need ...that's why in advertisement agency you always have the account manager and the creative manager going together to the client and playing that two type of role. *You need that creative behavior in your organization ... and that clashes with discipline (laughs).*

• Lack of fear of not being in control • Rational, linear process vs. "let's see how it goes" • Discontinuity of thought	• Freedom to think and behave differently	• Discipline vs. Creativity • Discontinuity of thought, "jumpy" process

Embracing discontinuity and openendedness	• Rational, linear process vs. "let's see how it goes"

Freedom to Think and Behave Differently

Informant B (Nissan Design): [...] to narrow down at an earlier stage to one vision of the product. And there ...*If you have the tendency to narrow down too quickly you also limit the creativity.* The [are] various thoughts and philosophies, so this is where you really need to pay a lot of attention to what kind of balance you are going to install in this relationship.

Informant C (Philips Design): [...] I mean the ability to develop solution or ideas or concepts that are maybe not so grounded in reality, [...] one of the key differences between designers or say for example people in research is that the researchers would take an iterative, step-by-step process towards an end conclusion, whereas designers might start with a hypothesis of an end conclusion or several end solutions and work backwards and see which one is best, based on intuition or certain research, trends[...] socio-cultural research, user research, sort of different ways of working but so. Obviously one of the things in the design industry is creativity. The other thing ... and that not only relates to sort of freedom and *abstract thinking* but also in terms of creating ...

Example of Initial Coding

Initial Coding	Interview Statement
Having design skills Being entrepreneurial Making voices heard, standing up for what one believes in Taking risks willingly Accepting uncomfortable positions when the outcomes are unknown Creating plans while acknowledging uncertainty	*Interviewer:* So what sorts of behaviours do you encourage? If you employ somebody, what sort of things will you be looking for in this person? *Informant:* Looking for people who are, who have great design skills and so on...but then looking for people who could be really entrepreneurial and do things, kind of be leaders... you know...have opinions on things, not be afraid to voice their opinions, those are the couple of things we're looking for. Not all these people have great design skills, which is obviously a very important thing, but it's also about people who are willing to be risky, and not necessarily comfortable in knowing exactly what the outcome of the project is going to be. We get lots of what we call "foggy projects", where gosh, we don't even know... it's not as simple as sitting down and saying, OK here are our plans for doing this but wow, we don't know what the outcome of this would be and being OK with this sort of, this kind of foggy world...

References

Alexander, C., Ishikawa, S. and Silverstein, M. 1977. A Pattern Language: Towns, buildings, construction. New York: Oxford University Press.

Argyris, C. and Schön, D. 1978. Organizational learning: A theory of action perspective. Reading: MA: Addison-Wesley.

Becher, T. 1981. Towards a definition of disciplinary cultures. Studies in Higher Education 6/2: 109–122.

Bernstein, D. 1988. "The design mind." In P. Gorb and E. Schneider (Eds), Design talks. London: The Design Council/ London Business School, Design Management Seminars.

Bloor, G. and Dawson, P. 1994. Understanding professional culture in organizational context. Organization Studies, 15/2: 275–295.

Boland, R. J. and Collopy, F. 2004. Design matters for management. In R. J. Boland and F. Collopy (Eds), Managing as designing: 3–18. Stanford, CA:Stanford University Press.

Broja de Mozota, B. 2003. Design management: Using design to build brand value and corporate innovation. New York: Allworth Press.

Bruce, M. and Bessant, J. 2002. Design in business: Strategic innovation through design. Harlow, UK: Financial Times Prentice Hall.

Bruce, M. and Harun, R. 2001. Exploring design capability for serial innovation in SMEs'. European Design Academy Conference, Portugal, April 2001.

Buchanan, R. 1995. Rhetoric, humanism, and design: In R. Buchanan and V. Margolin (Eds.), Discovering design: Explorations in design studies: 23–66. Chicago: University of Chicago Press.

Buchanan, R. 2004. Management and design. In J. Boland Jr. and Fred Collopy (Eds.), Managing as designing: 54–63. Stanford: Stanford University Press.

Chandler Jr., A. D. 1962. Strategy and structure. Boston, MA: MIT Press.

Charmaz, K. 2003. Qualitative interviewing and grounded theory analysis. In J. A. Holstein and F. Jaber Gubrium (Eds.), Inside interviewing: New lenses, new concerns: 311–330. Thousand Oaks, CA: Sage Publications.

Cooper, R. and Press, M. 1995. Design management: Managing design. Chichester. Wiley.

Cross, N. 1999. Natural intelligence in design. Design Studies, 20/1: 25–39.

Dumas, A. and Mintzberg, H. 1989. Managing design, designing management. Design Management Journal, 1: 37–43.

Dunbar, R.L.M. and Starbuck, W. 2006. Learning to design organizations and learning from designing them. Organization Science, 17/2: 171–178.

Eisenhardt, Kathleen, M. 1989. Building theories from case study research. Academy of Management Review, 14/4: 532–550.

Friedman, K. 2002. Towards an integrative design discipline. In S. Squires and B. Byrne (Eds.), Creating Breakthrough ideas: The collaboration of anthropoligsts and designers in the product development industry: 199–214. London: Bergin & Gravey.

Galbraith, J. R. 1973. Organizational design. Reading, MA: Addison-Wesley.

Galbraith, J. R. 1995. Designing organizations: An executive briefing on strategy, structure and process. San Francisco, CA: Jossey-Bass.

Gillham, W. 2000. Case study research methods. London: Continuum.

Glaser, B. G. 1978. Theoretical sensitivity. Mill Valley, CA: Sociology Press.

Glaser, B. G. and Strauss, A. L. 1967. The discovery of grounded theory: Strategy for qualitative research. Chicago: Aldine Publishing Co.

Gorb, P. 1986. The business of design management. Design Studies, 7/2: 106–110.

Goulding, C. 2002. Grounded theory: A practical guide for management, business and market researchers. Thousand Oaks, CA: Sage Publications.

Gregory, K. 1983. Native-view paradigms: Multiple cultures and culture conflicts in organizations. Administrative Science Quarterly, 28: 359–376.

Guba, E. G. and Lincoln, Y.S. 1994. Competing paradigms in qualitative research. In N.K. Denzin and Y.S. Lincoln (Eds.), Handbook of Qualitative Research.

Hofstede, G. 2001. Culture's consequences: International differences in work-related values, 2nd ed. Thousand Oaks, CA: Sage Publications.

Johannson, U. and Svengren, L. 2002. One swallow doesn´t make a summer: About the need for critical mass of designers to make a design strategy. 11th International Forum on Design Management Research & Education, Boston, MA, 10–12 June 2002.

Kelley, T. 2001. The art of innovation. New York: Random Books.

Kotler, P. and Rath, A. G. 1984. Design: A powerful but neglected strategic tool. Journal of Business Strategy, 5/2: 16–21.

Krippendorff, K. 2006. The semantic turn: A new foundation for design. Boca Raton, FL: Taylor & Francis.

Lester, R. K., Piore, M. J. and Malek, K. M. 1998. Interpretive management: What general managers can learn from design. Harvard Businesss Review, March–April 1998.

Lojacono, G. and Zaccai, F. 2004. The evolution of the design-inspired enterprise. Sloan Management Review, 45/3: 75–79.

Martin, J. 1992. Cultures in Organizations: Three Perspectives. New York: Oxford University Press.

Martin, J., Feldman, M. S., Hatch, M. J. and Sitkin, S. 1983. The uniqueness paradox in organizational stories. Administrative Science Quarterly, 28: 438–453.

Marzano, S. 1999. Creating value by design: Thoughts and facts. London: Lund Humphries.

Meyer, C. B. 2001. A case in case study methodology. Field Methods, 13/4: 329–352.

Miles, M.B. and Huberman, M.A. 1994. Qualitative data analysis: An expanded sourcebook. Thousand Oaks, CA: Sage Publications.

Mintzberg, H. 1998. Strategy safari: A guided tour through the wilds of strategic management. New York: Financial Times Prentice Hall.

Myerson, J. 2001. Ideo: Masters of innovation. London: Laurence King.

Nadler, D.A. and Tushman, L.M. 1997. Competing by design: The power of organizational architecture. New York: Oxford University Press.

Nussbaum, B. 2004. The power of design. Business Week, 17 May: 86–94.

Olson, E. M., Cooper, R. and Slater, S.F. 1998. Design strategy and competitive advantage. Business Horizons, March–April.

Partington, D. 2000. Building grounded theories of management action. British Journal of Management, 11: 91–102.

Peters, T. 1997. The circle of innovation. London: Hodder & Stoughton.

Polanyi, M. 1966. The tacit dimension. Garden City, NY: Doubleday.

Press, M. and Cooper, R. 2003. The design experience: The role of design and designers in the twenty-first century. Aldershot, UK: Ashgate.

Ravasi, D. and Lojacono, G. 2005. Managing design and designers for strategic renewal. Long Range Planning, 38: 51–77.

Rich, H. 2004. Proving the practical power of design. Design Management Journal, 15/4: 28–34.

Romme, A. G. L. 2003. Making a difference: Organization as design. Organization Science, 14/5: 558–573.

Sacher, H. 2002. Semantics as common ground: Connecting the cultures of analysis and creation. In S. Squires and B. Byrne (Eds.), Creating breakthrough ideas: The collaboration of anthropologists and designers in the product development industry: 175–196. London: Bergin & Gravey.

Sackmann, S. 1991. Cultural knowledge in organizations: Exploring the collective mind. Newbury Park, CA: Sage Publications.

Schön, D. 1983. The reflective practitioner: How professionals think in action. New York: Basic Books.

Squires, S. and Byrne, B. (Eds.) 2002. Creating breakthrough ideas: The collaboration of anthropologists and designers in the product development industry. Westport. CT: Bergin & Garvey.

Van Aken, J. E. 2004. Management research based on the paradigm of design science: The quest for field-tested and grounded technological rules. Journal of Management Studies, 41/2: 219–246.

Van Maanen, J. and Barley, S. R. 1984. Occupational communities: Culture and control in organizations. In B.M. Staw and L.L. Cummings (Eds.), Research in organizational behavior, Vol. 6: 287–366. Greenwich, CT: JAI Press.

Walker, D. 1990. Managers and designers: Two tribes at war? In M. Oakley (Ed.), Design management: A handbook of issues and methods: 145–154. Cambridge: Blackwell.

Weick, K. E. 2004. Rethinking organizational design. In R.J. Boland and F. Collopy (Eds.), Managing as designing: 36–53. Stanford, CA: Stanford University Press.

Yoo, Y., Boland, R.J. Jr. and Lyytinen, K. 2006. From organization design to organization designing. Organization Science, 17/2: 215–229.

"IT WILL BE FOUND, IN FACT, THAT THE INGENIOUS ARE ALWAYS FANCIFUL, AND THE TRULY IMAGINATIVE NEVER OTHERWISE THAN ANALYTIC."
(EDGAR ALLAN POE)

185

Design thinking in business has been conspicuously discussed by practitioners such as Tim Brown (IDEO) and academics such as Roger Martin from the Rotman School of Management. This type of thinking, whilst unfamiliar to many organizations in new industries and in service organizations, is inherently a part of Shell's technical DNA, perhaps to such an extent that it is not specifically labeled. The following note traces a few examples of innovation and implementation from the Shell stable and seeks to explain how the thought process behind solving an ostensibly small (though complex) problem can be applied at a larger scale. Furthermore, the note describes one particular method of innovation organization that has been successful within the technology wing of Shell, and which by default encapsulates many of the ideas behind design thinking. This process is called the Hunters Network.

As a company that believes its technology brings competitive advantage, Shell encourages all sections of the innovation curve, from discovery through to deployment. For a discovery to have an impact, the inventive team needs to understand on a global level how their discovery will impact their particular problem (the production of cleaner hydrocarbons, for example), their product (novel catalysts and other hi-tech process technologies, or smart lubricants) or the target clients (new fuels for consumers, or new energy solutions for major resource holders). Since the primary industry and energy domains are complex systems, maintaining a global perspective can be very challenging.

This complexity lies both in the interactions of external players such as government, macroeconomic trends and geopolitics, and in the internal machinery of the industry.

WHEREAS THE FORMER TOPIC CAN BE ENDLESSLY DISCUSSED TO NO AVAIL, THE LATTER CAN BE BROKEN DOWN MORE EASILY.

Capital costs of development and implementation are high, the regulatory frameworks are exceptionally stringent and the many of the incremental improvements in conversion technologies nevertheless require a huge sunk cost in terms of intellectual and material resources. Furthermore, new engineering projects are inevitably "mega-projects"; in order to be competitive, they need to be well executed and the balance between the most elegant solution and the most robust can be uneasy. However, some of the great feats of innovation, such as digital signal processing in the 1950s, conversion technologies for clean-burning methane, extraction of oil from oil-sands and the development of solar cells have emerged over the last 50 years from the various oil and gas multi-nationals. The reason behind this is simple. Energy consumption per capita has grown significantly over the last half-century and will continue to grow as more people from the developing world achieve higher quality of life, yet the production of energy is a complex and technically difficult process. Since the stakes are high, some countries and companies are willing to invest heavily in the innovative eco-system that will allow both energy security and energy sustainability.

In order to maintain the global view of complex inventive steps that is necessary to maintain a competitive advantage through technology, ideas are gathered into streams, developed and in a Darwinian mode of survival, are pitted against each other using long and short term economic parameters. The challenge, as always is to ensure that higher risk but potentially higher value projects are not left on the shelf, and that ideas not relevant to the company's business strategy today are also considered. The latter is important since interesting ideas attract interesting people and many ideas at the bleeding edge fit uneasily into short term business models. Historical examples of this span supercomputers, micro-sensing and more recently, synthetic biology which may be of great significance for the bio-fuel/bio-energy domain. Furthermore any company needs to future-proof any business through a diversification of ideas: one relies on the wisdom of senior thinkers, strategists and scenario-planners to paint the overall landscape of interest.

IT IS NATURAL TO QUESTION WHY THE ENERGY DOMAIN IS INNOVATIVE BY NECESSITY. IT MIGHT BE ARGUED THAT INNOVATION IN THE INDUSTRY HAS COME IN WAVES.

Post-war, the emergence of energy-hungry societies, especially the suburban design concept of post-war America contributed to the growing sophistication in the search for energy. Signal processing, computation and novel physical methods attracted young scientists and engineers eager to explore new territory, develop new technologies and apply their entrepeneurial spirit. The chemical richness of the hydrocarbon resource resulted in the spin-out of high-technology materials—polymers—without which much of 20th century life and certainly many aesthetic movements would not have existed. The rate of innovation in the chemicals domain led to a brain-gain into that sector in the 60s and 70s but it was the energy shock of the 70s that undoubtedly led to a major flurry of activity. Many companies looked in earnest at the front of the innovation funnel to see what concepts and technologies might allow them to continue being profitable in the face of a global downturn and limited access to straightforward resources. As companies have nurtured research and development departments, much work, though peripheral to the needs of the companies themselves, has developed. The roots of First Solar, one of the top photovoltaic companies can be traced back to oil-and-gas companies.

THE DEVELOPMENT OF GAS-TO-LIQUIDS TECHNOLOGY, A FEAT WHEREBY CLEAN NATURAL GAS (WHOSE RESERVES EXCEED THAT OF OIL) CAN BE MONETIZED BY CONVERTING IT INTO LIQUID FUELS, HAS TAKEN 40 ARDUOUS YEARS OF COMMITMENT.

The conversion of the power sector piece by piece from coal fired power stations to more environmentally friendly methods, from gas-turbines to fuel cells has required innovation at every stage of the supply chain. All these processes have been groundbreaking in their entirety yet have needed incremental developments at each stage and it is critical to note the patience that true innovation requires. Presently, the orthogonal relationship between difficult hydrocarbon recovery, the critical CO_2 challenge and global warming, and growing energy demand is fostering another innovation period. Smart ideas from computation,data mining, multi-variate testing, synthetic biology and nanotechnology, sometimes initiated in the laboratories and fields of oil and gas firms years ago, then developed in academia and small companies worldwide, are coming back to address many of the problems that we currently face. The development of biodegradable plastic through a synthetic biology process that forms poly-lactic acid derives its chemistry from experiments done in the 40s and 50s; however, it is only now that other technologies in reactor design and biology have caught up to make something like this a potentially viable process. The screening of catalysts, to find the compound that allows the least wasteful and most efficient production of chemical feedstocks used to be a mixture of inspiration, perspiration and luck; now, with the optimization of micro-fluidics, computational data-mining and data storage, compound libraries are being created and ideal catalysts are being rapidly developed. As a final

What is Design Thinking?

- A methodology to address dynamic, generative and social complexity…
  - Energy security and sustainability

- Innovation driven by behavioural norms, tools and rules
  - Ingenuity of engineers & scientists to anticipate/shape norms, develop tools and co-develop rules

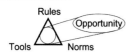

- Notions of "design", inherently a part of the innovative engineer's DNA
  -Understand the product, hold long-term view, be pragmatic

A Technologist's Approach to Design Thinking

- 100 years ago, great inventors could masterfully survey the technological and business landscapes….Wedgewood, Siemens, Brunel, Marconi
- But not always….Edison, Bell, Rockerfeller
- Currently, dynamic (D), generational (G) & social (S) complextiy and rate of change generally requires teams for discovery, landscaping & interlinking domains
- The "thinking methodology" to solve DGS scales to the problem

example, process control, the means by which complicated reactor processes are monitored and controlled depending on a stochastic (time dependent) outcomes, is being revolutionized by the growing cross-fertilization of ideas between previously disparate disciplines. For example, signal processing, once the domain of electronic and sound engineers, is entering the lexicon of chemists, chemical engineers and technical managers.

MUCH OF THIS IS DUE TO OPEN SOURCES OF INFORMATION, AND THE GROWING RESOURCE OF THE INTERNET.

How does design thinking fit into today's innovation space within the energy world? Design thinking encapsulates a range of practices which claim to be heterodox to traditional analytical approaches to business problems and include the development of ideas through stages of ideation and divergence, followed by convergence and implementation.

Some of the processes used within this context include storyboarding, workshops, the use of facilitated brainstorming sessions, Goldfire and TRIZ software, and good old-fashioned symposia. In fact, these are familiar tools within the innovation community at Shell, and in

particular the Gamechanger group, which as the name suggests, looks at potentially game-changing ideas. In the 150 years since Kingdom Brunel, the interconnectedness and complexity of the world has meant that specialization is increasingly required: no-one person can understand the whole. Although the innovation community is driven by creative engineers and scientists, there are strong links between the arena of ideas and the arena of implementation via technical manages, various strategists and scenario planning.

IN ORDER TO EFFECTIVELY USE THE INTELLECTUAL AND MATERIAL RESOURCES WITHIN THE INNOVATION DOMAIN, IT IS NECESSARY TO ENSURE THAT THE TECHNOLOGISTS' INFLUENCE IS EMBEDDED IN AN UNDERSTANDING OF DYNAMIC, GENERATIONAL AND SOCIAL COMPLEXITY.

Dynamic complexity in design thinking captures the concept that cause and effect of problems are distant in time. Generation complexity implies solutions that may unfold in an unpredictable and unfamiliar manner. Finally, societal

A Technologist's Approach to Design Thinking

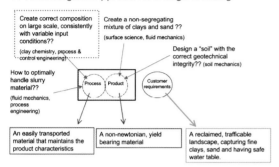

A Technologist's Approach to Design Thinking

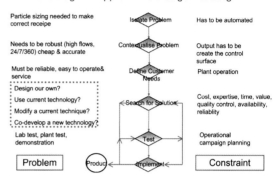

complexity captures the concept that various stakeholders will view the situation differently. To ensure that this understanding is present, there is a system of mentoring or coaching where senior, experienced strategists and technologists pair with less experienced staff. This often happens naturally and is self-organised to a large extent. In addition, the formation of various panels for technical and business challenge sessions after the initial exploratory stage has been completed is based on creating the correct blend of characters, skills and motivations.

To give an example of the variegated skillset that needs to be assembled for any task, we take an example of innovation within an environmental remediation project. In this case, the process and product are irrevocably interwined and it was hoped that developments therein would result in the desired product for the customer. But in order to understand this problem, it is clear that a large number of skillsets are needed to be brought together.

Taking one section of this puzzle, and expanding it, one can get a better picture of the design-driven thought process that lies behind the solving the problem. In this case, we expand on the creation of a material with the correct composition, consistently and at a large scale. If the thought process were to be broken down explicitly it would likely look like the middle column in the slide below.

THE TECHNICAL THINKING THEN BEGINS IN THE HIGHLIGHTED BOX: THIS CORRELATES TO THE STEP "IN THE SEARCH FOR THE SOLUTION".

An example of a potential solution in this case is using the difference in refractive index of the two components of different sizes in the mixture to measure a ratio. In reality, we took a method used in the bio/pharma industry, had meetings with a world class team of researchers at an academic institute and then took apart the tool and modified it. No-one has used it for the control purposes we were intending and thus, through this process we had created value through innovation.

In the example given above, there is technical ambiguity (do we need to know each particle's size—a particle distribution— or will a binary distribution be sufficient information for the process) and an ambiguous environment (what does "reliable" mean, is the cost structure in 3 years time going to prevent implementation, is the timeline fixed and if so how?). The thought process is no different when looking at a large scale problem. The technical solution requires constant feedback with the customer (the constraints), which sometimes results in changing some of the constraints themselves. The complexity can, again, be derived from the technical challenge or by the ambiguous environment in which the questions are posed.

Technology Futures; Identification

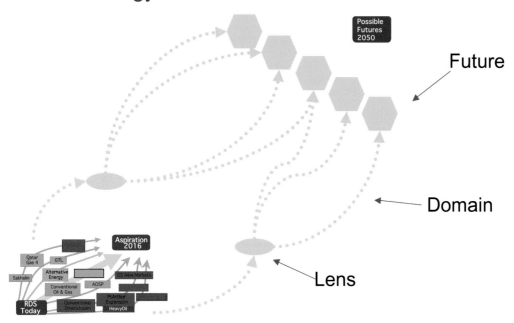

Future

Domain

Lens

WHEN LOOKING TO IDENTIFY TECHNOLOGY FUTURES, THE AMBIGUITY OF THE FUTURE POSSIBILITIES IS A REAL CHALLENGE AND OPPORTUNITY.

Choosing to focus on the correct suite of technologies, maintaining them at different levels within the innovation funnel is critical. The slide above gives a good representation of the pathway that needs to be charted to move an organization from where it is today to where it will be in 20 or 50 years time. One method to do this is to look at where a company is today and then look through lenses (technical, socio-political, competitive, socio-economic) to understand market and technical uncertainties. This then leads to domains, or areas where technology may add value to the business, and simultaneously contribute to the development of that future path. As these are dynamic processes, such diagrams and the preferred pathways therein ebb and flow with time, as certain technologies encounter the perfect storm (and collapse) whilst others encounter the virtuous circle (and thrive).

Had this exercise to search for technology futures been done 10 years previously, we may have come out with many conclusions including the following. *Due to various socio-economic and geopolitical factors (lenses), monetizing*

difficult-to-access hydrocarbons in politically friendly countries becomes a critical pathway.

Difficult hydrocarbons may imply high levels of impurity, higher processing energy requirements and novel extraction techniques. These hypotheses, based on limited experiences in the domain, lead to exploratory domains where real technical actions can be taken. In the first of these domains, sulphur markets and opportunities, the assumption is that much of the impurity is sulphur and if this can be isolated and then sold, a waste product becomes a valuable byproduct.

THE CHALLENGE IS THEN HOW CAN THIS BE ACHIEVED, AND INDEED, IF IT IS WORTHWHILE.

The value of any innovative activity needs to be measured differently to typical cost-profit methodologies. Typical discounted cash flow measures and net-present value concepts will typically push innovations (especially those that provide licenses to operate rather than sellable product) to the end of a project lifetime. Unfortunately, innovation cycles are long when the product is complex. Therefore other considerations are taken when approximating value.
The generation of intellectual and intangible resources can be critical to the company and the benefit of such

Technology Futures; an Example

An example of a future, had this exercise been carried out 10 years ago

A future: Monetizing difficult hydrocarbons in politically friendly/benign countries

The market and technical uncertainties scrutinized under lenses
-Cap and trade mechanisms
-Cost/price of ethylene monomer vs polyethylene,
-Price of crude oil
-In-situ technologies
-Energy policy assessment

A domain : a technical topic for this future wherein real actions could be taken

-Sulphur market and opportunities
-Improvements in refining catalysts
-CO_2 mitigation technologies
-In-situ upgrading
-Solids handling

Technology Futures; Measures of value

A future: Monetizing difficult hydrocarbons in politically friendly/benign countries

Type of Resource:
-Intellectual
-Economic
-Tangible
-Intangible

Measured by considerations of :
-Adaptability
-Approximation
-Measurability
-Risk

a body of experience and knowledge can yield rewards at the most unexpected places. Measurements around the four parameters of adaptability, approximation of the solution, and risk and measurement parameters allow for movements in the external business and technical environments.

THIS GIVES A SENSE OF THE ROBUSTNESS OF THE INNOVATION OVER A FUTURE TIME PERIOD.

Once some domains have been identified, one way to populate an innovation funnel for a domain is to ask a cluster of technologists to act as scouts, bring in ideas from their departments and from the external world, create simple experimental programmes and then pitch the idea to "angel" investors within the company. The process has been sponsored by the Gamechanger group and has been called the Hunters network. In essence it is an organized network designed to instigate and investigate non-standard ideas and bring them to sufficient maturation for a business to take over. A schematic showing the way it has operated is shown below.
Once an idea has been generated and preliminarily tested, it reaches a pre-panel where senior technologists/managers challenge the idea.
Should it pass, it reaches the panel of "angel" investors,

drawn from various business units that might be interested in the project. Should it pass this panel, some funding is allocated to develop the project further.

IF THE WORK IS SUFFICIENTLY ATTRACTIVE TO THE BUSINESS UPON THE REPORT-OUT, THEN THE PROJECT MOVES ALONG THE FUNNEL AND IS TAKEN INTO THE BUSINESS UNIT ITSELF FOR SUBSEQUENT DEVELOPMENT.

The major questions that the Hunters network poses to itself are in the following slide.
They ensure that the idea is tethered to some sort of business reality and company strategy. At the same time, they ensure that correct questions around resource allocation have been addressed. The Hunters network therefore acts as a useful pathway to populate the innovation funnel, allowing gamechanging ideas which are potentially high impact if successful to be tested with low risk. A number of very interesting ideas and projects have emerged from this network including work on concentrated solar power, unconventional process engineering and photochemistry.

Gamechanger; The Hunter's Process

•Hunters-an Input mechanism for Gamechanger funded ideas

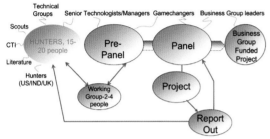

Gamechanger; The Hunter's Process

What is the value of the opportunity that this idea represents (revenue stream, order of magnitude)?

Is the idea consistent with strategy?

Why will the Business not fund the idea—why does it need seed funding?

Who would fund the idea further if the initial GameChanger seed money leads to successful results?
What is needed to test the idea? Are the resources required available, inside or outside the company? Can GameChanger help to find resources?

What are the key unknowns that should be tackled before doing an experimental program (e.g. a short economic evaluation, literature review)?

How much money do you need to test the idea?

ONE EXAMPLE THAT FOCUSED ON UNCONVENTIONAL PROCESS ENGINEERING WAS THE CONVERSION OF WASTE PLASTIC TO FUEL.

Plastic is an essential part of modern life. Without plastic packaging, it has been estimated that the tonnage of alternative packaging materials would increase by a factor of four, emissions of greenhouse gases by a factor of 1.9, costs by a factor of 1.9, energy use by a factor of 1.5, and waste by a factor of 1.6 in volume. Traditionally, plastics at the end of their normal useful life are regarded as a waste. Its disposal, owing to its lack of biodegradability, causes a major concern to the society. As the entire commodity plastics are made from the non-renewable petroleum feedstock, its consumption and later, the disposal leads to the loss of resources.The initial proposal was philosophical in nature: Shell supplies the chemical building blocks for plastic manufacture so is there a business case for cradle-to-cradle design in this instance. There was personal buy-in since waste polyethylene, in the shape of cheap and thin plastic bags litter Indian metropoles, and one of the originators of the idea was based in Bangalore. The potential business case centred around the idea of converting a cheap feedstock into a valuable product whilst simultaneously enhancing the company's reputation,

especially in India. The technical discussion centred around gasification projects at power stations in the Netherlands in comparison with known technologies of plastic conversion. The initial proposal was shaped with detailed calculations around supply chain and mass/energy (exergy) flows. Further work showed several interesting and non-intuitive findings and allowed the businesses to make a reasoned judgement on how to proceed with allocating resources to this project.

THE WHOLE PROCESS, WHILST RELATIVELY INEXPENSIVE AND RELIANT ON THE ENTHUSIASM OF THE PROPONENTS, CREATED REAL, TANGIBLE INTELLECTUAL RESOURCES.

There are many other areas of work within the primary and energy industries where innovation and design thinking are occurring without being identified explicitly. It can be said that engineers and scientists in the innovation domain work within a complex, and often ambiguous environment. At Shell, several structures exist to aid relevant idea generation. Non-traditional collaborations are made explicit through the use of scouting networks such as the Hunters and porous interfaces exist through strong extra-mural engagement with external institutes and professionals.

The Hunter's Process; Example 1

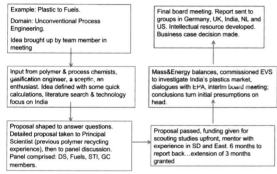

Example: Plastic to Fuels.

Domain: Unconventional Process Engineering.

Idea brought up by team member in meeting

↓

Input from polymer & process chemists, gasification engineer, a sceptic, an enthusiast. Idea defined with some quick calculations, literature search & technology focus on India

↓

Proposal shaped to answer questions. Detailed proposal taken to Principal Scientist (previous polymer recycling experience), then to panel discussion. Panel comprised: DS, Fuels, STI, GC members.

→

Proposal passed, funding given for scouting studies upfront, mentor with experience in SD and East. 6 months to report back…extension of 3 months granted

↑

Mass&Energy balances, commissioned EVS to investigate India's plastics market, dialogues with EPA, interim board meeting; conclusions turn initial presumptions on head.

↑

Final board meeting. Report sent to groups in Germany, UK, India, NL and US. Intellectual resource developed. Business case decision made.

193

In order to continue developing real energy solutions for the future, the open, collaborative and inquisitive mindset needs to nurtured through effective management and allocation of resources. Despite the current economic downturn, the future for innovation and technology looks bright. As a practitioner of design thinking, and participants in the energy innovation cycle, I believe that some of ideas developed in this environment will reach fruition and help solve some of the critical issues facing humanity today.

To Kathy, with Love.

In recent years, design thinking increasingly gained the attention of academic scholars (Boland Jr. and Collopy, 2004b) as well as of business practitioners (Brown, 2008). Based on these readings I understand design thinking as a special way of problem solving which creates more value by better satisfying human needs in the long run than other ways of problem solving might do.

IN THIS REGARD, DESIGN THINKING CAN HELP TO CREATE BETTER FUTURES AND IS THEREFORE WORTH BEING FURTHER DISCUSSED AND STUDIED.

In this essay I will first critically reflect on the current conceptualization of design thinking and suggest an alternative viewpoint. Second, I will critically reflect on the empirical focus on specific professionals such as architects or graphic designers. Based on this reflection I suggest that design thinking should additionally be studied within management practices and that one should be aware of the reasons why certain practitioners such as architects or graphic designers are often regarded to be more experienced in design thinking than other professionals.

195

Towards a new Conceptualization of Design Thinking
Tim Brown (2008), CEO and President of IDEO, an innovation
and design firm with headquarters in California, defines
design thinking in a recent article as "a discipline that uses
the designer's sensibility and methods to match people's
needs with what is technologically feasible and what a
viable business strategy can convert into customer value
and market opportunity" (p. 86). Boland and Collopy (2004a:
6) regard design thinking as a process of finding the best
answer possible, given the skills, time, and resources and
taking for granted that it will require the invention of new
alternatives. They contrast design thinking to analytical
thinking which implies that there is a good set of options
already available and that the core of the human ability lies
in choosing the best option.

Based on the existing literature, design thinking can be
regarded as a certain way of problem solving which creates
more value by better satisfying human needs in the long
run. Today's management practices often seem to consist
of copying and slightly improving the established and
well known and only a few companies truly differentiate
themselves within most of the markets and industries. Their
way of problem solving might create economic value but not
create enough of the other values that satisfy human needs
as well: e.g. beauty, easy handling, or sustainability. Let
us consider Apple computers which is a good example to
exemplify design thinking and which are very successful in
the computer and entertainment industry. Why are they this
successful? They differentiate themselves through products
and communication. Their products show very simple and
appealing designs, they are easy to handle, they are small
and they are lightweight. Until Apple's iPod and MacBook
were created, mp3-players and notebooks were ugly, heavy
and very difficult to navigate. Interestingly enough, no
competitor really managed until now to imitate the success
factors of Apple even though these factors appear very
clear and simple from the outside perspective. Why are the
competitors not able to copy this success? Apple seems to
be better at problem solving and creating value that better
satisfies human needs in the long run, than its competitors
are. Regarding the value creation, Apple seems to be a good
example of an organization practicing design thinking.
The definitions of Brown (2008) and Boland and Collopy

(2004a: 6) contain such a way of problem solving which creates more value. However, these conceptualizations do not describe how the value is created in the making but that the value has already been created when we are aware of this value post-hoc. Brown's definition promotes the idea that design thinking distinguishes itself from other ways of thinking through integrating usually separated practices of matching people's needs, of achieving technological feasibility and of converting ideas into customer value and market opportunities.

THE MAIN ASPECT OF THE DEFINITION IS REPRESENTED BY THE ABILITY OF INTEGRATING DIFFERENT DEMANDS WHICH ARE DIFFICULT TO ALIGN, BUT IF ACHIEVED CREATE NEW VALUE EXACTLY THROUGH THE INTEGRATION ITSELF.

According to Brown, design thinkers should know better than others what the people's needs are and they are better able to transform these needs into technologically feasible products which can then be exploited as a promising market opportunity. When looking back to well-known success stories, such a definition seems adequate. Though, the conceptualization does not tell how the value was created without being totally aware of what the value consists of and if it will be successful. I assume that when the iPod was created, Apple was only aware of very simple customer needs such as for example that the handling of an mp3-player should not be complicated and that an mp3-player should show an appealing design. The core value Apple created with the iPod was the idea to navigate a very simple user interface by just one button and a wheel and that this idea has enabled the creation of a very minimalistic and thus appealing design. The combination of these ideas builds one of the main success-factors of the iPod. Of course, Apple attempted or at least hoped the iPod to become such an economic success as we are aware of today. However, Apple could not have known that people want a wheel, a button and a very simple user interface ex-ante. This means that Brown's definition of design thinking is true post-hoc but does not tell exactly what design thinking is in

the making when we do not know what the people's needs are, if new ideas are technologically feasible and if it will become a success. On the other hand, Boland and Collopy (2004a: 6) define design thinking by explicitly distinguishing it from analytical thinking, which is assumed to be the opposite of design thinking. The main aspect of their idea is the ability of creating new alternatives in order to invent and deliver new products, processes and services which serve human needs (p. 7). While this conceptualization does refer to the value creation in the making it does not tell how these alternatives are being invented and how the successful alternative has been chosen and commercially exploited.

In my opinion, a new conceptualization of design thinking should include the way *how* people's needs, technological feasibility and market success can be matched at a time when we do not know enough about the needs, the feasibility and the market success. And a new conceptualization should include the way *how* new alternatives are created, chosen and commercially exploited. To do this, my suggestion is to regard design thinking as a special way of problem solving. It is important to be aware that the problem can be positively connoted (e.g. a promising customer need) as well as negatively connoted (e.g. a successful product of a competitor). Furthermore, neither the problem nor the solution is clearly defined until we know post-hoc what the problem was and which solution is successful. In this sense, design thinking involves working intensively on the problem and solution spaces (see figure 1):

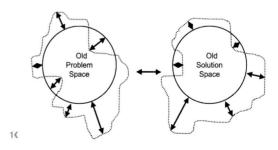

1<

Design thinking regarded as working on and matching problem and solution spaces (source: author)

In addition to an extensive and continuous opening up and closing of problem and solutions spaces, design thinking involves as well a continuous matching and even blurring of these spaces. It may sometimes be difficult to distinguish between problem and solution in reality. However, this conceptual distinction stresses that design thinking involves working on the problem and the solution at the same time and that matching the two is crucial in design thinking. Referring once more to the iPod example, the wheel, the single button, the simple user interface and the minimalistic design are the outcome of a design thinking process and may be regarded post-hoc as a being part of a redefined problem space as well as of a redefined solution space. However, during the designing process the boundaries of the problem space as well as of the solution space must have been changed continuously until they matched in a promising way. One could argue that every problem-solving-process involves changing and matching problem as well as solution spaces. Though, my thesis is that the process of design thinking works differently and more extensily with the problem and solution spaces than is usually done.

WHILE THIS CONCEPTUALIZATION OF DESIGN THINKING IS THEORETICAL, EMPIRICAL RESEARCH SHOULD CHALLENGE THIS IDEA AND REVEAL FURTHER INSIGHTS ON HOW SUCH BOUNDARY WORK MAY OCCUR IN PRACTICE.

Empirical Focus for Further Studies on Design Thinking

In order to further study design thinking, empirical research needs to be conducted that describes and possibly explains design thinking in more detail. One way of further studying this phenomenon is to analyze organizations and practitioners which seem to conduct design thinking and to compare them to other organizations and practitioners. Often, some specific professionals such as architects, graphic designers or engineers are thought to be experienced practitioners of design thinking (Boland

Jr. and Collopy, 2004b: xi). Boland and Collopy (2004a) refer for example to the process of designing a new university building by reflecting on the way how the architect Frank O. Gehry interacted with the users and ultimately created the university building. The authors experienced this problem-solving-process as to be quite different from their own processes and the ones of the managers they observed. In the following, I will critically reflect on the empirical focus on the practices of specific professionals such as architects or graphic designers in comparison to the practices of other professionals and especially managers.

For some authors a basic assumption behind the idea of design thinking is that the traditional management and the business world lacks this specific way of problem solving whereas some professionals such as architects, graphic designers or engineers are regarded to be more experienced practitioners of design thinking (Boland Jr. and Collopy, 2004b: xi). I agree that the problem-solving-processes of such professionals may differ to a certain degree from other problem-solving-processes and that studying their way of problem-solving can help us better understand design thinking. However, I agree as well with other authors (Orlikowski, 2004) that comparing design thinking to managing needs to be done cautiously and that we should not succumb to the temptation to romanticize the problem-solving-processes of specific professionals such as architects or graphic designers. My thesis is that design thinking can be observed not only in the practice of such specific professionals but also in the practice of every other professional. Especially when trying to learn how design thinking occurs in management we should try to further study design thinking within management practices itself and be aware of the reasons why specific professionals, such as architects, are regarded to be more experienced practitioners of design thinking, to what degree their way of problem-solving really differs and why these differences can be observed.

Are managers and professionals of a computer manufacturer less design thinkers than for example architects? Not necessarily. When we conceptualize design thinking as a certain way of problem solving which creates more value by better satisfying human needs and which involves extensive working on and matching of problem and solution spaces, every organization and every individual can potentially do so. Let us consider again the example of Apple computers. In my opinion they are practitioners of design thinking as they created the iPod which better satisfies human needs. The iPod provides a better handling and shows a more appealing design than the other mp3-players did until the introduction of the iPod. Therefore, it is not only important to study design thinking outside of management practices and to transfer the learning into the management practices but to additionally look for and analyze design thinking that already occurs within management practices. Moreover, insights from design thinking within management practices may be easier to be transferred to management practices whereas insights from the outside of management practices may be more innovative and more surprising from the point of view of managing.

Why are certain professionals such as architects or graphic designers still regarded to be more experienced practitioners of design thinking than other professionals? Three main reasons can be identified:

1. The reproduction of previous output is more difficult for certain professionals (negative stimulation to innovate)

Architects or graphic designers cannot easily reproduce their previous outputs. An architect for example will never create the same building twice even though he might be famous for his specific style of architecture and therefore recognizable. But the building itself is never the same. The architect is obliged to create a new building. It stands on a different ground, in a different region and it is built for different inhabitants with different needs and purposes. Of course, there are certain parts of a building that have been successful previously and will be reused in a new project. Though, every new project starts on a white paper and is created more or less from scratch. Management, on the other hand, can reproduce previous outputs more easily. The same products and services may be economically successful for a long period of time and are only refined on a small scale without creating considerably more

value and without the need to extensively work on the boundaries of the problem and solution spaces.

2. The innovativeness is a prerequisite for the success of certain professionals (positive stimulation to innovate)

Some professionals such as architects or graphic designers are more successful the more creative and different their ideas are, while still meeting the requirements and demands of their clients. A graphic designer needs to create a logo that differentiates itself from other logos while communicating the values of the product or the company it represents. At the same time the logo needs to meet the existing or future taste of the customers. A logo that is overlooked by the target customers or that is mistaken for the logo of another company will not be successful. This means, that the output of a graphic designer needs to be different and innovative in order to be successful. Furthermore, the awareness and image within the respective professional community and of the potential clients of an architect or a graphic designer depends as well on how creative and new the output is. An architect becomes famous because of outstanding and innovative projects that are recognized as such by his peers and by potential clients. Management, on the other hand, may be successful without being creative or without creating innovative products or services. Innovativeness is not per se a quality and success factor of management. Though, post-hoc everybody is aware if an organization missed an important trend and was overtaken by its competitors. Microsoft did not see the value and could not profit well enough from the emerging internet in the late 1990. Now we are aware that Microsoft should have invested more into the internet idea in the late 1990. On the other hand, managers that are too innovative and act too riskily may be unsuccessful and destroy value as well.

3. The innovativeness of certain professionals can be more easily observed (nature and value of artifacts)

Architects or graphic designers create outputs in the form of artifacts which are easy to be observed by others and which represent directly the value created by these professionals. A building or a logo represents the value that is created (e.g. living facilities, esthetics, recognizability). Furthermore, a building or a logo can be communicated and multiplied to demonstrate its value. On the other hand, management does not produce outputs directly in the form of artifacts. Of course, artifacts such as management letters, excel sheets or power point presentations are created as well. However, the end product such as, for example, the iPod of Apple has not been created by the management directly. Correspondingly, the value that is created by the management is not as easily recognized and communicated as it is for architects or graphic designers.

THE SAME HOLDS AS WELL FOR ALL SERVICES WHICH ARE NOT TANGIBLE AND REPRESENTABLE BY ARTIFACTS.

As the reflections above show, it is worth looking for and analyzing design thinking in management practices in addition to particular professionals such as architects, graphic designers or engineers. Furthermore, if studying and analyzing the practices of such specific professionals and, if comparing them to management we should be aware that they are stimulated to be innovative, and that their value creation, which stems from design thinking activities, is equal to the output of their work and may be observed as artifacts which represent the value created. On the other hand, innovativeness is not per se a quality and success factor of management and the value creation of design thinking within management practices is more difficult to be observed.

Conclusion

The critical reflection of the current definitions and conceptualizations of design thinking shows that design thinking can be regarded as a certain way of problem solving which creates more value by better satisfying human needs in the long run than other ways of problem solving might do. However, the value creation is observed post-hoc and missing is for example *how* people's needs, technological feasibility and market success can be matched at a time when we do not know enough about the needs, the feasibility and the market success and *how* new alternatives are created, chosen and commercially

exploited. A new conceptualization should therefore include the specific practice of design thinking in the making. A suggestion for such a conceptualization might be to look at design thinking as a specific way of extensively working on and matching problem and solution spaces.

The critical reflection of the usual empirical focus on specific professionals such as architects or graphic designers reveals that, when trying to transfer insights to management practices, it is worth additionally studying design thinking within the management practices themselves. In my opinion, certain management professionals and organizations such as Apple practice a way of design thinking which can be observed and analyzed. Furthermore, when studying and analyzing specific practitioners such as architects or graphic designers and when comparing them to management, one should be aware that they are stimulated to be innovative and that their value creation, which stems from design thinking activities, is equal to the output of their work and may be observed as artifacts which represent the value created. On the contrary, innovativeness is not per se a quality and success factor of management and the value creation of design thinking within management practices is more difficult to be observed. Being aware of such basic conditions helps to further investigate on design thinking empirically. While the conceptualization of design thinking suggested in this essay is theoretical, empirical research should challenge this idea and reveal further insights on how such extensive working on and matching problem and solution spaces may occur in practice.

References

Boland Jr., R. J., and Collopy, F. 2004a. Design matters for management. In F. Collopy and R. J. Boland Jr. (Eds.), Managing as designing: 3–18. Stanford: Stanford Business Books.

Boland Jr., R. J., and Collopy, F. (Eds.). 2004b. Managing as designing. Stanford: Stanford Business Books.

Brown, T. 2008. Design thinking. Harvard Business Review, 84–92.

Orlikowski, W. J. 2004. Managing and designing: Attending to Reflexiveness and Enactment. In F. Collopy and R. J. Boland Jr. (Eds.), Managing as designing: 90–95. Stanford: Stanford Business Books.

CASES ON DESIGN METHODOLOGY: SUSTAINABILITY ‹

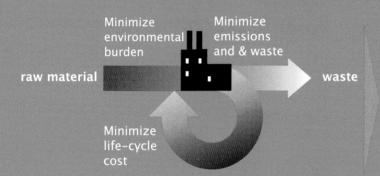

Minimize environmental burden

Minimize emissions and & waste

raw material

waste

Minimize life-cycle cost

Environment:
(Possible) Efficiency factor is far below factor necessary to **not** stress the earth's natural system beyond recovery.

Business:
Leads to antagonism towards long–term economic growth

❮ Linear industrial production system (concept of effectivity)

The impact of environmental issues on firm strategies has led to a variety of academic and professional perspectives. For the most part, these views suggest a model of industrial production exhibiting a linear sequence of extraction, production, and disposition, which, by nature, leads to negative consequences for the environment. This negative impact or ecological footprint is then to be reduced by mere reactive responses such as pollution control through end-of-pipe solutions or proactive initiatives towards pollution prevention through resource reduction and process innovation.

IN VIEW OF CURRENT GLOBAL GROWTH RATES OF INDUSTRIAL PRODUCTION AND RESOURCE CONSUMPTION, HOWEVER, THESE STRATEGIES ENTAIL AN ANTAGONISM TOWARDS LONG-TERM ECONOMIC GROWTH. THESE STRATEGIES ARE NOT COMPREHENSIVE ENOUGH TO AVOID THE RISK OF FURTHER IRREVERSIBLE DAMAGE TO THE EARTH'S ECOLOGICAL SYSTEM.

For instance, current possibilities to minimize processes of dematerialization, of extracting raw material from the earth's crust, are well below a factor that does not stress the earth's natural system beyond recovery. Across all industries, less than 10% of everything extracted from the earth becomes usable product. The rest becomes waste from production. Moreover, after use, discarded products produce still more waste. Recycling hardly resolves the problem of waste since products' materials are usually mixed and contaminated with others, which thereby leads to a process of down-cycling in which materials lose value as they circulate through subsequent industrial cycles. Likewise, over the past half century, human beings have multiplied their own population, their physical possessions, and the material and energy flows they utilize by factors of 2, 4 and 10 respectively. Therefore, today's resource productivity should have already improved well beyond a factor of 10 to avoid stressing the earth's natural system beyond recovery. But current efficiency gains are well below that. Take the following example: On a global level, the amount of energy used in metallurgical aluminum production per ton of product dropped by 10% in the period between 1991 and 2000. During the same period, however, total global production of metallurgical aluminum increased by over 40%. The few available studies on efficiency gains

raw material   no waste

Biological metabolism   technical metabolism

Environment: Eliminating the very concept of waste

Business: Key resources/ capabilities sustain competitive advantage. Antagonism towards long–term– growth economic growth dissolved

‹ Cycling industrial production system (concept of effectivity)

from manufacturing with respect to the environment suggest reductions of resource consumption and waste generation up to a maximal factor of 3. The OECD has projected that member countries' energy efficiency per unit of GDP will increase only by a factor of 1.5 to 2.1 over the next 30 years.

Recent findings in design and engineering suggest strategies towards eco-effectiveness encompassing a positive link between industrial production, the ecological system, and long-term economic growth.

ECO-EFFECTIVENESS, AS OPPOSED TO RESOURCE AND WASTE REDUCTION OR "ECO-EFFICIENCY," IS A DESIGN CONCEPT THAT IS INSPIRED BY UNDERSTANDING HOW NATURAL SYSTEMS WORK.

In natural systems, there is no waste as they follow cycles of production, recycling, and regeneration. All byproducts of one process become nutrients for another. Therefore, whereas eco-efficiency seeks to reduce the possible negative impact of the linear industrial model on the environment by minimizing waste emissions and resource use, eco-effectiveness suggests a cycling model that focuses on the development of products and industrial systems that maintain or enhance the quality and productivity of materials through subsequent life cycles.

This section of the book shows how design is capable of rendering new models of sustainability.

Fred Dust and Ilya Prokopoff start this section by directing our attention to the potential of design to create (eco-) systems at scale. That is to say, in too many cases, products and services are conceived to impact massive change, yet the offerings lack an awareness of their overall systems. Systems at scale comprise a series of design methods for directing behavioral change on a large scale by inspiring people to embrace a system as a shareholder.

Alejandro Gutierrez introduces six ideas for sustainability at work in the world-famous design and consultancy company Arup. Arup's methodology consists of challenging conventional wisdom by proposing holistic thinking that takes into account the life cycle of products or projects on the premises of resource flows.

John Thackara suggests re-conceiving design as a regenerative activity that necessarily operates in ways that are sensitive to context, to relationships and to consequences. We should cease imagining the built world as a landscape of frozen objects, but as a complex of interacting ecologies: energy, water, mobility and food.

Michael Braungart and William McDonough, both pioneers of the cradle-to-cradle design concept, along with their collaborating partners Albin Källin and Andrew Bollinger, conclude this section by presenting a design and production concept that is an alternative to the linear industrial model of zero emission and eco-efficiency. Their concepts of eco-effectiveness focus on the development of products and industrial systems that maintain or enhance the quality and productivity of materials through subsequent life cycles and address the major shortcomings of eco-efficiency approaches.

Wander into Mission Pie, a corner café in San Francisco best known for its namesake baked goods, and the place looks familiar enough. The 10 or so wooden tables, all in close proximity, are filled with pie-eating, warm-beverage-sipping customers. Some people chat, while others read leftover newspapers or peck out e-mail messages from their laptops. Swap the pie for bagels, and you could be in another San Francisco café.

BUT STICK AROUND AWHILE, AND THE PECULIARITIES OF MISSION PIE BECOME APPARENT.

This article originally appeared in Rotman Magazine published by the University of Toronto's Rotman School of Management

First off, roughly half of Mission Pie's 14-person staff is young—really young. But they're not the usual grad-school Lit majors or aspiring musicians working in so many of the city's eateries. They're either current or former students from Mission High, a nearby public high school with 68 per cent of the kids eligible to receive free and reduced-cost lunches. San Francisco native *Karen Heisler*, Mission Pie's owner, is largely paying the kids to understand where their food comes from and its impact on their bodies, their neighborhood and the world at large.

There's a surprisingly complex system behind a slice of Mission Pie's plum frangipane or mixed-berry tart. Mission Pie is part of a larger system: *Pie Ranch* is a 27-acre parcel about 90 minutes from the café and well positioned above the historic Steele Ranch. Named for its shape when viewed from atop a nearby ridge, it operates as an educational non-profit with the goal of inspiring urban youth to transform their relationships to food, and to work with their communities in building healthier local food systems. Not only does Pie Ranch supply the café with berries, pumpkins and apples, it welcomes the café's Mission High staff to work the land, contemplate the crops and sample the fresh food.

As both Mission Pie and Pie Ranch have found, the simple task of showing people where their food comes from and pointing to the impact of industrialized farming touches off all sorts of big system challenges, from obesity and education to sustainability and personal food-related attitudes and behaviors.

TO DESIGN COMPELLING, EFFECTIVE SOLUTIONS FOR CHALLENGES OF ALL SIZES, AN ORGANIZATION MUST CONSIDER THE OVERARCHING SYSTEM IT HOOKS INTO.

Heisler is a firm believer in the necessity of the human element—the community as a manifestation of the system. "Lose the human aspect," she says, "and the system falls apart."

In our work, we see system disconnects around us all the time. As networks grow and mutate, designers are forced to tackle issues of scale, legacy and influence. This reminds us that life is complex, and as designers, business people and other creative thinkers, we must resist both the seduction of simplicity and the safety of Byzantine networks that allow good ideas to fade and humans to be lost or forgotten. When tackling major challenges, we think about "systems at scale', which involves two distinct elements: designing systems that work and influencing people's thinking at mass scale. The best design solutions do both.

Balancing the Ecosystem

EVERY ECOSYSTEM IS COMPRISED OF BOTH MICRO AND MACRO ELEMENTS, AND WHEN ANY ELEMENT GETS OUT OF WHACK, THE REST OF THE SYSTEM SUFFERS.

In too many cases, products and services are conceived to impact massive change, yet the offerings lack an awareness of their overall systems.

Consider, for instance, the Segway. The two-wheeled transporter didn't catch on for a lot of reasons, from cost and practicality to a mountain-high learning curve for use. Still, an overarching issue was that it wasn't intentionally designed to be a part of a larger-scale system; rather, it was an individual product at odds with a larger ecosystem. The Segway clashed with local road and sidewalk regulations and has yet to be approved by the Food and *Drug Administration* as a medical device, which would allow for expanded use in public spaces.

Worse still, it didn't perform on the human scale—when it functioned, the rider still looked and often felt silly. How might creative thinkers at Segway have considered the broader range of real-world. When attempting to solve "wicked" problems, creative thinkers must design systems that influence people's behaviour on a mass scale. Design challenges that could make or break the relevance of their new technology?

At the other end of the spectrum, there are examples of efforts that influence people's thinking, but are not complemented by the systems needed to make them succeed at a large scale. *Al Gore's "An Inconvenient Truth"* is an interesting example. The documentary focused on educating people through a PowerPoint presentation about global warming. When Gore's road show took off in a way few expected—ultimately becoming the fourth-highest-grossing documentary film to date in the U.S.—the effort struggled to move from knowledge to action.

THE TASK AT HAND—LESSENING THE IMPACT OF GLOBAL WARMING—SEEMED, TO MANY VIEWERS, HOPELESS.

When the final credits rolled in Gore's slideshow, viewers were given a long list of small changes to make in their lives to offset global warming. For some, these suggestions felt too individually based and incremental, missing out on a proposal for a system-level solution as a complement. Gore and his team are now working to address the system at scale by bringing in more stake-holders from the governmental and business sectors. Problem-solving for big systems often leads designers to ask tough questions: how can an organization turn its workers, partners and customers into believers, people who buy into the current system, yet continue to help grow it? How can an organization avoid making only incremental changes or giving in to the temptation of defining a problem as "unsolvable" or "inevitable"? How can we make changes that impact multiple organizations and ultimately solve really big problems? The following examples—hard-earned success stories—show the potential for what balanced ecosystems can achieve through human-centered design, sticky systems, and reciprocity.

Growing Influential Networks

Following are three approaches that specifically deal with the idea of humanizing big problems to influence people to change and grow influential networks.

1. Human-Centered Systems: Design for People, Not the System
The notion of designing human values into big systems

isn't new. How-to business books the world over talk about building and maintaining that human connection. But often, the advice seems hollow, like a poster in the employee break room reminding everyone to smile at the customer. The point isn't to simply humanize a system, but to embed specific human elements within it.

One of our favorite success stories comes from an unlikely place: Bogotá, Columbia, a place typically known for corruption, violence and general indifference to chaos.

In 1995, after 18 years in academia, *Antanas Mockus* was elected mayor of Bogotá, a position he held intermittently between forays into presidential politics until 2004. While mayor and in his subsequent work, Mockus showed a knack for human-centered design by putting himself directly into the mix.

For him, this entailed literally bumping shoulders with the city's inhabitants and personally reaching out to them. When Bogotá's water was in short supply, Mockus had himself filmed showering for local TV broadcasts, during which he turned off the water as he soaped. The goal? Get city dwellers to curtail their showers to less than 20 minutes. Show them, as Mockus explained, "that even in a very private space, your behavior can be linked to a citizen's duty. You cooperate because of the fun of doing it." Within two months, people were using 14 per cent less water.

Humor as a human element can certainly be used as a generalized way of creating robust systems. But Mockus showed real genius in systems design when he incorporated more specific cultural insight into his approach to changing human behavior. In 1998, he hired 420 mimes to help calm traffic by standing at major intersections and poking fun at scofflaw drivers. In doing so, Mockus used a deep insight in the Columbian nature: the citizens of Bogotá were far more uncomfortable with being mocked than they were with being fined. Faced with public humiliation, albeit humoros, they opted to change their behavior. Within the year, traffic fatalities dropped from 1,300 to about 600 in the city.

"Mimes defeated pessimism," explained Mockus, adding, "Feel confidence in unexpected solutions."

Mockus' antics are more than one-trick wonders. They reveal a deep understanding of his constituents and a confidence to use humour, reality, and cultural insight to aid in big system change. Too often, solutions for big problems are subdivided into component parts.

When designing systems at scale, we must consider the whole ecosystem that needs to be engaged and more viral but profound behaviorial change. In short, he understands what it takes to design for impact at scale. Mockus shows the value of looking past what a system should simply accomplish to ask, What should the system feel like? In doing so, he brought the human into the mix in a way that had significant impact on the broader system.

Alas, Mockus' political career hasn't been a complete success: he has failed to win presidential campaigns twice, and it's fair to wonder how conscious he was of the system at the start of his city-turn-around campaign. Still, Mockus is clearly on to something, with his ability to build both a directed and an organic system and identify insights that can lead to behaviorial change. Enough so that the John F. Kennedy School of Government at Harvard brought him in as a visiting fellow at its Institute of Politics.

Professor *Jane Mansbridge* had him talk to her class "Democracy, from Theory to Practice." "He focused," she explained in the Harvard University Gazette in 2007, "on changing hearts and minds—not through preaching but through artistically-creative strategies that employed the power of individual and community disapproval." She added that Mockus "made it clear that the most effective campaigns combine material incentives with normative change and participatory stakeholding."

There is brilliance in this approach. As we design our way out of difficult problems, we need to harness influences that can become viral and, eventually, create ever-expanding loyalty and adherence that becomes organically self-sustaining and able to reach a broad range of stakeholders in a system. The citizens of Bogotá may have laughed when Mockus spoke while wearing yellow Spandex tights and a red cape, dressed as "Supercitizen", but they listened. More importantly, many changed their behavior.

2. Sticky Systems: Design for Scale

Solutions—not only people—can be trapped inside silos. Too often, solutions for big problems are subdivided into component parts: Let's make a system that solves this, or Let's get people to change their beliefs, so they do this. This approach rarely leads to robust solutions, and it can be counterintuitive, making people feel disempowered.

WHEN DESIGNING SYSTEMS AT SCALE, WE MUST CONSIDER THE WHOLE ECOSYSTEM THAT NEEDS TO BE ENGAGED. WITH MULTIPLE NETWORKS WITHIN AN ECOSYSTEM, SHAREHOLDERS NEED TO UNDERSTAND—AND BUY INTO—THE DESIRED IMPACT.

Functioning "silos" can be effective at a particular task, but the overall system eventually threatens to bottom out or limp along (think back to Gore's *Inconvenient Truth*.)

It is only by combining components into a whole that we see the potential for a solid, sustainable ecology—something we call "sticky systems".

The *American Red Cross* has long had an effective system for collecting donated blood, but it turned to IDEO when it recognized the need to improve its long-term influence with donors and become more proactive in attracting new and younger donors. Many people outside the organization, Red Cross officials realized, didn't associate the organization with the donation process: rarely were donors seeking opportunities to give blood independently and directly to the Red Cross. Rather, they waited to be spurred into action by a local school or church blood drive. The individual donor experience became the chance to influence donors to give as though it were their jobs or personal passions. As IDEO worked with the Red Cross to gain greater emotional relevance with potential new donors, the question posed to donors shifted from "how much blood?" to "why I give." Everyone had a story to tell.

Putting human sensibilities at the center of the solution for scaling influence also allowed staff and volunteers to reconnect with their humanitarian mission, as opposed to becoming cogs in the system. Workers posted donor-generated "why I give" answers on walls and a Web site. Surprisingly, privacy wasn't an issue: donors wanted to share their stories broadly. The "Why I Give Campaign" became the centerpiece of a community-building experience that reminds donors that there's no need for a middle-man when giving blood. As one donor from North Carolina explained, "It's great to find out why someone donates. It gives you more of a reason to donate yourself."

3. Reciprocal Systems: Connect by Sharing
Convincing people to give back to a system as a means of connecting to it is, in some respects, a telltale sign of system success. It can also be incredibly difficult to do. Yet, when the other key elements such as human-centered design and influential systems are working, it becomes possible. *Wikipedia* and other open-source systems certainly make it look seamless.

BEST BUY IS ANOTHER EXAMPLE.

With a complex ecosystem of 140,000 employees, hundreds of retail stores, and a legacy of more than 40 years, the company leverages the power of its scale, but the focus is not on consistency or predictability (though it generally delivers on these points). Rather, it's on building simple systems that engage people in focusing their creative energy on making things better for themselves and their customers. It's an acknowledgement that no one person at the top will have all the solutions, and that people on the frontline want to do their best and contribute to the continual improvement of the whole.

Another interesting element of Best Buy's system is that it's been designed deliberately to be "fuzzy" at the edges, to allow and encourage room for people to generate and try new ideas and to give back when and how they can. The scale of the organization is harnessed by creating venues and processes by which employees can see themselves as part of a local team that has global reach.

Best Buy's women's leadership forum, known as "WoLF", shows this in action. *Julie Gilbert*, a senior vice president at Best Buy, started WoLF in 2004 as an innovation engine and employee resource group after noticing that women needed a loyal pack of cohorts who would help them advance and better engage female customers. At Best Buy, a "WoLF pack" is a group of 27 people (25 women and two men) who come together from all parts and ranks of the company.

Together, they network, brainstorm and focus on the fact that women make up roughly 45 per cent of all retail consumer electronic purchases in an industry built by men for men. The WoLF packs have paid off. More than 20,000 female customers and employees have been pulled into the effort; the number of female job applicants has increased by 37 per cent; and female-employee turnover has dropped by 5.7 per

cent. Quarterly events let participants volunteer their time back to society in the form of events and fundraising.

WOLFS CAN ALSO MENTOR INDIVIDUALS OR PACKS IN ANOTHER PART OF THE COUNTRY, AND THEIR EFFORTS HAVE ORGANICALLY LED TO A JOB-SHARE PILOT PROGRAM.

In the realm of systems at scale, WoLF exemplifies an ecosystem developed to a point in which each component can give back as a valued shareholder in the form of consumer information, new products and volunteer work. The quid pro quo or social contract for this kind of giving back must be carefully considered. Esteem, visibility, and pride of affiliation are the currency of being part of a WoLF pack, part of the community.

Wikipedia, as its founder Jimmy Wales explained in a TED Talk in 2005, wouldn't work if its editors were paid. The system benefits from people wanting to feel valued and employed to make a difference in the organization through an authentic, personal way that cannot be bought.

As these examples show, the forces around any endeavor result in its ultimate design. Often, in order to manage the complexity of what we chose to bite off in a project, we frankly leave much of the design to chance. As Mission Pie's Heisler suggests, the community—its people and all its components—is a manifestation of the system. The question isn't, Do organizations get the system they deserve? Rather, as a creative thinker, How can you design the system your organization deserves? Can you acknowledge and own your part in effecting and improving the overall organization, not just one element in a system filled with silos?

The underpinning promise of a human-centered approach is that designers can rely on people and their behaviors and the things that entice them to find large-scale solutions that fit with—and thereby change—the bigger world around them. Let's face it: in order to take on the design of really big solutions, creative thinkers need to tap the most powerful (and most human) of design tools: optimism. By its very nature, thinking like a designer requires us to believe that we can change things for the better. Thinking like a designer keeps us from becoming stunned by the complexity and seeming impossibility of a goal. It also allows us to create a balance, from the big view to little view, and involve stakeholders, even those at the fuzzy edges.

Despite the relative early days of Mission Pie, Heisler is already working with a long list of individuals, from fellow Pie Ranch co-directors *Jered Lawson* and farmer/educator *Nancy Vail* to Mission High kids and the café's bakers, customers, and food distributors to more distant people working on emerging projects that borrow from Mission Pie's approach. Her plan to "lay out the landscape, so people can see the value of the system, the value of community-supported agriculture" allows for both freshly-baked pies on a daily basis and impact in the realms of education, health, and farming over time.

THE LONG VIEW, OPTIMISM, AND DETERMINATION LEADS TO SYSTEMS AT SCALE THAT WORK AND ADAPT, WHILE MAKING THEIR SHAREHOLDERS PROUD PARTICIPANTS.

In Closing

Systems at scale comprise a series of methods for directing behavioral change on a large scale by inspiring people to embrace a system as a shareholder. In a world increasingly plagued by "wicked" problems, this is one approach to tackling seemingly-unsolvable problems.

Ilya Prokopoff and Fred Dust are partners at IDEO, in Palo Alto, California. Ilya co-founded IDEO's Transformation practice, which helps clients use the tools and methods of design to work in new ways to address the challenges of the future. Fred leads IDEO's Smart Space practice, the group responsible for helping clients with their strategic and innovation goals around space, real estate and communities.

The Five Principles of Systems at Scale

1. *Ask how the system feels, not just how it works.*
   Design isn't just about making something work: it's about asking what something feels like when it does work. Many brilliant systems fail because they feel stupid, humiliating, or dull to the humans who use them.

2. *Recognize that a good system is often the best influencer.*
   Sticky systems keep people interested and coming back, and each visit is an opportunity to have your actions change their actions.

3. *Let the user close the loop.*
   A system's recipients will either make it a success or a failure. Letting them influence and shift the system dynamically means they can buy into the system, and that's what will make it work over the long run.

4. *Go micro with the human factors.*
   Human values matter, but vague isn't helpful: specific human insights give real clues for changing behavior.

5. *Start with hope, and take the long view.*
   Systems that are purely reactionary (as opposed to visionary) fail, or worse, they limp along, alienating everyone from staff to customers and communities.

213

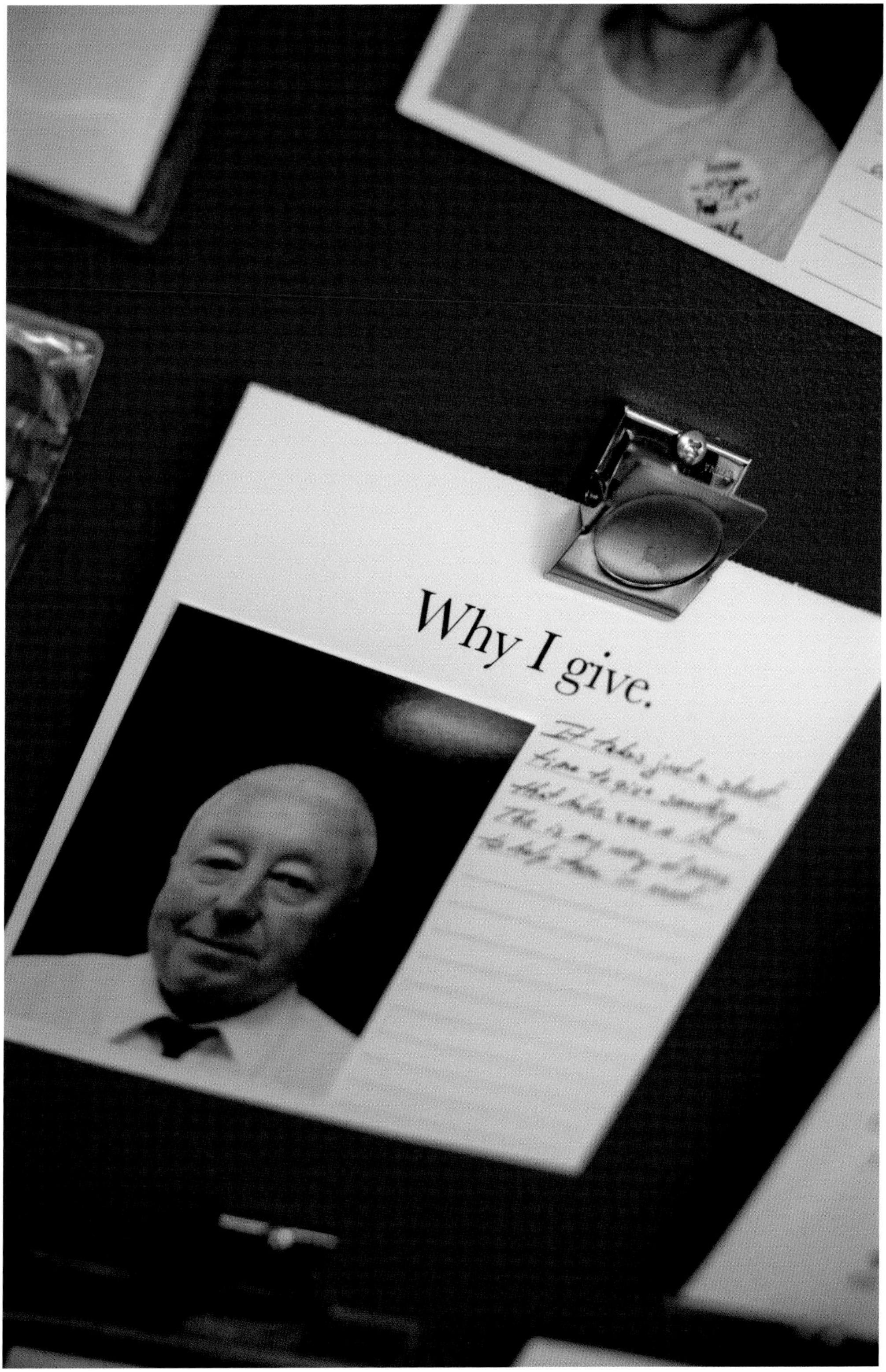

American Red Cross Donor Experience

Redefining the donor experience
Experience blueprint for the American Red Cross

To increase the national donor base, the American Red
Cross (ARC) sought IDEO's help redefining and elevating
the donation experience. Spurred by conversations with
donors and non donors, IDEO looked at ways the ARC could
refocus its emphasis on the donor as its most valuable
asset and gain greater emotional relevance with potential
donors. As a result, IDEO is helping the ARC to identify
opportunities, journeys, and brand principles that can be
implemented nationwide in the form of donor centered
mobile drive environments and service interactions. IDEO
has designed and prototyped full-scale, spatial layouts,
furniture components, and service tools and protocols, many
of which are currently being piloted in select regions of the
United States.

Organizational Transformation for Productos Cementeros Mexicanos

Guiding a start-up to the leading edge of an industry
Service concepts and innovation framework for PCM

To develop a strategic foothold in a highly established industry, Mexican start-up Productos Cementeros Mexicanos (PCM) approached IDEO to help understand the opportunities for innovation in the concrete industry—specifically, the potential for creating and testing new products and services—and to begin defining a culture of continuous innovation. With the project run almost entirely in Mexico, IDEO and PCM observed a variety of local concrete use situations and stakeholders, including employees at corporate and operational levels, clients, foremen, and architects. The initial fieldwork and synthesis led to six customer-facing innovation platforms, with two prototypes piloted for further development. The team also developed frameworks that describe how PCM can build and sustain its own culture of innovation.

Arup is a design company in a broad sense. This engineering company was founded in 1946 in the UK by Ove Arup. We now have 90 offices worldwide and about 10,000 engineers, architects, designers, economists, sociologists, anthropologists and archaeologists on staff. Basically, we are a consulting firm; our gross revenues are about $1.4 billion.

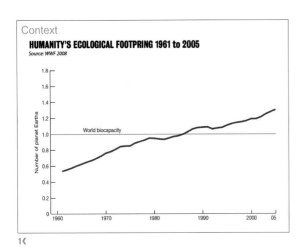

1❮

2❮

1❮ We reached our biological capacity a while ago, 10 years ago, and we are living on credit. That is scary now that we have seen what happened with financial markets, let alone what happens with "ecological" credit.

2❮ We've experienced a great deal of suffering and frustration. We have lost jobs due to the financial crisis. We have seen very weak and difficult and improper and misaligned reactions to the financial crisis by world and national governments. We can hardly cope with this international financial crisis. What would happen with a more complex set of events, with events such as the melting of the polar ice caps? How will we deal with that crisis? Do we have robust, responsive and effective international governance to deal with this? Do we have the state of mind and the resources and the knowledge to deal with this? The run-away scenarios that can unfold are so scary that there is a very strong rationale for doing something now instead of later. And that is, we at Arup believe, very much related to well-designed regions, well-designed cities. The biggest task is not how we do the next cities; rather, it is how we retrofit, how we re-do, how we re-invent existing cities so that they perform in a way that is suited to the Ecological Age.

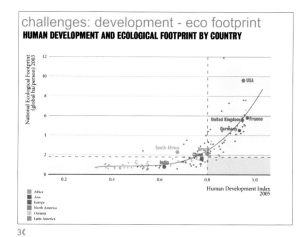

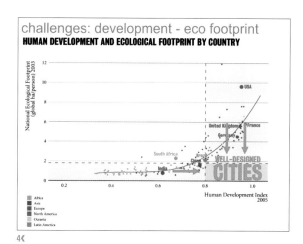

3❮

4❮

3❮ On the left hand side on the vertical axis, we see the ecological footprint per nation, and on the horizontal axis we have the human development index which is a more sophisticated version of measuring development compared to GDP only. We need to retrofit developed cities in the West and bring them down into a kind of performing environment.

4❮ The rationale for doing this is quite clear. If we don't act now, the costs—the economic costs—accruing later will be much, much higher.

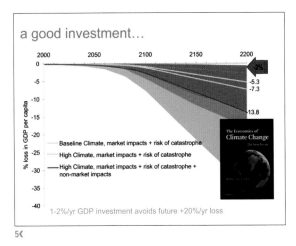

a good investment…

1-2%/yr GDP investment avoids future +20%/yr loss

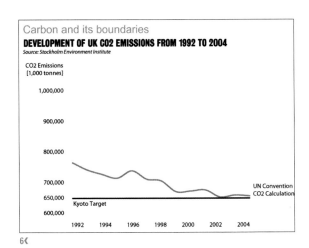

Carbon and its boundaries
DEVELOPMENT OF UK CO2 EMISSIONS FROM 1992 TO 2004
Source: Stockholm Environment Institute

5‹ The recommendation of the "Economics of Climate Change" report, which has been mentioned quite often recently, is that the world has to spend between 1 and 2 percent of its total aggregated GDP in order to introduce a change in how we use energy, how we consume, how we use our buildings and how we actually live in our cities and regions. What is the most effective way of getting there?

6‹ Getting there is very difficult because if you measure the UK footprint in terms of carbon emissions and take the measurements from the Kyoto protocol, the UK is doing pretty well, as is every European country.

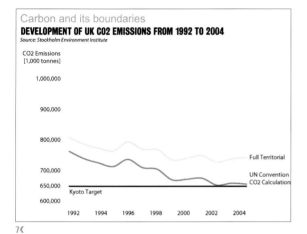

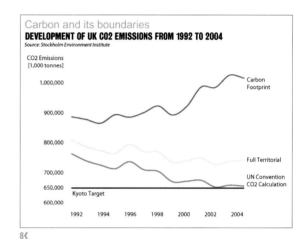

7❬

8❬

7❬ However, if you take the full territorial impact of our emissions, then we are not doing so well. For example, in the UK the actual supply chains of the consumer market (e.g. if you buy a pair of jeans that was produced in China, or if you buy a dishwasher that was produced in Thailand, etc.) are taken into account in measuring the full territorial impact of our emissions.

8❬ The UK, as any other country that has tried to curve down their emissions according to the measurements of the Kyoto protocol, is doing really well. But if you start adding the real impact of the economy, the country is doing badly. So how do governments and global governments address the issue of full territorial impact of their carbon emissions?

urban regions

50 % of the worlds population lives in cities

75% of the worlds energy are consumed by cities
80% of the world's GHG are emitted by cities

source: Clinton Climate Initiative

six ideas

Challenging conventional wisdom

Thinking holistically

Using resources efficiently

Allowing for change

Monitoring and reporting

Aiming high!

9❮ Urban regions are very important in this equation. They are responsible for most of the emissions and most of the consumption. Cities are like energy sinks because they consume and consume energy and don't give anything back to the system. Therefore, the challenge is how we manage to retrofit cities.

10❮ How do we start, how do we do things, how do we work in this environment, in these countries? We at Arup like to work with six ideas. One is "challenging conventional wisdom." We tend to think that things are like they are and we can't change them, so we have to challenge conventional thinking and wisdom.
"Thinking holistically" means that urban design or any type of design has to take into account the life cycle of products or projects and the premises of resources efficiency.
"Allow for change" is a very important element of design, particularly when you consider long-term design decisions like in master planning or infrastructure.
The other very important issue is that you can't stop when you've finished a design and build it. You have to monitor and improve performance of designs.
And, finally, "aim high." Among the things that I've learned through the experience of working in China, in the Middle East and in Europe on large-scale design projects is that if you don't aim high, you will never get there. It is very simple.

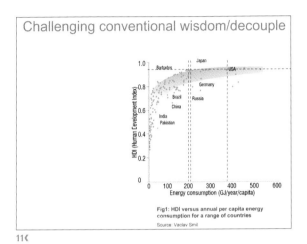

Challenging conventional wisdom/decouple

Fig1: HDI versus annual per capita energy
consumption for a range of countries

Source: Vaclav Smil

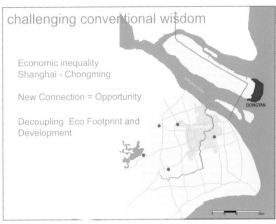

challenging conventional wisdom

Economic inequality
Shanghai - Chongming

New Connection = Opportunity

Decoupling Eco Footprint and
Development

11‹

12‹

11‹ "Challenging conventional wisdom"
In our business, people say: "if you want to grow, you need to have more energy. If you want to
be a wealthy, developed country, you have to use more energy. There is no way out." We at Arup
challenge this thinking. According to the UN, Japan and Germany use half of the energy per capita of
the US and nevertheless maintain the same quality of life.

12‹ Dongton, a project in which Arup challenges conventional wisdom. Arup got a call from a client
in China asking us to develop a city for about half a million people. We wanted to demonstrate that it
is possible to develop a city in an ecologic form by equally providing the means for economic growth.
The concept is very simple: This island is the poorest part of that region. Every person living there
earns on average one sixth as much as people living on the other side.
The national government built a tunnel and a bridge to connect the island to Shanghai in the south
and to Jiangsu Province in the north with the intention of enabling economic development in a
conventional manner.

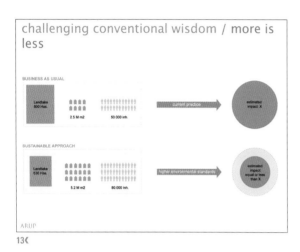

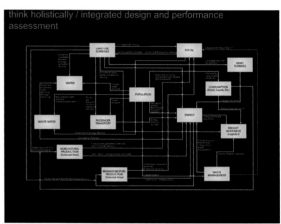

13‹ The original idea of the client was to build a suburban dormitory town for Shanghai. However, we suggested settling more people and more activities there to have high revenue on the project. This higher revenue may pay for higher standards, which will decrease the footprint in absolute terms of the population.

14‹ Think holistically. Arup wasn't told to look only at the buildings; we were asked to look at the infrastructure, transport, agriculture, etc. too.

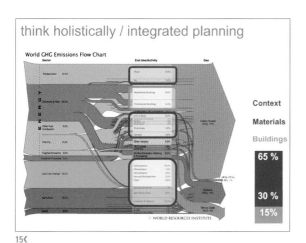

think holistically / integrated planning

World GHG Emissions Flow Chart

Context

Materials

Buildings

65 %

30 %

15%

think holistically / urban agriculture

15❮

16❮

15❮ All the transport connections, the resources of food and energy generation inputs that we needed to create a whole sustainable city were relevant as well.

16❮ Beijing, Wanzhuang—another example of thinking holistically. In Wanzhuang we were facing a 5,000 hectare site with 60,000 people already living in it. One of the key problems in China is its practice of displacing farmers to develop real estate on their former fields. We at Arup were aiming to retain this population, the particular economy, and the social fabric within that city centre to merge it with a new development.

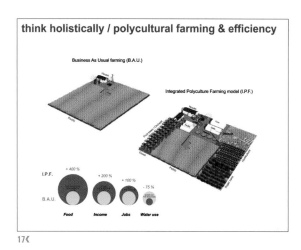

think holistically / polycultural farming & efficiency

Business As Usual farming (B.A.U.)

Integrated Polyculture Farming model (I.P.F.)

I.P.F.
+ 400 %
+ 200 %
+ 100 %
- 75 %
B.A.U.

Food   **Income**   **Jobs**   **Water use**

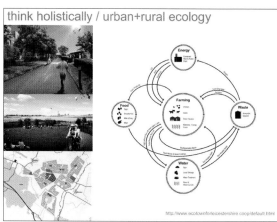

think holistically / urban+rural ecology

http://www.ecotownforleicestershire.coop/default.html

17‹ How could we actually make those two cultures coexist in close proximity? How could the design support the conceived business model?

18‹ We suggested supporting these people financially and legally to run their own businesses and to create a living out of it in order to have a local market for the additional population coming to the site, which was planned for up to 320,000 people.

Our efforts resulted in proposing twice as many jobs in this particular industry. These farmers were more or less fully employed already. Hence, there was a need to import about 200% more people, reduce water consumption by 75% and increase food production by 400%.

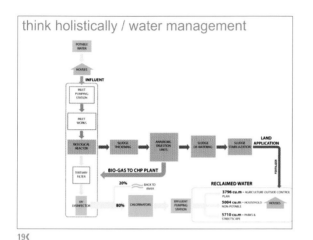

think holistically / water management

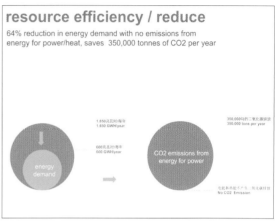

resource efficiency / reduce

64% reduction in energy demand with no emissions from
energy for power/heat, saves 350,000 tonnes of CO2 per year

229

19‹ One of the key drivers defining the size of the additional population was the amount of available resources on site. Water is a key constraint in Beijing. Thus, the availability of water determines the size of the population. Normally in urban design, it is done the other way round: First, there is a business case for the real estate development, second, population size becomes determined, and finally required water demand is calculated. Ultimately, one has to solve the "water problem." In Beijing, Wanzhuang we did it the other way around. And there was a massive discussion and challenge to the planning system and to the authorities.

20‹ Ecotown—a project, in the UK. Arup was asked to develop an eco-town outside the city of Leicester where agriculture and food production were central to the population.
Arup again applied system thinking or holistic thinking. Food was at the core of the designed systems. Food was going to serve this particular town, which was creating waste; and that waste was creating biomass and that biomass was going back in the form of CO_2, heat and electricity to produce more food—system thinking applied to urban rural environments.

Reducing energy demand was a very important element of the equation. We reduced the demand by 65%. The total demand for energy in Dongton, with of population of 80,000 in the first phase, went from 1,650 GWh/year to 600 GWh/year. By means of a large-scale design, we managed to develop passive measures and small scale specification measures for the buildings and eliminating 350,000 tons of CO_2 per year at that site.

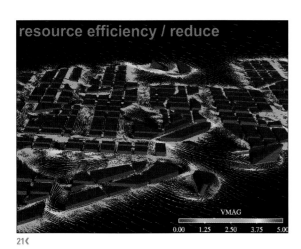

resource efficiency / reduce

VMAG
0.00   1.25   2.50   3.75   5.00

21‹

resource efficiency / looking around

22‹

21‹ How can one reduce energy consumption by design? There are certain measures, such as specifying ways of improving the performance on the envelope, and locating buildings in an optimal position. In that particular case, we had the opportunity to do much more than that. We could put the whole city layout in an optimal position. Hence, we could model the whole city and test all the scenarios—for example, the impact of wind or the sun in various positions, or the optimal heat peak loads in winter or cold peak loads on summer. In this particular case, we could reduce the size of the energy plant for the city by about 10%. Thus, sustainability and thinking one more minute about these things is not more expensive; it is cheaper, more cost effective.

22‹ The whole region produces rice. Rice husks are cut and burned, and rice husks have a high calorific value. We could use it as a biomass resource to provide energy.

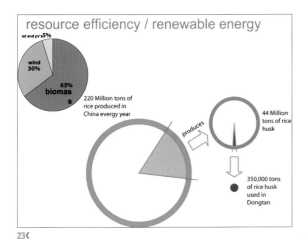

resource efficiency / renewable energy

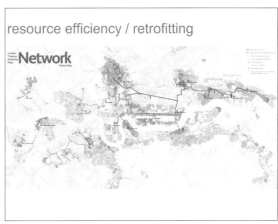

resource efficiency / retrofitting

23❮

24❮

23❮ The total amount of rice production in the region is 220 million tons, and 44 million tons of rice husks are produced as agricultural waste. 0.7% is taken for our project. Though there are a lot of rice husks, it is possible to replicate this idea.

24❮ In London, there is a power station in Barking, just down the river from central London. It's been there for 40 years. What is happening in this power station today? For 40 years it has been dumping the waste heat of energy generators into the river. On the other hand, there are several new developments in London which are in need of energy and heat. The London Development Agency and Arup put these two things together. The heat produced by the waste of the existing power plant station are captured and provide heating for 120,000 new homes. This is retrofitting on a large scale. This is what everybody needs to be doing.

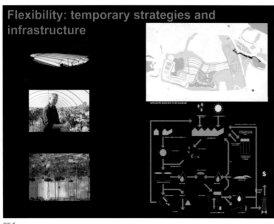

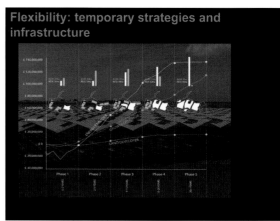

25❮ Allowing for change—Another big issue in planning is the focus on planning horizons of about 20-25 years. How do you deal with uncertainty and the ability to modify scenarios? One of the things that we are looking at is how you can make use of the land as an interim phase and produce positive value out of it today without having the need to hold on for future real estate development. Our proposition was to have an agricultural industry, which is very common in the Netherlands, but we are justifying that concept as a temporary use for urban development.

26❮, 27❮, 28❮ Create employment for 20 years, create value for the land and positive economic impact, and then reconvert it incrementally again and develop it as real estate when market conditions are suitable. Basically, the business model is based on the idea that rents are taken from farmer who lease the land for a given period or time. This money pays for the infrastructure that is needed to build for future developments. At the end of the day, developers are better off as they get an additional income stream. Furthermore, it generates employment and leads to local food creation, which can be marketed locally. It generates a win-win situation.

Flexible approach to planning: accommodating change

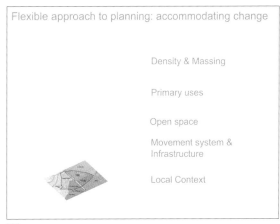

Flexible approach to planning: accommodating change

Density & Massing

Primary uses

Open space

Movement system &
Infrastructure

Local Context

27❬

28❬

Flexible approach to planning: performance guidance

And building it up ....

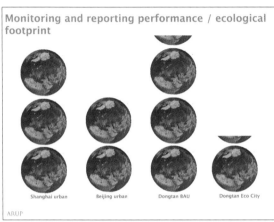

Monitoring and reporting performance / ecological footprint

Shanghai urban   Beijing urban   Dongtan BAU   Dongtan Eco City

ARUP

29‹ For strategic planning, the actual picture, the "tangible" city, the form of the master plan and how the city looks in detail, is something that we at Arup try not to focus on. Our vision and what we try to share with our clients and stakeholders in the project is not so much the image of a city or district; it is first and foremost the process and the performance of it.

This process of negotiation and testing of performance allows us to get to its form, but we are guided by the performance, not by the actual image. I think that's a very subtle but important difference with respect to how we think about planning and design in the long-term in regard to master planning.

30‹ Monitoring / reporting is an important aspect. Take for example ecological footprinting. In the case of Dongtan and all the projects that we are doing now, we are pursuing different tests to show local authorities that what we are doing is robust and much better than a standard solution. If Dongtan had been built the way they were initially considering, its impact would have been 6.5 global hectares per person. Such an impact would be completely unacceptable, as it would mean that if everyone would live like them, we would need 3 planets to sustain our life.

With all the ideas discussed above, we managed to get that figure down to 2.3 global hectares per person. That is very close to the one planet target.

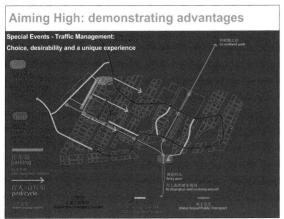

31❮

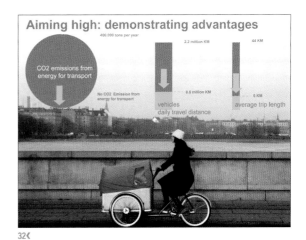

32❮

31❮, 32❮ Aiming high has a very tangible value. For this city, aiming high was to be a city of zero emissions for all its functions and activities. The vehicles are running by means of electricity and the distance between buildings and streets is diminished. Ultimately, this is also relevant for the quality of life for people in Dongton. If you live in Dongton and work in Dongton, which would be the case for approximately 75% of the people, you would save 20 days a year of commuting.

Peak debt. Peak energy. Peak protein. Peak climate change. Each of these challenges is daunting on its own. Taken together, they mean that business—as usual is over—for good. The old ways will not return. There are green shoots, if you choose to look—but they are not the same old plants.

THEY ARE THE FIRST SIGN THAT NEW ECONOMIC AND SOCIAL LIFE FORMS ARE EMERGING.

Does this mean that architects should not expect to design buildings? or designers, products, or posters? My question is not a rhetorical one. The inputs and outputs of industrial society are wildy out of balance—and that includes its buildings and infrastructure.

Many of the troubling situations in our world are the result of design decisions. Eighty percent of the environmental impact of the products, services, and infrastructures around us is determined at the design stage. Design decisions shape the processes behind the products we use, the materials and energy required to make them, the ways we operate them on a daily basis, and what happens to them when we no longer need them. We may not have meant to do so, and we may regret the way things have turned out, but we designed our way into the situations that face us today.

A good example is what is inaccurately described as "mindless" sprawl in our urban environment.

WE DEPLORE THE RELENTLESS SPREAD OF LOW-DENSITY SUBURBS OVER MILLIONS OF ACRES OF FORMERLY VIRGIN LAND.

We worry about its environmental impact, about the obesity in people that it fosters, and about the other social problems that come in its wake. But nobody seems to have designed urban sprawl, it just happens—or so it appears.

On closer inspection, however, urban sprawl is not mindless at all. Sprawl is the result of zoning laws designed by legislators, low-density buildings designed by developers, marketing strategies designed by ad agencies, tax breaks designed by economists, credit lines designed by banks, geomatics designed by retailers, data-mining software designed by hamburger chains, and automobiles designed by car designers. The interactions between all these systems and human behavior are complicated and hard to understand—but the policies themselves are not the result of chance.

So What to Do?

We need to re-imagine the built world not as a landscape of frozen objects, but as a complex of interacting ecologies: energy, water, mobility, food. We need to reconceive design as a regenerative activity that necessarily operates in ways that are sensitive to context, to relationships, and to consequences.

A second core task of design will be to make it easier to share resources—resources such as energy, matter, time, skill, software, space, or food. A key concept here is that of enabling solutions—solutions that re-assert human agency in our systems-filled world.

There is much work for architects to do, even as they cease designing buildings. The architect's understanding of space, time, and process will be valuable as our focus shifts to closed-loop systems and services that meet the needs of daily life in new ways.

Food

I recently found myself in the town centre of Carlisle, in the north west of England, at 7am. The town square was empty except for a large truck whose driver was unloading packaged food into a shop. An incredible, raw-edged roar of noise came from the refrigeration unit on top of his cab. The noise was so extreme that I couldn't hear a word when someone called my mobile phone. I retreated into the railway station cafeteria, but it was little better in there: Two large refrigerated drinks machines were roaring so loudly that the sales assistant had to shout to tell me the price of a coffee.

THAT NOISE, WHICH REPRESENTS WASTED ENERGY, WAS FOR ME AN AUDIBLE WARNING SIGNAL THAT GLOBAL FOOD SYSTEMS ARE LURCHING INTO CRISIS.

As I write, there are empty shelves in Caracas, food riots in West Bengal and Mexico, and warnings of hunger in Jamaica, Nepal, the Philippines and sub-Saharan Africa.

Global food prices have risen by 75 per cent since 2000, and soaring prices for basic foods have forced some governments to control the cost of bread, maize, rice and dairy products. According to the UN Food and Agricultural Organisation, global food reserves are at their lowest in 25 years. (Energy Bulletin, 2007)

Little of this appears in mainstream media in the North, where the rich have been the last to be hit. Food costs are ten percent of household expenditure in rich countries, whereas in China the figure is 30 per cent. In sub-Saharan Africa, 60 per cent of houshold income goes on food, the crisis is acute already.

MANY CIVILISATIONS, FROM THE SUMMERIAN TO THE MAYA, HAVE FALTERED WHEN THE SCALE AND COMPLEXITY OF FOOD PRODUCTION PRODUCED RUINOUS DIMINISHING RETURNS.

On American farms in the early 1800s, the balance between calories expended, and calories produced as food, was about even. Under today's system, it takes sixteen calories of input to produce one calorie of meat. Up to 40 per cent of the ecological impact of a modern city can be attributed to its food and water systems. (Manicore, 2004)

In a report titled "What will we eat as the oil runs out?" Richard Heinberg mapped four coordinates of the evolving food crisis. First is the direct impact on agriculture of higher oil prices; increased costs of tractor fuel, agricultural chemicals, and transport, add cost to farm inputs and outputs. Second, increased demand for biofuels leads farmland being turned from food production to fuel production; 70 per cent of vegetable oil grown today in Europe is destined to power cars. A third dimension of the crisis is climate change and extreme weather events caused by fuel-based greenhouse gas emissions. The fourth problem described by Heinberg is the degradation or loss of basic natural resources—principally, topsoil and fresh water supplies—as a result of high and unsustainable methods of production stimulated by decades of cheap energy.

"Each of these problems is developing at a somewhat different pace regionally, and each is exacerbated by the continually expanding size of the human population" Heinerg writes; "as these dilemmas collide, the resulting overall food crisis is likely to be profound and unprecedented in scope". (Heinberg, 2007)

Thanks to cheap fuel, agriculture and food now account for nearly 30 per cent of goods transported on Europe's roads. We also ship millions of bottles of water from one country to another despite the fact the carbon emissions of one bottle are 600 times higher than the same amount of water drawn from a tap. On the island of Fiji, citizens suffer from typhoid in the vicinity of a foreign-owned water bottling plant that exports designer water all over the world. (Harp, 2008) There are even more bizarre exports of water. Notoriously, one supermarket flew planeloads of turnips from New Zealand to the UK in order to drive down the prices being asked by home growers. Turnips contain 70 per cent water—so the company was in effect flying planeloads of water across the world to drive down prices of a root crop that could once have been found within a couple of miles of where most of the population lives.

PRODUCERS HAVE BENEFITTED FROM CHEAP MONEY AS WELL AS CHEAP FUEL.

Every head of cattle in Europe gets a subsidy from the taxpayer worth $2.20 a day at a time when half the world's population—three billion people—scrapes by on an income less than that. (Elliott, 2005)

Most processed foods are packaged, and manufacturing the packaging (steel, aluminium, plastics) accounts for 70–80 per cent of the overall emissions of the food industry. Once packaged, processed food is generally purchased in supermarkets which consume electricity to keep foods frozen—especially in open display units. Food retailers also spend insanely on energy—seven times more than is used in an ordinary office. In larger food stores up to a quarter of their energy budget goes on lighting—to make the food look good, not for it to be good. Most of the rest is used for refrigeration. More than 50 per cent of food in developed countries is retailed under refrigerated conditions. A single open-fronted freezer costs a retailer 20,000 euros per year to run in energy bills alone—and that does not include the embergy (embodied energy) involved in each unit's manufacture.

Supermarkets generate wasteful mobility in deciding to locate their shops in places that we can only reach by car. In the UK, 25 per cent of car journeys are to get food. We increasinlgy eat food whilst moving, too. "Dashboard dining" is a fast-growing and energy-squandering chunk of the food industry; seventy percent of fast-food sales in the US are at the drive-through window, and a lot of energy is needed to speed up the service. At San Diego-based Jack in the Box restaurants, for instance, where it takes 3.8 minutes to get burgers out the drive-through window, a research firm told the company that speeding up delivery by six seconds could improve profits substantially. (Green, 2005) The British, for their part, purchase three billion pre-packed sandwiches a year from outlets whose every wall is lined with energy-intensive chiller cabinets. Once back home, our reliance on processed stimulates energy use in fridges and freezers, stoves, ovens, and microwaves. (Young, 2007)

When food is forced into the formal economy and industrialised, indirect costs skyrocket. Poor diet and physical inactivity account for 35 per cent (and rising) of avoidable causes of deaths in the US; the on-costs of obesity alone amount to 10 per cent of total health costs. In Europe, grab-and-go consumers probably do not realise is that the sandwiches they eat contain the same amount of salt as seven bags of crisps. (BBC News, 2007)

PROCESSED FOOD DOES NOT JUST CLOG OUR ARTERIES.

Two geographers, Simon Marvin and Will Medd, found that fat deposits from fast food outlets and homes was increasing the number of sewer blockages and overflows across cities in the United States. Cities become fat, they say, as restaurants and fast food chains pour cooking residue into drains. Local governments lack the resources

to monitor grease disposal or to enforce the relevant regulations. (Urban Vulnerability, 2004)

Food madness is not confined to the North. The obesity pandemic has reached India, too; 29 per cent of school-age children in Delhi are obese—possibly because the sugar content of their diet has risen 40 per cent during the last 50 years, and its fat content by 20 per cent. Bizarrely, Delhi authorities now want to ban the city's 300,000 street food vendors (few of whom use much sugar or fat) in the name of "hygiene" and "modernisation" ahead of the 2010 Commonwealth Games. The financial pressure to industrialise food in emerging economies is immense. In a Western food shop, for every ten dollars you or I spend at the checkout, only 60c ends up with the farmer.

THE REMAINING $9.40—THE "ADDED VALUE"—REPRESENTS TURNOVER AND PROFIT FOR THE INDUSTRIES INVOLVED.

Compare that to formal stores in India (also known as organised retail); they account for only three percent of India's $300 billion food retail sector. Most food shopping is still done through hole-in-the-wall stores, roadside vendors, and open-air markets. A report published for the Indian government by McKinsey promoted the idea that India become the "food factory of the world" in the next few years. The firm promoted the twin concepts of "efficiency" and "innovation" as the basis for an Indian drive into the $640 billion global packaged food industry. "Efficient products at extremely low cost...that's where the heartland of the Indian consumer is going to be". The likely costs to social and environmental quality, and public health, were not mentioned in McKinsey's report. (www.mckinseyquarterly.com)

Plan B for Food

The impact of business on food is not all negative. Some multi-national corporations in the food sector are moving faster than most governments in response to the unfolding food and water crisis. Patrick Cescau, for example, Group Chief Executive of Unilever, talked to an industry conference about "seismic shifts in the world we do business in" and warned of a "reality gap between where we are, and where we need to be". Cescau proposed to apply new design principles to "drive down our usage of resources and move towards ever more sustainable consumption".

Easy to say, of course; harder to do. When I asked people in Unilever about this pledge, it seemed to me that many of Cescau's 234,000 colleagues remain vague, to put it mildly, about what these "new design principles" are—let alone how they are to be implemented. But this also means there's a design opportunity here: If huge companies like Unilever are in the market for sustainable design principles, it seems to me we should provide them. (http://www.unilever.com/Images/ir_pc_montreux091006_tcm13-70144.pdf)

For its part WalMart, another giant company, is facing in both directions at once. Its India operation is complicit in the drive to wipe out the informal sector—but back in the USA the company required all its managers to watch Al Gore's movie. Confusion, but not inaction, also describes Marks and Spencer's position. Britain's most active food retailer is committed to make all its UK and Irish operations carbon neutral within five years. "We'll maximise our use of renewable energy and only use offsetting as a last resort" pledges the firm. It has committed to act on waste, raw materials, healthy eating, and fair trade; it has banned white veal and calves liver from its shelves; and the firm is playing a leading role in a government programme called WRAP that is tackling the packaging issue. (http://www.wrap.org.uk/retail/about_us/index.html) M&S's glaring omission is refrigeration.

THIS SLEIGHT OF HAND IS SIMILAR TO THE DECISION OF GOVERNMENTS TO OMIT AVIATION FROM THEIR NATIONAL FOOTPRINT CALCULATIONS.

More than 50 per cent of food in developed countries is retailed under refrigerated conditions. Shopping for a snack in central London recently I counted out 78 metres (256 feet) of chiller cabinets in one small central London branch. A single open-fronted freezer costs 15,000 pounds (22,000 euros) per year to run in energy bills alone—and that does not include the embergy (embodied energy) involved in each unit's manufacture. Unchecked, air conditioning units and chiller cabinets will cause hundreds of billions of tons of CO_2 to be released into the atmosphere in the next 50 years.

Of course, M&S may reply, if food were not refrigerated, a good proportion of it would rot or spoil. Up to 40 per cent of fruit is lost post-harvest in some food systems. Such a loss of produce represents a waste of energy on its own account, since wasted food embodies the energy used in its production, processing and transport. Nonetheless, as things stand today, it looks as if M&S is resigned not to reduce, but to offset, the massive energy emissons from its supply, storage and retail operations when its five year deadline for Plan A expires.

The alternative would be for food retailers to change their business model to one of shopless shopping, and close down most of their retail outlets. And why not? Refrigerated trucks, warehouses, and high street stores are expensive and wasteful steps in the journey from farm to table. It would not require much infrastructure investment to re-purpose retail outlets into hubs in a warehouse and delivery system. Many intermediaries in food systems would disappear, but the big players like M&S are well-placed to become the radically de-centralized distribution and quality assurance platform that all towns and cities need to relocalize their food systems.

Measure what Matters

As awareness of crisis of food systems has grown, so too has demand for information about what we are eating. As public awarness about food issues has grown, food miles have come to emblemise the problem. Some experts point out, correctly, that the energy efficiency of food systems is not just about miles covered by the various ingredients. One study found that transportation accounted for 11 per cent of the energy use within the food system in the United States, compared to agricultural production (17.5 per cent) and processing (28.1 per cent). Friends of the food industries use these anomalies to draw misleading conclusions. *The Economist*, for example, opinioned that it is "better for the environment to truck in tomatoes from Spain during the winter, than to grow them in heated greenhouses in Britain" (Economist, 2006). A British government minister argued that that "flowers flown from Africa can use less energy overall than those produced in Europe because they're not grown in heated greenhouses". A total-energy-used metric was also used to show that tomatoes grown outdoors in Spain, then flown to the UK, were "responsible for fewer carbon emissions than UK tomatoes grown in heated greenhouses." Nobody lied here, but "better" in this context does not mean "sustainable." It just means less bad. The fact that a product flown from another country is responsible for fewer carbon emissions than its equivalent where it is consumed does not mean it its import is sustainable." (Saunders et al. 2006) The term "greenwashing" applies when companies (or governments) devote more resources to advertising and communications, than to actions that materially change the way a system impacts on the biosphere. The worst greenwashing involves changing the name or label of an otherwise unchanged product. Images of trees, birds, or dew drops are warning signs.

National and transnational governments are taking important steps against greenwashing. In the UK for example, the Carbon Trust and Defra, the environment ministry, are co-sponsors of the Publicly Available Specification (PAS). (Defra, 2007) A standardised system for measuring embodied greenhouse gas emissions in products and services will be applied across a wide range of product and service categories and their supply chains, including food. The aim is to enable companies to measure the life-cycle climate change impacts of their products and highlight significant emission reduction opportunities.

IN THE MEDIUM-TERM IMPROVED FOOD SYSTEM *STANDARDS*, SPECIFICATIONS, METRICS, AND SCORECARDS, WILL MAKE GREENWASHING MUCH HARDER.

Harder, but not impossible. If we are to re-localise food, a new generation of information systems will be needed as support. Many of today's food systems rely on closed networks in which access to information is controlled by entities (such as supermarkets) that are not keen on localisation. Many food and agriculture companies have deployed private information and labelling systems that they have designed and they operate. This allows them to decide what variables will be measured, and which benchmarks will be used to plot progress. The result has been to confuse matters. The good news is that open source software for food systems are already emerging. (Thackara, 2005)

EFFORTS BY INTERNATIONAL INSTITUTIONS TO IMPOSE ORDER AND TRANSPARENCY ON REPORTING SYSTEMS WILL BE A CONTINUOUS BATTLE.

A challenge for designers is to develop new ways to reveal data as they are uncovered. With a system called ThingLink, for example, the Finnish designer Ulla Maaria Mutanen has made it possible, simply by touching items with a mobile phone, their unique story can be told. The phone is used as a scanning device, linking with individual tags placed on items. The phone then uses a database called Thinglink to access the full history of the item and send this information back to the mobile phone. The details of the item are displayed on the phone in various forms including audio messages.

Urban Farming

When the civic and business leaders of thirty world cities convened in New York in 2007 for the Large Cities Climate Summit, food did not figure on the agenda. Delegates discussed Congestion, Energy, Water, Buildings, Business, Urban Transit, and Waste—but not food systems. This was a remarkable omission: Up to forty percent of the ecological footprint of a modern city can be traced back to its food systems—the transportation, packaging, storage, preparation and disposal of the things we eat. (Toronto Food Policy Council, 2000)

It's a measure of the speed with which things are changing that food now figures prominently in the ways some cities are planning their futures. An unexpected best-seller,

Continuous Productive Urban Landscapes (Cpuls) by Andre Viljoen and Katrin Bohn, persuaded many planners and architects that food systems to accord food systems the same priority as transport, or housing. City farming is spreading fast and some 800 million people worldwide are involved in urban agriculture. (http://journeytoforever.org/cityfarm_link.html#unbook)

In cities as diverse as Rosario, Argentinia, the South Bronx, Portland, Curitiba, Freiburg Mexico City and Barcelona, citizens are rediscovering how to grow fruits, vegetables, and herbs, as well as raise livestock. The core belief system modern urban design—that cities are for people to live and work in, and the countryside is for growing food—is being swept away. A curious side-effect of the shift to urban farming is the attention now paid to Cuba as a whole nation model and laboratory for sustainable development.

CUBA COULD ASSUME GLOBAL LEADERSHIP IN DESIGNING SUSTAINABLE PRODUCTS, PROCESSES, AND POLICIES—WITH URBAN AGRICULTURE FOOD SYSTEMS AS ITS CORE COMPTENCE.

Urban farming brings together the disparate disciplines of architecture, engineering, landscape, ecology, land-use planning, embodied energy studies, recycling and pollution control to create what the Malaysian architect Ken Yeang describes as "a single approach to ecological design." Another architect, Chris Hardwick, a member of Toronto's food policy council, describes as *ecosystem planning* an approach that includes the whole food system, not just parts of it, and understands that humans are part of nature, not separate from it. Ecosystem planning recognizes the dynamic nature of the ecosystem and incorporates the concepts of carrying capacity, resilience and sustainability.

When I became the programme director of a new national design biennial, Dott 07, I contacted Viljoen immediately for advice on how best to develop a large urban agriculture

project. Today, thousands of people living and working in the town of Middlesbrough are participants in a project devoted to the cause of local food production and reduced food miles. Young, old, rich and poor have begun to work together work to grow and eat food, and to realise new relationships with local food producers and existing growers in the town and its surrounding area. (http://www.dott07.com/go/food/urban-farming)

The Dott project set out to help schools, communities and businesses grow their own fresh food in small, medium and large urban growing spaces; these ranged from window boxes to larger planter boxes and open-sided skips. The project included the establishment of Meal Assembly Centres (MACs) in different locations, and culminated in a big "Meal for Middlesbrough" in the city centre. In parallel with this community action, the town commissioned a revision to its strategic plan which identifed and mapped new opportunities for growing food.

THIS MAP CONNECTED THE LOCATION OF THE CONTAINERS AND INTERESTED PUBLIC GROWERS WITH EXISTING ALLOTMENT SITES AND "DEAD LAND".

Food systems are a key part of the agenda in making towns and cities sustainable. The design challenge is knit of together diverse resources and opportunities. The ecology of a city is complicated, and a tremendous level of coordination is needed among service providers, consumers and producers. Urban Farming, in this sense, is more about the design of services and infrastructures than it is about stand-alone artefacts. New services and infrastructures are needed to support food co-ops, collective kitchens and dining rooms, community gardens, and other enhancements of community food systems.

References

BBC News. 2007. Sandwiches "rival crisps on salt". July, 5. http://news.bbc.co.uk/2/hi/health/6266164.stm

Defra. 2007. http://www.defra.gov.uk/news/2007/070530a.htm

Dott 07. Urban farming. http://www.dott07.com/go/food/ urban-farming Economist. 2006. Food Politics. December, 7.

Elliott, L. 2005. Subsidising cows while milking the poor. The Guardian, October 17. http://www.guardian.co.uk/business/2005/oct/17/eu.internati onalaidanddevelopment

Energy Bulletin. 2007. Food & Agriculture. November 3. http://www.energybulletin.net/36686.html

Green, F. 2005. Not-as-fast food. Sign on San Diego, October 29. http://www.signonsandiego.com/news/business/20051029- 9999-1b29fastfood.html

Harp, T. 2008. Bottled water: Who needs it? BBC Panorama, February 18.

Heinberg, R. 2007. What will we eat as the oil runs out? Energy Bulletin, December 3. http://www.energybulletin. net/38091.html

Journey to forever. Resources for city farms. http://journeytoforever.org/cityfarm_link.html#unbook

Manicore. 2004. How much greenhouse gases in our plate? March. http://www.manicore.com/anglais/documentation_a/ greenhouse/plate.html

http://www.mckinseyquarterly.com

Saunders, C., et al. 2006. Food Miles Comparative Energy/ Emissions Performance of New Zealands's Agriculture Industry. http://www.jborganics.co.nz/saunders_report.pdf

Thackara, J. 2005. Infra for food. Doors of perception. August, 10. http://www.doorsofperception.com/ archives/2005/08/infra_for_food.php

Toronto Food Policy Council. 2000. Food Secure City. February, 18. http://www.toronto.ca/health/tfpc_secure.pdf

http://www.unilever.com/Images/ir_pc_montreux091006_ tcm13-70144.pdf

Urban Vulnerability. 2004. http://www.surf.salford.ac.uk/ Events/UrbanVulnerabilityAbstracts.htm

Wrap. Retail Innovation Programme. http://www.wrap.org. uk/retail/about_us/index.html

Young, J. 2007. Jeffrey Young Allegra Strategues Presentation to the British Sandwich Association. November 1. www.allegra.co.uk

MICHAEL BRAUNGART, WILLIAM MCDONOUGH, ALBIN KÄLIN AND ANDREW BOLLINGER ❮

Cradle-to-Cradle Design: Creating Healthy Emissions—A Strategy for Eco-Effective Product and System Design

ECO-EFFECTIVENESS AND CRADLE-TO-CRADLE DESIGN PRESENT AN ALTERNATIVE DESIGN AND PRODUCTION CONCEPT TO THE STRATEGIES OF ZERO EMISSION AND ECO-EFFICIENCY.

Where eco-efficiency and zero emission seek to reduce the unintended negative consequences of processes of production and consumption, eco-effectiveness is a positive agenda for the conception and production of goods and services that incorporate social, economic, and environmental benefit, enabling triple top line growth.

Part of this article originally appeared in Journal of Cleaner Production 15 (2007), 1337–1348. Elsevier.

Eco-effectiveness moves beyond zero emission approaches by focusing on the development of products and industrial systems that maintain or enhance the quality and productivity of materials through subsequent life cycles. The concept of eco-effectiveness also addresses the major shortcomings of eco-efficiency approaches: their inability to address the necessity for fundamental redesign of material flows, their inherent antagonism towards long-term economic growth and innovation, and their in-sufficiency in addressing toxicity issues.

A central component of the eco-effectiveness concept, cradle-to-cradle design provides a practical design framework for creating products and industrial systems in a positive relationship with ecological health and abundance, and long-term economic growth. Against this background, the transition to eco-effective industrial systems is a five-step process beginning with an elimination of undesirable substances and ultimately calling for a reinvention of products by reconsidering how they may optimally fulfill the need or needs for which they are actually intended while simultaneously being supportive of ecological and social systems.

THIS PROCESS NECESSITATES THE CREATION OF AN ECO-EFFECTIVE SYSTEM OF "NUTRIENT" MANAGEMENT TO COORDI-NATE THE MATERIAL FLOWS AMONGST ACTORS IN THE PRODUCT SYSTEM. THE CONCEPT OF INTELLIGENT MATERIALS POOLING ILLUSTRATES HOW SUCH A SYSTEM MIGHT TAKE SHAPE, IN REALITY.

The concept of eco-effectiveness offers a positive alternative to traditional eco-efficiency approaches for the development of healthy and environmentally benign products and product systems. Eco-efficiency strategies focus on maintaining or increasing the value of economic output while simultaneously decreasing the impact of economic activity upon ecological systems (Verfaillie and

Bidwell, 2000). Zero emission, as the ultimate extension of eco-efficiency, aims to provide maximal economic value with zero adverse ecological impact—a true decoupling of the relationship between economy and ecology.

ECO-EFFICIENCY BEGINS WITH THE ASSUMPTION OF A ONE-WAY, LINEAR FLOW OF MATERIALS THROUGH INDUSTRIAL SYSTEMS: RAW MATERIALS ARE EXTRACTED FROM THE ENVIRONMENT, TRANSFORMED INTO PRODUCTS AND EVENTUALLY DISPOSED OF.

In this system, eco-efficient techniques seek only to minimize the volume, velocity and toxicity of the material flow system, but are incapable of altering its linear progression. Some materials are recycled, but often as an end-of-pipe solution since these materials are not designed to be re-cycled. Instead of true recycling, this process is actually downcycling, a downgrade in material quali-ty, which limits usability and maintains the linear, cradle-to-grave dynamic of the material flow system.

In contrast to this approach of *minimization* and *dematerialization*, the concept of *eco-effectiveness* proposes the transformation of products and their associated material flows such that they form a supportive relationship with ecological systems and future economic growth. The goal is not to minimize the cradle-to-grave flow of materials, but to generate cyclical, *cradle-to-cradle* "metabolisms" that enable materials to maintain their status as resources and accumulate intelligence over time (*upcycling*). This inherently generates a *synergistic relationship* between ecological and economic systems—a positive *recoupling* of the relationship between economy and ecology.

1. Eco-Effectiveness and Zero Waste

The eco-effective approach contrasts with zero emission strategies in that it deals directly with the issue of maintaining (or upgrading) resource quality and productivity through many cycles of use, rather than seeking to eliminate waste. The characteristic of zero waste (no production of negative side-products) arises as a natural side-effect of efforts to maintain the status of materials as resources, but is not the focus of eco-effective strategies. The maintenance of a high level of quality and productivity of resources is, by contrast, not necessarily a side effect of zero waste approaches.

This difference in focus between the concepts of zero waste and eco-effectiveness is reflected in the array of strategies which they employ. The zero waste concept encompasses a broad range of strategies including volume minimization, reduced consumption, design for repair and durability and design for recycling and reduced toxicity (http://www.zwia. org/standards.html; http://www.productpolicy.org/assets/ resources/DuncanMartin2004ZW.pdf; http://www.zerowaste. co.nz/assets/Reports/TheEndofWaste.pdf)

Whether changes are made in product design, manufacturing processes, consumer behavior or material flow logistics, reduction and minimization remain a central component of the zero waste concept.

In contrast to this, eco-effectiveness emphasizes strategies such as cradle-to-cradle design and intelligent materials pooling, which deal directly with the question of maintaining or upgrading the quality and productivity of material resources. Eco-effectiveness does not call for minimization of material use or prolonged product lifespan. In fact, it celebrates the creative and extravagant application of materials and allows for short product lifespans under the condition that all materials retain their status as productive resources. Even the application of toxic materials is acceptable as long as it takes place in the context of a closed system of material flows and the quality of the material is maintained. In the context of eco-effectiveness, strategies of reduction and minimization are not even steps in the right direction unless they contribute to the ultimate aim of achieving cyclical material flow systems that maintain material quality and productivity over time.

Definitions of Eco-Efficiency from Different Sources

Source	Definition
Australian Government	Eco-efficiency is a management process that is designed to "produce more from less". Eco-efficiency can be achieved by increasing mineral recovery, using fewer inputs such as energy and water, recycling more and reducing emissions (Australian Government website: erin.gov.au/industry/finance/glossary.html)
European Environmental	Agency Eco-efficiency is the amount of "environment" used per unit of "economic activity" (European Environmental Agency website: http://reports.eea.eu.int/)
Global Development Research Center	The relationship between economic output (product, service, activity) and environmental impact added caused by production, consumption and disposal (Global Development Research Center website: www.gdrc.org/uem/ait-terms.html)
Joseph Fiksel	The ability of a managed entity to simultaneously meet cost, quality, and performance goals, reduce environmental impacts, and conserve valuable resources. (Fiksel J. (ed.) 1996. Design for environment: creating eco-efficient products and processes. McGraw-Hill.)
Klaus North	Eco-efficiency, cleaner production and lean production are based on a common philosophy: to reduce "waste" in all steps of a production process. Eliminating waste will lead to improvements in eco-efficiency and thus contributes to: less energy consumption, less waste material, less materials handling, and less intermediate storage. (North K. 1997. Environmental business management. 2nd revised ed. Geneva: International Labour Organisation.)
Laurent Grimal	This strategy induces the integration of cleaner production technology into the production process, aiming at a reduction in materials and energy consumption and thus at a decrease in pollution. (Grimal L. 2003. The adoption of cleaner production technology and the emergence of industrial ecology activity: consequences for employment. In D. Bourg and S. Erkman (Eds). Perspectives on industrial ecology. Alsace, France.)

LEAN Advisors	The means by which more and better goods and services are created using fewer resources and minimizing waste and pollution. In practice, eco-efficiency has three core objectives: increasing product or service values, optimizing the use of resources, and reducing environmental impact. (LEAN Advisors website: http://www.leanadvisors.com)
Nokia	Eco-efficiency means producing better results from less material and energy. For us this means: minimizing energy intensity, minimizing the material intensity of goods and services, extending product durability, increasing the efficiency of processes, minimizing toxic dispersion, promoting recycling, and maximizing the use of renewable resources. (Nokia website: http://www.nokia.com)
PrintNet	Eco-efficiency is a concept that links environmental and financial performance. It does this by focusing on the development, production and delivery of products and services that meet human needs while progressively reducing their environmental impact throughout their lifecycles. Eco-efficiency essentially means doing more with less—using environmental resources more efficiently in economic processes. The application of eco-efficiency is undertaken, but not limited, by approaches and tools such as cleaner production and environmental management systems. (PrintNet website: http://www.printnet.com.au.)
Toshiba Group	Eco-efficiency is calculated by dividing the "value" of a product by the product's "environmental impact". The smaller the environmental impact and the higher the value of the product, the greater is the eco-efficiency. The value of a product is calculated based on its functions and performance, taking the voice of customer into consideration. The environmental impact of a product is calculated, taking into consideration various environmental impacts throughout its life cycle. (Toshiba Group website: http://www.toshiba.co.jp)
WMC Resources Ltd.	Maximizing efficiency of production processes while minimizing impact on the environment. Eco-efficiency can be achieved by using new technology, using fewer inputs per unit of product such as energy and water, recycling more and reducing toxic emissions. In summary doing more with less. (WMC Resources Ltd. website: http://www.wmc.com.au/sustain/envrep97/glossary.htm)

2. Eco-Efficiency: Less Bad is No Good

Eco-efficiency is a broad concept that has been supplied with various definitions by a number of groups since its inception in 1989. The World Business Council for Sustainable Development originally defined eco-efficiency as "being achieved by the delivery of competitively priced goods and services that satisfy human needs and bring quality of life, while progressively reducing ecological impacts and resource intensity throughout the life cycle to a level at least in line with the earth's carrying capacity". (http://www.wbcsd.ch/templates/TemplateWBCSD5/lay-out. asp?type¼p&;MenuId¼NzA&doOpen¼1&ClickMenu¼LeftM enu.)

The Wuppertal Institute defines eco-efficiency as a "social action strategy" seeking to "reduce the use of materials in the economy in order to reduce undesirable environmental impacts and produce a relatively higher degree of economic affluence which is more fairly distributed" (Schütz and Welfens, 2000).

THIS MORE MATERIAL-BASED AND SOCIALLY-ORIENTED APPROACH REFLECTS THE MULTITUDE OF SLIGHTLY VARYING DEFINITIONS FOR THE TERM "ECO-EFFICIENCY".

Table 1 provides a sampling of these variations. Despite various definitions, the core of the eco-efficiency concept can generally be understood as to get more from less: more product or service value with less waste, less resource use or less toxicity. In this context: eco-efficiency can be said (in the material realm) to encompass the concepts of:
- Dematerialization
- Increased resource productivity
- Reduced toxicity
- Increased recyclability (downcycling)
- Extended product lifespan

Each of these strategies starts with an assumption of the linear, cradle-to-grave flow of materials through industrial systems. They presuppose a system of production and consumption that inevitably transforms resources into waste and the Earth into a graveyard. Strategies of dematerialization and increased resource productivity seek to achieve a similar or greater level of product or service value with less material input. (http://www.productpolicy. org/assets/resources/DuncanMartin2004ZW.pdf; Schmidt-Bleek, 1998)

With cradle-to-grave material flows as a background, strategies for generating increased recyclability and extended product lifespan seek to prolong the period until resources acquire the status of waste, for instance by increasing product durability or reprocessing post-use material for use in lower value applications. Though recycling strategies begin to approach eco-effectiveness, the large majority of recycling actually constitutes "downcycling" because the recycling process reduces the quality of the materials, making them suitable for use only in lower value applications. Some materials still end up in landfills or incinerators. Their lifespan has been prolonged, but their status as resources has not been maintained. Though some have commented that zero emissions cannot be achieved through the practice of eco-efficiency. (Pirker, Pschernig, Gwehenberger and Schnitzer, 2002) parallels certainly exist between eco-efficiency strategies and the zero emission concept. Both strategies concern themselves directly and primarily with the reduction of waste, and neither focuses directly on the maintenance of resource quality and productivity.

THIS, HOWEVER, IS A NECESSARY CHARACTERISTIC OF ECO-EFFECTIVE INDUSTRIAL SYSTEMS.

The mode of action of eco-efficiency strategies—reductions in the quantities, velocities, and toxicities of the waste stream—are not adequate solutions. Less bad is no good—to destroy less is not positive, as has been stated by the authors before. (Berkhout, Muskens, Jos, Velthuijsen, 2000) By extension of this point, with zero emissions as the ultimate though unattainable target of eco-efficiency, "no bad" is not good either, when compared to eco-effective systems where the products and outputs are inherently positive.

In the short-term, eco-efficiency strategies present the potential for tangible reductions in the ecological impact of a business's activities and an opportunity for (sometimes significantly) reduced costs. In the long-term, however, they are insufficient for achieving economic and environmental objectives on several accounts:

1. Eco-efficiency is a reactionary approach that does not address the need for fundamental redesign of industrial material flows.
2. Eco-efficiency is inherently at odds with long-term economic growth and innovation.
3. Eco-efficiency does not effectively address the issue of toxicity.

2.1. Eco-Efficiency is a Reactionary Approach that does not Address the Need for Fundamental Redesign of Industrial Material Flows

Eco-efficiency is principally a strategy for *damage management and guilt reduction*. It begins with an assumption that industry is 100% bad, and proceeds with the goal of attempting to make it *less bad* (Fig. 1). While being eco-efficient may indeed reduce resource consumption and pollution, and provide temporary economic advantage in the short-term, it lacks a long-term vision for establishing a truly positive relationship between industry and nature. Eco-efficiency strategies do not address the deep design flaws of contemporary industry. They address problems instead of the source, setting goals and using practices that sustain a fundamentally flawed system. The ultimate result is an unappealing compromise that takes for granted, even institutionalizes, the antagonism between nature and industry.

This tendency can be seen in resource use patterns over recent decades, where the absolute quantities of materials extracted from, and wastes and pollution disposed into, the natural environment have continued to grow despite significant efficiency improvements. For instance, on a global level, the amount of energy used in metallurgical aluminum production per tonne of product dropped by 10% in the period between 1991 and 2000. (UNIDO, 2003) During the same period, however, total global production of metallurgical aluminum increased by over 40%, causing the total energy used for aluminum production to increase as well. (Pirker, Pschernig, Gwehenberger and Schnitzer, 2002). Rebound effects like this unavoidably connect increased efficiency with a greater total rate of destruction. Because of its largely inefficient industry, for instance, the former East Germany did a much better job of "protecting" the environment than did the West. Its greater level of efficiency allowed industry in West Germany to much more successfully and completely destroy the local ecology.

Recycling is hardly a magic bullet solution. As previously noted, the large majority of recycling done today is actually downcycling where materials lose value as they circulate through industrial systems. When plastics are recycled into countertops, for example, valuable materials are mixed and cannot be recycled again. Their trip to the landfill has only been slowed down and the linearity of the material flow system has been maintained. From this same perspective, mixing metals dilutes their value and increases the impact of the materials.

WHEN RARE AND VALUABLE METALS LIKE COPPER, NICKEL AND MANGANESE ARE BLENDED IN THE RECYCLING PROCESS, THEIR DISCRETE VALUE IS LOST FOREVER. CREATING NEW STOCKPILES IS EXTREMELY COSTLY, BOTH ECONOMICALLY AND ECOLOGICALLY.

Recycled paper offers another example of the difficulty in recycling products that were not designed for this purpose. The range of materials—often including plastics, dyes, inks and various chemical additives—that are included in modern papers make recycling a highly awkward process necessitating the use of even more toxic chemicals and in a product of inevitably lower quality. In "Recycling is Garbage", John Tierney claims that recycling newsprint produces 5000 gallons more polluted water than creating newspaper from virgin wood. (Tierney, 1996)

CRADLE TO GRAVE : TARGET IS ZERO

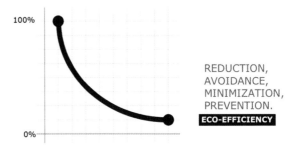

REDUCTION, AVOIDANCE, MINIMIZATION, PREVENTION.
ECO-EFFICIENCY

1‹ Eco-efficiency strives to minimize damage to ecological systems.

2.2. Eco-Efficiency is Inherently at Odds with Long-Term Economic Growth and Innovation

The ultimate aim of eco-efficiency approaches is to achieve a state of zero:zero waste emission, zero resource use and zero toxicity. Within the context of a system of cradle-to-grave material flows, however, the goal of zero is inherently unreachable. Despite the immense dematerialization possibilities of the digital era, it will never be possible to provide the vast majority of goods and services without the use of any material resources. The digital realm will always require the hardware to keep it running, and humans will always need food to nourish them, clothes to cover them, physical shelters to protect them and a transportation infrastructure to move them.

Eco-efficiency promotes incremental reductions in the ecological impact of industrial processes and products. While this type of incremental change has been a worthwhile (and maybe necessary) initial step with regards to laying a groundwork and getting hold of the "the low-hanging fruits", it cannot be regarded as an end in itself or even a feasible long-term strategy.

WHILE SUCH IMPROVEMENT CAN LEAD TO COST SAVINGS IN THE SHORT-TERM, OPPORTUNITIES FOR MARGINAL IMPROVEMENT INEVITABLY DECREASE AS DEMATERIALIZATION LIMITS ARE REACHED.

The subsequent maintenance of this dematerialized system limits possibilities for innovation and growth. Innovation is impossible because the priority for dematerialization suffocates creative approaches to the use of materials while simultaneously directing funding towards the generation of decreasingly beneficial incremental improvements. Growth becomes a problem because it threatens to result in increased resource use and waste emissions.

The constant pursuit of the goal of zero: *zero* waste, *zero* resources, *zero* impact—results in an uneasy marriage between financial and ecological objectives reflected for instance in the concept of the *triple bottom line*. In reality, triple bottom line strategies do not result in a balance amongst economic, environmental and social aims, because economic objectives remain paramount.

THE GOAL WITH REGARD TO ENVIRONMENT IS TO BE *LESS BAD*.

This approach is reflected amongst others in the vision statements of major corporations committed to a triple bottom line approach: "Philanthropy is important to Hewlett-Packard, but we at HP want our contribution and involvement in global citizenship initiatives to have a far greater impact than simply writing a check would .... On the environmental front, we have an explicit goal of designing new products so as to minimize their ecological impact, from production through disposal." (Dunn and Yamashita, 2003) Despite a positively-stated vision within the social realm, the implicit goal in the environmental realm is to achieve a state of *zero* impact.

2.3. Eco-Efficiency does not Effectively Address the Issue of Toxicity

Whether a telephone, an electric razor, athletic shoes, a newspaper or a mobile phone, all products emit chemicals. The concentration of these emitted chemicals is generally so small that they do not acutely sicken the user, but rather present an additional chemical load with an undefined long-term effect. The increasing contamination, especially of interior air, can lead to a multiplicity of health problems, including allergies, chronic fatigue syndrome and multiple chemical sensitivity. (Braungart and Soth, 1999) Statistics over the past several decades indicate two- to three-fold increases in various types of allergies in Europe, including allergic asthma, atopic dermatitis and others. (Watson, 1997). The increasingly ubiquitous application of certain chemicals in everyday products is highly suspect as a contributing factor. Common plastics, for instance, contain a wide spectrum of additives, including antioxi-dants, lubricants, antistatic agents, blowing agents, mineral fillers, pigments, plasticizers, flame retardants, heat stabilizers, impact modifiers, UV absorbers, longer life additives and others. The toxicological and ecotoxicological profiles of some of these substances are often not well defined. A recent study led by the Swedish National Testing and Research Institute, for instance, found a link between phthalates, a common plasticizer in PVC plastics, and allergic symptoms in children. (Bornehag, Sun-dell, Weschler, Sigsgaard, Lundgren and Hasselgren, 2004)

Global sourcing and lean production have resulted in products with undefined material and chemical compositions. A product assembled in Germany, for instance, may be made up of components produced in India and sub-components produced in China. The result is that companies often are unfamiliar with the material composition of their products, which may be wholly unsuitable for the purpose for which the products are intended.

FIG. 2 SHOWS THE OFF-GASSING DIAGRAM OF A BRAND-NAME CHILDREN'S TOY SOLD IN THE UNITED STATES AND PRODUCED IN CHINA.

Each peak in the diagram indicates a chemical emitted from the product into the air around it. Some of these peaks indicate the presence of a spectrum of aromatic hydrocarbons and other potentially toxic components, clearly unsuitable for application in a product intended for young children.

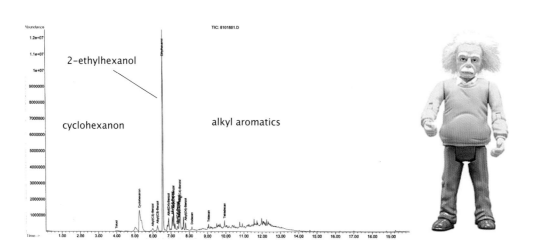

2◖ Off-gassing of a brand name children's toy sold in the United States.

When dealing with toxic chemicals, a minimization approach is insufficient. Even very small amounts of some toxic chemicals pose a significant risk because of their extreme bioaccumulation or eco-/toxic potential. Even more, existing knowledge about the toxicity of substances is for the most part limited to the toxicity of single substances. Studies show that significant allergenic potential also exists in synergies amongst multiple chemicals. (Bashir and Maibach, 1997) This presents an especially increased risk in the context of products that employ a larger set of chemicals and chemical combinations. Penetration enhancers used in cosmetics, for instance, can increase the ability of certain toxic chemicals to enter the body through the skin, enabling small amounts to have a multiplied effect.

As the levels of chemicals present in indoor air climbs, ecoefficient building construction guidelines call for more heavily insulated and tightly sealed interior spaces. While this helps to reduce energy requirements for maintaining constant interior temperatures, it also traps chemicals released into interior spaces, potentially leading to an acute incidence of indoor air pollution known as the *sick building syndrome*. (Brinke, Selvin, Hodgson, Fisk, Mendell, Koshland, Hägerhed-Engman, 1999)

ONE APPROACH TO REDUCING THE ISSUES ASSOCIATED WITH TOXIC CHEMICALS IN PRODUCTS IS TO REPLACE KNOWN TOXIC SUBSTANCES.

If a toxic substance is replaced with another substance that has a better eco-/toxicological profile, then this is certainly a step in the right direction. Such free of strategies may be problematic, however, because known toxic substances are sometimes replaced by others with similar, or even worse, toxicological characteristics. This may occur, for instance, if the toxicological profile of the replacement substance is unknown, or if inconsistent regulations call for the elimination of a particular high-profile substance while leaving open the possibility for the application of potential replacement substances with similar toxicological characteristics. A 1989 ban of the wood preservative

pentachlorophenol in Germany, for instance, did not automatically result in the banning of tetrachlorophenol, despite their comparable toxicological properties.

The zero emissions concept contradicts thermodynamics: existence creates emissions.

BY STRIVING TO ELIMINATE EMISSIONS FROM THEIR ACTIVITIES, PEOPLE ARE ATTEMPTING TO SEVER THE LINK BETWEEN THEMSELVES AND THEIR ENVIRONMENT.

An eco-effective approach takes the position that the quantity of the emissions is not the problem, it is the quality of the outputs that must be addressed by making the emissions healthy. To illustrate this, consider that the biomass of ants on the planet is greater than that of humans, yet the Earth suffers no ill effect from ants' emissions, rather it is continually nourished by them. (McDonough and Braungart, 2003) Eco-effectiveness designates all outputs from human activity as positive—healthy waste is good—and make people native to the planet once more by re-establishing a positive link between human activity and natural systems. In this, eco-effectiveness eliminates the need to associate guilt with human activity, and celebrates the relationship between man and nature as mutually beneficial.

3. Eco-Effectiveness and Cradle-to-Cradle Design

In contrast to eco-efficiency that begins against an assumption of linear, cradle-to-grave material flows, eco-effectiveness encompasses a set of strategies for generating healthy, cradle-to-cradle material flow metabolisms. Use of the term metabolism in this case is indicative of a similarity between cradle-to-cradle material flow systems and the internal processes of a living organism. Ayres and Simonis (1994) note the similarities between biological organisms and industrial activities on multiple levels. Just as the metabolic systems of biological organisms include the synthesis and breaking down of substances for the maintenance of life, the metabolic systems of eco-effective material flow systems include the synthesis and breaking down of products for the maintenance of a healthy economy and provision for human needs.

Eco-effectiveness is modelled on the successful interdependence and regenerative productivity of natural systems. In nature, all outputs from one process become inputs for another. The concept of waste does not exist. The blossoms of a cherry tree bring forth a new generation of cherry trees while also providing food for microorganisms, which in turn nourish the soil and support the growth of future plant-life.

Each element within a natural system may also be highly inefficient. The growth and release of thousands of cherry blossoms, only a few of which may become new cherry trees, is a travesty of material intensity per service unit. When the cherry tree is viewed in the context of the interdependent natural system of which it is a part, however, the overall effectiveness of the system becomes clear.

In eco-effective industrial systems, the material intensity per service unit of each individual element is irrelevant to the effectiveness of the whole.

AS LONG AS THOSE MATERIALS THAT ENTER INDUSTRIAL SYSTEMS ARE PERPETUALLY MAINTAINED AT THE STATUS OF RESOURCES, THE SYSTEM IS PERFECTLY EFFECTIVE AND NO WASTE IS PRODUCED.

If the trimmings from the production of a textile system are composed in such a way that they become nutrients for ecological systems, then it is ecologically irrelevant when they are not included in the saleable product. Even if the material intensity per service unit of the textile mill were astronomically high, the system as a whole would be highly eco-effective because the trimmings would become productive resources for natural systems.

Efficiency and effectiveness can be complementary strategies. If efficiency is defined as "doing things the right way", effectiveness means "doing the right things". (Drucker,

2002) The concept of efficiency in itself has no value; it can be either good or bad. If industry is driven by systems that are inherently destructive, making them more efficient will not solve the problem, and may even aggravate it (e.g. the rebound effect). (Berkhout, Muskens, et. al, 2000) The slimming down of material flows per product or service unit (eco-efficiency) is only beneficial in the long-term if the goal of closing material flows (eco-effectiveness) has first been achieved. Once effectiveness has been achieved, efficiency improvements are not an environmental necessity, but a matter of equity. They are necessary to ensure the fair distribution of goods and services.

Where eco-efficiency begins with an assumption of industry that is 100% bad, Eco-effectiveness starts with a vision of industry that is 100% good (Fig. 3), that supports and

258

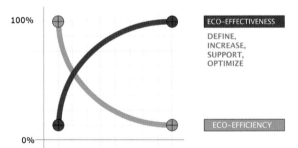

3⟨ Eco-effectiveness strives to generate an entirely (100%) beneficial impact upon ecological sys-tems.

regenerates ecological systems and enables long-term economic prosperity. This perspective is the basis for the concept of the triple top line. (McDonough and Braungart, 2002) Pursuit of triple bottom line objectives promotes awareness within companies of the environmental and social impacts of their activities and a drive to minimize ecological footprint. In contrast to this, pursuit of triple top line growth begins with recognition of the inherent business value of natural and social capital, and promotes a celebration of the potential synergies amongst economic, environmental and social business aims.

3.1. Cradle-to-Cradle Design

Cradle-to-cradle design enables the creation of wholly beneficial industrial systems driven by the synergistic pursuit of positive economic, environmental and social goals. The practical, strategic expression of the eco-effective philosophy, *cradle-to-cradle design* defines a framework for designing products and industrial processes that turn materials into nutrients by enabling their perpetual flow within one of two distinct *metabolisms*: the *biological metabolism* and the *technical metabolism*.

Materials that flow optimally through the biological metabolism are called biological nutrients. As defined for cradle-to-cradle products, biological nutrients are biodegradable materials (or the result of biodegradation processes) posing no immediate or eventual hazard to living systems that can be used for human purposes and be safely returned to the environment to feed biological processes. Biological nutrients can be natural or plant-based materials, but include also materials like biopolymers and other potentially synthetic substances that are safe for humans and natural systems.

THE BIOLOGICAL METABOLISM INCLUDES PROCESSES OF RESOURCE EXTRACTION, MANUFACTURING AND CUSTOMER USE, AS WELL AS THE EVENTUAL RETURN OF THESE MATERIALS TO NATURAL SYSTEMS WHERE THEY CAN AGAIN BE TRANSFORMED INTO RESOURCES FOR HUMAN ACTIVITY.

Products conceived as biological nutrients are called *products of consumption*. This, for instance, includes products that may actually be consumed (e.g. through physical degradation or abrasion) during the duration of their lifespan, such as textiles, brake pads, shoe soles, etc. Because they are designed as nutrients for living systems, products of consumption can be returned to the natural environment after use to become nutrients for living systems. A biological nutrient textile, for example, can be used as garden mulch after its useful life as an upholstery fabric. An ice cream wrapper can be designed to contain seeds and liquefy at room temperature so that when thrown away, it not only dissolves safely into the ground but also supports the growth of plant-life.

A technical nutrient, on the other hand, may be defined as a material, frequently synthetic or mineral, that has the potential to remain safely in a closed-loop system of manufacture, recovery, and reuse (the technical metabolism), maintaining its highest value through many product life cycles. Technical nutrients are used as *products of service*, which are durable goods that render a service to customers. The product is used by the customer but owned by the manufacturer, either formally or in effect. The product of service strategy is mutually beneficial to the manufacturer and the customer.

THE MANUFACTURER MAINTAINS OWNERSHIP OF VALUABLE MATERIAL ASSETS FOR CONTINUAL REUSE WHILE THE CUSTOMERS RECEIVE THE SERVICE OF THE PRODUCT WITHOUT ASSUMING ITS MATERIAL LIABILITY.

The manufacturer or commercial representative of the product also fosters long-term relationships with returning customers through many product life cycles. Consider, for instance, a television or a washing machine that is leased to a customer for a defined period, and then afterwards returned to the company so that the materials can be recovered and used again in the creation of new products (either by the same or a different company, but at an equivalent or higher level of quality).

BIOLOGICAL CYCLE

Consumer Goods (natural fibers, cosmetics, detergents, etc.) are designed so that they can be used in the biological cycle over and over again. They will decompose to organic nutrients and promote biological nutrients and systems such as plant growth. The renewable raw materials are in turn the basis for new products.

Trigema: T-Shirt

100% Organic Cotton, short sleeve TRIGEMA was jointly developed with the Environmental Institute EPEA as the world's first COMPOSTABLE Polo SHIRT, particularly skin-friendly, best ware physiological properties: Durable, as well as best wash and light fastness. Short sleeve, with a no buttons collar. Women's Cut.

Material: Piqué (100% Organic Cotton)

The textiles and garments which have been developed are composed of a variety of material components (threads, labels, threads, dyes), all of which have been defined as part of the secure biological cycle system.

The "Wellness Polo Shirt" by TRIGEMA® is the world's first 100% organic cotton T-Shirt in Cradle to Cradle®. It is characterized by specific skin-friendliness, excellent ware-physiological properties, durability as the best wash and light fastness.

Rohner Textil AG: Climatex®

"Climatex Lifecycle®" is durable, safe for biological cycles, and made from renewable resources with Cradle to Cradle® Gold certification.
Not only the raw materials, but also the production processes of these materials meet the stringent criteria of eco-effective principles of Cradle to Cradle®. For example, 1600 different dyes were assessed, of which 16 were recognized as safe and free of heavy metals.
"Climatex Lifecycle®" is completely biodegradable. Even waste from production is made into felt which may be used, for example, as garden mulch for strawberries and cucumbers.

www.gessner.ch

26

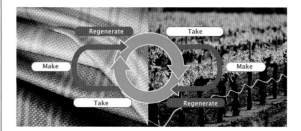

Strategy Biological Cycle:

The refund system
How to reward the customer

• 1 € for a used T-Shirt
• Business to Customer Relation Network

TECHNICAL CYCLE

Service Products (TV sets, cars, synthetic fibers, etc.), the so-called technical nutrients, are seperated to enable the production of new commodities after fulfilling their initial function. The users/consumers purchase only the relevant services, e.g television. The materials remain the property of the manufacturer, which retains them through collection and reenters them into the technical cycle.

Backhausen Interior Textiles: Returnity®

Backhausen developed jointly with the German environmental research institute EPEA International Umweltforschung GmbH, Returnity®, the world's first environmentally friendly and 100% cyclable flame-retardant Trevira CS fabrics. Based on the Cradle to Cradle® philosophy, the environmentally friendly chemical optimization method was developed and implemented including the entire manufacturing process of furniture and decorative fabrics.

The chemical substances of concern, especially in the yarn dyeing and the final finishing treatment, have been extracted and replaced with ingredients harmless to humans and which are not harmful to the environment. The flame resistent fiber Trevira CS can therefore circulate in a technical cycle. Returnity® fabrics will be taken back after use. Under license, this technology can be adopted by qualified mills worldwide.

The first Backhausen collection called "Elements", which consists of 100% Returnity®, was first presented in Autumn 2008 and is on the way to conquering the market. The application of the fabric is used in the fields of seat manufacturing and office furniture and in the production of made-up textile products (except apparel). Since the 1st of July 2009 Backhausen produces all Trevira CS fabrics in Returnity® quality.

www.backhausen.com
www.returnity.at

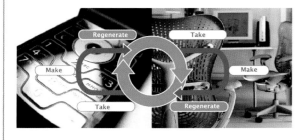

Strategy Technical Cycle:

The leasing system
How to re-use a chair

- 3 year lease
- take back system
- repolymerize materials making endless lifecycles a reality

CHAIR MANUFACTURE   CHAIR SALE AND USE   CHAIR RECOVERY

REPOLYMERIZATION   DISSASSEMBLY

4. From Efficiency to Effectiveness

The shift from efficiency to effectiveness necessitates a fundamental redesign of products and the system of industrial material flows within which they circulate. Cradle-to-cradle design defines a broad framework for creating eco-effective industrial systems, but for businesses to put this framework into practice they need both the right technologies and the right strategies.

Standard life cycle assessment (LCA) is an unsuitable approach for generating eco-effective products and processes because its linear nature does not allow for optimization in the context of cradle-to-cradle design. Braungart and McDonough (2001a, 2001b, 2001c, 2001d, 2001e) have defined a step-wise strategy for businesses to realize the transition from eco-efficiency to eco-effectiveness on the level of product design:

Step 1: Free of ...
Step 2: Personal preferences
Step 3: The passive positive list
Step 4: The active positive list
Step 5: Reinvention

This five-step process begins with an elimination of undesirable substances and moves towards the positive definition of desirable substances (Step 4). Ultimately, Step 5 calls for a *reinvention* of products by reconsidering how they may optimally fulfill the need or needs for which they are actually intended while simultaneously being supportive of ecological and social systems.

4.1. Step 1: Free of ...

Most companies today have a very limited knowledge of the toxicological and eco-toxicological characteristics of the substances that make up their products. An automobile, for instance, may contain thousands of different materials and chemicals. Gaining an understanding of the impact that each of these materials may have on the natural environment and human health is an immense undertaking, and something that the large majority of businesses have not done and do not immediately have the capacity to do.

Most companies, however, have a general knowledge of the most dangerous substances in their products (referred to as X-substances in the context of eco-effectiveness). For companies like this, a first step in moving towards eco-effectiveness is to find replacements for the X-substances in their products.

THIS INCLUDES SUBSTANCES LIKE MERCURY, CADMIUM AND LEAD THAT ARE KNOWN OR SUSPECTED CARCINOGENS, TERATOGENS, MUTAGENS OR ENDOCRINE DISRUPTORS.

Removal of X-substances is almost always a step in the right direction, but as noted previously, such a *"free of"* approach has to be applied carefully to ensure that replacement substances are indeed better than those that are replaced.

4.2. Step 2: Personal Preferences

Once the most undesirable substances have been removed from a product, the next step is to begin to make educated choices about those substances that should be included in the product. Though the best way to do this is to have a detailed knowledge about the impacts of a particular substance on ecological and human systems throughout its life cycle, this is often impractical or even impossible. Furthermore, different substances have different types of impacts. Should a company prefer a substance which is potentially sensitizing or one which is persistent in the environment; a substance that may contribute to global warming or one that might end up harming marine life?

Without a detailed scientific knowledge of a substance's toxicological profile and its fate throughout the life-cycle of a product, these decisions can be difficult to make. At the same time, design decisions have to be made and products have to be brought to the market. With incomplete knowledge, the best way to make decisions about which chemicals and materials to include in a product comes down to personal preferences based upon the best available information. Though decisions guided by *personal preferences* may not always result in the most eco-effective

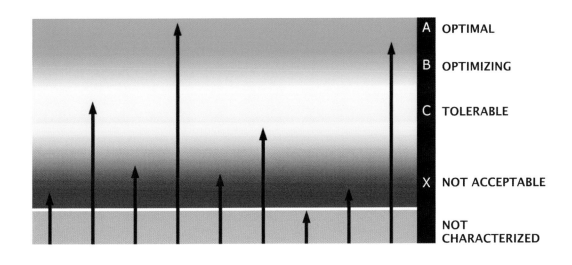

A	OPTIMAL
B	OPTIMIZING
C	TOLERABLE
X	NOT ACCEPTABLE
	NOT CHARACTERIZED

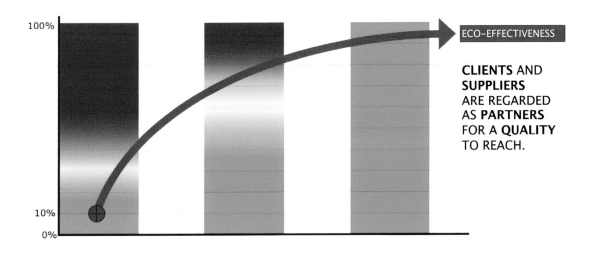

ECO–EFFECTIVENESS

CLIENTS AND **SUPPLIERS** ARE REGARDED AS **PARTNERS** FOR A **QUALITY** TO REACH.

design choices, they generally will result in a product that is at least less bad than its predecessors.

4.3. Step 3: The Passive Positive List

Step 3 includes a systematic assessment of each ingredient in a product to classify them according to their toxicological and eco-toxicological characteristics, especially their capability to flow within biological and technical metabolisms. For products of consumption, criteria to examine should include for instance: toxicity to humans (acute, delayed, developmental, reproductive), aquatic toxicity, persistence and bio-accumulation in nature, sensitization potential, mutagenicity, carcinogenicity and endocrine disruption potential. Based upon the assessment of a material or chemical according to these criteria, a *passive positive list* can be generated which classifies each substance according to its suitability for the biological metabolism. This list can be used to determine the degree of additional optimization necessary for a particular product to be a true product of consumption.

This same process applies for products of service as well, though the criteria are somewhat different. Cadmium, for instance, is a highly toxic heavy metal, and is often applied in photovoltaics in the form of cadmium telluride. Though cadmium telluride is far from an ideal substance from an ecological perspective, its careful application in photovoltaics in the context of a product of service concept may be considered acceptable until a suitable replacement is found.

AS PART OF A DEFINED MATERIAL FLOW METABOLISM THAT ENSURES THE SAFE HANDLING AND RECAPTURE OF THE MATERIAL AFTER USE, THE RISK OF THE CADMIUM COMING INTO CONTACT WITH NATURAL SYSTEMS IS MINIMAL.

4.4. Step 4: The Active Positive List

Step 4 includes the optimization of the passive positive list to the point until each ingredient in the product is positively

defined as a biological or technical nutrient. Whereas step 3 establishes knowledge of the degree to which each component in a product needs to be optimized, step 4 implements this optimization to the fullest degree. Climatex® Lifecycle™ upholstery fabric is an example of a product whose constituent materials are positively defined as biological nutrients. Created in a collaboration amongst EPEA Internationale Umweltforschung GmbH, McDonough Braungart Design Chemistry and Rohner Textil, Climatex® Lifecycle™ is a completely biodegradable and compostable fabric. Each component was selected according to EPEA's positive listing methodology for its positive environmental and human health characteristics and its suitability as a biological nutrient.

The fabric is made from natural fibers, including wool from free-ranging, humanely sheared New Zealand sheep, and Ramie, a tall, fibrous plant grown in Asia. To identify suitable dyes for the fabric, 60 major dye producers were asked to provide the necessary information on their best dyes to enable an assessment of their suitability as biological nutrients.

FROM A SELECTION OF 1600 DYE FORMULATIONS, EPEA UTILIZED THEIR METHODOLOGY TO IDENTIFY 16 THAT MET BOTH THE DESIRED TECHNICAL AND ENVIRONMENTAL SPECIFICATIONS. (KÄLIN, 2001)

The optimization of the materials and dyes used in the product also has an impact upon the environmental profile of the production process. Before eco-effective optimization of the product, trimmings from the mill were classified as hazardous waste requiring special (and expensive) disposal. After optimization, waste material from the mill could be made into felt to be used as garden mulch, and in the cultivation of strawberries, cucumbers and a wide range of other plants.

Step 4 also applies for products of service. An automobile, for instance, might be designed so all of the materials and components it contains are biological or technical nutrients.

Brake pads, tires and interior upholstery might be designed as biological nutrients because these are components that will likely degrade over the period of use of the car. The frame and body, on the other hand, might optimally be designed as technical nutrients like steel and polypropylene so they can be regained and upcycled into new automobile components or other products after the use period of the car.

The Ford Model U concept car reflects an initial effort to put this concept into practice. It contains a number of biological and technical nutrient materials, including a polyester upholstery fabric optimized for flow in closed-loop cycles and a car top made from polylactic acid, a potential biological nutrient. From packaging (Newcorn, 2003) and textiles (Rodie, 2003) to buildings (Gissen, 2002) and furniture (Smith, 2005), the practicality of this approach has been illustrated again and again. Once a product's material components have been positively defined as biological or technical nutrients, Step 4 has been achieved.

4.5. Step 5: Reinvention

Where step 4 stops at the level of redefining the substances in a product, step 5 involves a *reinvention* of the relationship of the product with the customer. The concept of reinvention addresses the inter-connected nature of ecological, social and economic systems by pushing the idea of the biological and technical metabolisms beyond the confines of existing product and service forms.

STRATEGIES FOR REINVENTION VIEW PRODUCTS FROM THE PERSPECTIVE OF THE SERVICES THEY PROVIDE AND THE NEEDS THEY FULFILL FOR CUSTOMERS AND FOR THE BROADER CONTEXT OF SOCIAL AND ECOLOGICAL SYSTEMS.

The product of service concept offers an ideal strategy for this. One might think about a washing machine, for instance, in terms of the service it provides: a convenient cleansing system for clothes. When customers purchase a washing machine, they are not paying for ownership of the materials it contains but for this service that it provides. If companies began to sell the service of a convenient cleansing system for clothes instead of the material object of the washing machine, a new set of immediate benefits becomes apparent. A company could potentially still provide a washing machine to customers, but perhaps under the form of a time-limited lease, or 3000 cycles of washing including service and possibly even detergent and water. Ownership of the washing machine itself would not change hands.

One benefit of such a system is that customers are no longer confronted with the liability associated with owning a product which contains potentially hazardous materials, connected with the dilemma of what to do with them at the end of the product's useful life. Another benefit for customers is that their interests are now aligned with those of their service provider. Under a traditional situation of ownership transfer, it is at least partially in the interest of the company to provide a product that fails as quickly as possible because this enables them an opportunity to sell yet another washing machine to their customer. This system encourages the production of cheap, low-quality goods. When products are provided in the form of a service scheme, however, companies are interested in producing the best product possible, because the better the needs of customers are fulfilled the more likely they are to remain customers after the end of the service period. Furthermore, when products are constructed using biological and technical nutrient materials, companies have the added benefit of getting these valuable nutrients back after the product's defined use period. This enables the application, for instance, of high quality technical nutrient materials like polysulfonic polymers, which are too expensive for application in most products when they are not regained after use. The result is higher quality and less expensive products.

Going back to the example of the automobile, reinvention means considering how the services that an automobile provides may be fulfilled with broader ecological and social benefits. This might mean, for instance, designing a nutrivehicle that not only releases no negative emissions, but releases positive emissions that have a nourishing effect on the environment. Instead of making the catalytic converter as small as possible, methods could be developed so that the nitrogen could be used as a fertilizer. Cars could be constructed so that as much nitrogen as possible is produced and collected during use. Likewise, perhaps using fluid mechanics, tires could be designed to attract and capture harmful particles, thus cleaning air instead of further dirtying it.

If in twenty years there are three times as many cars on the streets, then their relationship with ecological systems will only be a part of the issue.

THE AMOUNT OF RESOURCES (BOTH LAND AND MATERIAL) REQUIRED TO SUSTAIN SUCH WIDESPREAD USE OF THE AUTOMOBILE WOULD HAVE A SIGNIFICANTLY DETRIMENTAL SOCIAL EFFECT BY PLACING SEVERE LIMITS ON RESOURCE AVAILABILITY.

In this case, reinvention means considering how systems of mobility might be redesigned to have a beneficial impact on social conditions while better fulfilling the need for mobility.

The concept of the *community car* (McDonough and Braungart, 2001d) addresses these issues. As part of a local or regional transportation plan, the community car could automatically respond to electronic calls to provide door-to-door transportation service twenty-four hours a day. Operating within a smaller area, the cars could eventually even be driven automatically, providing the service of transportation amongst others to children, the elderly, the handicapped, and a broad spectrum of others who are often excluded from current forms of transportation, while at the same time reducing the number of cars on the road.

5. Eco-Effective Nutrient Management

Products designed as biological or technical nutrients need to be embedded in an eco-effective system of *nutrient flows*. The effective management of nutrient flows associated with the biological and technical metabolism necessitates the formation of collaborative business structures with the role of coordinating the flow of materials and information throughout the product life cycle.

Individual businesses generally have control only over a small portion of material flow system of which their product is a part, and are incapable of directing the flow of materials or exchanging intelligence with other actors throughout the product's life-cycle. Manufacturers may be able to positively define the materials in their products as biological or technical nutrients, but once the product has been passed on to customers they have little control over the fate of its constituent materials.

Extended producer responsibility legislation like the EU's End-of-Life Vehicles (ELV) Directive requires manufacturers to begin to ensure the safe handling of their product's materials after the customer use phase. The ELV Directive has stimulated the formation of automobile industry collaborations for the safe take-back and recycling of automobiles within the EU. In this case, the producer links the upstream (supplier) and downstream (collector, dismantler, and shredder) portions of the vehicle's life cycle through coordinated collaboration with actors on both ends as well as with other vehicle manufacturers. Though the ELV Directive and other similar legislative initiatives have generally not spurred the development of true cradle-to-cradle metabolisms, they have resulted in the beginnings of collaborative mechanisms for handling the flow of materials throughout the product life cycle.

THE SHIFT TO ECO-EFFECTIVE INDUSTRIAL SYSTEMS AND THE ENABLING OF UPCYCLING REQUIRES NOT ONLY A REDIRECTION OF MATERIAL FLOWS, BUT ALSO THE ESTABLISHMENT OF NEW FORMS OF SUPPORTIVE INFORMATION AND FINANCE FLOW NETWORKS.

Manufacturers require information from suppliers concerning the exact composition of their intermediate products and disassembly capabilities at recovery sites; customers need information on how to deal with the product after its use period; recyclers need information on appropriate dismantling processes and material composition. The exact structure of the network that supplies this information and the manner in which information is shared may vary amongst situations. Kamejima and Ejiri (1993) suggest the use of automized computer-based systems for the sharing of information between suppliers/manufacturers and recyclers in the context of achieving cyclical material flow systems.

As an initial move in the direction of cyclical material flows for automobiles, the ELV Directive has given rise to a new network of information flows amongst relevant actors. Original equipment manufacturers (OEMs) are required to release dismantling information within 6 months of the release of a new vehicle, and to provide information to prospective buyers about design changes that increase vehicle recyclability. Likewise, the International Material Data System (IMDS) was developed in collaboration amongst automobile OEMs as a tool to integrate and share supplier data relating to the constituent substances of varying tiers of an automobile construction.

The ELV Directive establishes the OEM in a central role as a coordinator of information and material flows, but structures for realizing cradle-to-cradle metabolisms may take many different forms. Regardless of their configuration, the central role of these structures remains the same: *to optimize or ensure the integrity of cyclical nutrient flow metabolisms and the maintenance of the status of materials as resources.*

IN ADDITION TO COORDINATING THE FLOW OF MATERIALS THE STRUCTURE ALSO PLAYS A KEY ROLE IN MANAGING THE EXCHANGE OF INFORMATION AND INTELLIGENCE AMONGST ACTORS.

In some cases, this role may best be fulfilled by an entity (an organization or group of organizations) external to the

network of material flows. Such an entity could ensure that all actors within the material flow metabolism have access to the information that they need, while also ensuring that proprietary information remains proprietary.

A CHEMICAL COMPANY PRODUCING A PARTICULAR DYE FORMULATION, FOR INSTANCE, MAY WISH TO KEEP THE SPECIFICS OF THEIR FORMULATIONS CONFIDENTIAL TO ENSURE THAT THEY ARE NOT COPIED BY COMPETITORS.

At the same time, a fabric manufacturer wishing to dye their products with the chemical company's product may want to be able to ensure the compatibility of the dye formulation with the criteria for a product of consumption. A third party external to the material flow system may be in an ideal position to mediate the exchange of information in this situation by analyzing and certifying the formulation as a biological nutrient while ensuring the safe handling of proprietary information. In other contexts as well, this external entity could provide each actor throughout the material flow metabolism with the necessary information to ensure the eco-effective integrity of the system as a whole.

6. Intelligent Materials Pooling

Another type of structure for the management of eco-effective nutrient flow metabolisms is intelligent materials pooling. (McDonough and Braungart, 2003) Intelligent materials pooling is a framework for the collaboration of economic actors within the technical metabolism which allows companies to pool material resources, specialized knowledge and purchasing power relating to the acquisition, transformation and sale of technical nutrients and their associated products. The result is a mutually beneficial system of cooperation amongst actors along the supply chain that supports the formation of coherent technical metabolisms and the enabling of product-service strategies.

The heart of an intelligent materials pooling community is a *materials bank*, which maintains ownership of technical nutrient chemicals and materials. The materials bank leases these substances to participating companies, who in turn transform them into products and provide them to consumers in the form of a service scheme. After a defined use period, the materials are recovered and returned to the materials bank. The materials bank also manages the information associated with these materials, integrating and sharing related information amongst relevant actors. In this manner, it ensures the accumulation of intelligence relating to a particular material over time, and a true *upcycling* of the material.

As illustrated in Fig. 4, the duties of a materials bank are ideally performed by the product chain actor responsible for post-use reprocessing of the material (e.g. a polymer or steel producer). This actor is responsible for reprocessing and intermediate storage of the material, as well as for leasing it to others for transformation into products.

The formation of an intelligent materials pooling community is a four-step process:

- Phase 1. Creating community: identification of willing industrial partners with a common interest in replacing hazardous chemicals with technical nutrients, targeting of toxic chemicals for replacement;
- Phase 2. Utilizing market strength: sharing lists of materials targeted for elimination, development of a positive purchasing and procurement list of preferred intelligent chemicals;
- Phase 3. Defining material flows: development of specifications and designs for preferred materials, creation of common materials bank, design of a technical metabolism for preferred materials;
- Phase 4. Ongoing support: preferred business partner agreements amongst community members, sharing of information gained from research and material use, co-branding strategies.

The formation of intelligent materials pooling communities has the potential to result in economic advantage for all actors involved. By establishing a framework for materials to be regained after use, intelligent materials pooling enables the application of higher quality materials at lower cost.

THIS IN TURN RESULTS IN THE POTENTIAL FOR HIGHER QUALITY, SAFER AND LESS EXPENSIVE PRODUCTS.

The prospects for realization of this potential depend upon the specific material metabolism in question, namely the relationship between the costs of material recovery and recycling and those associated with disposal and raw material acquisition.

In the steel industry, for instance, value is often lost when a range of grades is mixed in the recycling process. A materials pool could preserve the value of steel over many life cycles by specifying the separation of different grades. Rare, valuable constituent elements such as chromium, nickel, cobalt and copper could also be preserved and reused at the highest level of quality. With cooperation

4◀ Material flows in the context of an Intelligent Materials Pooling community.

between steel producers (the materials banks) and the manufacturers of a wide variety of products, from automobiles to trains to refrigerators, the steel loop could begin to be closed and the value of its nutrients preserved over time. The aim is not just zero waste, but the maintenance or upgrading of the quality and productivity of materials through subsequent cycles of production and use.

7. Conclusions

Eco-effectiveness is a concept for the production and consumption of goods and services that goes beyond the reduction of negative consequences implied in eco-efficiency and zero emission. Eco-effectiveness positively defines the beneficial environmental, social, and economic traits of goods and services, thereby eliminating the fundamental problems (material flow quality limitations, antagonism to economic growth and innovation, and toxicity) that arise in eco-efficiency strategies.

ECO-EFFECTIVENESS ENCOMPASSES A SET OF STRATEGIES: CRADLE-TO-CRADLE DESIGN, POSITIVE LISTS, INTELLIGENT MATERIALS POOLING, ETC. THAT ENABLE THE FORMATION OF CYCLICAL MATERIAL FLOW METABOLISMS.

Eco-effective material flow systems not only empower materials to maintain their status as resources, but by establishing a coherent network of information flows amongst actors in the material flow chain, they enable a continual accumulation of knowledge that forms the basis for true *upcycling*. This continuously accumulating intelligence becomes a perpetual source of added value to products and services, and provides for a supportive relationship between eco-effective industrial systems and long-term economic prosperity. The aim is not only to achieve zero emissions, but to utilize materials in a way that maintains or increases their value and productivity over time.

Coherent biological and technical metabolisms ensure the availability of raw materials for industrial processes. In the technical metabolism, material reprocessing is conducted by industry and generates added employment and further economic activity. Within the biological metabolism, material reprocessing is carried out by ecological processes, and results in the regeneration and replenishment of natural systems.

THIS SUPPORTIVE RELATIONSHIP BETWEEN THE BIOLOGICAL METABOLISM AND THE HEALTH OF NATURAL SYSTEMS IS THE BASIS FOR A *POSITIVE RECOUPLING* OF THE RELATIONSHIP BETWEEN ECOLOGY AND ECONOMY.

References

Australian Government. http://erin.gov.au/industry/finance/glossary.html

Ayres, R.U. and Simonis, U.E. 1994. Industrial metabolism: restructuring for sustainable development. Tokyo: United Nations University Press.

Bashir, S. and Maibach, H.I. 1997. Compound allergy. An overview. Contact Dermatitis, 36: 179–83.

Berkhout, P., Muskens, H.G., Jos, C., Velthuijsen, J.W. 2000. Defining the rebound effect. Energy Policy, 28(6–7): 425–32.

Bornehag, C.G, Sundell, J., Weschler, C.J., Sigsgaard, T., Lundgren, B., Hasselgren, M., et al. 2004. The association between asthma and allergic symptoms in children and phthalates in house dust: a nested case-control study. Environmental Health Perspectives, 112(14): 1393–7.

Braungart, M. and Soth, J. 1999. Allergieprävention durch intelligentes Produkt-Design. Medizin und Umwelt, 12: 54–8.

Brinke, J.T., Selvin, S., Hodgson, A.T., Fisk, W.J., Mendell, M.J., Koshland, C.P., et al. 1999. Development of new volatile organic compound (VOC) exposure metrics and their relationship to "sick building syndrome" symptoms. Indoor Air, 8(3): 140.

Drucker, F.E. 2002. The effective executive. 4th ed. New York: HarperCollins.

Dunn, D. and Yamashita, K. 2003. Microcapitalism and the megacorporation. Harvard Business Review, August: 1–9.

European Environmental Agency. http://reports.eea.eu.int/

Fiksel J. (Ed.) 1996. Design for environment: creating eco-efficient products and processes. McGraw-Hill.

Gissen, D., (Ed.). Big & green: toward sustainable architecture in the 21st century. Princeton Architectural Press; 2002.

Global Development Research Center. www.gdrc.org/uem/ait-terms.html

Grimal L. 2003. The adoption of cleaner production technology and the emergence of industrial ecology activity: consequences for employment. In D. Bourg and S. Erkman (Eds). Perspectives on industrial ecology. Alsace, France.

Kälin, A. 2001. Positiv definierter Chemikalieneinsatz als Voraussetzung für die Schließung von Material- und Wasserkreisläufen: Das Beispiel des Möbelbezugstoffes Climatex Lifecycle der Rohner Textil AG. In E.U. von Weizsäcker, B. Stigson and J.D. Seiler-Hausmann (Eds.) Von Ökoeffizienz zu nachhaltiger Entwicklung in Unternehmen. Wuppertal: Wuppertal Institute.

Kamejima, K. and Ejiri, M. 1993. Recycling on network: an information-control architecture for ecologically-conscious industry. In: Proceedings of the 1993 International Conference on Advanced Robotics, Tokyo.

LEAN Advisors. http://www.leanadvisors.com

Martin, D.J. Zero waste: useful target or dangerous delusion? http://www.productpolicy.org/assets/resources/DuncanMartin2004ZW.pdf (accessed February 2006).

McDonough, W. and Braungart, M. 2001a. Reinventing the world, Green@Work, 8: 43–5.

McDonough, W. and Braungart, M. 2001b. Reinventing the world: step two, Green@Work, 9: 37–40.

McDonough, W. and Braungart, M. 2001c. Reinventing the world: step three, Green@Work. 10: 33–5.

McDonough, W. and Braungart, M. 2001d. Reinventing the world: step four, Green@Work. 11: 29–32.

McDonough, W. and Braungart, M. 2001e. Reinventing the world: step five, Green@Work. 12: 32–5.

McDonough, W. and Braungart, M. 2002. Design for the triple top line: new tools for sustainable commerce. Corporate

Environmental Strategy, 9(3): 251–8.

McDonough, W. and Braungart, M. 2003. Intelligent materials pooling: evolving a profitable technical metabolism through a supportive business community. Green@Work, 20: 50–4.

Newcorn, D. May 2003. Cradle-to-cradle: the next packaging paradigm? Packaging World. http://www.packworld.com/ articles/Features/16105.html. (accessed February 2006).

Nokia. http://www.nokia.com

North K. 1997. Environmental business management. 2nd revised ed. Geneva: International Labour Organisation.

Pirker, U., Pschernig, G., Gwehenberger, G. and Schnitzer, H. 2002. Implementation of zero emissions waste technologies. 8th European Roundtable on Cleaner Production Conference, Oct. 9–11, Cork, Ireland. http://zeria.tugraz.at/pics/zeria_ round_table.pdf (accessed January 2006).

PrintNet. http://www.printnet.com.au

Rodie, J.B. March 2003. Survival tactics. Textile World. http:// www.textileworld.com/ News.htm?CD ¼1371&;ID¼3533. (accessed February 2006).

Schmidt-Bleek, F. 1998. Das MIPS-Konzept—Faktor 10. Munich: Droemer.

Schütz, H. and Welfens, M.J. 2000. Sustainable development by dematerialization in production and consumption — strategy for the new environmental policy in Poland. Wuppertal Institute, June, no. 103.

Smith, R. 2005. Beyond recycling: manufacturers embrace "C2C" design. The Wall Street Journal, March, 3: B1–2.

Tierney, J. 1996. Recycling is garbage. The New York Times Magazine, June, 30:2–8.

Toshiba Group. http://www.toshiba.co.jp

UNIDO. 2003. Industry and environment: the need for a new industrial revolution. UNIDO position paper. 30 September, 2003.

Verfaillie, H.A. and Bidwell, R. 2000. Measuring eco-efficiency: a guide to reporting company performance. World Business Council for Sustainable Development, June 2000.

Watson, R. 1997. Europe urged to tackle rise in allergies. BMJ, 314:1641.

WMC Resources Ltd. http://www.wmc.com.au/sustain/ envrep97/glossary.htm

World Business Council for Sustainable Development (Ed.) Ecoefficiency. http://www.wbcsd.ch/templates/ TemplateWBCSD5/ lay-out.asp?type¼p&;MenuId¼NzA&doO pen¼1&ClickMenu¼LeftMenu. (accessed January 2005).

Zero Waste International Alliance. Standards. http://www. zwia.org/standards.html (accessed February 2006).

Zero Waste New Zealand Trust. The end of waste. http:// www.zerowaste.co.nz/assets/Reports/TheEndofWaste.pdf (accessed February 2006).

MANAGEMENT STRATEGIES BY DESIGN ❮

MICHAEL SHAMIYEH ❮

Today, men and women running businesses are beginning to understand that, in light of the increasingly diverse forms of the complexities of our world, the field of business strategy is in need of new approaches. The ill-suitedness of traditional approaches to strategy formulation in the sense of scientific planning is evident. Whereas controlling, integrating and coordinating—as fundamental to "business administration"—are all potentially important tasks, the emphasis on science and excessive emphasis on analysis at the expense of creative conjecture dramatically underestimates the value and necessity of conceiving and designing new futures at times of manic cycles of change.

THERE IS A NEED FOR PROCESSES THAT MOVE BEYOND THE STERILITY OF SCIENTIFIC STRATEGIC PLANS, RESPOND BETTER TO THE CHALLENGES OF TOMORROW, AND INTEGRATE REALITY IN CREATING DESIRED FUTURES.

The design approach suggests a highly participatory, dialogue-based and issue-driven approach whose iterative nature aims at continuous invention and learning rather than stability and control.

In this section, authors see great benefits in regarding processes of strategy formulation as synonymous with design processes.

Kamil Michlewski establishes the basis of this section by hypothesizing about the channels through which design rhetoric, sensitivities and ethos can permeate people and organizations. He also hypothesizes about the main challenge of spreading the benefits hidden in the design approach.
Jeanne Liedtka, in her seminal work in defense of strategy as design, suggests viewing the process of strategy formulation and implementation as one of iteration and experimentation, and paying sequential attention to idea generation and evaluation in a way that attends first to possibilities before moving on to constraints.
Heather Fraser too calls for new ways of strategizing for future success and identifies in design some important clues. By broadening the definition of "design" and expanding the application of design methodologies and mindsets to business, Heather argues that enterprises can move beyond mere survival and incremental change, and open up new possibilities for breakthrough growth strategies and organizational transformation.
Simon Grand links the inherently dynamic, processual and open nature of design processes to processes of strategizing, and addresses the importance of interpreting strategy-making as a creative, imaginative, future-oriented, risk-taking, assertive activity for entrepreneurial thinking.
Jamshid Gharajedaghi concludes this section with a detailed account of the design process as a process for operationalizing the most exciting vision of the future that the men and women running a business are capable of producing. A clear operational definition is given about how to arrive at successful solutions by design in complex business contexts.

TELL ME, AND I WILL FORGET. SHOW ME, AND I MAY REMEMBER. INVOLVE ME, AND I WILL UNDERSTAND. (CONFUCIUS, 450 B.C.)

Design thinking, design attitude, design culture and design-driven innovation are just a few design-led concepts which have been generating significant amount of interest and debate in a variety of environments including business schools (Rotman, Said, Weatherhead), commercial organisations (Apple, Steelcase, IDEO) and governmental institutions (British National Health Service).

THE CONVERSATION APPEARS TO BE SHIFTING AWAY FROM THE EARLY THRUSTS OF DISCOVERY TO MORE RECENT ONES FOCUSED ON APPLICATION AND UTILITY.

In this article I propose that there are essentially three channels through which design rhetoric, sensitivities and ethos permeate people and institutions. These are *design frameworks* (distributed via argument and persuasion), *design artefacts* (experienced aesthetically, ergonomically, economically and ecologically) and *design professionals* (infecting organisations with design attitude). I also submit a thesis that the main challenge of spreading the benefits hidden in the design approach does not necessarily lie in how persuasive design practitioners and scholars are or how delightful the products and services can be, but to what extent professional designers are integrated into the wider organisational culture.

---

¹❮ Vector (molecular biology)—vehicle used to transfer genetic material to a target cell

Channels of Design's Influence

There are many ways to address *design's* impact on organisations. The literature focuses, for example, on the financial impact of investment in industrial design (Roy and Potter, 1993; Rich, 2004; Hertenstein, Platt and Veryzer, 2005), the strategic importance of design (Kotler and Rath, 1984; Bruce and Bessant, 2002; Borja de Mozota, 2003; Lojacono and Zaccai, 2004; Ravasi and Lojacono, 2005), design's own knowledge and impact (Buchanan, 1992; Cross, 2000; Jimenez Narvaez, 2000; Bertola and Teixeira, 2003), design's impact on innovation (Thackara, 1997; Bruce and Harun, 2001; Squires and Byrne 2002) political, ethical and social implications of design (Papanek, 1971; Margolin and Buchanan, 1995; Papanek, 1995), epistemological implications of design in management research (Romme, 2003; Van Aken, 2005) and organisational design (Weick, 2004).

There are many different interpretations of what *design* is and how it affects organizations. Some of the above authors use *design* as a signifier of a particular processes that utilizes aspects of the epistemology of pragmatism represented in design. Others have started using more focused terms such as *design thinking* (Kelly, 2001; Brown, 2009; Martin, 2009) or *design attitude* (Boland and Collopy, 2004; Michlewski, 2008).

A large number of meanings of the word *design* (i.e. process, product, function, plan, conception, intent, pattern, blueprint, art, activity, creativity, industry, etc.) does not help with the creation of precise arguments and persuasive narratives. Using broad constructs arguably obscures the picture of what is precisely meant by *design*, especially when it is thought that design is "what we all do" (Cross, 1995) and that designing is all about "changing current situations into preferred ones" (Simon, 1996). A fundamental question remains, however: How *design*—seen as theories, concepts and sensibilities implicitly grasped by the participants of the *design-led* discourse—finds its way to the hearts and minds of the people in organisations?

I PROPOSE A MODEL FOR ANALYSING THE WAYS IN WHICH *DESIGN* CARRIES ITS DNA INTO ORGANIZATIONS (SEE FIG. 1).

The model is based on the assertion that all *design* has to offer, both to an enterprise and through it to a broader economy, is essentially channelled by three vectors: *design frameworks* inspired by design theories and design thinking, *design artefacts* which are the outcomes produced during the design process and *design professionals* with their professional culture and design attitudes.

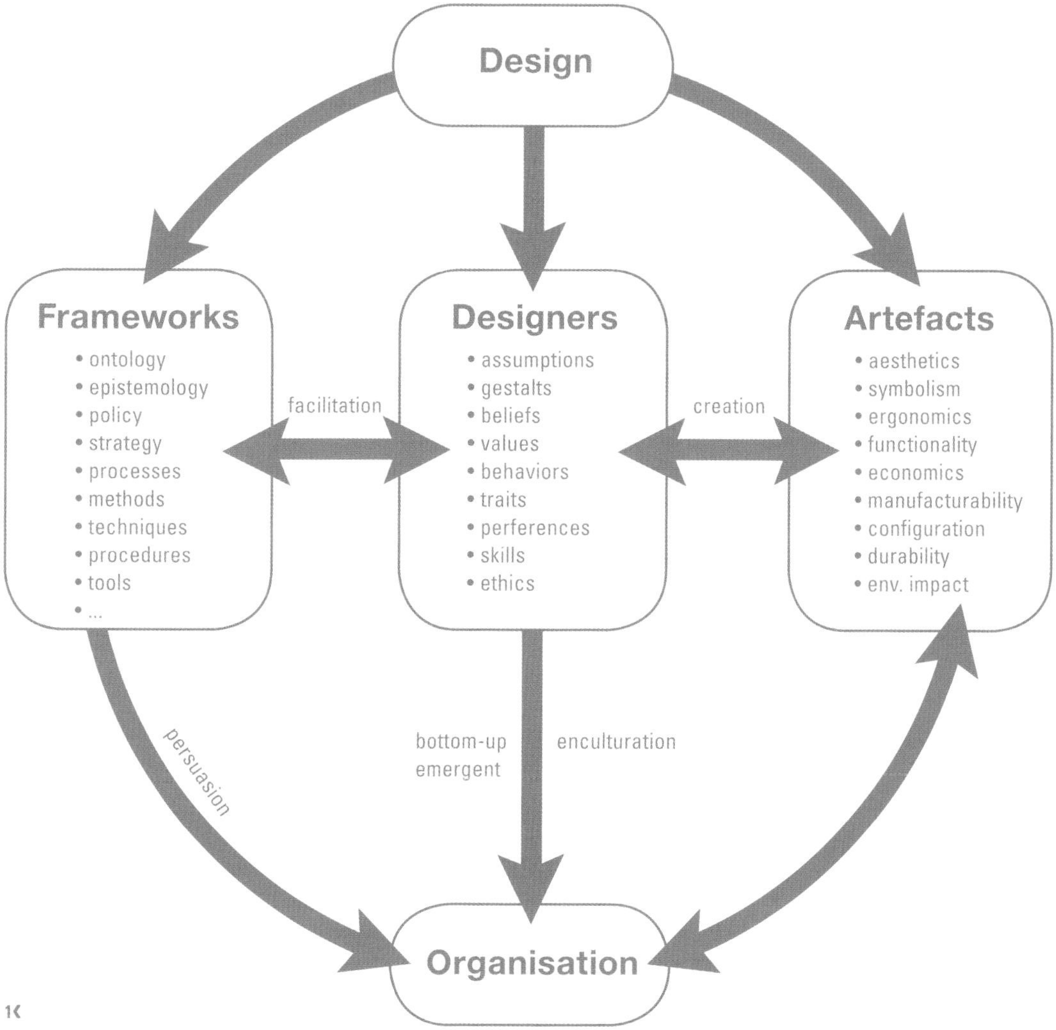

Design

Frameworks
- ontology
- epistemology
- policy
- strategy
- processes
- methods
- techniques
- procedures
- tools
- ...

facilitation

Designers
- assumptions
- gestalts
- beliefs
- values
- behaviors
- traits
- perferences
- skills
- ethics

creation

Artefacts
- aesthetics
- symbolism
- ergonomics
- functionality
- economics
- manufacturability
- configuration
- durability
- env. impact

persuasion

bottom-up
emergent

enculturation

Organisation

1〈

Frameworks

The first vector takes the form of *design-inspired frameworks*, epistemologies, theories, methods, tools and techniques. The examples here include: design as an underlying epistemology and mode of management research (Romme, 2003; Van Aken, 2004; 2005); seeing "managing as designing" with emphasis on the process and nuances of *design* (Boland Jr. and Collopy, 2004; 2004; Weick, 2004); epistemological influences of Dewey's experiential and cultural approach to learning (Dewey, 1934; 1991; Eickmann, Kolb and Kolb, 2004); the use of reflectivity and deep-level learning (Argyris, 1977; 1978; 1982; Schön, 1983; 1985; 1990; Senge, 1990); design-inspired polices (Cooper and Press, 1995; Papanek, 1995; Press and Cooper, 2003). All of the above share a common way of influencing actions in and outside organizations, namely *persuasion*. The strategy, in this instance, is to argue the case of design-inspired theories and frameworks, in other words use the rhetoric, often supported by the current research fashions, to achieve the desired impact. The proposed solutions of some of the design frameworks range from bridging the "relevance gap" in management academia (Tranfield and Starkey, 1998; Huff, 2000; Huff and Huff, 2001; Starkey and Madan, 2001; Romme, 2003; Van Aken, 2004; Van Aken, 2005) through increasing the innovative powers of companies through the design thinking and the design process (Kelly, 2001; Squires and Byrne, 2002; Weick, 2004; Ravasi and Lojacono 2005), to bringing tangible, economic benefits to the organisations (Rich, 2004; Hertenstein et al., 2005). Arguably, those efforts also contribute to making design more visible and more important along the lines of the professional project which aims to elevate design's stature in the society. Institutions such as the Design Council in the UK, the Design Management Institute in the US and numerous consultancies promote design-inspired policies, theories and tools in the society. The process of proposing those frameworks to the research community, managers and wider public is, to use Mintzberg's (1993) language, mostly top-down and planned. Subsequently, the impact of those frameworks is felt more broadly after the process of peer verification and exhaustive debate. As can be expected it takes time to take root and

the success of the adoption is contingent upon the current research trends and scientific "meta-narrative" (Nowotny, Scott and Gibson, 2001).

Continuum of Design-Inspired Frameworks

Design-informed frameworks are one of the channels through which *design* rhetoric imprints itself onto organisations. Those frameworks, theories, methods and tools could be attributed to different kinds of professional values and motivations. Their characteristics and overall messages follow on from who the authors are, what their chosen field of practice is, and what their professional agenda is. Broadly speaking the work can be mapped onto a continuum between two poles: (a) one driven by practical concerns and usually advocated by professional designers, (b) the other driven by epistemic concerns, usually driven by non-professional designers (see Table 1). The frameworks proposed by (a) and (b) suggest that the former is more concerned with practical advice which concentrates on achieving particular results, is usually heuristic and unstructured, and uses evocative and emphatic rhetoric.

THE LATTER, ON THE OTHER HAND, IS ENGAGED IN MORE PHILOSOPHICAL DEBATE WHICH SEEKS STRUCTURING DEVICES, METHODICAL TOOLS AND USES LOGICAL-DESCRIPTIVE RHETORIC.

Frameworks, including: epistemologies, theories, methods, processes, techniques, tools etc.		
Driven by practical concerns (usually by professional designers)		Driven by epistemic concerns (usually by philosophers, economists and organisation science scholars)
• practical and immediate • concentrated on achieving particular results • heuristic • evocative and emphatic rhetoric		• philosophical • concentrated on achieving understanding and conceptual distinctiveness • methodical • logical and descriptive rhetoric

⟵——————————————————————————————————⟶

Kelly (2001) Brown (2009) (IDEO) • design thinking principles • design process often flexible and open-ended • design tools: brainstorming, rapid prototyping, shadowing, observation etc.	Schön (1983) • reflection in action • conversation with materials and situations	Simon (1969) • "natural" and "design" sciences • bounded rationality
Olins (1995) • totally integrated and coherent branding, emotional and evocative content etc.	Papanek (1971) and Manzini (1995) • ethical conduct of designers • environmental consequences of designers" work	Romme and Van Aken (2003; 2004; 2005) • epistemology and research methods informed by design
Marzano (1999) (Philips) • ambient intelligence	Alexander (1977) • pattern language	Weick (2004) • organisation design
(Peto 1999) • random nature of design • importance of "accidents" and errors in design process	Cross (1992; 1996) • design thinking and design intelligence • design methods	Csikszentmihalyi (1981; 1996) • self identity and designing
Martin (2009) • design thinking as the source of competitive advantage	Cooper and Press (1995; 2003) • policies informed by design • design's role in economy	Dewey (Dewey 1934; 1991) • design, culture, experience, learning Peirce (Peirce 1992) • abductive logic and serendipitous exploration

Table 1. Continuum of Design-Inspired Frameworks

As an illustration of how *design frameworks* impact organisations, I would like to briefly introduce the case of the themes advocated by California-based IDEO, a company which some consider "the world's most successful design firm" (Byrne and Sands 2002).

Commercial Design Process as a Practical, Design-Inspired framework

IDEO have long been primary advocates of pragmatic set of design-inspired frameworks. In their books and articles we find a source of practical inspiration on how to create a culture in which innovation flourishes and product and process boundaries are re-written. Instead of focusing their attention on epistemological clarity and academic soundness, authors such as Kelly (2001) introduce ways in which designers at IDEO successfully collaborate. Their enlightening case studies and success stories (Brown, 2009) offer an excellent *framework* which is being advocated, argued, persuaded and adopted by practitioners across industries and institutions.

A MAJOR PART OF THE IDEO NARRATIVE IS THE UBIQUITY OF THEIR DESIGN PROCESS.

It has not only been highlighted by the founders and managers of the company (see: IDEO, 1991; Kelly, 2001, General Director IDEO London, own interview; Brown, 2009) but also discussed by various commentators (see: Myerson, 2001; Nussbaum, 2004). In itself, the process creates a backbone for the innovation mechanisms and is used to

focus project leaders' attention. Myerson (2001) reports one of the founders of IDEO as saying:

"At IDEO we have steadily moved away from a sequential idea of design process towards a set of values which contribute to a rich design and innovation culture. These values provide a framework within which *chaos, risk, experimentation, innovation* and *vision* can thrive." *(italics added) (ibid: 91)*

However, as a Managing Director of IDEO London acknowledged in an interview, this process is an important galvanizing tool for designers and other professionals working on projects (interview with Managing Director IDEO London).

The process, or as Kelly (2001) calls it "methodology", has five basic steps or parts: (a) understand, (b) observe, (c) visualize, (d) evaluate and refine, (e) implement (ibid: 6–7). It is also presented as: (a) observation, (b) brainstorming, (c) rapid prototyping, (d) refining, (e) implementation (Nussbaum, 2004).

Observation/Understanding

Usually the first step in the process is aimed at trying to understand the situation. Here designers utilise one of the most effective customer research tools, namely observation (for more in-depth discussion on anthropological methods and design, see Squires and Byrne, 2002). Instead of asking the customers what they want, which they are usually unable to articulate well, IDEO use empathy whilst engaging directly in a number of ways. Together with cognitive psychologists, anthropologists, sociologists they use a number of techniques to aid the process.

Brainstorming

At IDEO brainstorming follows observation and understanding as the first step in generating potential avenues for exploration. It is thought that brainstorming "[...] is not just a valuable creative tool at the fuzzy front end of projects" (*ibid*: 5), but also an important *cultural engine* (Sutton and Hargadon, 1996). The skill of brainstorming is evidently an important ingredient but what perhaps is more important is the intensity, playfulness and pervasiveness with which brainstorming is practised at IDEO: "brainstorming is practically a religion" says Kelly (2001).

Rapid Prototyping

Prototyping and physically making things has a special place in IDEO's culture. Kelly (2001) writes that prototyping is "both a step in the innovation process and philosophy about moving continuously forward, even when some variables are still undefined" (*ibid*: 5). In this respect it gives a sort of visual and tactile guidance in the mode of action based on *discontinuity* and *openendeness*. It is clearly an encouragement to *reflect in action* and "listening to the situation back-talk" (Schön, 1983).

On a deeper level, experimentation with prototypes is the heart of the moment when creative and emotional tensions are being resolved. As John Dewey writes:
"With the realization, material of reflection is incorporated into objects as their meaning. Since the artist cares in a peculiar way for the phase of experience in which union is achieved, he does not shun moments of resistance and tension. He rather cultivates them, not for their own sake but because of their potentialities, bringing to living consciousness an experience that is unified and total." (in: Eickmann et al. 2004)

THIS EXAMPLE OF DESIGN-INSPIRED FRAMEWORK PROMOTED BY IDEO ATTEMPTS TO PERSUADE THE AUDIENCE TO PAY MORE ATTENTION TO ISSUES CONCERNING *DESIGN*.

Arguably, IDEO's approach is closely linked with the *professional designers* and *design attitude*. Hence, one of the ways in which to judge and analyse the frameworks that subscribe to *design* as their focal point might be on the basis of their relationship with the professional design culture and its members. The values of *openendedness, exploration, bringing to life, polysensoriality, consolidation of meanings and personal and commercial empathy* (Michlewski, 2008) will most likely be displayed and encouraged by those who have been a part of this particular professional culture. It is not inconceivable to see those values expressed and advocated by a different professional group but the impact is bound to be less strong.

An additional and fertile approach to introducing *design* into organizations and into management practice, is through the two other channels of *design's* influence—*design artefacts* produced by professional designers and *design professionals* themselves. In addition to seeing design theories and frameworks as mediators between design and science, and between exploration and exploitation (Martin, 2009), seeing design professionals as "cultural change-agents" can be beneficial.

Artefacts

A second vector through which *design* makes its mark is by the *aesthetic* (non-cognitive), *symbolic*, (cognitive) and *physical* (ergonomic, economic and ecologic) impact of the artefacts professional designers create. Those include the visible and tangible artefacts such as spaces, environments and logos, as well as the intangible cultural components such as brands, experiences and fashions (Olins, 1995; Gobé, 2001). Artefacts have substantial evocative powers and in a direct way influence all consumers/users (as external recipients of designers' work) and employees (see: Gagliardi, 1990; Strati, 1999; 2000). Unlike in *design frameworks'* case, the impact of the *artefact* of designers can be instantaneous. They have the capacity to imprint themselves onto a particular culture (Dormer, 1997; Julier, 2000) or shape the inner-workings of an organization.

Holding an Apple iPhone in one's hand, admiring the architecture of Frank Gehry, sitting in an Aeron chair or experiencing the sound of Bang & Olufsen speakers has the power to affect us on a very deep, personal level. Indeed, when many people from outside of the field of design talk about design they only have those types of artefacts as their reference point. The plethora of beautiful and often equally functional products, which design professionals love to create, is a visible remainder that the world around us is saturated with outcomes of designers' work.

WE ENJOY THE RELATIONSHIP WITH TANGIBLE OBJECTS, DESPITE THE FACT THAT OUR CONSUMPTION OF THEM HAS LED DIRECTLY TO MANY ENVIRONMENTAL HEADACHES OF OUR TIMES.

Unfortunately, we continue to find it difficult to rid ourselves of the desire to buy and the desire to own physical products. Many prominent design thinkers call onto the design profession, policymakers and consumers to re-examine how we design and how we consume (Papanek, 1995; Thackara, 2005; Thackara and Design Council. 2007). We must remain hopeful that through a collective action we be able to move

closer to a more sustainable model of existence. In the meantime, however, design continues to manifest itself mainly through things we can see, feel, smell, taste and hear. As Gagliardi (1990) argued, artefacts and spaces that surround us are not just an expression of deep underlying assumptions (as in Schein's (1992) view) but, rather, equally shape how cultures are carrying deeply symbolic meaning. The artefacts we buy and consume have an extraordinary impact on our day-to-day lives. They delight us, as in the case of a humble iPod, or terrify us, as in the case of the same iPod seen from the ecological footprint's point of view. Physical properties, usability, impact on the environment and price are all decided and designed in by the design professionals. It is this group's values, attitudes, ideas, sensitivities and dreams that find their way into the end products and into our homes.

THE IMPACT OF DESIGN HERE IS CLEAR FOR EVERYONE TO SEE AND, IT MUST BE SAID, NOT ALWAYS EASY TO ADMIRE.

The gradual shift from within the field of design away from products and towards designing services continues to gain momentum with some young consultancies coming to the fore (Engine, LiveWork) and the work of Design Council. There is still a long way, though, before every young designer's dream is first and foremost the creation of sustainable services.

In the workplace the value of artefacts can have significant impact too. Probably the most famous recent case relates to the offices of Google. The Googleplex, as the campus is called, achieved a legendary status due to the way it breaks the traditional office paradigm (Vise and Malseed, 2008). A particularly configured workplace such as the one at IDEO (Kelly, 2001; Brown, 2009) or Google might not only be an expression of the creativity of the people working there but might also be the catalyst for innovation. Even though the research in this field is very limited (Martin, 2002; Haner, 2005) one could envisage a situation where a uniform and inadequately configured office will have an impact on the lack of innovation and vice versa. This category of influencing and interfacing agents also includes the ergonomic dimension. There are considerable gains available if the quality of ergonomics of a workplace are carefully attended to by designers (Cooper and Press, 1995; see also Myerson, 1998).

There are a number of sub-fields dealing with how the products interface and how they interact with customers and culture (Heskett, 1980; Csikszentmihalyi, 1981; Norman, 1988; Heskett, 2002). Areas include: product semantics, product semiotics, product interaction, interface design, communication design, human factors all address the outcome-user connection. An extensive literature on evocative and culturally significant products can also be referred to (see: Sudjic, 1985; Forty, 1986; Juller, 1993; Woodham, 1997). As my aim here is mainly to propose a way of looking at how design impacts organizations, I will not be delving deeper into these subjects.

SUFFICE TO SAY THAT DESIGN ARTEFACTS HAVE A DIRECT IMPACT ON US AS INDIVIDUALS AND THE ORGANISATIONS WE WORK FOR.

Design Professionals

Designers as a professional group provide the third vector through which design makes a direct (social integration, socialisation and acculturation) and indirect (*design frameworks* and *design artefacts*) impact on organizations. They do so by interacting with other professionals in an organisation on a social and decision-making level. It is arguably the strongest, most powerful way of creating a lasting impact and implanting the design DNA into organizations.

Firstly, I examine the relationship between marketers and designers. The reason for including it is two-pronged: (a) designers are often subcontracted by the marketing function, hence are in close cultural contact with them, and (b) design in an organisation is, from a managers' point of view, often interpreted through the prism of marketing.

Secondly, I look at the strategic dimension of incorporating a professional design culture. In this instance I offer an example of a company that successfully integrated designers into the heart of its culture.

The Interface between Designers and Marketers

The fact that design is in close proximity to and in a symbiotic relationship with marketing (Bruce and Bessant, 2002) suggests analyzing the interface between professional design culture and marketers is a viable starting point to investigate its impact on other professions within an organization. Probing this close relationship should give some insights into how designers fit into management-driven organizational cultures.

Back in 1984, marketing guru Philip Kotler made a statement that design is misunderstood and under-appreciated as a *strategic marketing tool*. Many design management publications since have cited his article when discussing the strategic implications of design (Lorenz, 1990; Borja de Mozota, 2003; Cooper and Press, 2003; Ravasi and Lojacono, 2005). In Kotler and Rath's (1984) article *"Design: A powerful but neglected strategic tool"*, design is seen as a device in marketing's hands with the unique capability to differentiate the product offering or, as Kotler puts it, to "stand out from the crowd" (*ibid*: 16).

The benefits of "well-managed", "high-quality" design according to Kotler are: (a) creation of corporate distinctiveness; (b) creation of personality for a newly launched product; (c) reinvigoration of product interest for mature products; (d) communication of value to the consumer; (e) entertainment and highlighting visual impact (*ibid*: 17). Designers' role in this respect is to "blend creatively major elements of the design mix" (*op. cit.*). These components include: performance, quality, durability, appearance and cost. This heavily marketing-centric approach has far-reaching consequences in relation to the place and status of design in an organization. Arguably, the single most important reason why design has failed to effectively communicate its message and true identity has been the full ownership of design in organizations exercised by marketing staff and within the marketing function. Design as part of marketing has no separate voice and is a subject to the governing values and rules created and interpreted by people in marketing. This interpretation for the last fifty years has been heavily influenced by marketing's utopian quest to become a "real science" (Brown, 1996). As Brown admits in self-flagellating fashion, "the heroic but utterly wrongheaded attempt to acquire the unnecessary trappings of 'science', a self-abusive orgy of mathematical masturbation which rendered us [marketers] philosophically blind, intellectually deaf and spiritually debilitated" (ibid: 260). Here, whilst describing design use words such as "optimization of consumer satisfaction", "design-tool", even the form "to manage design" denotes a high degree of control and predictability. Design seen through the eyes of marketers is simply a device which should be managed to increase the visibility of the product. It also must be accountable and predictable along the lines of the "scientific" expectations.

IF IT DOES NOT THEN IT IS DISMISSED OR DEEMED FLIMSY OR FUZZY BY THE MARKETERS FOCUSED ON.

Morello (1995), whilst discussing drawbacks of a marketing approach in addressing users' needs, points to consequences of maintaining competitiveness mainly through product differentiation (the primary mode in which marketing uses design). These are:
• an overcomplication of performances
• the dominant idea that design is mainly a way to communicate
• the separation of product form from structure and the reduction of design to styling, an overdecoration of products (ibid: 72).

Seeing design as subordinate to marketing is so pervasive it has even penetrated the work of the key proponents of design as a unique contributor to corporations success (see for example Broja de Mozota, 2003). The function of design, as stipulated by Kotler, has been recognized as one of the three ways in which design inputs into an organization. Instead of being "strategic" as the author suggests, the

approach could be better described as operational. Broja de Mozota outlined those three ways as: design as *differentiator* (here the Kotlers' view fits best), design as *coordinator* and design as *transformer*.

The problem with the superiority of marketing over design is as follows: When looking at designing and designers through the prism of the marketing "science quest" they do not appear as predictable, controllable, accountable, quantifiable and hence are deemed inadequate or subsequently seen as highly problematic. Taking them seriously also does not contribute to making marketing look more predictable and "scientific". This in turn brands designers as "arty", "serendipitous" and "flimsy".

IT CONSEQUENTLY PUTS DESIGNERS AND DESIGN MANAGERS IN THE POSITION WHERE THEY HAVE TO DEFEND THEMSELVES AGAINST ATTACKS ON THEIR SEEMINGLY FLIMSY METHODOLOGIES.

They feel the need to argue their case and to show evidence of accountable process, controlled tools and respectable behavior. It is not, in my view, because they want to, but because of their struggle for recognition and reward with the people who historically have had more kudos in organizations.

In order to contribute and create value, designers need to go through the marketing gate keepers who are influenced by values only partially compatible with those of designers. As it has been pointed out, the relationship between marketers and designers can be somewhat problematic (Lorenz, 1986; Bruce and Docherty, 1993; Roy and Potter, 1993; Thomas, 1993; Bruce and Cooper, 1997; Shaw, Shaw and Tressider, 2002). Bruce and Docherty (1993) list the following problems which may exist between designers and marketers: (a) differences in goals and objectives; (b) misunderstandings and lack of agreement which leads to the rejection of each others ideas; (c) lack of trust, respect and cooperation; (d) different educational backgrounds; (e) different methods of working and the lack of common language; (f) lack of personal chemistry; (g) reluctance to be directed by someone outside their area of expertise. This long list of sources of conflict is indicative of the deep, underlying differences between those groups. The calls for more understanding and appreciation of each other by researchers, such as Bruce and Cooper's and Kotler's, fall largely on deaf ears.

THE REASON, IT APPEARS, DOES NOT LIE WITH THE LACK OF WILLINGNESS TO LEARN FROM EACH OTHER BUT FROM POLARIZED POLITICAL AND CULTURAL POSITIONS OF THE TWO GROUPS.

Design and Marketing have two different evolutionary routes. Design, after the industrial revolution, followed the more art-oriented values in its quest for identity and relevance in society. Marketing, on the other hand, as part of the "scientific management" tradition which was initiated by the likes of Taylor, Fayol, Bernard, followed the route of the scientific values (Brown, 1996; Squires, 2001).

Marketers can arguably be considered the closest representatives of the "management camp" to designers. The similarities between design and marketing have even prompted some authors to state that they are the same thing (Thomas, 1993). This appears to be in stark contrast to what has been observed. Arguably, marketers are the "interpreters" of designers to the rest of the organization. By attaching their own interpretation they often misrepresent designers. Bruce and Bessant (2002) describe barriers to integrating design expertise. One of them is "design illiteracy" whereby managers do not know what is involved in design activities, and do not have the experience to appreciate designers' contribution. The authors note that this fact, in many cases, may be led by "design segregation [which] occurs in companies which repeatedly outsource design expertise and therefore may have a tunnel view of what the design function is" (*ibid:* 50). The outsourcing of the design function may have consequences going far beyond simple misunderstanding of designers by managers (I will discuss this in the next section). Other barriers to integrating design include high risk associated with design by managers; failing to acknowledge the potential benefits for strategy and growth; underappreciation of the value of creativity (*op. cit.*).

The ownership of *design* in organizations where professional design culture is not dominant will most likely belong to the marketing function. If this is the case, design is filtered through a different set of professional values instilled during formal education and on-the-job socialization of marketers.

Design Professionals and Strategy

Bruce and Bessant (2002) write "Designers play a key role in providing firms with raw materials for making decisions. If they are performing their proper function, they open 'doors of opportunity'. They help decision makers to explore alternative futures" (*ibid:* 65). What is hidden in this statement which highlights positive contribution of designers to strategy formation is that designers are "helpers" to somebody who is their superior and who makes strategic decisions. This view places designers as useful but somewhat lesser members of the strategic team. Broja de Mozota (2003) notes that design has an "identity problem" when it comes to being successfully integrated into some companies. She writes that designers are often to blame for the opposition design meets in organizations (*ibid:* 51).

IN THEIR VIEW, SOME DESIGNERS WANT TO CREATE PERFECTLY DESIGNED OBJECTS FOR MARKETS WHERE "BAD TASTE" DOES NOT EXIST.

Moreover, Broja De Mozota critizises designers for being too eager to claim their strategic role: "Designers are sometimes tempted to confound the strategic character of certain design projects with conviction that they can be strategists of the firm" (*ibid:* 51). Her view is that the objective of the design profession is to make the strategy visible and to "help the firm to conceptualize [its] fundamental values" (*op. cit.*), not to take a leadership role in the company. Furthermore, designers are not prepared to work with management despite the fact that design education is changing to include marketing and strategy courses. Broja De Mozota remarks that "creative" staff often cultivate an "ego" but lack confidence and communicate badly (*ibid:* 51). Her assessment of the reasons why design struggles to be fully integrated into a company mentions such factors as: a lack of design management courses and research policies with long term mission; young age of the design profession; small library of references; poor communication of methodologies by designers which creates a "fuzzy" working environment (*op cit*). In order to embrace design: "Managers need strong reference marks, reliable information and assurance that they will be able to finance design with security" (*ibid:* 66). This statement demonstrates, in my opinion, the flawed thinking of managers rather than the inadequacies of designers. Firstly, "strong reference marks" in a constantly changing market place do not exist, "reliable information and 'security' of investment are as rare in managers' output as they are in designers". The difference is in the "style" and "rhetoric" of presenting the "security" and "reliability". In the designers' case, as it has been observed, this will most likely be dressed up in rather colourful clothes and playfulness (signifying to managers qualities such as flimsiness and unreliability). In the managers' case it will be much more professional looking (signifying reliability, stability and security). These culturally ascribed symbols of reliability and of security are one of the issues which prevent both groups from effectively engaging in a productive, strategically-driven dialogue.

One of the most significant roles of *design professionals* in organizations is their influence as *change agents* enabling the process of transformation of value to take place.

AN IMPORTANT FACTOR IN THEIR SUCCESS IS THE PERVASIVENESS OF PROFESSIONAL DESIGNERS IN ANY GIVEN ORGANIZATION.

Establishing critical mass may enable them to leverage their cultural significance and strategic integration. Johansson and Svengren (2002) made an observation in relation to the effects of numbers of designers in an organization and the strategic integration of design. The authors conducted qualitative research in a company which attempted to turn design into a strategic resource. Initially this job was assigned to only one designer. The

person was the personification of the design profession to the rest of the company's employees. She struggled to be adequately understood and was trying to build up a "critical mass" (a sufficient number of in-house designers) to have "more influence" (*ibid:* 9–10). As she was able to bring more full-time designers on board, the appreciation of design increased and became richer. When a core team came into existence and a design laboratory was established the level of design involvement into the operational and strategic decision making process became more central. As this was happening, other groups such as engineers and managers started to benefit from the more transparent and effective communication. The learning became a collaborative venture drawing especially on designers' experimental nature. There was a marked improvement of the position of design in the company after creating the critical mass. Now not only did the rest of the organisation find out for themselves how designers work and what design is about but the designers' own professional development was also stimulated. What could be said about this case is that a single designer with her professional design values has not been able to *culturally connect* to others in organisation. Managers and engineers were not able to comprehend and adequately respond to the challenges of a lone designer. Johansson and Svengren (2002) reported her saying, after she was finally in a group of designers "now I have others to talk with" (*ibid:* 14).

THIS IS INDICATIVE OF THE DIFFERENT LANGUAGE AND VALUES DESIGNERS AS A PROFESSIONAL GROUP USE IN THEIR CORPORATE LIFE.

The authors conclude that, in order to stimulate establishing design as a strategic resource, companies should consider the "critical mass" of designers present amongst their staff. This observation, although as Johansson and Svengren admit was only based on one single case, adds to the debate about the role and place of designers as a *professional group* in an organization. It is likely that a considerable group presence of in-house designers contributes to successful integration of design on a strategic level.

Spreading the Design Culture

Another case of integration of designers into an organization is associated with previously discussed design consultancy firm IDEO. Even though this example is as much about the systems and methods developed by a company as about the people, it illustrates the reactions by people not familiar with the professional design culture.

IDEO claim that as a result of customers requests, they have launched a service which they call IDEO "U" (for University) whereby they "teach" others their way of innovating (own interview, Senior Manager, IDEO, London). This began with IDEO engaging its corporate clients in their five-stage design process. Firms experienced: (a) observation and the input of cognitive psychologists, anthropologists; (b) brainstorming, the cultural engine of IDEO (Sutton and Hargadon, 1996), with heavily visual and tactile content; (c) rapid prototyping and speedy creation of simple mock-ups; (d) trial-and-error refining within strict time and specification constraints; (e) implementation (Nussbaum, 2004).

After being exposed to such a visually rich and tactile process, which in my belief is something most designers would quickly recognise as they do, clients of IDEO became convinced of the merits and benefits of such an approach to innovation (including strategic innovation).

One of their customers is an FMCG giant and one of the oldest companies in the world (De Geus, 1997), Procter and Gamble. The CEO, Alan Lafley is reported to have teamed up with IDEO to create "a more innovative culture" (Nussbaum, 2004: 91). This statement is nothing unusual in the business world itself but when it is expressed by the head of one of the most innovative companies it signifies the appreciation of the corporate executive of the IDEO approach. In the process of "learning" how to innovate the IDEO way, Lafley took his Global Leaders Council of 40 strategic business unit heads to San Francisco (where the company's headquarters are based) for a one day "immersion" in IDEO's culture. The result was astonishment and praise for the "approach". In my mind it showed in what exposure to the culture of designers by managers can result.
I can sympathize with those comments as a similar

experience happened to me when I was "immersed" in the design culture of a different organization.

As part of the IDEO "U" program, more permanent and long-term relationships are in place. During weekly workshops and monthly stays in IDEO, P&G managers are taught the techniques that go with observation, brainstorming, prototyping and fast implementation (*ibid:* 92). Additionally, IDEO built an innovation centre for P&G where employees are acculturated into the process and arguably design culture as well. Claudia Kotchka, vice president for design innovation and strategy at P&G, said that "they [IDEO] opened our eyes to new ways of working" and "they solved problems in ways we would never have thought" (*ibid:* 92). Her statements can also be read from the viewpoint that she is an accountant by training and she has been made responsible for making design part of P&G's' "DNA", i.e. organizational culture (Reingold, 2005). Kotchka is reported to have said: "Design used to be soiled at P&G, viewed by most as peripheral and unimportant. Now most designers work directly with researchers within each unit.

THIS SPARKS NEW SORTS OF INNOVATION AND MAKES IT EASIER FOR NON-DESIGNERS TO UNDERSTAND WHAT DESIGN IS." (REINGOLD, 2005).

The "new ways of working" to which she is referring, in my view, comprise the professional design culture. Instead of being unique to IDEO, it is present in environments where design professionals work.

Hence, it could be stated that the *problem* might not reside solely on the designers' side (as unable to *sell* the qualities of design to managers) but might also stem from managers who fail to appreciate *design* for what it is. Managers, are conditioned by their education to mistrust the colourful, serendipitous and open-minded yet this is how they themselves need to behave in order to respond to the unexpected problems they face in a turbulent business environment. The reason why design and designers are not seen as "business-like" is, therefore, predominantly culturally based.

Summary

This article engaged in a discussion around a devised model representing three different vectors through which *design* impacts organizations. Among other things, it attempted to demonstrate that there is an alternative way of looking at the influence of design on organizational milieu other than the epistemic, top-down perspective. In addition to debating and advocating the design-led concepts such as design thinking one can investigate the effects of design artefacts and the impact of a direct involvement of groups of design professionals and the design attitudes they bring with them into organizations.

The main point of the article has been the introduction of the design influence model, which was also used as a narrative tool. With professional design culture as the common denominator, the discussion examined several key issues:

The article looked at how design is being debated in mainstream organizational research and in the ways the culture of designers appears to modify the message and format of the frameworks and theories inspired by design. The narrative then explored the fact that design artefacts are equally important vectors affecting our culture and organizations.

Designers themselves impact on organizations by the means of socialization and acculturation. This notion has been explored on two levels: (a) the level of cultural interfaces between arguably the closest professional group to designers, namely marketers and (b) the strategic level of integrating designers as significant change agents who are transforming broader organizational cultures. The discussion pointed to the necessity of re-examining of the culturally subordinate role of designers to marketing and deliberately freeing them from its contextual grip. Finally, it has been suggested that the examples of "teaching" companies' design culture might indicate the realization, on the part of the commercial world, of the benefits of the professional design culture as a catalyst for innovation and organizational transformation.

References

Alexander, C., Ishikawa, S. and Silverstein, M. 1977. A pattern language: towns, buildings, construction. New York: Oxford University Press.

Argyris, C. 1977. Double loop learning in organizations. Harvard Business Review, September 1.

Argyris, C. 1982. The executive mind and double-loop learning. Organizational Dynamics. Autumn.

Argyris, C. 1990. Overcoming organizational defences: Facilitating organizational learning. Boston, Allyn and Bacon.

Argyris, C., Putnam, R. and McLain Smith, D. 1985. Action science. Concepts, methods, and skills for research and intervention. San Francisco, Jossey-Bass.

Argyris, C. and Schön, D. 1978. Organizational learning: a theory of action perspective. Reading: MA, Addison-Wesley.

Bertola, P. and Teixeira, J. C. 2003. Design as a knowledge agent. How design as a knowledge process is embedded into organizations to foster innovation. Design Studies, 24(2).

Boland Jr., R. J. and Collopy, F. 2004. Design matters for management. In R. J. Boland Jr. and F. Collopy (eds.), Managing as Designing: 3–18. Stanford: Stanford University Press:

Boland Jr., R. J. and Collopy, F. Eds. 2004. Managing as Designing. Stanford: Stanford University Press.

Borja de Mozota, B. 2003. Design management: Using design to build brand value and corporate innovation. New York: Allworth Press.

Brown, S. 1996. Art or science? Fifty years of marketing debate. Journal of Marketing Management, 12(4): 243–267.

Brown, T. 2009. Change by design. New York: HarperCollins Publishers.

Bruce, M. and Bessant, J. 2002. Design in business: strategic innovation through design. Harlow: Financial Times Prentice Hall.

Bruce, M. and Cooper, R. 1997. Marketing and design management. London: Thompson Business Press.

Bruce, M. and Docherty, G. 1993. It's all in a relationship: A comparative study of client-design consultant relationships. Design Studies, 14(4): 402–422.

Bruce, M. and Harun, R. 2001. Exploring design capability for serial innovation in SME's. European Design Academy Conference, Portugal.

Buchanan, R. 1992. Wicked problems in design thinking. Design Issues, 8(2): 5–22.

Byrne, B. and Sands, E. 2002. Creating collaborative corporate cultures. In S. Squires and B. Byrne (eds.) Creating Breakthrough Ideas: The collaboration of anthropologists and designers in the product development industry: 45–70. Westport. Bergin & Garvey.

Cooper, R. and Press, M. 1995. Design agenda: A guide to successful design management. Chichester: John Wiley and Sons Ltd.

Cooper, R. and Press, M. 2003. The design experience: The role of design and designers in the 21st century. Ashgate Publishing Limited.

Cross, N. 1995. Discovering design ability. In R. Buchanan and V. Margolin (eds.), Discovering design: explorations in design studies: 105–120.Chicago: University of Chicago Press.

Cross, N. 2000. Designerly ways of knowing: design discipline versus design science. Design Plus Research, Milan.

Cross, N. and Christiaans, H. (Eds). 1996. Analysing design activity. Chichester: John Wiley and Sons Ltd.

Cross, N. (Ed.) 1992. Research in Design Thinking. Delft: Delft University Press.

Csikszentmihalyi, M. 1981. The meaning of things: Domestic symbols and the self, Cambridge University Press.

Csikszentmihalyi, M. 1996. The idea of design. Cambridge: MIT Press.

De Geus, A. 1997. The living company. Boston: Harvard Business School Press.

Dewey, J. 1934. Art as experience. New York: Perigee.

Dewey, J. 1991. How we think. Amherst, NY: Prometheus.

Dormer, P., Ed. 1997. The culture of craft: status and future. Manchester: Manchester University Press.

Eickmann, P., Kolb, A. and Kolb, D. 2004. Designing learning. In R. J. Boland Jr. and F. Collopy (Eds.), Managing as Designing: 241–247. Stanford: Stanford University Press.

Forty, A. 1986. Objects of desire: design and society since 1750. London: Thames & Hudson.

Gagliardi, P., Ed. 1990. Symbols and artifacts. Views of the corporate landscape. New York: Aldine de Gruyter.

Gobé, M. 2001. Emotional branding: the new paradigm for connecting brands to people. Oxford: Windsor.

Haner, U. 2005. Spaces for creativity and innovation in two established organizations. Creativity and Innovation Management, 14(3): 288–298.

Hertenstein, J. H., Platt, M. B. and Veryzer, R.W. 2005. The impact of industrial design effectiveness on corporate financial performance. Journal of Product Innovation and Management, 22: 3–21.

Heskett, J. 1980. Industrial design. London: Thames & Hudson.

Heskett, J. 2002. Toothpicks and logos: design in everyday life. Oxford: Oxford University Press.

Huff, A. S. 2000. Changes in organizational knowledge production. Academy of Management Review, 25(2): 288–293.

Huff, A. S. and Huff, J. O. 2001. Re-focusing the business school agenda. British Journal of Management, 12 (Special Issue): 49–54.

IDEO 1991. Methodology handbook: IDEO product development.

Jimenez Narvaez, L. M. 2000. Design's own knowledge. Design Issues, 16(1): 36–51.

Johansson, U. and Svengren, L. 2002. One swallow doesn't make a summer: About the need for critical mass of designers to make a design strategy. The 11th International Forum on Design Management Research and Education, Boston: Massachusetts.

Julier, G. 2000. The culture of design. London: Sage.

Julier, G. 1993. Encyclopedia of 20th century design. London: Thames & Hudson.

Kelley, T. 2001. The art of innovation. New York: Random Books.

Kotler, P. and Rath A. G. 1984. Design: A powerful but neglected strategic tool. Journal of Business Strategy, 5(2): 16–21.

Lojacono, G. and Zaccai, G. 2004. The evolution of the design-inspired enterprise. Sloan Management Review, 45(3): 75–79.

Lorenz, C. 1986. The Design Dimension: Product strategy and the challenge of global marketing. Oxford: Basil Blackwell.

Lorenz, C. 1990. The design dimension: The new competitive weapon for product strategy and global marketing. Oxford: Basil Blackwell.

Manzini, E. 1995. Prometheus of the everyday. The ecology of the artificial and the designer's responsibility. In R. Buchanan and V. Margolin, Discovering design: explorations in design studies: 219–243. Chicago: University of Chicago Press.

Margolin, V. and Buchanan, R. (Eds.) 1995. The idea of design. Cambridge: MIT Press.

Martin, J. 2002. Organizational culture: Mapping the terrain. London: Sage.

Martin, R. 2009. The design of business: Why design thinking is the next competitive advantage. Boston: Harvard Business Press.

Marzano, S. 1999. Creating value by design: Thoughts and facts. Lund Humphries.

Michlewski, K. 2008. Uncovering design attitude: Inside the culture of designers. Organization Studies, 29(2): 229–248.

Mintzberg, H. 1993. The rise and fall of strategic planning. New York: Free Press.

Morello, A. (1995). "Discovering Design" means [re-] discovering users and projects. In R. Buchanan and V. Margolin, Discovering design: explorations in design studies: 69–76. Chicago: University of Chicago Press.

Myerson, J. 1998. New workspace, new culture: office design as a catalyst for change. Aldershot.

Myerson, J. 2001. IDEO: Masters of innovation. London: Laurence King.

Norman, D. A. 1988. The psychology of everyday things. New York: Basic Books.

Nowotny, H., P. Scott and Gibson, M. 2001. Re-thinking science: knowledge and the public in an age of uncertainty. Malden: Blackwell Publishers Inc.

Nussbaum, B. 2004. The power of design. Business Week: 86–94.

Olins, W. 1995. International corporate identity 1. London: Laurence King Publishing.

Papanek, V. 1971. Design for the real world: Human ecology and social change. New York The essential Peirce: selected philosophical writings, vol. 1. Pantheon Books.

Papanek, V. 1995. The green imperative: Natural design for the real world. London: Thames & Hudson.

Peirce, C. S. 1992. The essential Peirce: selected philosophical writings, vol. 1. N. Houser and C. Kloesel (Eds.). Bloomington: Indiana University Press.

Peto, J. (Ed.) 1999. Design, process, progress, practice. London: Design Museum.

Press, M. and Cooper, R. 2003. The design experience: The role of design and designers in the twenty-first century. Aldershot: Ashgate.

Ravasi, D. and Lojacono, G. 2005. Managing design and designers for strategic renewal. Long Range Planning, 38: 51–77.

Reingold, J. 2005. Creating a design-centric culture. Fast Company, 95.

Reingold, J. 2005. The interpreter. Fast Company, 95.

Rich, H. 2004. Proving the practical power of design. Design Management Journal, 15(4): 28–34.

Romme, A. G. L. 2003. Making a difference: Organization as design. Organization Science, 14(5): 558–573.

Roy, R. and Potter, S. 1993. The commercial aspects of investment in design. Design Studies, 14(2): 171–193.

Schein, E. 1992. Organizational culture and leadership. San Francisco: Jossey-Bass Publishers.

Schön, D. 1983. The reflective practitioner: how professionals think in action. New York: Basic Books.

Senge, P. 1990. The fifth discipline: The art and practice of the learning organisation. New York.

Shaw, V., Shaw, C. T and Tressider, J. 2002. Conflict between designers and marketers: A study of graphic designers in New Zealand. Design Journal, 5(3): 10–22.

Simon, H. A. 1996. The sciences of the artificial. Cambridge Mass: MIT Press.

Squires, G. 2001. Management as a professional discipline. Journal of Management Studies, 38(4): 474–487.

Squires, S. and Byrne, B. (Eds.) 2002. Creating breakthrough ideas: The collaboration of anthropologists and designers in the product development industry. Westport: Bergin & Garvey.

Starkey, K. and Madan, P. 2001. Bridging the relevance gap: Aligning stakeholders in the future of management research. British Journal of Management 12 (Special Issue): 3–26.

Strati, A. 1999. Organization and aesthetics. London: SAGE.

Strati, A. 2000. The aesthetic approach in organization studies. In S. Linstead and H. Höpfl, The Aesthetics of Organization: 13–34. London, Sage.

Sudjic, D. 1985. Cult Objects: the complete guide to having it all. London: Paladin.

Sutton, R. I. and Hargadon, A. 1996. Brainstorming groups in context: effectiveness in a product design firm. Administrative Science Quarterly, 41: 685–718.

Thackara, J. 1997. Winners! How today's successful companies innovate by design. Aldershot: Gower.

Thackara, J. 2005: In the bubble: Designing in a complex world. Cambridge, Mass.: MIT Press.

Thackara, J. and Design Council. 2007. Wouldn't it be great if—we could live sustainably—by design? London: Design Council.

Thomas, H. 1993. Designers don't want to agree. Marketing, 26.

Tranfield, D. and Starkey, K. 1998. The nature, social organization and promotion of management research: Towards policy. British Journal of Management, 9: 341–353.

Van Aken, J. E. 2004. Management research based on the paradigm of design science: The quest for field-tested and grounded technological rules. Journal of Management Studies, 41(2).

Van Aken, J. E. 2005. Management research as a design science: Articulating the research products of mode 2 knowledge production in management. British Journal of Management, 16(2): 19–36.

Vise, D. A. and Malseed, M. 2008. The Google story. New York: Bantam Dell.

Weick, K. E. 2004. Rethinking organizational design. In R. J. Boland and F. Collopy (Eds.), Managing as designing: 36–53. Stanford: California, Stanford University Press.

Woodham, J., M. 1997. Twentieth-Century Design. Oxford: Oxford University Press.

JEANNE LIEDTKA ❮ In Defense of Strategy as Design

The field of business strategy is in need of new metaphors. We stand at the frontier of a business world in the midst of fundamental change, in which much of the traditional thinking about strategy formulation and implementation seems potentially ill-suited to escalating imperatives for speed and flexibility. We need new metaphors that better capture the challenges of making strategies both real and realizable, metaphors that bring life to the human dimension of creating new futures for institutions, that move us beyond the sterility of traditional approaches to strategic planning in large organizations. In that spirit, I attempt here to interest the reader in the resuscitation of an old metaphor that I see as offering new possibilities—the metaphor of strategy as a process of design.

This article orignially appeared in California Management Review, University of California, Berkeley

The centrality of design skills to the practice of management has long been recognized. In 1969, Herbert Simon noted: "Engineering, medicine, business, architecture, and painting are concerned not with the necessary but with the contingent—not with how things are but with how they might be—in short, with design ... Everyone designs who devises courses of action aimed at changing existing situations into preferred ones... Design, so construed, is the core of all professional training."

THE CONCEPT OF DESIGN, HOWEVER, HAS TAKEN ON A PEJORATIVE MEANING IN THE FIELD OF STRATEGIC MANAGEMENT SINCE HENRY MINTZBERG ISSUED HIS INFLUENTIAL INDICTMENT OF THE APPROACH TO STRATEGY MAKING THAT HE LABELED THE "DESIGN SCHOOL."

(Mintzberg, 1994) The Design School, as he defined it, represented a hierarchical, top-down approach that was ill-suited for the realities of changing environments. With this important work, the term "design", in particular, and the concept of planning, in general, fell into disfavor. In this article, I take issue, not specifically with Mintzberg's critique of the elements of the "Design School's" approach, but with his use of the nomenclature of design.

THE METAPHOR OF DESIGN OFFERS RICH POSSIBILITIES FOR HELPING US TO THINK MORE DEEPLY ABOUT THE FORMATION OF BUSINESS STRATEGY, AND IT IS TIME TO LIBERATE THE IDEA OF DESIGN FROM ITS ASSOCIATION WITH OUTMODED APPROACHES TO STRATEGY.

Such liberation would allow us to see one important goal of strategy formulation as the design of a "purposeful space"— virtual rather than physical—in which particular activities, capabilities, and relationships are encouraged. These, in turn, produce a particular set of associated behaviors and hence, outcomes in the marketplace. Theories of design have much to teach us about the creation of such spaces.

The Idea of Design

The story of the design of the University in which I teach—the University of Virginia—offers an interesting place to begin a conversation about design (see Exhibit 1). At one level, the UVA story illustrates a traditional view of strategy making as occurring at the nexus of an institution's external environment, internal competencies, and values. It also demonstrates the power of strategic intent. What it conveys even more vividly, however, is the process through which Thomas Jefferson's design for UVA unfolds and the assemblage of the components that, taken together, create the purposeful space. He begins with clarity of purpose and a very specific view of the outcomes that he is trying to produce. He then works backward from this to design the space in which the capabilities, resources, and relationships exist to bring these outcomes to life.

As we move into the literature of the design field itself, a set of themes and issues emerge over time in the discussion of the design process. The notion of synthesis—the creation of a coherent harmonious whole emerging with integrity from a collection of specific design choices—constitutes the earliest and most fundamental notion of what constitutes "good" design, in architecture as well as in business strategy. Vladimir Bazjanac, a Berkeley Architecture professor, traces the evolution of thinking about architectural design. (Bazjanac, 1974) He notes that early theories of architecture, dating back as early as Babylon and the first pyramids of Egypt, were primarily concerned with the concept of beauty and emphasized fundamental principles such as order, symmetry, and harmony.

More recent views, Bazjanac notes, have tended to emphasize the concept of the "best" solution to a stated problem. Perhaps most emblematic of this shift in focus was the emergence of the "Bauhaus" School in Germany in the 1920s, with its emphasis on flexibility, function, and connecting design to what Walter Gropius called "the stuff of life." Together, these themes of beauty and utility illustrate modern design's interest in serving two functions: utilitarian and symbolic.

The history of the influential "Prairie School" of Architecture in the United States at the turn of the twentieth century illustrates the interaction of symbolism and cultural context in the acceptance and rejection of innovative design. Early architectural critics noted that these designs were seen as "echoing the spirit of the prairies of the great middle West, which to them embodied the spirit of democracy." (Pond, 1918) This was seen as in stark contrast to the architecture of the East—wedded

EXHIBIT I

Mr. Jefferson's University

Thomas Jefferson was the third President of the United States, author of the Declaration of Independence, initiator of the Lewis and Clark expedition and the Louisiana Purchase, and President of the Philosophical Society, among many other roles. He was a scientist, an architect, an inventor, a farmer, an agnostic, and a slaveholder. He remains one of the most enigmatic and complex figures in American history.

He also had a passionate, lifelong interest in the field of education, and devoted the last decade of his life to the creation of the University of Virginia, which he called the "hobby of my old age," "the last of my mortal cares, and the last service that I can render my country," Jefferson himself was personally responsible for every aspect of its design and implementation from the architecture of its buildings and grounds to the composition of its curriculum and the selection of its faculty. The story of UVA's creation provides a vivid example of the creation of a purposeful space.

The original portion of the UVA campus that Jefferson designed—the "main grounds" as it is referred to today—remains remarkably unaltered from that which Jefferson built in the 1820s.
It is widely regarded as one of the most architecturally significant college campuses in the United States today. To stand in the center of Mr Jefferson's lawn on an October day, with students sprawled on the expanse of lawn, many deep in conversation, framed by the beauty and harmony of Jefferson's pavilions and gardens is, for many visitors, to experience almost viscerally the ideal of the university as it *ought* to be—bustling with activity and energy, yet beautiful and intimate, with an ethereal sense of serenity, harmony and community To the modern observer Jefferson's genius may appear to lie in the beauty of the architecture that he created. In reality, he took much of his architectural inspiration rather directly from the sixteenth century Italian architect Palladio. His true genius lay with the power of the space that he created and its ability to evoke so vividly the purpose for which it was designed—in Jefferson's own words, "the illimitable freedom of the human mind to explore and expose every subject susceptible of its contemplation ...For here, we are not afraid to follow truth wherever it may lead, nor to tolerate any error so long as reason is left free to combat it," For Jefferson, the link between democracy and education was clear—without an educated populace, there was no hope of protecting self-government. Education would replace a strong central government. As one of Jefferson's many

biographers noted: "Liberty was his chief concern, and his major emphasis was on freedom of the spirit and the mind." Jefferson's University would differ from prevailing American practice in many ways. It would be a community where faculty and students worked as partners to pursue the kind of learning that democracy required.The typical large central building such as the one Jefferson had lived, studied, and worked in at the College of William and Mary, would be replaced with a collection of smaller buildings, an "academical village." As early as 1810, Jefferson had developed a clear image of the future campus:
I consider the common plan followed in this country, but not in others, of making one large and expensive building, as unfortunately erroneous. It is infinitely better to erect a small and separate lodge for each professorship, with only a hall below for his class, and two chambers above for himself: joining these lodges by barracks for a certain portion of the students, opening into a covered way to give a dry communication between all of the schools. The whole of these arranged around an open square of grass and trees would make it, what it should be in fact, an academical village, instead of a large and common den of noise, of filth, and of fetid air.

The hilly terrain of Charlottesville necessitated a more intimate scale than Jefferson had originally envisioned. Craftsmen from Italy were ultimately imported to do much of the work, as local craftsmen lacked the skill to execute Jefferson's design.

This garden-encircled village would be a community of learning where students would have unprecedented freedom in both the choice of curriculum and in governing their own behaviors, Jefferson spoke of the importance of "uncontrolled choice" of subject matter by the students:

Our institution will proceed on the principle of doing all the good it can without consulting its own pride or ambition: of letting everyone come and listen to whatever he thinks may improve the condition of his mind.

The available curriculum would include the new "scientific" and "pragmatic" fields like botany and agriculture, as well as the classical courses in literature, philosophy, and Greek and Latin. Perhaps most significantly, student self-government would be the principle upon which the new university would run:
It may be well questioned whether fear; after a certain age, is a motive to which we should have ordinary re-

course. The human character is susceptible to other inci-
tements to correct conduct, more worthy of employ, and
of better effect. Pride of character; laudable ambition, and
moral dispositions are innate correctives of the indiscre-
tions of that lively age: and when strengthened by habitual
appeal and exercise, have a happier effect on future cha-
racter than the degrading motive of fear.

Thus, Jefferson set out to create a spoce capable of
evoking a desired set of behaviors and relationships—a
particular kind of learning. He did not set out to design
a set of buildings. All aspects of UVA's design, from the
architecture to the curriculum to the selection of faculty
and methods of governance emerge out of an image that
Jefferson held of the type of educational experience that
he was committed to creating. This idealized image, in turn,
was inextricably linked with the set of values and beliefs
that he held most dear—in the promise of democracy and
self-government, the power of knowledge and community,
the primacy of freedom of choice. Like all great design, our
campus inspires as it puts us to work.

This, then, is the design process—one in which the values
and purpose, the nature of the terrain, the capabilities of
the craftsmen, and a host of other elements are brought
together to create a purposeful space—a space that
recognizes the power of both form and function, of both
the aesthetic and the pragmatic.

Sources: All quotations here are taken from Jefferson's
letters, dated 1810 and 1823.

298

to formality, still dominated and made subservient by a sense of inferiority to European styles. Frank Lloyd Wright, one of the Prairie School's most well-known designers, laid out a set of design principles that reflected a multi-faceted approach that sought fit, utility, and harmonizing with context simultaneously. For Wright, the central design "principles" that he developed in his early Prairie School designs would be elaborated on throughout the remainder of his career. These principles were built around harmony with context, the primacy of purpose, and the unity of parts: in his words, "kinship of building to ground," "imaginative design to specific human purposes," and the "organic" design in which "site, structure, furnishing— decoration too, planting as well— all these become one." (Wright, 1960)

Models of the Design Process

Within this context of the goals and principles of design, serious attention to the process of design is a fairly recent phenomena, Bazjanac *(1963)* argues, occurring in the middle of this century and in tandem with developments in the fields of mathematics and systems science, which had a major impact on design thinking: "All early models of the design process have one thing in common: they all view the design process as a sequence of well defined activities and are all based on the assumption that the ideas and principles of the scientific method can be applied to it." 1‹

299

DESIGN THEORISTS OF THIS ERA GENERALLY DESCRIBE THE DESIGN PROCESS AS CONSISTING OF TWO PHASES: ANALYSIS AND SYNTHESIS.

In the analytical phase, the problem is decomposed into a hierarchy of problem subsets, which in turn produce a set of requirements. In the ensuing stage of synthesis, these individual requirements are grouped and realized in a complete design. Parallels with the design of business planning processes and the almost mathematical detail of processes like Igor Ansoff's come to mind here. (Ansoff, 1965)

Unlike in business, however, these early models with their emphasis on "systematic procedures and prescribed techniques" met with immediate criticism for the linearity of their processes and their lack of appreciation for the complexity of design problems. These are some of the same reasons that Henry Mintzberg later used to critique strategic planning processes. Hoerst Rittel first called attention to what he described as the "wicked nature" of

design problems. (Rittel, 1972) Such problems, he asserted, have a unique set of properties. Most importantly, they have no *definitive* formulation or solution. The definition of the "problem" itself is open to multiple interpretations (dependent upon the *Weltanschauung*, or worldview, of the observer) and potential solutions are many, with none of them able to be *proven* to be correct. Writers in the field of business strategy have argued recently that many issues in strategy formulation are "wicked" as well, and that traditional approaches to dealing with them are similarly incapable of producing intelligent solutions. (Rittel, 1972)

Rittel asserted that these "first generation models" were ill-suited for dealing with wicked problems. Instead, he saw design as a process of argumentation, rather than merely analysis and synthesis. Through argumentation, whether as part of a group or solely within the designer's own mind, the designer gained insights, broadened his or her *Weltanschauung*, and continually refined the definition of the problem and its attendant solution. Thus, the design process came to be seen as one of negotiation rather than optimization, fundamentally concerned with learning and the search for emergent opportunities. Rittel's arguments are consistent with recent calls in the strategy literature for more attention to "strategic conversations" (Liedtka; Liedtka and Rosenblum, 1996, Westle, 1990), in which a broad group of organizational stakeholders engage in dialogue-based planning processes out of which shared understanding and, ultimately, shared choices emerge.

The Role of Hypotheses in the Design Process

More recently, design theorists have explored a number of these issues in greater depth. The issue of the role of the scientific method in the design process has been an on-going focus of discussion. In general, studies of design processes frequently suggest a hypothesis-driven approach similar to the traditional scientific method, Nigel Cross, in reviewing a wide range of studies of design processes in action, notes, "It becomes clear from these studies that architects, engineers, and other designers adopt a problem-solving strategy based on generating and testing potential solutions," (Cross, 1995) Donald Schon (1983), after studying architects in action, described design as "a shaping process" in which the situation "talks back" continually and "each move is a local experiment which contributes to the global experiment of reframing the problem". Schon's designer begins by generating a series of creative "what if" hypotheses, selecting the most promising one for further inquiry. This inquiry takes the form of a more evaluative "if then" sequence, in which the logical implications of that particular hypothesis are more fully explored and tested.

THE SCIENTIFIC METHOD THEN— WITH ITS EMPHASIS ON CYCLES OF HYPOTHESIS GENERATING AND TESTING AND THE ACQUISITION OF NEW INFORMATION TO CONTINUALLY OPEN UP NEW POSSIBILITIES—REMAINS CENTRAL TO DESIGN THINKING.

However, the nature of "wicked problems" makes such trial and error learning problematic. Rittel makes this point from the perspective of architecture—a building, once constructed, cannot be easily changed, and so learning through experimentation in practice is undesirable. This is the ultimate source of "wickedness" in such problems: their indeterminacy places a premium on experimentation, while the high cost of change makes such experimentation problematic. As in business, we know that we might be able or be forced to change our strategies as we go along—but we'd rather not. This apparent paradox is what gives the design process—with its use of constructive forethought— its utility. The designer substitutes mental experiments for physical ones. In this view, design becomes a process of hypothesis generating and testing, whose aim is to provide the builder with a plan that tries to anticipate the general nature of impending changes.

A concern of the design process, however, is the risk of "entrapment," in which a designer's investment in early hypotheses make them difficult to give up as the design progresses, despite the presence of disconfirming data.

DESIGN IS MOST SUCCESSFUL, THEN, WHEN IT CREATES A VIRTUAL WORLD, A "LEARNING LABORATORY," WHERE MENTAL EXPERIMENTS CAN BE CONDUCTED RISK-FREE AND WHERE INVESTMENTS IN EARLY CHOICES CAN BE MINIMIZED.

As Schon (1983: 162) points out: "Virtual worlds are contexts for experiment within which practitioners can suspend or control some of the everyday impediments to rigorous reflection-in-action. They are representative worlds of practice in the double sense of "practice." And practice in the construction, maintenance, and use of virtual worlds develops the capacity for reflection-in-action which we call artistry."

Thus, rather than seeing planning as doomed and dysfunctional in times of change, the use of the design metaphor suggests that planning's value is maximized in times of change. Design's value lies in creating a "virtual" world in which experiments (mental rather than physical) can be conducted on a less costly basis. This offers a very different perspective from which to think about the creation of business strategies. Traditional approaches to strategic planning have shared the perspective of early design theorists and assumed that planning creates value primarily through a process of controlling, integrating, and coordinating—that the power of planning is in the creation of a systematic approach to problem-solving—de-composing a complex problem into sub-problems to be solved and later integrated back into a whole. While integration, coordination, and control are all potentially important tasks, a focus on these dramatically underestimates the value of planning in a time of change. The metaphor of design calls attention to planning's ability to create a virtual world in which hypotheses can be generated and tested in low cost ways.

Invention versus Discovery

Contemporary design theorists have been especially attentive to the areas in which design and science *diverge*, however, as well as converge.

THE MOST FUNDAMENTAL DIFFERENCE BETWEEN THE TWO, THEY ARGUE, IS THAT DESIGN THINKING DEALS PRIMARILY WITH WHAT *DOES NOT YET EXIST*; WHILE SCIENTISTS DEAL WITH EXPLAINING WHAT *IS*.

A common theme is that scientists *discover* the laws that govern today's reality, while designers *invent* a different future. Designers are, of course, interested in explanations of current reality to the extent that such understanding reveals patterns in the underlying relationships essential to the process of formulating and executing the new design successfully, but the emphasis remains on the future. Thus, while both methods of thinking are hypothesis-driven, the *design* hypothesis differs from the *scientific* hypothesis. Rather than using traditional reasoning modes of induction or deduction, March (1976) argues that design thinking is adductive: "Science investigates extant forms. Design initiates novel forms. A scientific hypothesis is not the same thing as a design hypothesis ... A speculative design cannot be determined logically, because the mode of reasoning involved is essentially adductive."
Adductive reasoning uses the logic of conjecture. Cross

borrows from Philosopher C.S. Peirce this elaboration of the differences among the modes: "Deduction proves that something must be; induction shows that something actually is operative; adduction merely suggests that something may be." Thus, a capacity for creative visualization—the ability to "conjure" an image of a future reality that does not exist today, an image so vivid that it appears to be real already— is central to design. Successful designers—in business or the arts— are great conjurers, and the design metaphor reminds us of this.

UNDERLYING THIS EMPHASIS ON CONJECTURAL THINKING AND VISUALIZATION IS AN ON-GOING INQUIRY INTO THE RELATIONSHIP BETWEEN VERBAL AND NON-VERBAL MEDIUMS.

Design theorists accord a major role to the use of graphic and spatial modeling media—not merely for the purpose of *communicating* design ideas, but for the *generation* of ideas as well. "Designers think with their pencils" is a common refrain. Some theorists have argued that verbalization may, in fact, "obstruct intuitive creation," noting that the right side of the brain is mute. Arnheim (1992) asserts that the image "unfolds" in the mind of the designer as the design process progresses; and that it is, in fact, the unfolding nature of the image that makes creative design possible: "As long as the guiding image is still developing it remains tentative, generic, vague. This vagueness, however, is by no means a negative quality. Rather it has the positive quality of a topological shape. As distinguished from geometric shapes, a topological shape stands for a whole range of possibilities without being tangibly committed to any one of them. Being undefined in its specifics, it admits distortions and deviations. Its pregnancy is what the designer requires in the search for a final shape."

Thus, the designer begins with what Arnheim calls "a center, an axis, a direction," from which the design takes on increasing levels of detail and sophistication as it unfolds.

Architect Frank Gehry's description of the design of the Guggenheim Bilbao Museum captures these themes of experimentation in virtual worlds, and the role of sketches and models in the unfolding process (see Exhibit 2). In the story of Gehry's creation, we witness the designer bringing his or her own previous experiences to the new site and, through a process of iteration that moves back and forth between the general idea and the specific design of its subcomponents, the design evolves, gaining clarity and definition.

EXHIBIT 2

The Design of the Guggenheim Bilbao:
An Unfolding Process

In describing this Century's 100 "greatest design hits," *NewYorkTimes* architecture critic Herbert Muschamp included ten buildings, among them Antoni Caudi's Casa Mila (1906), Mies van der Rohe's Barcelona Pavilion (1929), Frank Lloyd Wright's Fallingwater (1936), Le Corbusier's Chapel at Ronchamp (1950), and I.M. Pei's Bank of China Tower in Hong Kong (1982). Number 100, and the only building listed designed in the last decade, was Frank Gehry's Guggenheim Museum in Bilbao. Writing in the Los Angeles Times, Architecture Critic Nicolai Ouroussoff effuses: "Gehry has achieved what not so long ago seemed impossible for most architects: the invention of radically new architectural forms that nonetheless speak to the man on the street. Bilbao has become a pilgrimage point for those who, until now, had little interest in architecture. Working class Basque couples arrive toting children on weekends. The cultural elite veer off their regular flight paths so they can tell friends that they, too, have seen the building in the flesh. Gehry has become, in the eyes of a world attuned to celebrity, the great America architect, and, in the process, he has brought hope to an entire profession."

Van Bruggen chronicles the story of the design of the Bilbao Museum, tracing, through a series of interviews with Gehry the unfolding nature of the design process, with its emphasis on experimentation and iteration, and its comfort with ambiguity. Gehry explains how the design process begins:

"You bring to the table certain things. What's exciting, you tweak them based on the context and the people ... Krens (Guggenheim Foundation Director), Juan Ignacio (future director of the Bilbao museum site), the Basques, their desire to use culture, to bring the city to the river And the industrial feeling ... I knew all of that when I started sketching."

Gehry's first sketches are on pieces of hotel stationery—they are "fast scrawls and mere annotations ... the hand functions as an immediate tool of the mind." Later on an airplane, as the design evolves, the sketches begin to capture the basics of his scheme for the site. As Van Bruggen notes, he has "begun to take hold of the complexities of the site ... Allowing the pen to take possession of the space helps him to clarify the program requirements and re-imagine the problem .... Elements shift and are regrouped to contribute to a different kind of understanding, a leap from the conditional, technical aspects of building into unrestrained, intuitive sense perception, into sculptural architecture. From here on, a delicate process of cutting apart while holding together takes place, a going back and forth from sketches into models in order to solve problems and refine the plastic shapes of the building."

Gehry explains: "I start drawing sometimes, not knowing where it is going ... It's like feeling your way along in the dark, anticipating that something will come out usually. I become a voyeur of my own thoughts as they develop, and wander about them. Sometimes I say 'boy, here it is, it's coming.' I understand it. I get all excited and from there I'll move to the models, and the models drain all of the energy, and need information on scale and relationships that you can't conceive in totality in drawings. The drawings are ephemeral. The models are specific; they then become like the sketches in the next phase. The models change scale and materials as the project progresses, becoming increasingly detailed, and moving from paper to plastic to wood to industrial foam. In total, six different models were developed over the course of the Bilbao project.

Computer modeling plays a critical role as the physical models evolve. "The Guggenheim Museum Bilbao would not have stayed within the construction budget allotted by the Basque Administration had it not been for Catia, a computer program originally developed for the French aerospace industry, "Van Bruggen observes. Gehry's staff customized the software to model the sculptural shapes, accelerating the layout process and devising more economically buildable designs. These computer models were always translated back into physical models.

Throughout, the process remains iterative. Gehry observes that "often the models take me down a blind alley and I go back to sketches again. They become the vehicle for propelling the project forward when I get stuck." In the end, the process from first sketch into final building remains one of "unfolding": "In the first sketch, I put a bunch of principles down. Then I become self-critical of those images and those principles, and they evoke the next set of responses. And as each piece unfolds, I make the models bigger and bigger bringing into focus more elements and more pieces of the puzzle. And once I have the beginning, a toehold into where I'm going, then I want to examine the parts in more detail. And those evolve, and at some point I stop, because that's it I don't come to a conclusion, but I think there's a certain reality of pressure to get the thing done that I accept."

Sources: See H. Muschamp, "Blueprint: The Shock of the Familiar" New York Times, December 13, 1998, section 6, p. 6l, col. I: N. Ouroussoff, "I'm Frank Gehry," Los Angeles Times, October 25, 1998, home edition, p. 17; C. Van Bruggen, Frank O. Gehry: Guggenheim Museum Bilbao, (New York NY: Guggenheim Museum Publications, 1997), pp. 33, 31, 71, 103, 135, 104, 130.

The General versus the Particular

In addition to the prominent role played by conjecture and experimentation in design thinking, there is also a fundamental divergence between the concern of science for generalizable laws and design's interest in the particulars of individual cases. Buchanan (1995: 15–16) argues that there can be no "science" of design: "Designers conceive their subject matter on two levels: general and particular. On a general level, a designer forms an idea or a working hypothesis about the nature of products or the nature of the human-made in the world ... But such philosophies do not and cannot constitute sciences of design in the sense of the natural, social, or humanistic science. The reason for this is simple: design is fundamentally concerned with the particular, and there is no science of the particular ... Out of the specific possibilities of a concrete situation, the designer must conceive a design that will lead to this or that particular product... (The designer does not begin with an undeterminate subject waiting to be made determinate.) It is an indeterminate subject waiting to be made specific and concrete."

This quality of indeterminacy has profound implications for the design process. First, the tendency to project determinacy onto past choices—"prediction after the fact"—is ever present and must be avoided, or it undermines and distorts the true nature of the design process. (This is an assertion that has been used to argue against case method pedagogy, with its tendency towards retrospective rationalization of strategic choices). Secondly, creative designs do not passively await discovery—designers must actively seek them out. [2K] Third, the indeterminacy of the process suggests the possibility for both exceptional diversity and continual evolution in the outcomes produced (even within similar processes). Finally, because design solutions are always matters of *invented choice*, rather than *discovered truth*, the judgment of designers is always open to question by the broader public.

Each of these implications resonates with business experiences. Richard Pascale's contrasting stories of Honda's entry into the U.S. motorcycle market chronicles the kind of retrospective rationalization that can accompany well-known business success stories. (Pascale, 1984)

SIMILARLY, THE NEED TO SEEK OUT THE FUTURE IS ONE OF THE MOST COMMON PRESCRIPTIONS IN TODAY'S WRITINGS ON STRATEGY.

Similarly, the search for and belief in the ideal of the *one* right strategy can stifle creativity, cause myopia that misses opportunity, and paralyze organizational decision processes.

However, the final implication—this notion of the inevitable need to justify to others the "rightness" of the design choices made—is perhaps the most significant implication for the design of strategy processes in business organizations. Because strategic choices can never be "proven" to be right, they remain always contestable and must be made compelling to others in order to be realized. This calls into play Rittel's role of argumentation and focuses attention on others, and the role of rhetoric in bringing them into the design conversation.

PARTICIPATION BECOMES KEY TO PRODUCING A COLLECTIVE LEARNING THAT BOTH EDUCATES INDIVIDUALS AND SHAPES THE EVOLVING CHOICES SIMULTANEOUSLY.

Thus, design becomes a shared process, no longer the province of a single designer.

The Role of Values in Design

Participation is critical, in part, because of the role that values, both individual and institutional, play in the design process. As we saw in the UVA story, values drive both the creation of the design and its acceptance. However, there is a sad footnote to that story. History tells us that UVA's early students did not share Jefferson's values and sense of purpose, apparently preferring gambling, horses, and drinking to the pursuit of truth. As a result, key elements of his design, like student self-governance and faculty living in community with students, did not achieve their intended purpose. The buildings were just as beautiful, yet without the invisible infrastructure of shared values and purpose, the space could not evoke the intended behaviors. In the last year of his life, Jefferson is reported to have sat in his great Rotunda at the head of UVA's sweeping lawn, and wept openly at the reports of student misbehavior, including that of his own nephew, and their failure to share his dream.

Successful designs must embody both existing and new values simultaneously. "Designers persuade," Williamson argues, "by referencing accepted values and attributing these to a new subject." (Williamson, 1983) It is the linkage to values already present in the Weltanschauung of the observer that allows the new design to find acceptance. The ability to establish and communicate these links is essential to achieving a successfully implemented design. Designs that embody values and purpose that are not shared—however innovative—fail to persuade.

Given the indeterminacy of the choices made, the ability to work with competing interests and values is inevitable in the process of designing. Buchanan notes that the question of whose values *matter* has changed over time, evolving from 1950s beliefs about the "ability of experts to engineer socially acceptable results" for audiences that were seen as "passive recipients of preformed messages," towards a view of audiences as "active participants in reaching conclusions." (Buchanan and Margolis, 1995: 10)

THE "CHARETTE" PLAYS A FUNDAMENTAL ROLE IN MAKING DESIGN PROCESSES PARTICIPATIVE AND MAKING COLLEAIVE LEARNING POSSIBLE.

Charettes are intensive brainstorming/planning sessions in which groups of stakeholders come together. Their intention is to share, critique, and invent in a way that accelerates the development of large-scale projects. The charette at the Guggenheim Bilbao, for example, lasted for two months. One of the most well-known users of charettes is the architectural firm Duaney, Plater-Zyberg, who specialize in the design of new "traditional towns" like Seaside, Florida, or Disney's Celebration. In their charette for the design of a new town outside of Washington, D.C, Duaney, Plater-Zyberg brought together architects, builders, engineers, local officials, traffic consultants, utility company representatives, computer experts, architecture professors, shopping mall developers, and townspeople for a discussion/critique that lasted seven days. (Washington Post, June 9, 1988) The more complex the design process, the more critical a role the charette plays. The charette offers a new model for planning processes in business.

Design as Dialectical

In the design literature, there is a clear recognition of the fundamentally paradoxical nature of the design process and its need to mediate between diverging forces. Findeli (1990) notes: "The discipline of design has got to be considered as paradoxical in essence and an attempt to eliminate one pole to the benefit of the other inevitably distorts its fundamental nature, [The goal becomes] to perceive this dualism as a dialectic, to transform this antagonism into a constructive dynamic."

Echoing a similar theme, Buchanan situates design as a dialectic at the intersection of constraint, contingency, and possibility. (Buchanan and Margolis, 1995) Successful design remains ever mindful of the constraints imposed by the materials and situation at hand, as well as the changing, and contingent, preferences of the audience that it serves. Simultaneously, however, it holds open the promise of the creation of new possibilities—available by challenging the status quo, reframing the problem, connecting the pieces, synthesizing the learning, and improvising as opportunities emerge.

The design of New York's Central Park by Frederick Law Olmsted and Calvert Vaux in the 1850s offers a look at the way in which successful design mediates the tension between constraint, contingency, and possibility. In the competition held to award the contract for the design of the park, only Olmsted and Vaux were able to envision a design that succeeded in meeting all of the requirements set forth—that the Park must allow carriages to transverse it, rather than go around it, while retaining a park-like feel—requirements that other designers had seen as impossible to satisfy. They did this by envisioning the park space as three dimensional, rather than two, and proposing the construction of buried roadways that would allow cross-town vehicular traffic, but would be out of site to those enjoying the park.

This tension created by the often diverging pulls of necessity, uncertainty, and possibility define design's terrain. It is a landscape where a mindset that embraces traditional dichotomies—art versus science, intuition versus analysis, the abstract versus the particular, ambiguity versus precision—finds little comfort.

Implied Characteristics of Design Thinking

To summarize, despite the avowed plurality that design theorists use to describe the field more precisely, a set of commonalties does emerge from the recent work on the attributes of design thinking.

First, design thinking is *synthetic*. Out of the often disparate demands presented by sub-units' requirements, a coherent overall design must be made to emerge. The process through which and the order in which the overall design and its sub-unit designs unfold remains a source of debate. What is clear is that the order in which they are given attention matters, as it determines the "givens" of subsequent designs, but ultimately successful designs can be expected to exhibit considerable diversity in their specifics.

Second, design thinking is *adductive* in nature. It is primarily concerned with the process of visualizing what might be, some desired future state, and creating a blueprint for realizing that intention.

Third, design thinking is *hypothesis-driven*. As such, it is both analytic in its use of data for hypothesis testing and creative in the generation of hypotheses to be tested. The hypotheses are of two types. Primary is the design hypothesis. The design hypothesis is conjectural and, as such, cannot be tested directly. Embedded in the selection of a particular promising design hypothesis, however, are a series of assumptions about a set of cause-effect relationships in today's environment that will support a set of actions aimed at transforming a situation from its current reality to its desired future state. These explanatory hypotheses must be identified and tested directly. Cycles of hypothesis generation and testing are iterative. As successive loops of "what if" and "if then" questions are explored, the hypotheses become more sophisticated and the design unfolds.

Fourth, design thinking is *opportunistic*. As the above cycles iterate, the designer seeks new and emergent possibilities. The power of the design lies in the particular. Thus, it is in the translation from the abstract/global to the particular/local that unforeseen opportunities are most likely to emerge. Sketching and modeling are important tools in the unfolding process, as Gehry's description of the Guggenheim Bilbao design illustrates.

Fifth, design thinking is *dialectical*. The designer lives at the intersection of often conflicting demands—recognizing the constraints of today's materials and the uncertainties that cannot be defined away, while envisioning tomorrow's possibilities. Olmsted's Central Park testifies to the ability of innovative design to both satisfy and transcend today's constraints to realize new possibilities.

Finally, design thinking is *inquiring and value-driven*—open to scrutiny, welcoming of inquiry, willing to make its reasoning explicit to a broader audience, and cognizant of the values embedded within the conversation. It recognizes the primacy of the Weltanschauung of its audience. The architect imbues the design with his or her own values, as Jefferson's design of the University of Virginia and Gehry's of the Guggenheim Bilbao reflect.

SUCCESSFUL DESIGNS, IN PRACTICE, EDUCATE AND PERSUADE BY CONNECTING WITH THE VALUES OF THE AUDIENCE, AS WELL.

Implications for Strategy-Making as a Design Process

Having developed a clearer sense of the process of design itself, we can begin to describe the possibilities that the use of such a metaphor might hold for thinking about business strategy, in general, and the design of strategy-making processes, in particular.

First, strategic thinking is *synthetic*. It seeks internal alignment and understands interdependencies. It is systemic in its focus. It requires the ability to understand and integrate across levels and elements, both horizontal and vertical, and to align strategies across those levels. Strategic thinking is built on the foundation of a systems perspective. A strategic thinker has a mental model of the complete end-to-end system of value creation, and understands the interdependencies within it. The synthesizing process creates value not only in aligning the components, but also in creatively re-arranging them. The creative solutions produced by many of today's entrepreneurs often rest more with the redesign of aspects of traditional strategies rather than with dramatic break-throughs. (see Petzinger, 1999)

Strategic thinking is *adductive*. It is future-focused and inventive, as Hamel and Prahalad's popular concept of strategic intent illustrates. (Hamel and Prahalad, 1994) Strategic intent provides the focus that allows individuals within an organization to marshal and leverage their energy, to focus attention, to resist distraction, and to concentrate for as long as it takes to achieve a goal. The creation of a compelling intent, with the sense of "discovery, direction, and destiny" of which Hamel and Prahalad speak, relies heavily on the skill of alternative generation. As Simon has noted, alternative generation has received far less attention in the strategic decision making literature than has alternative evaluation, but is more important in an environment of change. (Simon, 1993)

Yet, it is not merely the creation of the intent itself, but the identification of the gap between current reality and the imagined future that drives strategy making. The ability to link past, present, and future in a process that Neustadt and May (1986: 251) have called "thinking in time": "Thinking in time (has) three components. One is recognition that the future has no place to come from but the past, hence the past has predictive value. Another element is recognition that what matters for the future in the present is departures from the past, alterations, changes, which prospectively or actually divert familiar flows from accustomed channels. ... A third component is continuous comparison, an almost constant oscillation from the present to future to past and back, heedful of prospective change, concerned to expedite, limit, guide, counter, or accept it as the fruits of such comparison suggest."

Strategic thinking is *hypothesis-driven.* In an environment of ever-increasing information availability and decreasing time to think, the ability to develop good hypotheses and to test them efficiently is critical. Because it is hypothesis-driven, strategic thinking avoids the analytic-intuitive dichotomy that has characterized much of the debate about strategic thinking. Strategic thinking is *both* creative and critical, in nature. Figuring out how to accomplish both types of thinking simultaneously has long troubled cognitive psychologists, since it is necessary to *suspend* critical judgment in order to think more creatively. Strategic
thinking accommodates both creative and analytical thinking sequentially in its use of iterative cycles of hypothesis generating and testing. Hypothesis generation asks the creative question "what if... ?" Hypothesis testing follows with the critical question "if. . ., then . . .?" and brings relevant data to bear on the analysis, including an analysis of a hypothetical set of financial flows associated with the idea. Taken together, and repeated over time, this sequence allows us to pose ever-improving hypotheses, without forfeiting the ability to explore new ideas. Such experimentation allows an organization to move beyond simplistic notions of cause and effect to provide on-going learning.

Strategic thinking is *opportunistic.* Within this intent-driven focus, there must be room for opportunism that not only furthers intended strategy, but that also leaves open the possibility of new strategies emerging. In writing about the role of "strategic dissonance" in the strategy-making process at Intel, Robert Burgelman has highlighted the dilemma involved in using a well-articulated strategy to channel organizational efforts effectively and efficiently against the risks of losing sight of alternative strategies better suited to a changing environment. (Burgelmann, 1991) This requires that an organization be capable of practicing "intelligent opportunism" at lower levels. He concludes: "One important manifestation of corporate capability is a company's ability to adapt without having to rely on extraordinary top management foresight."

Strategic thinking is *dialectical.* In the process of inventing the image of the future, the strategist must mediate the tension between constraint, contingency, and possibility. The underlying emphasis of strategic intent is stretch—to reach explicitly for potentially unattainable goals. At the same time, all elements of the firm's environment are not shapeable and those constraints that are real must be acknowledged in designing strategy. Similarly, the

"unknowables" must be recognized and the flexibility to deal with the range of outcomes that they represent must be designed in.

Finally, strategic thinking is *inquiring* and, inevitably, *value-driven.* Because any particular strategy is invented, rather than discovered—chosen from among a larger set of plausible alternatives—it is contestable and reflective of the values of those making the choice. Its acceptance requires both connection with and movement beyond the existing mindset and value system of the rest of the organization. Such movement relies on inviting the broader community into the argumentation process—the strategic conversation. It is through participation in this dialogue that the strategy itself unfolds, both in the mind of the strategist and in that of the larger community that must come together to make the strategy happen. The conversation is what allows the strategist to pull his or her colleagues "through the keyhole" into a new Weltanschauung.

Taken together, these characteristics borrowed from the field of design—synthetic, adductive, dialectical, hypothesis-driven, opportunistic, inquiring, and value-driven—describe strategic thinking.

Concerns with the Design Metaphor

Having delineated the characteristics of design thinking, I return now to Mintzberg and his stated concerns with the design metaphor. The most prominent of these include: Design suggests that strategy is a process of thought, decoupled from action.

1. In design, implementation must wait for formulation to be completed.
2. Design gives too much emphasis to creativity and uniqueness.
3. Design gives too central a role to THE designer—the CEO in the business.
4. Application of the term.
5. Design is overwhelmingly concerned with fit and focus. (Mintzberg, 1990) ³<

Design as Decoupling Thought from Action

Mintzberg (1990: 182) is concerned that the design process is primarily a process of reflection—of cognition rather than action—and that, as such, it precludes learning: "Our critique of the design school revolves around one central theme: its promotion of thought independent of action, strategy formation above all as a process of conception, rather than as one of learning."

Mintzberg's preference for action appears to be rooted in a belief that in environments characterized by complexity, change, and uncertainty, learning can only occur in action. The process of constructive forethought that this article suggests, however, is not "independent of action." Much of the forethought in the design process is directed specifically at iterative cycles of hypothesis generating and testing whose very purpose is to examine the likely consequences *in action* of the hypotheses being tested. In support of Mintzberg's point, however, these "experiments" are conducted mentally rather than physically. Rather than a liability, this is, for design theorists, one of the key *benefits* of design—the ability to create a virtual environment for risk-reduced, entrapment-minimizing decision-making. Who would choose to construct a building "as you go along," rather than laying out the design in advance? The likely efficiency, quality, coherence, and integrity of the result using the latter process would appear to be far superior to the former. Similarly, to use Mintzberg's own example of the potter at her craft, (Mintzberg, 1987) do we want to suggest that it is preferable for the potter to think of her creation *only* while sitting at the wheel, and never beforehand? The mistakes made at the wheel are clearly more expensive and difficult to undo. The same logic would appear to be compelling for business, especially to the extent to which we accept strategic problems as "wicked." Given the ability to do either, would we actively choose to experiment on our customers in the marketplace instead of on "virtual" customers living in a virtual world? At times, of course, new possibilities may only present themselves at the potter's wheel, necessitating the conduct of actual experiments in the "real" versus the virtual world. An important aspect of the design process lies with identifying those areas of uncertainty and potential opportunism.

THE CHALLENGE IS NOT TO CHOOSE CORRECTLY BETWEEN PLANNING AND OPPORTUNISM— AN EITHER/OR—IT IS HOW TO DEVELOP CAPABILITIES TO DO BOTH IN PRODUCTIVE WAYS.

One hypothesizes that it is Mintzberg's assumption that strategists lack, and cannot reasonably be expected to develop, the ability to conduct high-quality thought experiments—those that truly model reality. This is an assumption on which disagreement exists. It is one generally not shared by a group of influential learning theorists (Senge, 1990) who have devoted significant attention to the ways in which skills in systems thinking and mental modeling can improve the capability for more

effective action. Further, the contention that managers are, in fact, clearly more capable of "learning from their mistakes" after the fact, rather than at thinking their way to successful choices before the fact, remains unsubstantiated. A review of the design literature suggests that, rather than abandoning the process of design, we could more fruitfully turn our attention to enhancing strategists' capabilities to be better designers.

Emphasis on Creativity and Uniqueness

Here, Mintzberg has two concerns about using the design metaphor: first, design's insistence that the resulting design be "unique," second that the "best" designs emerge from a creative process. There can be no disagreement that a shared emphasis on creative process exists between Mintzberg's design school and the larger design literature, and that this process occurs for both within the context of an emphasis on the particular rather than the generalizable. Where there is less clarity is around what constitutes "unique" and "best." The design literature argues strongly for the *possibility* of diversity in design, even in the case of similar purpose and circumstance; it does not, however, insist that such diversity, or "uniqueness," will inevitably be the result of good design. Similarly, "best" in the design world is strongly linked with purpose—both utilitarian and symbolic—rather than with uniqueness, as it might be in a purely creative process. Thus, we might expect that the "best" design in situations sharing a common purpose and experiences and in similar circumstances might look a lot alike. Achieving uniqueness might require reducing the emphasis on achieving purpose. While the world of fine arts might view this as a worthy trade-off, the world of design would not.

Formulation Precedes Implementation

As above, it is literally true in the design field that the act of creation precedes the act of implementation. However, the generative cycle described here is ultimately always repeated and is issue, rather than calendar, driven. For some issues, the loop is continually in motion—a movement back and forth between mental designing and physical implementation that may appear almost simultaneous. Where major new commitments are required, the cycle operates in a more visible, episodic way. It does not insist that the world stand still while lengthy planning cycles operate. Again, though the process of design separates thinking and action, it does not separate "thinking" from "thinking about the consequences of action"—these are, in fact, one and the same for design theorists.

What is also clear, however, is that while design theorists talk very little about implementation as an explicit topic, in practice, designers such as Frank Gehry devote tremendous attention to the ultimate reality that their designs represent and what it will take to realize them. In fact, the distinction between formulation and implementation becomes wholly artificial in the *practice* of designing. What part of design thinking is *not* fundamentally about implementation—making reality of an image of some future state? The question is not whether implementation precedes, succeeds, or occurs simultaneously with formulation. *Within* the design process itself, the distinction simply does not make sense. The important issue behind the formulation/implementation dichotomy is the separation of who is involved in each.

The Prominence of the Architect /CEO in the Design Process

Mintzberg's equates "the CEO" with "the Architect" and objects to the extent to which this devalues the role of other organizational members. This is understandable, given the recent history of the architecture field, which has had as much, or perhaps even more, of a "great man" tenor than the management field. However, the "great man" obsession of the architecture field should not be confused with the nature of the design process.

In the recent practice of architecture, the roles of designer and builder have, in fact, been made distinct. However, today's notion that architects have the overwhelmingly dominant role in the design process and that builders are mere executors of completed designs only emerged within the last century. In the building of the great cathedrals of Europe, the architects' role was seen as the communication of a *general* direction, and builders had great latitude in interpreting these design prescriptions, using their knowledge base. (DeForge, 1990)

THE QUESTION OF WHETHER DESIGN SUFFERS WHEN CREATED BY SOMEONE WHO DOES NOT UNDERSTAND *BUILDING* AS A PROCESS, IS AN IMPORTANT ONE.

Leading architects like Frank Lloyd Wright and Frank Gehry would have answered an emphatic yes. What remains lost, despite an understanding of building, is the opportunity to continually reshape the original design, while under construction, to take advantage of emergent opportunities or to deal with unanticipated constraints. No mental experiments, however carefully conceived and repeated, can anticipate all relevant future developments. Conversely, there is nothing in the idea or process of design itself that suggests that designers ought not to be builders, or vice-versa. While this distinction has emerged in practice in the field of architecture, it is not necessarily as aspect of design practice that we would want to incorporate into business practice, for many of the reasons that Mintzberg reviews. In exploring the transition of the design metaphor to business in a more complete way, the opportunity is to see all managers as designers (and builders as well), each with responsibility for the design of a different piece of the system, within the context of a shared sense of overall purpose.

Design as Primarily Concerned with Focus and Fit

Mintzberg's last concern is that design is primarily concerned with the fit between current competencies and external opportunities, that a well-articulated design's likelihood of providing focus impedes change, and that flexibility, rather than focus, should be the dominant criteria.

The concept of fit carries with it the same two connotations in the design world that it does in the strategy literature. One is fit as internal cohesion and alignment among sub-systems. The second is fit as what Wright called "kinship," or harmony, with the surrounding environment. Both are seen as critically important aspects of design. Interestingly, however, both are considered as "constraints" in the design process. That is, they are important aspects of current reality that must be attended to. The way that they are attended to, however, is in the context of an ever-present tension between them and some different view of a new future. Constraints are not allowed to drive the design process; nor can they be ignored. Instead, they are an important part of the dialectic always underway which the designer tries to mediate through a process of invention. This is a much more powerful view of the natural antagonism between constraint and possibility than has existed in the business strategy field. In business strategy, we have tended to capture this tension as a dichotomy that firms must choose between—labeling them the "strategic fit" and "strategic intent" perspectives. The design field sets the bar far higher: designers are expected to find creative higher level solutions that honor both the current reality and some different future.

PERHAPS WE SHOULD EXPECT THE SAME OF BUSINESS STRATEGISTS—AT WHATEVER POSITION THEY OCCUPY IN THE ORGANIZATION.

Mintzberg's second point argues that a well-articulated strategy impedes change and that on the focus-flexibility continuum, a design approach locates itself too close to the focus end, forfeiting necessary flexibility to deal with change. Mintzberg's contention that the more articulated the strategy, the harder it is to change and its corollary—the "fuzzier" the strategy, the more it welcomes change—must be seriously questioned. For several decades, change theorists have argued the opposite—that a clear picture of the desired future state is an essential ingredient in achieving change. In the views of these theorists, the enemy of change is more likely to be the

lethargy and lack of action introduced by confusion and "fuzziness," rather than active resistance mobilized by clarity. In twenty years of work with managers of companies attempting to implement new strategies, I have yet to hear a manager lament, "if only the strategy was less clear, I would have more freedom to act." The refrain is universally the opposite—"if only they would lay out where they think we're headed, I would be happy to do my part!" The goal of achieving clarity in the ultimate design does not imply that such clarity is present throughout the design process. Clearly, things start "fuzzy" and get clearer. They get clearer through a process of iteration, as needed for implementation. Once implemented, things get fuzzy again as the design evolves in a process similar to the cycles of "chaos" and "single-minded focus" that Andy Grove describes at Intel. (Grove, 1996)

The focus/flexibity conundrum remains one of the central strategic questions of this decade, but the issue here is not primarily one of design versus opportunism. Design, by its nature, is open to emergent opportunity, if viewed as an on-going process. Flexibility can, in fact, be designed into systems. In fact, it must be *designed* into systems in order to be achieved. The mere lack of constructive forethought offers no guarantee of openness to opportunity—quite the opposite, if we believe in the old dictum that "luck finds the prepared mind." The trade-off between focused commitment to a particular strategy and an alternative strategy that maximizes flexibility is, instead, often reflected in the former strategy's superior ability to deliver efficiently against a particular purpose and the latter's ability to change purpose. That difference in performance is not a choice made by choosing design, it is a choice made in the process of designing.

Leveraging the Design Metaphor

The metaphor of design offers a window into a deeper understanding of the process of strategy making. It does this by calling attention to the process of creating a purposeful space. Such spaces "work" because of much more than the structures visible to the eye. They work because they create an environment that fuses form and function; that builds relationships and capabilities and targets specific outcomes; that inspires, at an emotional and aesthetic level, those who work towards a shared purpose. Values play a vital role here, as do hypothesis generating and testing, and the ability to conjure a vivid picture of a set of possibilities that do not yet exist.

What would we do differently in organizations today, if we took seriously the design metaphor? A lot, I believe.

It would call for significant changes in the way that strategic planning is approached today, especially in large organizations. The problems with traditional approaches to planning have long been recognized. (Lenz, 1987) They include: the attempt to make a science of planning with its subsequent loss of creativity, the excessive emphasis on numbers, the drive for administrative efficiency that standardized inputs and formats at the expense of substance, and the dominance of single techniques, inappropriately applied.

Decades later, strategists continue to struggle to propose clear alternatives to traditional processes. Design offers a different approach and would suggest processes that are more widely participative, more dialogue-based, issue-driven rather than calendar-driven, conflict-using rather than conflict-avoiding, all aimed at invention and learning, rather than control. In short, we should involve more members of the organization in two-way strategic conversations. We should view the process as one of iteration and experimentation, and pay sequential attention to idea generation and evaluation in a way that attends first to possibilities before moving onto constraints.

FINALLY, AND PERHAPS MOST IMPORTANTLY, WE WOULD RECOGNIZE THAT GOOD DESIGNS SUCCEED BY PERSUADING, AND GREAT DESIGNS BY INSPIRING.

1❰ in particular, the writings of C. Alexander, Notes on the Synthesis of Form (Boston, MA: Harvard University Press, 1964); L. Archer, "Systemation Method for Designers," Design (1963), pp. 172–188.

2❰ There exists a fascinating literature on the neurological processes at work when a creative break through suddenly "presents itself" in the conscious mind without clear forethought, which Simon [(1969), op. cit.] reviews, noting that such unsought "illuminations" are always preceded by periods of preparation and incubation.

3❰ Mintzberg states seven specific concerns with the "Design School." Several of these, however, are inconsistent with our use of the term "design" (e.g., numbers 3 and 5: designs must be kept simple and designs emerge fully formed from the process), and so I have focused my attention on those concerns that remain significant, given our use of the term "design."

References

Ansoff, I. 1965. Corporate strategy: An analytic approach to business policy for growth and expansion. New York, NY: McGraw-Hill.

Arnheim, R. 1992. Sketching and the psychology of design. In V. Margolis and R. Buchanan (Eds.) The idea of design: 70–74. Cambridge, MA: MIT Press.

Bazjanac, V. 1974. Architectural design theory: Models of the design process. In W. Spillers (Ed.) Basic Questions of Design Theory: 3–20. New York, NY: American Elsevier.

Buchanan, R. and Margolis, V. 1995. (Eds.) Discovering design. Chicago, IL: University of Chicago Press.

Burgelman, R. 1991. Intraorganizational ecology of strategy making and organizational adaptation. Organizational Science, 2/3: 208, 239–262.

Cross, N. 1995. Discovering design ability. In R. Buchanan and V. Margolis (Eds.) Discovering design: 105–120. Chicago, IL: University of Chicago Press.

DeForge, Y. 1990. Avators of design: Design before design. Design Issues, 6/2: 43–50.

Findeli, A. 1990. The methodological and philosophical foundations of Moholy-Nagy's design pedagogy in Chicago (1927–1946). Design Issues, 111: 4–19, 32–33.

Grove, A. 1996. Only the paranoid survive. New York, NY: Doubleday.

Hamel, G. and Prahalad, C. K. 1994. Competing for the future. Boston, MA: Harvard Business School Press: 129–130.

Lenz, R. 1987. Managing the evolution of the strategic planning process. Business Horizons, 30/1: 34–39.

Liedtka, J. and Rosenblum, J. 1996. Shaping conversations: Making strategy, managing change. California Management Review, 39/1, Fall: 141–157.

Liedtka, J. Generative planning. European Journal of Management (forthcoming)

March, L. 1976. The logic of design. In L. March (Ed.) The architecture of form. Cambridge, MA: Cambridge University Press.

Mason, R. and Mitroff, I.1981. Challenging strategic planning assumptions. New York, NY: Wiley.

Mintzberg, H. 1987. Crafting strategy. Harvard Business Review, 64/4: 66–75.

Mintzberg, H. 1990. The design school: Reconsidering the basic premises of strategic management. Strategic Management Journal, 11/3: 171–195.

Mintzberg, H. 1994. The rise and fall of strategic planning. New York: The Free Press.

Neustadt, R. and May, E. 1986. Thinking in time: The uses of history for decision-makers. New York, NY: The Free Press.

Pascale, R.T. 1984. Perspectives on strategy: The real story behind Honda's success. California Management Review, 26/3: 47–72.

Petzinger, T. 1999. The new pioneers. New York, NY: Simon and Schuster.

Pond, I. 1918. The meaning of architecture: An essay in constructive criticism. Boston: Marshall Jones Company.

Rittel, H. 1972. On the planning crisis: Systems analysis of the first and second generations. Bedrift Sokonomen, 8: 309–396.

Schon, D. 1983. The reflective practitioner: How professionals think in action. New York, NY: Basic Books.

Senge, P. 1990. The fifth discipline. New York, NY: Doubleday.

Simon, H. 1996. The sciences of the artificial. Cambridge, MA: MIT Press.

Simon, H. 1993. Strategy and organizational evolution. Strategic Management Journal, 14: 131–142.

Westley, F. 1990. Middle managers and strategy: Microdynamics of inclusion. Strategic Management Journal, 11: 337–351.

Williamson, J. 1983. Decoding advertisements. New York, NY: Marion Bryars Publishers.

The Washington Post. 1988. In seven days. Designing a new traditional town. June 9: Cl, C6.

Wright, R. and Kaufman, E., Raebu, R. (Eds.) 1960. Frank Lloyd Wright: Writings and buildings. New York, NY: Meridian Books.

313

In an environment where the challenge for businesses to stay ahead of the curve calls for new ways of strategizing for future success, design holds some important clues. By broadening the definition of "design" and expanding the application of design methodologies and mindsets to business, enterprises can move beyond mere survival and incremental change, and open up new possibilities for breakthrough growth strategies and organizational transformation.

Part of this article originally appeared in Journal of Business Strategy
VOL. 28, NO. 42007, pp.66–74, © Emerald Group Publishing Limited, ISSN 0275-6668

Drawing from a number of wide-ranging projects, case studies and executive education initiatives at Rotman DesignWorks™ we have gleaned some promising insights into how to achieve breakthrough strategies for success, by design. This article articulates how to embed design methods and mindsets into an organizations strategic planning practices. It articulates how to unearth new and breakthrough opportunities to strengthen business strategies and create sustainable competitive advantage in a competitive marketplace.

Design as a Catalyst for Growth

What forces in the marketplace are driving the need for new methods to create strategies for growth? A number of significant game-changing forces are at play. Here are just a few of the seismic shifts that set the scene today:

- Global access to new markets and expanded sources of people and components are breaking down barriers and creating new opportunities for some and threats to others.

- Technology has profoundly changed the way people connect and business gets done locally and globally. Virtual access, interactions and transactions have transformed the physical world and created new ways to connect and compete.

- Marketplace demands are increasing as consumers have come to expect better, more sophisticated offerings and greater customization within the plethora of goods and services. The "category walls" are breaking down as consumers look for more integrated solutions to meeting their needs across products and services, demanding more from manufacturers and service providers than ever before. This expectation transcends all markets—it is now believed that all people in all markets should have access to life-enhancing solutions of all kinds.

- Social values are shifting, with higher expectations on good citizenship and the corporation's social and environmental role and responsibilities. The "green movement" will radically change future expectations of corporations and governments.

Within this context, many companies are slow to respond to these forces because their historically successful models and infrastructures are making it challenging to shift organizational cultures and evolve rigid business models.

In the face of these dynamic forces of change, companies are searching for better, faster, more effective means of reinvigorating their human capital to get ahead of the curve.

THE AIM: TO CREATE NEW ECONOMIC AND HUMAN VALUE.

Economics of Design versus Design of Economics

Herein lies the opportunity to leverage design practices for both cultural transformation and strategic growth, moving from a framework of the "economics of design" to the "design of economics". The economics of design are indisputable: good design of products and service experiences creates satisfaction, connections, desire and value to the ultimate user, taking a commodity product to a premium position. A smart redesign can also yield economic rewards through greater operational efficiencies. No one can debate that. But where design has its highest value is in applying design thinking to strategy and business modeling—in designing the sustainable competitive advantage of an enterprise. By embracing design methods and mindsets, an enterprise can not only design new products, services and experiences, but they can also fundamentally drive the design of economics in support of dramatic new growth strategies.

While this is not yet a broadly embraced interpretation of "design" it is one where the evidence for success is mounting. While at first this model may seem either radical or abstract, those who discover its advantages find it surprisingly intuitive and practical—just what the business world needs in the face of high-stakes complexities and change.

How it Works—The Methods

Drawing from the many tools and techniques used in both the design world and the business world, this methodology can be distilled into what we call the "three gears of design" (see Fig. 1) that drive strategy and business design: empathy and deep user understanding, concept visualization and multiple-prototyping, and strategic business design. This is not a 1-2-3 linear process, but rather an iterative process anchored in the needs of the user or ultimate customer target. By cycling through these three gears, work teams can get to bigger breakthroughs faster—applying user insights to stimulate high-value conceptual solutions and extracting strategic intent from the concepts to reform strategic business models.

EMPATHY & DEEP HUMAN UNDERSTANDING
A deep dive with a broad lens

CONCEPT VISUALIZATION
Ideation, Prototyping & User Evaluation

STRATEGIC BUSINESS DESIGN
Activity System Design & Evaluation

Setting the Foundation

Before beginning the design journey, it is beneficial for the business team to frame up its current operating strategy, articulating what the organization is doing today that is driving current business results. Understanding the current business models, operational focus areas and market challenges and opportunities helps to get everyone grounded in the same view of the current state. Furthermore, not only does this help frame up the current business model, but also the team's mental model that is conditioned by the ongoing, well-entrenched activities of an organization. These are the points of reference for the business team that are both valuable and limiting in driving business.

KNOWING ONE'S WORKING MODEL, ORGANIZATIONAL COMPETENCIES AND STRATEGIC FOCUS AREAS KEEP AN ENTERPRISE MOVING FORWARD PRODUCTIVELY.

At the same time, if the current framework is viewed as a fixed model, this "mental model" can also be a source of constraint in exploring future possibilities outside current practices and capabilities.

The limiting forces: a drive for "narrow perfectionism" and a reliance on current capabilities and measurements to squeeze more out of the current activity system which may yield diminishing returns over time. Often we hear executives discount opportunities because "We're not in that business. We're a manufacturer, not a service provider." The position that "that's not what we do today" is not a reason for not doing it in the future. Consider where Apple would be today if they had subscribed to old school thinking of "sticking to their knitting"; we would never have witnessed the revolutionary success of a computer company introducing iTunes and iPod, and setting up for another potential step change with the iPhone. Apple does not live within the constraints of their current business model; they follow their user to new opportunities, which is what the first gear of design is all about.

The Three Gears of Design

First gear
The first step is to reframe your business wholly through the eyes of the user. This may sound like Marketing 101, but companies are so often consumed by their current development initiatives, business challenges, budgets, deadlines and quarterly plan delivery that they find it difficult to really turn the telescope around and view their business entirely through the eyes of their end-user in a holistic manner.

To broaden the lens, it is important to look beyond the direct use of a company's product or service and explore the activity surrounding it to gain deeper insight and a broader behavioral and psychographic perspective on the user's life. It is also critical to understand the "whole person" in the context of a given activity—not just what they do, but how they feel and how their needs surrounding the activity link to other parts of their life in terms of other activities, other people, and other cues to their needs.

As an example, Nike's focus on its deep understanding of the runner goes way beyond the utility of the running shoe. The runner is deeply motivated by their drive for "personal best", achievement of personal goals, the achievements and standards set by winning athletes, and their need to ascribe to a "winning mindset." A perfect example of the manifestation of this deeper understanding is the Nike + offering: a chip in a specialized running shoe that measures and motivates personal performance and connects you to a community of runners. In this example, everyone wins. The avid runner wins through a new means of motivating personal performance, and Nike wins because they have established a deeper and more engaging relationship with their consumer than ever before.

To gain a deeper understanding of the user, we leverage one of the tools mastered by one of our academic partners, the Institute of Design at Illinois Institute of Technology (Whitney and Kumar, 2003), as presented in this journal. In applying their POEMS ethnographic technique, users bring photographs of people, objects, environments, messages and services of significance in an activity.

❮ Rotman DesignWorks Associate conducts an interview, focusing on the POEMS framework.

THROUGH A NON-DIRECTIVE INTERVIEW, THE PHOTOGRAPHS ARE USED AS TRIGGERS TO STORIES THAT ULTIMATELY REVEAL SURPRISING INSIGHTS.

Interviewers on the business team get a much deeper sense of what the design world calls a persona, the "whole person" as defined by their intellectual, emotional and practical needs surrounding the activity of interest, and in the context of their everyday life. Through this exploration, the team discovers a broader range of adjacent needs that can serve as a springboard for innovation and strategic opportunities that go far beyond an incremental product upgrade or direct line extension. Furthermore, against conventional wisdom rooted in a culture of surveys and focus groups, studies have shown that by conducting a relatively small number of in-depth, holistic interviews with the appropriate cross-section of users, we can glean more than 90 percent of the insights we would gather through a much larger sample (Griffin and Hauser, 1993).

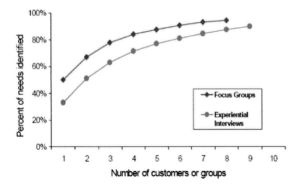

❮ Source: John R. Hauser/Voice of the Customer/MIT

So this methodology is an accessible, cost-effective means of discovering unmet needs early in the strategic planning process.

To illustrate the power of deep user understanding, a hospital that is focused on objective operational improvements to enhance efficiencies may discover that the "healing process" is enhanced by a multitude of factors beyond the essential medical expertise and "patient flow." The patient's need for reduced anxiety may be rooted in many dimensions—their connection to the outside world (physical cues to nature and spirituality), the physical design of the hospital (the width of the halls, the flicker rates of the florescent lighting or the artwork on the walls) or a sense of control or empowerment (the information they receive in communications before, during and after their hospital visits) or the practices and manner of the people on staff. All of these cues—people, objects, environment, messages and services—can enhance or hinder the healing process. A beautiful example of this deeper understanding of patient needs is brought to life by the success of the North Hawaii Community Hospital (available at: www.northhawaiicommunityhospital.org). This is a case where medical acumen and "patient flow" were successfully complimented by a holistic design of the patient experience based on physical and emotional needs.

A DESIGN APPROACH RESULTS IN A BETTER PATIENT EXPERIENCE, OPERATIONAL EFFECTIVENESS AND, MOST IMPORTANTLY, BETTER PATIENT OUTCOMES AND COMMUNITY WELLNESS.

Second gear
With a renewed empathy and broader set of criteria for innovation as the springboard, we move into gear 2—concept visualization through the process of ideation and multiple-prototyping. Through a number of these workshops and projects, we have seen that user empathy unleashes creativity. We have seen more ideas emerge when a health care organization wholly shifts from an operational focus to a patient focus, or a technology company shifts its focus from wireless infrastructures and revenue-per-unit to community or cultural needs.

In another health care example, Toronto's Princess Margaret Hospital Breast Cancer Centre looked beyond the treatment of cancer to the more holistic needs of the breast cancer survivor. They created a beautiful "unhospital-like" setting resembling a high-end salon, a program for "beauty" in which survivors can get counsel on how to feel and look their best, and a community for women to enhance their emotional well-being through counsel and support.

In the world of packaged goods, a number of companies have thought beyond their manufacturing products to serve deeper needs. One example is the Kraft Food and Family Program—a multi-channel customer relationship program with customizable solution-based meal ideas (versus straight product push). This program delivers to meet the needs of time-starved consumers, helping them get meals on the table quickly, skillfully, nutritionally and creatively. Another example is Dove's multi-layered "self esteem" initiative which not only reframes "beauty" in its advertising, but extends their support for young women by offering mother/daughter dialogue content on the subject and sponsoring altruistic programs to fight against the emotionally-damaging media stereotyping of "unachievable beauty."

All of these initiatives have been inspired by a deeper understanding of human needs. And what better way to leverage the discovery of new needs and capture the creativity of an organization than through ideation and prototyping, generating possibilities of how to meet those human needs in a more imaginative and compelling way before locking down a tightly-defined strategy?

BY USING CONSUMER NEEDS AS A POINT OF DEPARTURE TO EXPLORE MULTIPLE SOLUTIONS, ONE CAN GENERATE A WIDE RANGE OF POSSIBILITIES OUTSIDE ONE'S CURRENT REPERTOIRE OF SOLUTIONS AND BUSINESS FRAMEWORK.

❮ PCMA Workshop at the Rotman School of Management

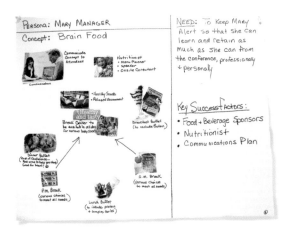

❮ A concept board, generated during the workshop, depicts the "brain food" idea.

In a recent workshop with 180 executives from the Professional Convention Management Association, participants followed this methodology to think beyond how to perfect logistics and delivery of a well-run convention. In teams, this seasoned group of professionals prototyped 36 breakthrough ideas for better meeting convention-goers needs. For the conventioneer who needed to be alert at all times, they created an on-site "brain food" service. For the time-starved participant they created a technology-driven "personalized scheduling program". For the ambitious professional who is looking to advance his career, they created a "personal advancement coaching" program to help the participant get the most out of the convention and set himself on a path to personal success.

ALL OF THESE CONCEPTS WERE OUTSIDE THEIR PREVIOUS SET OF CONSIDERATIONS.

All of them were multi-dimensional and richly constructed around the deeper needs of their user. And all of them were new and valuable to the market they serve. Whether or not they got the concept perfect in two days is not important. What is important is that they discovered new needs and new strategies to meet those needs that had previously not been pursued.

These and many other experiences demonstrate that making solutions tangible is an intuitive and risk-free way to "quick test" ideas as the basis for strategy. Strategy therefore becomes the summation of tangible concepts that satisfy user needs. Through rapid-prototyping and iteration, teams build solutions that facilitate a more concrete basis for discussion, which can be later translated into strategic intent. This is in contrast to conventional practices that analyze and build off existing knowledge and frameworks to lock down strategies before exploring possible expressions of those strategies. Executive teams frequently say that they have sometimes bought into a strategy that makes sense on paper, only to discover that their leadership team all had different interpretations of how that strategy would actually manifest itself much later in the game, when it can be more difficult and costly to reconcile. This is a function "domain

perspective"—seeing the strategy through each individual's base of functional expertise and experience. This occurs naturally even in the most collaborative teams—one person's view of "reality" is different from another's. Anchored in a common understanding of the end user's deeper needs, the prototyping process becomes a "thinking and communication tool" for making the abstract concrete and stimulating productive dialogue within business teams and with users. In addition, when prototyping is done by multi-disciplinary teams early on in the process, both the solutions and the buy-in are more complete, fueling greater momentum down the development path. The design approach is about discussing strategy in the spirit of asking "What if it looked like this? How would that better serve our user's needs and what would that mean to our business? What would we need to do to in order to bring that to life in terms of our capabilities and our organization's activities?" That leads into the third gear of business design.

Third gear
With defined user-driven solutions in hand, the next step is to align strategic concepts with future reality through strategic business design. In this third gear, we explore and define what it would take in order for the "big idea" to become both viable and valuable by articulating the strategies and capabilities required. One useful visualization and development tool for this step is Porter's (1996) "activity system." Applying the activity system tool against a new solution, we define the core strategies that would be critical in bringing this concept to life—the strategic hubs and the mutually reinforcing activities of the self-standing activity system.

FOR EXAMPLE, A HEALTH CARE COMPANY MAY DECIDE THAT THEIR PATIENTS NEED MORE PERSONALIZED AND RESPONSIVE SUPPORT.

In order to deliver that in real-time, they may need a significant investment in database systems, access and management. It may require new channels of communication to proactively and reactively support patient needs. It will also impact organizational structure and operating procedures. Further, each of these components will cost money, save money and generate stronger revenue and retention—all at the same time. While at first glance this may seem like a tall order with a high price tag, through iterative integration it can be designed to be a net gain for the enterprise.

Like the prototyping process in gear 2, this phase entails prototyping the business model to integrate the parts and assess the impact of the activity system as a whole. What is critical is to identify what will strategically drive the success of the solution, prioritize which activities an organization must undertake to deliver those strategies, define the relationship of those parts strategically, operationally and economically, and determine what net impact the new model will have.

With the "stand-alone" model defined, the final step of business design is to integrate this stand-alone system back into the current operating model, always asking: What can we leverage in our current activity system? What tensions (barriers, issues, conflicts) must be resolved in our current activity system? For each tension point, what are possible strategies and tactics for resolution? How can we lock up this system so it is proprietary and sustainable to our enterprise, therefore justifying the investment required to support this breakthrough strategic plan? Through several iterations will come an ownable working model that can deliver value to all stakeholders (the end user and the enterprise) and do so responsibly with a well-planned build-and-transition plan.

TO ILLUSTRATE THIS POINT, WE CAN IMAGINE HOW THE IPOD ACTIVITY SYSTEM MAY LOOK: A COMPLEX NETWORK OF INTER-RELATED STRATEGIES AND TAC-TICS THAT REDEFINE THE GAME RULES OF AN INDUSTRY WHILE LEVERAGING AND EXTENDING APPLE'S EQUITIES IN DESIGN

(beyond just the aesthetics, and including the entire user experience), a distinct and intuitive interface and the brand's reputation for "radical innovation" and breakthrough marketing. Figure 6 visualizes Apple's long-standing base of equities and capabilities in support of delivering an intuitive and seamlessly integrated user experience. The dark blue hubs represent Apple's core strategies used to build its historical foundation and create a system of competitive advantage. Specific initiatives and supporting activities are indicated in green.

What is critical in this particular case is the leveraging of current equities and capabilities and the creation of new activities and capabilities both within the company (iTunes as an intuitive interface to content and an enhanced retail presence) and through partnerships (content alliances and peripherals integration). So while the parts of this activity system may not be entirely proprietary to Apple, the business design is locked up by an interrelated set of activities and partnerships that are not only pre-emptive, but also sustainable in that they cannot be easily replicated within a period of time for the plan to get traction and pay out the investment.

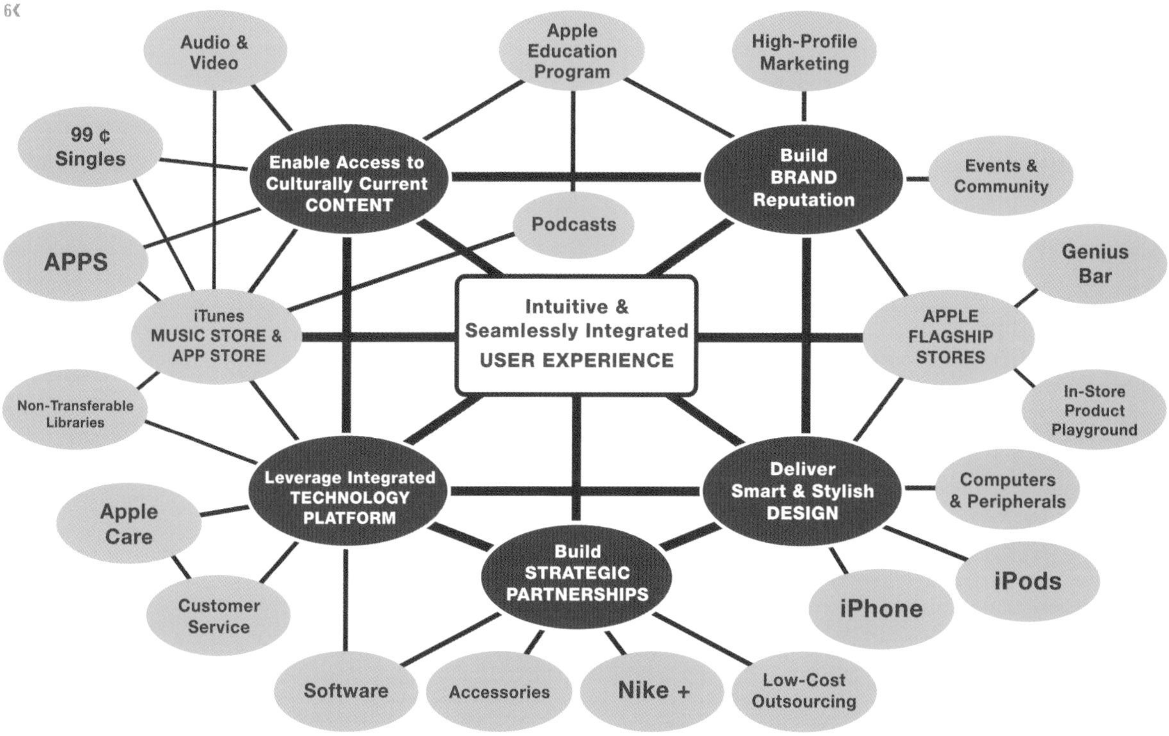

Audio & Video

99 ¢ Singles

Apple Education Program

High-Profile Marketing

Enable Access to Culturally Current CONTENT

Build BRAND Reputation

Events & Community

APPS

Podcasts

Genius Bar

iTunes MUSIC STORE & APP STORE

Intuitive & Seamlessly Integrated USER EXPERIENCE

APPLE FLAGSHIP STORES

In-Store Product Playground

Non-Transferable Libraries

Computers & Peripherals

Apple Care

Leverage Integrated TECHNOLOGY PLATFORM

Deliver Smart & Stylish DESIGN

iPods

Build STRATEGIC PARTNERSHIPS

iPhone

Customer Service

Software

Accessories

Nike +

Low-Cost Outsourcing

Through this iterative process, prototyping (first on a conceptual solution, then on the strategic business model) and constant assessment of user value (based on the identified user needs and considerations) along with the potential to create sustainable competitive advantage for the enterprise, one can formulate a strategy for a new level of innovation and competitive advantage. By challenging the current model and exploring new ways to drive success, one can find the strategic and operational point of sustainable equilibrium—what is unique and good for the user can be good for the enterprise.

Mindset Matters

With that as a methodological framework, the make or break ingredient is the mindset of both the individual and the team.

THE FOLLOWING ARE SOME OF THE MOST IMPORTANT EMOTIONAL CONDITIONS THAT ALLOW DESIGN THINKING TO FLOURISH.

Open-minded collaboration
Everyone on the team not only needs to be committed to "working together" but must also be receptive to new insights and ideas, whether they fit one's preconceived paradigm or not. Business designers feed off new insights and effectively build off the ideas of others, embracing both the friction and fusion that comes with intense collaboration.

Abductive thinking and the license to explore possibilities
In gathering new user insights and moving from what is "known" to the exploration of alternative solutions, an important capability is "abductive thinking", as defined and explored in this journal. What is critical is to allow for the "leap of inference" in tackling new opportunities and designing new possibilities. A perfect example of this: Swiffer—a phenomenon that revolutionized the market not as a conventional household cleaner "line extension", nor as a better version of the traditional mop. It signaled a leap into a new category of cleaning and became part of the cleaning vernacular (with a loyal franchise moving from "I've never

seen anything like that" to "I'll just Swiffer that before they arrive."). To take the leap toward game-changing solutions, it is vital to think beyond what is immediately observable and provable and imagine what could be possible as a radically new solution to unmet needs. Great design does not come without risk-taking and trying new things, with the very strong possibility of failure. There are countless stories of where a really "bad" or "crazy" idea became the germ of a brilliant concept or strategy. How often have we heard someone shut down an idea by saying "That's never been done before. What if it doesn't work? I may get fired." For those who need to mitigate risk, this method allows for consumer needs to "legitimize" far-out thinking and prototyping to provide a zero-risk way of exploring the otherwise seemingly extreme "what if" concepts.

Imperfection and iteration early in the process
This is not a clean and linear process; it is as messy as finger-painting. What is important early in the process is to explore lots of possible solutions, not perfecting a prototype so it becomes difficult to evolve it or even kill it. Iteration and constant change are necessary and good through every part of the process.

THAT KEEPS THE COST OF FAILURE LOW AND THE REWARDS OF POSSIBLE BREAKTHROUGH HIGH.

Challenge constraints toward creative resolution
No great design is realized without the absolute unwillingness to give in to constraints and obstacles, and that is doubly true for business design. Roger Martin, Dean of the Rotman School of Management at the University of Toronto, has long claimed that one of the single biggest attitudinal drivers in breakthrough success is a mindset of "no unacceptable trade-offs" (Martin, 2002). Good strategy involves making choices. Great strategy includes not making compromising trade-offs. Those who find ways to create new models instead of making unacceptable trade-offs find themselves ahead of the game, as shown be many model-changing successes like Southwest Airlines, Red Hat Software, Four Season's Hotels, and Apple's iPod, to name but a few. That is where the design method can help

in resolving model conflicts—keeping the user at the centre and prototyping various "what if" strategic business models to ultimately deliver both value to the user and viability, operationally and economically—the point of equilibrium noted before.

The design way

Whatever the sector or the nature of the business, any organization can benefit from the "design way". It naturally taps into team intelligence, creativity and the ambition to make a meaningful impact in the customer's life, both functionally and emotionally. The process itself is easy to follow, but should be embedded into an organization's strategic planning practices to realize the full potential of design thinking. At its core, the design approach is about combining the essential three gears of design with a "design mindset," and allowing an organization to discover opportunities to capitalize on new and unmet needs, exploring possibilities outside their activity system and then setting the strategies to evolve their business model (see Fig. 7).

A true "design organization" asks three questions of every opportunity: What is the need driving this initiative? Have we pushed out on the possibilities to best serve that need? How we can we embed that into our business model to create a sustainable advantage?

IT IS THE POWER OF ALL THREE GEARS THAT DRIVE BREAKTHROUGH STRATEGIES.

Once embedded into an organization's DNA, design methods can help generate ongoing possibilities for growth and evolution, recognizing that as the marketplace evolves, the needs of the user evolve and thus the business model must evolve to avoid extinction. The more an enterprise sees its business model or "activity system" as a living organism rather than a fixed model, the more a company will be poised to respond to ongoing opportunities to meet new needs. A company that views "design thinking" not as a one-shot vaccination but rather an ongoing fitness program for strategic growth will be better conditioned to stay ahead of the curve in an increasingly competitive global marketplace.

The result: bigger breakthroughs in thinking, more innovative strategies for success, and development of new business models to better meet user needs and create greater economic and human value.

FOUNDATION:
Frame the
Current State

Collaboration
from the start

Empathy

User Understanding:
See the activity wholly
through the eyes
of the user

Exploration:
Multiple-Prototyping

Abductive
Thinking

Challenging
Constraints

New Strategies &
Models for Success

References

Griffin, A. and Hauser, J.R. 1993. The voice of the customer.
Marketing Science, vol. 12, no. 1: 1–27.

Martin, R. 2002. Integrative thinking: a model takes shape.
Rotman Magazine, Fall: 6–11.

Porter, M. 1996. What is strategy? Harvard Business Review,
November/December: 61–78.

Whitney, P. and Kumar, V. 2003. Faster, cheaper, deeper user
research. Design Management Journal, vol. 14, no. 2: 1–9.

331

We observe a recent call for *entrepreneurial* thinking and acting in strategy research and strategic management.*
It is argued that entrepreneurial thinking and acting is important for dealing with the uncertainties and ambiguities, which are inherent in innovation and change.**

* (Hitt, Ireland, Camp and Sexton, 2002; Schendel and Hitt. 2007)
** (Meyer and Heppard, 2000)

In particular, this call for entrepreneurial thinking and acting addresses the importance of interpreting strategy making as a creative, imaginative, future-oriented, risk taking, assertive activity (Tsoukas and Knudsen, 2002). More recently, strategy making as a creative process has been labeled *strategizing*, to emphasize the inherently dynamic, processual, open nature of strategy making (Whittington, Molloy, Mayer and Smith, 2006). Entrepreneurial strategizing is seen as important for disclosing new worlds and creating possible futures for organizations and businesses (Spinosa, Flores and Dreyfus, 1997), and thus for establishing new strategic action spaces. Thereby, it must be considered that the future is uncertain, meaning that entrepreneurial strategizing implies strategic thinking and acting without knowing how the future will be; *but while uncertainty is often seen as a challenge, it turns into an opportunity in the perspective of entrepreneurial strategizing.*
We will discuss this in part one of this essay.

When carefully observing entrepreneurial strategizing, it is interesting to recognize that strategizing cannot be reduced to an analytical and conceptual process (Johnson, Langley, Melin and Whittington, 2007);

ENTREPRENEURIAL STRATEGIZING IS ALWAYS ALSO ABOUT IMAGINING POSSIBLE FUTURES, TELLING ATTRACTIVE STORIES, DESIGNING POSSIBILITIES FOR NEW PRODUCTS AND SERVICES, SOLUTIONS AND BUSINESSES.

This is what we identify as design (Simon, 1996): the particular nature of design processes is that they not only focus on the world as it is, but on the world as it could be (see also Grand, 2009). In other words, entrepreneurial strategizing as design practice is not primarily about exploring and discussing the actual reality, but moving into a space of future possibilities in a process of becoming (Tsoukas and Chia, 2002). This perspective is not only important and challenging for entrepreneurs and managers facing major future uncertainties, it also puts forth a particular understanding of design. Design is not only

associated with the design of artifacts and images, but it is understood as a *complex creation process, a particular way of knowing, and a transformation of possible worlds into actual futures* (Bonsiepe, 1996; Jonas, 2007). We will discuss this in part two of this essay.

As we learn from Joseph A. Schumpeter, the transformation of possible worlds into actual futures is not only playful and imaginative, but must be characterized as "creative destruction" (Schumpeter, 1942): not discussing, but building the future; not imagining, but materializing new possibilities; not drawing, but realizing innovative solutions is a *difficult, controversial process of value creation and value destruction. A new idea or option is inherently challenging the world as it is.* In this perspective, design practices in entrepreneurial strategizing are not just about disclosing new worlds and creating new possibilities, but always also about criticizing the world as it is (Boltanski, 2009), about favoring one possibility against alternatives, about establishing a new reference system (Thévenot, 2006), in relation to which the existing solutions lose their value, while new solutions gain attractiveness. In sum, entrepreneurial strategizing, understood in the perspective of strategy design, is a political and normative process, at the same time opening and closing controversies, provoking alternative world views and arguing possible alternatives away in order to reduce ambiguity (see also Latour, 1999).

We argue that this is the main reason why it is not just desirable and attractive, but very difficult and ambiguous to call for "entrepreneurial" thinking and acting in strategizing, and thus for "design" in strategy. Paraphrasing Bruno Latour, we have to make a difference between creativity, innovation, design, imagination *ex ante (thus controversial and in the making) and ex post (thus established and successful)* (Latour, 1987). Ex post, it is obvious whether a new strategy and the creation of a new business are successful and attractive (and this is what we are usually aiming for); however, ex ante, creation is highly controversial and ambiguous (and this is in most cases what we try to avoid). But there is no ex post strategic success without an engagement in the ex ante mess and uncertainty in entrepreneurial strategizing. More provocatively, we can argue with Peter Sloterdijk that no true actor (entrepreneur, manager, designer …) can know in advance (*ex ante*), whether he or she will be seen (*ex post*) as a fool and a lunatic, or rather as a genius and a visionary (Sloterdijk, 2005).

TO CALL FOR AN ENTREPRENEURIAL APPROACH TO STRATEGIZING, FOR DESIGN PRACTICES IN ENTREPRENEURIAL STRATEGIZING, AND THUS FOR STRATEGY DESIGN IS POTENTIALLY BENEFICIAL, BUT ALSO RISKY.

This essay operates at the interface of design and business, by focusing on the more specific interface between design and strategy. First, it contributes to our understanding and practice of strategy, by discussing the particularities of an entrepreneurial approach to strategizing; second, it contributes to our understanding and practice of design, by providing a particular re-interpretation of design as a particular way of knowing and acting, as well as by introducing series of strategy design practices, which benefit from a fruitful interplay between entrepreneurial strategizing and design practices. Thereby, this essay benefits from in-depth empirical research and theoretical perspectives, personal entrepreneurial experience and strategic dialogues with a series of entrepreneurs and entrepreneurial managers, in different industry contexts, including software engineering and life sciences, research institutions and technology corporations, entrepreneurial ventures and established companies, global public corporations and family-owned businesses, including critical companies in the context of art and design.

Part One: Entrepreneurial Strategizing under Uncertainty

Entrepreneurial thinking and acting in strategizing is characterized by a series of important practices, which are mutually interdependent and form a complex interactive process:

- *Questioning, challenging, reflecting the self-evident, unquestioned, taken-for-granted in strategy is a first series of fundamental practices:* Strategizing, as every organizational activity, is only possible if it can rely on a foundation of self-evident, taken-for-granted and thus unquestioned rules, themes, tools, definitions, and concepts (Gomez and Jones, 2000). For example, companies work with a company-specific pre-understanding of the industries in which they are operating (see also Spender, 1989), the main references of success which are used to evaluate major past, present and future activities and initiatives, core values which guide organizational action under uncertainty (Callon, 1998). To introduce entrepreneurial thinking and acting implies that the self-evidence of these success measures, core values and pre-assumptions is no longer taken-for-granted. It is itself continuously reflected, based on the fundamental insight that the world is contingent, meaning that it would be possible to discuss, define and conceptualize central strategic issues differently. Entrepreneurial thinking and acting is thus about looking for controversies and initiating controversial debates about fundamental issues; it is about criticizing the world as it is, in order to open new action spaces for future strategies; it is about reflecting unquestioned premises, in order to better understand how they guide current activities, as well as to identify productive alternatives to allow for new opportunities. *Entrepreneurial strategizing is emphasizing the fragility of the world as it is, by exploring possible future worlds as if they would be realizable* (Ortmann, 2004).

- *A complementary, second series of practices refers to the formation of alternative world views and the assertion of possible new realities:* The critical reflection and questioning of the existing world is only productive if it leads to the formulation, establishment, discussion and evaluation of alternative world views. Just challenging the world as it is does not lead very far, only by exploring, envisioning and realizing interesting and attractive alternatives, it becomes possible to think about innovating and changing the current state (Boltanski, 2009). It is easy to challenge existing concepts and industry recipes of innovation (which are often strongly formalized), but difficult to establish *new* ones (which take seriously the inherent uncertainty of innovation) (Burgelman, Christensen and Wheelwright, 2008). It is easy to question the ways in which certain companies are organized today, but difficult to create truly *new* organizational structures (which are both highly structured and enable for strategic agility). Furthermore, new realities and alternative world views require sufficient degrees of precision in order to increase their chance of survival against established world views (Burgelman, 2001). It is easy to criticize companies which rely on financial performance indicators as their measures for success, but difficult to formulate a robust performance measurement system, which explicitly considers creativity, responsibility, sustainability, cultural relevance as performance dimensions. *Asserting alternative world views is not enough, it is important to explicate, specify, justify, legitimate these alternatives,* in order to make them robust enough to survive in a controversial environment, in which the established and known is always inherently more powerful and better protected than the new and unconventional (Boltanski and Thévenot, 1991; Gomez and Jones, 2000).

- This leads to a *third series of fundamental practices, which are concerned with making a new alternative interesting, relevant, and attractive for other actors:* To assert new, unconventional, risky initiatives, it is not only important to criticize the world as it is and to assert alternative possible worlds, it is important to gain the interest and engagement of other parties, helping to make the idea happen (Christensen, 1997). In recent innovation, strategy and entrepreneurship research, this is explored under labels like "*collectivization*", emphasizing the importance for new initiatives to gain other relevant parties to join into a common belief and narrative (Hughes, Bijker and Pinch, 1989); ... "*interessement*", arguing that it is important to make

those beliefs and narratives attractive for other people as a reference, which supports them to realizing their own interests, initiatives and strategies (Callon, 1986); ... "*mobilization*", insisting that joining a common story is not enough, but that it is key to committing major relevant resources (including financial resources, expertise, competences, attention, time, work, ...) for new initiatives to be realized (Bower, 1970; Christensen and Bower, 1996; Bower and Gilbert, 2007). Building, developing, extending, and fostering a robust, relevant and reliable network of partners, which contribute to the realization of a shared belief or common initiative is essential. In the perspective of Clayton Christensen and his contribution to the strategic management of technological innovation, this requires constantly *re-building, re-assembling, and transforming the value constellations of relevant actors, actants, activities and artifacts* (Christensen, 1997).

- *Fourth, it is important to transform ideas, stories, concepts and possibilities into artifacts, which materialize important features towards tangible products, technologies, services:* While we tend to see realization and materialization as the ultimate phase in a creation process, we learn from successful entrepreneurial strategizing in practice that is important to continuously translate ideas into images, concepts into prototypes, possibilities into objects, stories into communicative efforts. It is the mutual interplay and translation between reflection and realization, conceptualization and materialization, thinking and acting, which characterizes entrepreneurial strategizing under uncertainty (Spinosa et al., 1997). On the one hand, this is important to ensure that the imagination is continuously validated and tested in relation to possible tangible outcomes; furthermore, it is only through materialization that the openness of ideas can turn into a well-founded common understanding or can lead to specific controversies, which are central for the further advancement of any new initiative (Latour, 1999). On the other hand, tangible outcomes and artifacts are much more attractive, if they communicate fascinating stories; it is this richness, density, complexity and heterogeneity, assembled and embodied in a convincing product or service, which makes the difference between just another artifact and a robust innovation. As a consequence, it is the complex *interplay between reflection and materialization, imagination and artifact, possible worlds and actual world, which make the difference.*

In sum, we can draw the following simple model (see Fig. 1) to summarize some key insights into entrepreneurial strategizing under uncertainty, and some central strategizing practices.
Based on this discussion, we now turn to interpreting and exploring this process of entrepreneurial strategizing as a design process.

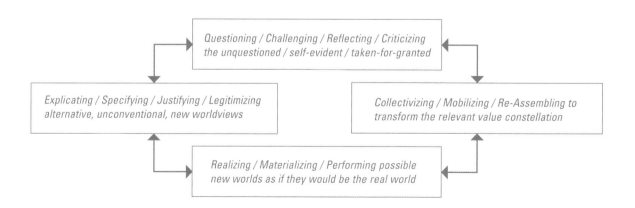

Questioning / Challenging / Reflecting / Criticizing the unquestioned / self-evident / taken-for-granted

Explicating / Specifying / Justifying / Legitimizing alternative, unconventional, new worldviews

Collectivizing / Mobilizing / Re-Assembling to transform the relevant value constellation

Realizing / Materializing / Performing possible new worlds as if they would be the real world

1◖ Central practices of entrepreneurial strategizing under uncertainty

Part Two: Strategy Design as a Promising Perspective

Only the fourth dimension of entrepreneurial strategizing, which is the materialization of ideas and stories as products and communication artifacts, is typically associated with design. In this respect, entrepreneurial strategizing is obviously a design process. At the same time, it is increasingly argued that a design perspective is important in all practices of strategizing, most recently discussed as the relevance of "design thinking" (Brown, 2008) or the creation of "desired futures" for business. But as long as we identify design primarily with the creation of objects and products, websites and logos, it is impossible to really advance in this discussion. We suggest another direction.

IF WE UNDERSTAND DESIGN AS THE CREATION OF POSSIBLE WORLDS, IT CAN BE SEEN AS A PERSPECTIVE AND ATTITUDE, WHICH IS RELEVANT IN ALL DIMENSIONS OF ENTREPRENEURIAL STRATEGIZING.

Furthermore, designers actually or potentially have the competences to develop tools and methods, practices and visualizations, which productively foster and enhance all entrepreneurial strategizing practices. The design disciplines thus not only contribute through the creation and materialization of artifacts and other outcomes, but through the *creation of processes and media for entrepreneurial strategizing in all four dimensions. This is what we call strategy design.* We will introduce a series of specific themes and practices, which are important for both research and practice, beyond "strategy" and "design" as separate disciplines.

We differentiate four areas of strategy design: *strategic content, strategy tools, strategizing practices, and strategy communication.* First, we introduce some practices for the design of *strategic content:*

- *Answering unanswerable questions:* We tend to exclude multiple issues and questions from a detailed debate by qualifying them as impossible to answer. An interesting example in architecture is the 5 minutes city project by MVRDV (Maas, 2003): Sketch a city where you can reach each point from each other point within five minutes or less. We know that this is impossible, but by drawing a city as if it would be possible, leads to important perspectives on the geometry and logic of a city, and to fascinating insights into (im)mobility. To draw a strategy, by assuming that the main core competence or core business will disappear within the next 12 months, forces a company to imagine the unimaginable. With such questions, we think in strategic alternatives and possible futures, and focus on the implicit, self-evident foundation of the current business, and thereby go beyond the typical scenario discussion in strategic planning. This approach particularly supports reflection of the self-evident, unquestioned, and taken-for-granted in strategy, as well as the formation of alternative world views and the assertion of new realities. It is an experimental practice, which generates unconventional and sometimes irritating new perspectives.

- *Changing strategic language:* We know from literature, but also from research on narratives and storytelling, that language and metaphors play a fundamental role for innovating our ways of talking and thus of thinking and acting (Czarniawska, 1999). In the perspective of Ludwig Wittgenstein, we know that the boundaries of our language are the boundaries of our world (Wittgenstein, 1921). By introducing new metaphors and by using new language, we trigger our imagination in strategic discussions, and change the direction of certain debates. Furthermore, the establishment of a firm-specific language implies a firm-specific way of talking and thinking about strategic issues. The field of strategy is itself characterized by a specific terminology, which mostly originates in military contexts. To move into a more design mode of discussing "strategy" can thus have a major impact (Hamel, 2002). While this approach supports the reflection of the taken-for-granted and the creation of new world views, it much more focuses from the beginning on ways in which new opportunities and interesting initiatives could be explained and justified, as well as communicated and leveraged in broader communities, within and outside the company.

- *Exploring visual implications:* Discussing and exploring strategic opportunities and initiatives in strategy making often remains at an abstract and general level, which makes it quite easy to agree on major ideas and concepts. However, if the implications of these strategic ideas and concepts are visualized, they typically become controversial again: by mapping the specific resource allocation streams inherent in a business model (who does pay and who does receive money) or by sketching the implications for the information hierarchy on the company website (which themes come first, and which come later), it becomes very tangible and clear whether a common understanding of a strategy has been achieved or not. By using Anthony Dunne's critical design (Dunne and Raby, 2002; Dunne, 2005) or IDEO's fast prototyping (Brown, 2008) in strategizing, the abstraction of many strategy debates transforms into tangible and visible issues. While the creative potential of this approach is evident, it also prepares for developing a robust intuition for tangible outcomes, which will be important for generating and mobilizing the relevant resources and activities to translate strategic ideas into relevant initiatives with an impact in the company (Johnson et al., 2007).

Second, we discuss some design practices related to the creation of *strategy tools*, which are used to represent controversial debates, to structure strategic content, and to analyze strategic themes:

- *Mapping strategic controversies:* Strategic issues are often uncertain and controversial. It is a fascinating task for concept design to imagine ways of mapping and representing the different relevant perspectives, interest constellations, argumentation structures of the parties involved in a controversy. Currently, there are various initiatives to develop such representations in the broader context of controversial political, social and technological issues, based on the work by Bruno Latour and other authors in the science and technology studies STS (Latour and Weibel, 2005). Developing such strategy maps would allow to recognize, whether and why different parties in such a controversy are often at cross-purposes. Interestingly, convincing tools for mapping strategic controversies are rare, opening up a fascinating space for design innovation (Birkinshaw and Mol, 2006; Hamel, 2007). This approach is helpful for better understanding and identifying the relevant perspectives, and for developing alternative, new perspectives which go beyond the current perspectives and interests, but in particular, it is an important tool to map the relevant audiences and parties, which play a role in mobilization: their attention and interest have to be gained, they have to be convinced and involved.

- *Re-assembling strategic products:* We learn from the technology studies as well as from industrial design that strategies, industry structures and value constellations can be seen through a careful formal analysis of the strategic products of a company or the flagship products of an industry: On the one hand, successful products are perceived as a coherent, functional, beautiful entities, which integrate technologies, product modules, product architectures, materials, interaction and product design into a convincing artifact. On the other hand,

each successful product becomes a black box for the parties involved (Latour, 1999). The multiple decisions, controversies, expectations, debates, interests and hopes, which were important for the creation process, are no longer visible (Latour and Weibel, 2005). By dis-assembling and re-assembling strategic products, their taken-for-granted nature can be critically reflected and made accessible to careful analysis and well-founded reflection (see also Latour, 2005). By better understanding how strategic products have become what they are today, it is possible to identify alternatives, which might turn into new opportunities, because the context has changed in a way which is favorable of such an alternative. Redesigning product architectures and modules become central innovation strategies.

- *Changing strategizing media:* Strategy making is characterized by a series of typical strategy tools, in particular Power Point, Excel and Word documents, which are distributed and presented in multiple modes; furthermore, strategy making takes place in particular formats, including meetings, video conferences and workshops. As we know, the media and formats shape and enact the content which they represent and incorporate (Manovich, 2001). By changing the media, as well as the particular formats, in which strategies are discussed, decided, communicated and documented, it thus becomes possible to critically reflect inherently unquestioned features, which result from a specific media usage (Grand, Müller-Beyeler and Bellicchi, 2005). By telling stories in parallel to presenting data, by drawing business models in parallel to conceptually discussing them, by mapping new organizational structures into the corporate architecture in parallel to displaying them in organization charts, by prototyping new technologies in parallel to discussing them on roadmaps, the particular qualities and challenges of different options become much more tangible, can be tested in heterogeneous respects, and will thus be more robust when realized and communicated (Gänshirt, 2007).

Third, it is key to reflect how strategy tools are used and how they shape firm- and industry-specific *strategizing practices*, as a basis for experimenting with alternative usages and new tools:

- *Translating strategizing tools:* Companies and industries are characterized by firm- and industry-specific ways of structuring, representing, visualizing and discussing strategic issues: in the Pharma and Life Sciences industry, strategizing is largely organized around product pipeline discussions and milestones, which relate to well-defined phases in the research and development process; in the fashion industry, companies work with mood boards and collages of images and materials from multiple sources, including fashion magazines, art exhibitions, archival material, photographs; in the context of information technology, technology roadmaps are a central tool. Knowing that our ways of representing and visualizing themes and issues influence our thinking and acting, it would be interesting to translate strategizing tools between industries and contexts. On the one hand, this contributes to the identification of alternative perspectives on current issues, and thus supports the reflection and critique of the world as it is; on the other hand, this introduces already known and justified strategizing tools, which have legitimacy in certain industries and companies, which is an important premise for introducing them in a new context.

- (*Mis-)using existing artifacts:* In current debates, it is argued by Wanda Orlikowski and others that the design process of a product or an interface is not completed with a prototype or artifact, but it is the actual usage and misuse, which complete the design process (Orlikowski, 2000). This provides a new view on the creation and usage of strategic tools and strategizing frameworks: There is not one appropriate way of interpreting, understanding, explaining and using a strategic tool, and there is no obvious linkage between the intentions, when developing a strategizing framework, and its actual use. How tools and frameworks are used in entrepreneurial strategizing process, but also in the mobilization of attention, commitment and resources, as well as in the internal and external communication of the strategy, influence how particular strategies are seen, interpreted, and realized (Johnson, Langley, Melin and Whittington, 2003). It is the performance of strategy communication, the multiple narratives, metaphors, stories, examples, and references used to talk about the strategy, which enact and shape strategy. Strategy design not only focuses on the creation of strategic tools and artifacts, but also on their firm-specific use.

- *Assembling heterogeneous tools*: Finally, companies tend to essentially focus on one or just a few tools and frameworks, when exploring particular issues and themes. While this serves as a productive complexity reduction, it might also imply that the complexity and ambiguity inherent in strategic issues is over-simplified. In order to correct for these biases, it is important to use different tools, and to assemble major insights and outcomes of different tools and frameworks within one strategy map (Law, 2004). By combining an conceptual and a visual analysis of the competition, in order to show differentiation strategies conceptually and aesthetically at the same time; by presenting a product (pipeline) map, a technology (road) map, a mood board and a competence map together in one outline, in order to explore the interplay of competitive forces, synergies and contradictions between these levels of strategizing; by not only discussing a strategy presentation, but exploring different ways of narrating a strategy, it is possible to understand the systemic interplay between different perspectives within the same entrepreneurial strategizing process (Latour and Hermant, 1998; Latour and Weibel, 2005).

Fourth, strategies only shape business if they are communicated in ways, which are related to relevant processes in the organization. The design of *strategy communication* requires additional practices:

- *Enacting dominant expectations:* As discussed in part one, it is important to gain the interest and attention of multiple parties within and outside a company, in order to successfully translate strategic ideas and opportunities into realized strategies and successful organizational action. In this process, it is on the one hand important to map strategic controversies and the heterogeneous perspectives, which determine these controversies. On the other hand, it is important to carefully understand the specific expectations, unquestioned beliefs and taken-for-granted references of these multiple parties. This allows to narrating a new strategy in a way, which leverages some of those expectations, beliefs and references in favor of the new strategy. As we can learn from the interview of François Truffaut with Alfred Hitchcock, we gain the interest and attention of the audience when developing storylines, which confirm and break those expectations, in order to make an unexpected, new story at the same time thrilling and evident, stretching and plausible (Truffaut, 1966). It is the continuous dynamic interplay between the known and the unknown, the established and the new, the expected and the unexpected, which allow for unconventional and unexpected possibilities to become believable and real.

- *Exploring multiple interactions:* Typically, entrepreneurial strategizing interacts with different audiences and multiple parties. At the same time, entrepreneurial strategizing processes can only involve a limited number of parties and perspectives, in order to remain efficient and productive. When talking to successful entrepreneurs and managers, but also designers and artists, we observe that they constantly talk about their work and their ideas, their context and their competition, their current initiatives and future perspectives. When interpreting this overemphasis of their own work as narcissistic and selfish, we miss an important process, which goes on in these interactions: it is a continuous evaluation and validation, reflection and discussion, experimentation and exploration of past activities and future projects, possible ideas and potential directions. These interactions are systematically (mis-)used as virtual laboratories for the design of possible futures. It is thus not surprising that conversations and interviews have been evolving into an art form of its own, from Andy Warhol to Hans-Ulrich Obrist (2003); in a similar perspective, various artistic collaborations can be interpreted as visual and material conversations in their own right.

- *Designing corporate interfaces:* Companies have multiple interfaces with internal and external parties. We can learn from successful design entrepreneurs that the systematic enactment of all these interfaces in the perspective of a robust strategy generates enormous communicative impact. We can learn from fashion companies like Maison Martin Margiela (2008) or Come des Garçons (Shimizu and NHK, 2005), how to focus on this plurality of relevant media and interfaces in order to create the myth, which makes the difference between just another label and an attractive brand. From the invitation letter to a new show to shop design, from corporate design to newspaper advertisement, from exhibitions on their own work to interaction with media, from strategic partnerships to the website, all media and interfaces are systematically understood as opportunities and platforms to make the strategic focus and differentiation strategy of these companies visible and tangible. There is actually a very direct, but also complex interdependence between entrepreneurial strategizing, visual communication and materialization in multiple media. Strategy design is an approach and a perspective, which allows to see these two as mutually interdependent and strongly related.

In sum, we can start to sketch the following strategy design toolbox for entrepreneurial strategizing (see Fig. 2), as a way of summarizing some key ideas from our discussion into one framework.
By systematically enriching entrepreneurial strategizing in the perspective of strategy design, it is thus possible to develop more innovative and at the same time more robust strategies.

Conclusion

When exploring a new approach such as strategy design for your own strategizing as entrepreneurs or designers, managers or artists, one basic question remains: Where do we start? While the entire setup and the multiple practices discussed look quite complex, they all follow a simple and straightforward logic: It is difficult to challenge, question and criticize the taken-for-granted and self-evident, because it is black boxed by the tools and artifacts, languages and narratives, metaphors and images we use in our strategizing practices. But while it is difficult to reflect those black boxes on an abstract level, it is rather simple to open these black boxes and to create and introduce new perspectives and world views, by trying out different design practices, as well as related tools and artifacts, metaphors and images. This is the core of strategy design:

TO GET BEYOND THE WORLD AS IT IS AND TO DRAW ALTERNATIVE POSSIBLE WORLDS, NOT BY CHANGING STRATEGIES, BUT BY CHANGING THE STRATEGIZING PRACTICES, IN THE FOUR DIMENSIONS OF ENTREPRENEURIAL STRATEGIZING, IN THE FOUR AREAS OF STRATEGY DESIGN.

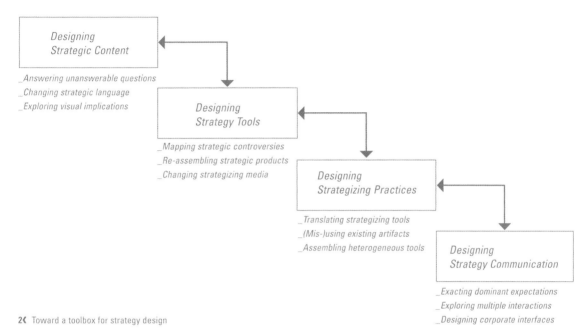

Designing
Strategic Content

_Answering unanswerable questions
_Changing strategic language
_Exploring visual implications

Designing
Strategy Tools

_Mapping strategic controversies
_Re-assembling strategic products
_Changing strategizing media

Designing
Strategizing Practices

_Translating strategizing tools
_(Mis-)using existing artifacts
_Assembling heterogeneous tools

Designing
Strategy Communication

_Exacting dominant expectations
_Exploring multiple interactions
_Designing corporate interfaces

2 Toward a toolbox for strategy design

References

Birkinshaw, Julian and Mol, Michael (2006): How management innovation happens, MIT Sloan Management Review, 47/4, pp. 81–88.

Boltanski, Luc and Thévenot, Laurent (1991): De la justification: Les économies de la grandeur, Paris: Gallimard.

Boltanski, Luc (2009): De la critique: Précis de sociologie d'émancipation, Paris: Gallimard.

Bonsiepe, Gui (1996): Interface: Design neu begreifen, Mannheim: Bollmann.

Bower, Joseph L. and Gilbert, Clark G. (Eds.) (2007): From resource allocation to strategy, Oxford: Oxford University Press.

Bower, Joseph L. (1970): Managing the resource allocation process, Boston, MA: Harvard Business School Press.

Brown, Tim (2008): Design thinking, Harvard Business Review, June, pp. 84–92.

Burgelman, Robert A. (2001): Strategy is destiny: How strategy-making shapes a company's future, New York: Free Press.

Burgelman, Robert A., Christensen, Clayton M., and Wheelwright, Steven C. (2008): Strategic management of technology and innovation, New York: McGraw Hill.

Callon, Michel (1986): Some elements of a sociology of translation: Domestication of the scallops and the fishermen of St. Brueuc Bay, in: Law, John (Ed.): Power, Action and belief. A new sociology of knowledge, London: Routledge, pp. 196–233.

Callon, Michel (Ed.) (1998): Laws of markets, Oxford: Blackwell Publishers.1998.

Christensen, Clayton M. and Bower, Joseph, L. (1996): Customer power, strategic investment, and the failure of leading firms, Strategic Management Journal, 17/3, pp. 197–218.

Christensen, Clayton C. (1997): Innovator's dilemma: When new technologies cause great firms to fail, Boston, MA: Harvard Business School Press.

Czarniawska, Barbara (1999): Writing management: Organization theory as a literary genre, Oxford: Oxford University Press.

Dunne, Anthony and Raby, Fiona (2002): Design noir: The secret life of electronic objects, Basel: Birkhäuser.

Dunne, Anthony (2005): Hertzian tales: Electronic products, aesthetic experience, and critical design, Cambridge, MA: The MIT Press.

Gänshirt, Christian (2007): Werkzeuge für Ideen: Einführung ins architektonische Entwerfen, Basel: Birkhäuser.

Gomez, Pierre-Yves and Jones, Brittany C. (2000): Conventions: An interpretation of deep structures on organization, Organization Science, 11/6, pp. 696–708.

Grand, Simon (2009): Design Fiction und unternehmerische Strategien, in: Wiedmer, Martin and Caviezel, Flavia (Eds.): Design Fiction: Perspektiven für Forschung in Kunst und Design, Basel: FHNW.

Grand, Simon, Müller-Beyeler, Ruedi A. and Bellicchi, John (2005): Beauty Case, in: Schwarz, Hans-Peter (Ed.): Aufträge: Hochschule für Gestaltung und Kunst Zürich, Zürich: Zürcher Jahrbuch der Künste.

Hamel, Gary (2002): Leading the revolution, Boston MA: Harvard Business School Press.

Hamel, Gary (2007): The future of management, Boston MA: Harvard Business School Press.

Hitt, Ireland, Camp and Sexton, 2002.

Hughes, Thomas P., Bijker, Wiebe E. and Pinch, Trevor (1989): The social construction of technological systems, Cambridge, MA: The MIT Press.

Johnson, Gerry, Langley, Ann, Melin, Leif and Whittington, Richard (2007): Strategy as practice: Research directions and resources, Cambridge: Cambridge University Press.

Jonas, Wolfgang (2007): Design research and its meaning to the methodological development of the discipline, in: Michel, Ralf (Ed.) (2007): Design research now, Basel: Birkhäuser.

Latour, Bruno and Hermant, Emilie (1998): Paris ville invisible, Paris: La Découverte.

Latour, Bruno and Weibel, Peter (2005): Making things public: Atmospheres of democracy, Cambridge, MA: The MIT Press.

Latour, Bruno (1987): Science in action: How to follow scientists and engineers through society, Boston: Harvard University Press.

Latour, Bruno (1999): Pandora's hope: Essays on the reality of the science studies, Boston: Harvard University Press.

Latour, Bruno (2005): Re-assembling the social: An introduction to actor-network theory, Oxford: Oxford University Press.

Law, John (2004): After method: Mess in social science research, New York: Routledge.

Maas, Winy (2003) Five minute city: Architecture and (im) mobility, Rotterdam: Episode Publishers.

Maison Martin Margiela (2008): 20, The exhibition, Antwerpen: Momu.

Manovich, Lev (2001): The language of new media, Cambridge, MA: The MIT Press.

Meyer, G. Dale and Heppard, Kurt A. (2000): Entrepreneurship as strategy: Competing on the entrepreneurial edge, Thousand Oaks: Sage Publications.

Obrist, Hans-Ulrich (2003): Interviews 1, Charta.

Orlikowski, Wanda (2000): Using technology and constituting structures: A practice lens for studying technology in organizations, Organization Science, 11/4, pp. 404–428.

Ortmann, Günther (2004): Als ob: Fiktionen und Organisationen, Wiesbaden: VS Verlag für Sozialwissenschaften.

Rumelt, Richard P., Schendel, Dan E. and Teece, David J. (1996): Fundamental issues in strategy: A research agenda, Boston: Harvard Business School Press.

Schendel, Dan E. and Hitt, Michael A. (2007): Strategic entrepreneurship: Comments from the editors, Strategic Entrepreneurship Journal, 1/1, pp.1–6.

Schumpeter, Joseph A. (1950): Kapitalismus, Sozialismus und Demokratie, München: Verlag Francke.

Shimizu, Sanae and NHK (2005): Unlimited: Comme des Garçons, Heibonsha.

Simon, Herbert A. (1996): The sciences of the artificial,

Cambridge, MA: The MIT Press, 3rd Edition.

Sloterdijk, Peter (2005): Im Weltinnenraum des Kapitals: Für eine philosophische Theorie der Globalisierung, Frankfurt a.M.: Suhrkamp.

Spinosa, Charles, Flores, Fernando and Dreyfus, Hubert L. (1997): Disclosing new worlds, Cambridge, MA: The MIT Press.

Thévenot, Laurent (2006): L'action au pluriel: Sociologie des régimes d'engagement, Paris: Editions la découverte.

Truffaut, François (1966): Le cinéma selon Hitchcock, Paris: Robert Laffont.

Tsoukas, Haridimos and Chia, Robert C.H. (2002): On organizational becoming: Rethinking organizational change, Organization Science, 13/5, pp. 567–582.

Tsoukas, Haridimos and Knudsen, Christian (2002): The conduct of strategy research, in: Pettigrew, Andrew, Thomas, Howard and Whittington, Richard (Eds): Handbook of strategy and management, London: Sage Publications, pp. 411–435.

Whittington, Richard, Molloy, Eamonn, Mayer, Michael and Smith, Anne (2006): Practices of strategizing / organizing: broadening strategy work and skills, Long Range Planning, 39, pp. 615–629.

Wittgenstein, Ludwig (1921): Tractatus Logico-philosophicus, Frankfurt a.M.: Suhrkamp.

I would like to thank my colleagues Daniel Bartl and David Griesbach from RISE Management Research for their detailed comments on earlier drafts of this paper, my business partners Thilo Fuchs, Oliver Mayer and Ruedi Alexander Mueller-Beyeler from Tatin Scoping Complexity for their openness to explore and discuss strategy design as part of our joint entrepreneurial activities, Martin Wiedmer from the Academy of Art and Design, Basel, as well as Matthias Georg and Wolfgang Jonas for inspiring discussions on design practice and design research.

347

In a global market economy with ever increasing levels of disturbance a viable business cannot be locked into a single form or function any more. Success comes from a self-renewing capability to spontaneously create structures and functions that fit the moment. In this context proper functioning of self-reference would certainly prevent the vacillations and the random search for new product/markets that have destroyed so many businesses over the past years.

In fact, creation of the ability to continuously match the portfolio of internal competencies with the portfolio of emerging market opportunities is the foundation of emerging concept of new business architecture.

This chapter was originally published in "Systems Thinking: Managing Chaos and Complexity," 2nd Edition, by Jamshid Gharajedaghi, pp 152–186, © 2006 Elsevier.

1 Multi-dimensional Modular Design

Business Architecture is a general description of a system. It identifies its purpose, vital functions, active elements, and critical processes and defines the nature of the interaction among them. Business architecture consists of a set of distinct but interrelated platforms creating a multidimensional modular system. Each platform represents a dimension of the system signifying a unique mode of behavior with a predefined set of performance criteria and measures. Designing business architecture follows the general rules of iterative idealized design described in chapter 5 of "Systems Thinking". It therefore starts by assuming that the system to be redesigned has been destroyed overnight but that everything else in the environment remains unchanged.

THE DESIGNERS HAVE BEEN GIVEN THE OPPORTUNITY TO DESIGN THE SYSTEM FROM SCRATCH. THE SCHEMATIC (FIG. 1) OUTLINES THE PROCESS OF DESIGNING BUSINESS ARCHITECTURE

| Portfolio of internal competencies | Matching internal competencies with market opportunities | Portfolio of market opportunities |

1 ◁

The System's Boundary and Business Environment

The first step in designing system architecture is to define the system's boundary and appreciate the environment in which it intends to operate.

To define the system's boundary we need to understand the behavior of its stakeholders. A stakeholder of an organization is any individual or group who is directly affected by what the organization does and therefore has a stake in its performance. Therefore, we need to know the following: Who are the major stakeholders? What are their expectations? What are the desired properties of the system from their perspective? What is their influence? Which critical variables do they control (or influence)?

For example, in a market economy the customer provides the operating income, the boss defines the membership, stockholders pay the capital, suppliers are the source of complementary technologies, and distributors provide access to customers. However, stake and influence do not necessarily go hand in hand. On the contrary, a high stake is often coupled with low influence, and vice versa. For example, customers with highest level of influence (refusing their patronage) show very low level of stake in the system. On the other hand, employees with a very high stake in the system often have low level of influence. Shareholders with very high influence have least at stake. If unhappy they simply would take their money out.

As we alluded before, the systems boundary is a subjective construct defined by the interest and level of influence and/or authority of the participating actors.
The system therefore consists of all variables that could be sufficiently influenced or controlled by the participating actors. Meanwhile, the environment in which the system must remain viable consists of all those variables that, although affecting the system's behavior, could not be directly influenced or controlled by the participating designers.
Since in this formulation business environment is to remain intact it is critical to get an appreciation of its behavior by understanding: How is the game evolving? What are the drivers for change? What are the bases for competition? Figure 3 is a schematic representation of how the game is evolving and the drivers for change in the energy business. Note how a single event, the oil crisis of 1979, by producing an unrealistic forecast for energy prices, triggered a chain of events to reduce consumption. But, in a fixed-cost and price-regulated environment, it counterintuitively resulted in higher prices and ultimately restructured the whole industry.

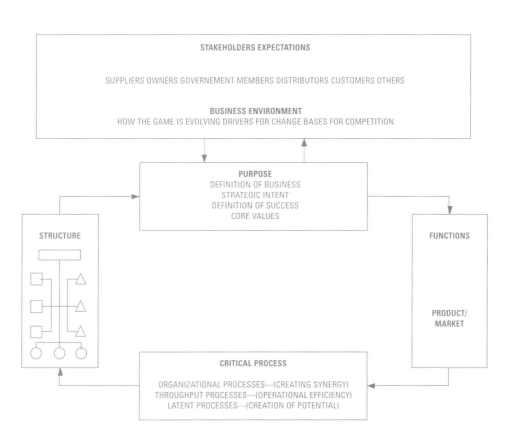

2‹ Schematic outline of a Design process

Figure 3:
How the Energy Business Environment is Evolving

Figure 4 captures the drama of health-care system.
The game is still evolving. The industry has yet to find
alternatives for the three villains of *third-party payer, cost
plus reimbursement*, and *fee for service*, which are assumed
responsible for creating insatiable demand. Note how a
counterintuitive event, General Motor's agreement with
the labor union, to cover the health care cost of workers in
exchange for a one-time concession on wages combined
with President Johnson Medicare & Medicaid programs led
to the "Health Care Bonanza" and a dynamics that no one
has yet figured how to deal with it.

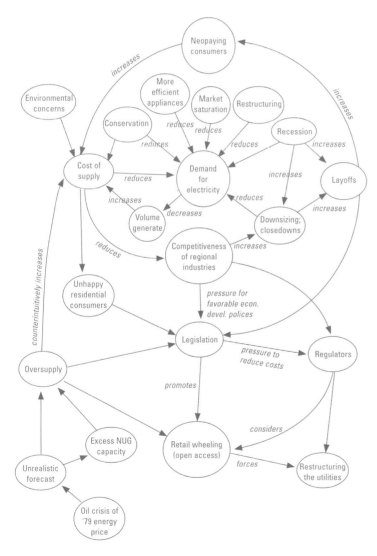

Figure 4:
How the Game is Evolving in the Health Care Industry

As for the change in the bases of competition consider the fact that past was the age of mass production based on the interchangeability of parts and labor. We have entered the mass customization era where success is defined by producing smaller batches of customized products at lower break-even points. Honda's break-even point for a given model is two thousand cars whereas Ford Motors Company requires five hundred units of the same model car to break-even. Mastery of a simple procedure was the cornerstone of mass production, but the multi-skilled knowledge worker is now the core requirement of mass customization. Globalization means that price is set in the global market place therefore it is considered to be uncontrollable variable and making the cost controllable variable (target costing) whereas in the "Cost Plus Economy" cost is considered to be uncontrollable and price is the controllable variable

(target pricing). Efficiency in performing a routine used to be a virtue when the cost of automation outweighed the cost of labor. Digital revolution has reversed the equation. Increasingly cheaper computers have rendered the 'narrow skill' and 'simple procedure' approach obsolete. In fact when it comes to performing a specific procedure the computer is the ideal actor. Knowledge workers of today are capable of putting together whatever pieces of know-how it takes to produce an integrated solution.
There was a time when problems could be neatly formulated and conveniently solved within the confines of a single discipline or department. Modern problems, however, are increasingly complex and interrelated. These problems are messy; they come in bundles and require a different approach. Knowledge workers of today are not only required to be competent in their own vocation but are supposed to be intimately aware of the total context and overall process within which, they are to collaborate.

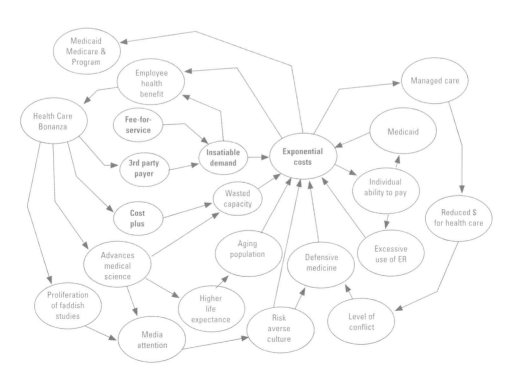

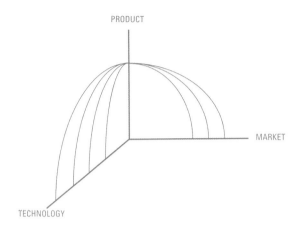

PRODUCT

MARKET

TECHNOLOGY

5‹ Business Defined by Product

2 Purpose

Many commonsense statements invoked in the process of developing organizations prove counterintuitive. The surprise element is not because people are knowingly disingenuous. Emerging consequences contradict expectations because the operating principles are rooted in assumptions that belong to different paradigms. Such surprises are inevitable unless the underlying premises are surfaced and their eventual consequences are mapped out. In fact Purpose of business enterprise is essentially defined by its implicit paradigm. If the organization in question operates in a mechanistic mode then it is considered to be a tool of its owner. Its purpose therefore would be to serve the purpose of its owner. Performance criteria of a tool, of course, would be efficiency and reliability. Purpose of organization in biological mode of operation is survival and thus its performance criterion would be growth at any cost. Profit as the means of growth would finds additional social value and overcomes the negative stigma of mechanistic era. However, since organization in a Socio-cultural mode of operation is considered to be a voluntary association of purposeful members its purpose would be to serve its members and its environment by doing more and more with less and less.

But, as stated so elegantly by Milton Friedman, ultimately "Business of a business is business" therefore, for designers of business architecture understanding the vision of the desired future of the enterprise and its business model are of the utmost importance.

The initial sketches of vision of the desired future usually can be put together after the first iteration of idealized design. Although, we are told that visions are escape mechanisms of daydreamers, but without a vision there will be no sense of direction. Without a vision all possibilities would have equal values; there would be no basis to judge the relevancy of the emerging opportunities.

Business model, on the other hand, defines the way a business generates value, creates a deliverable package and exchanges it with money. Now-a-days amazing originalities shown in developing new business models are radically influencing the traditional business concepts. Consider, for example, the case of Google the search engine

that, by providing free service to group of consumers,
can make so much money from advertisers that exceeds
the value of giants such as General Motors. Creating a
multibillion dollar business to create, package and sell
operating systems independently from computer hardware,
as is done by Microsoft, was inconceivable for those of us
who worked for IBM during the sixties. In early 90s, I was
involved with a Fortune 100 Company as a consultant in
acquisition of 10 billion dollar business. The total sum of
the money that all service providers—legal, financial and
management—charged the client was less than $500,000.
It was based on actual time spent multiplied by the hourly
rate. Today the same task would cost over $200 million
in commission based on a business model that works on
percentage.

In general, business is usually defined in terms of three
dimensions. A know-how or *technology*, that is transformed
into a set of tangible *products* or services and delivered via
an access mechanism to its target customers or *markets*.
Business architecture defines the nature of relationships
among three dimensions of: technology, product, and
market.

TRADITIONALLY ONE OF THESE DI-MENSIONS HAS BEEN DESIGNATED AS PRIMARY, FORCING THE OTHER TWO INTO SUBORDINATING ROLES.

When the product defines the business, technological
requirements and the markets to be served are determined
by product characteristics. Alternative technologies are
sought for making the product, and different markets are
sought for selling the product. (Fig. 5)

The success of a product-based business is usually
measured by the success of its product divisions. That is
why everything is easily compromised and subordinated to
the product. However, when the potential value of a given
technology somehow becomes more than the value of the
product it supports, the business faces a dilemma.
Unfortunately, experience shows that, in these cases,

technology has always been compromised. In a product-based business, product manager are the boss. They see technology only as a competitive advantage for their product; therefore, technology will never get the chance to realize its potential in the context of a product-based business. Quite a few cases will support this assertion, but the most conspicuous is the fate of the Apple operating system (the famous graphic interface). This phenomenal operating system had been used exclusively to sell Apple computers when its potential had been much higher than the maximum potential of the products it supported.

THIS WAS PROVEN BY MICROSOFT, WHOSE CLAIM TO FAME, WINDOWS 95, IS THE BEST IMITATION OF THE APPLE OPERATING SYSTEM OPEN TO BE USED BY ALL.

It is reported that IBM spent billions laying off about 200,000 people, some say the best available knowledge workers, but did not consider capitalizing on its advance "digital technology" and state-of-the-art "electronic packaging" to become the major player in the most potentially explosive markets of the future.

When the market is used as the basis for defining the business, then the characteristics of the market determine the product mix and the type of skills and technologies required to produce it (Fig. 6). Procter and Gamble, for example, provides as many of the products sold in supermarkets as it can profitably make. Pharmaceutical companies make a variety of different products for the same market segment.

However, the trauma of the defense industry, when its market collapsed overnight, was another confirmation that the price tag on selecting a single pattern of existence is very high. The industry's inability to take advantage of its access and knowledge of emerging Internet technology was not surprising. Managing technology requires a different set of criteria than those necessary to manage products and/or markets.

Finally, when the business is technologically defined, a variety of products are developed around a given core

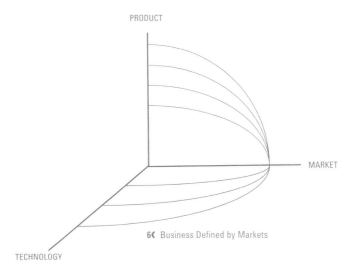

6‹ Business Defined by Markets

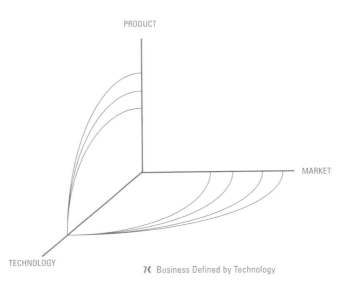

7‹ Business Defined by Technology

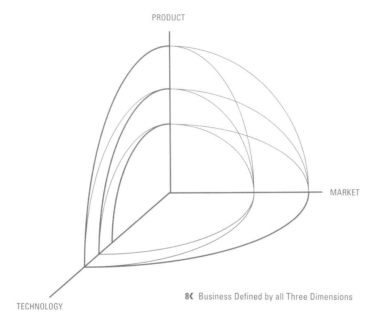

PRODUCT

MARKET

TECHNOLOGY

8‹ Business Defined by all Three Dimensions

technology, using the same base of know-how, and sold in different markets (Fig. 7). For example, 3-M defines itself as being in the "sticking" business. The company evolves around technologies used to bind different things together (from scotch tape and composite structures to electronic packaging). Using its materials science and processing technology, it continually searches for new products that it can produce and offer in different markets. Managing a technology-based business not only needs broader planning vision, but also the ability to use the same knowledge in different contexts.

The success or failure of each approach depends on its compatibility with the emerging competitive challenge at the time. Because competitive games change over time, they force companies to switch their strategic emphasis from one dimension to another. Since each strategy has organizational implications in terms of authority and responsibility, changes in strategy require changes in the organizational structure and the dominant culture of the business. As competition intensifies and the changes become more frequent, this unidimensional approach becomes more ineffective. Shifts from one dimension to another in search of the effective competitive base cause organizational turmoil and strategic confusion. The waste and frustration associated with periodic restructuring have necessitated a search for alternative solutions.

The interactive systems architecture uses product, market, and technology in an interactive mode. It recognizes the necessity for achieving competitive advantage in all three dimensions of market, product, and technology.
The objective is to capitalize on the totality of the value chain and actively generate synergy among the three dimensions.

AN INTERACTIVE ARCHITECTURE IS BASED ON MANAGING THE INTERACTIONS AMONG TECHNOLOGY, PRODUCT, AND MARKETS.

The emerging multidimensional structure and multiple business cultures dissolve the need for subordination or sub-optimization around any one business dimension,

eliminate periodic restructuring, and shift from one dimension to another in search of an effective competitive base.

In an unpredictable, turbulent environment, the viability of any design will depend on its capability to explore and exploit emerging opportunities all along the value chain. These opportunities, which emerge out of interactions among technology, product, and markets, remain inaccessible to unidimensional cultures and architecture. A platform that identifies the basic dimensions of the multicultural architecture is the starting point from which the initial elements of the value chain will evolve.

OF COURSE, AS THE BUSINESS GAINS MATURITY AND STABILITY, NEW ELEMENTS WILL BE ADDED.

In formulating the strategic intent of an enterprise we must remember that competitive advantage is a dynamic and relative phenomenon, different in different contexts and in reference to different classes of users. For example, the element of time, as a basis for competition, is not the same for supermarket shoppers at 10 a.m. and those at 5 p.m. Often the former are spending time, whereas the latter are interested in saving time. What might be an advantage in one context could be a disadvantage in another.

Now recall the concept of "experience curve," which is a volume-based learning. An important outcome of learning through an experience curve is *process control*. This type of control takes considerable time and resources to achieve in a given context. When this context is changed or even modified, the whole knowledge that was gained in controlling the particular process is lost. Now assume that, somehow, we have gained the ability to make this know-how context-free and are able to transfer it to different applications, without having to go through the time and resource-consuming notion of the experience curve each time. If we *can really do this, then we have created a* core competency, an unmatched opportunity for competitive advantage. Formulating and developing state-of-the-art knowledge that can be operationalized in different contexts is, in my opinion, a much more profound way of formulating a competitive strategy. For example, adding digital technology to miniaturization has recently provided Sony with a whole new dimension in its competitive strategy.

Strategic intent can be formulated as a core competency. In this context a core competency is the attribute of the organization as a whole; it cannot be housed in a single division. Creation of context-free transferable knowledge requires multiple sources of learning and application.

3 Functions

To serve its own interest in an exchange, a purposeful system ought to have something to give back to its environment. Therefore, it needs access to a group of potential users with a purchasing power who have a need or desire for the product or service it can produce. A true customer, in reality, is a pain in the neck. He/she has something you want; and his/her satisfaction, in competition with other sources of supply, is the price you have to pay in order to get it.

Selecting a product-market niche is the first step in defining an enterprise's function and designing its architecture. We need to answer the following questions: Whose problem are we trying to solve? What solutions are we offering? How we will access the target customers?

AND, FINALLY, WILL THE TARGET CUSTOMERS HAVE SUFFICIENT PURCHASING POWER TO PAY FOR THIS SOLUTION?

Competitive advantage is an attribute of outputs produced by an enterprise. It is a difference that makes a difference, for a given class of users, in affecting their choice. And it must be transferable to a value for the provider.

To select a desired product-market niche, it is necessary to differentiate the customer base. There are many different ways to segment a market. Each segment reveals something new about the nature of the market and the behavior of

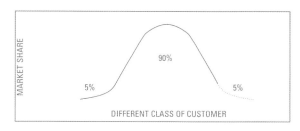

9◖ Traditional Assumption on Distribution of customer Base

10◖ Emerging Distribution of Customer Base

the target customers. Use as many criteria as you can
to differentiate user characteristics and identify their
purchasing habits. The most useful segmentation is the one
that identifies:

1) The group of customers for whom the desired
   properties of the product is more compatible with the
   organization's potential capabilities, and
2) Those potential customers who have less stake in the
   old product system and who therefore display less
   inertia and offer easier access.

Using the traditional bell-shaped distribution curve to
differentiate the customer base assumes that the majority
in the big category alone defines the market (Fig. 9). The
behavior of this single group, considered normal, is used to
determine the desired properties of outputs, while behavior
of the smaller groups, considered nerds, are conveniently
ignored as insignificant.

Struggle for a share of this monolithic market leads to a
game of intense competition between big powerful players.
However, increasingly it seems that the nerds are taking
over. And the bell-shaped curve is somehow flattening out
(Fig. 10). It seems that nerds are taking over. Targeting and
understanding behaviors of the smaller groups that are
emerging rapidly provides the best, and sometimes only,
window of opportunity for a new player to successfully enter
the game and skillfully avoid the intense competition.

Nerds are taking over!

4 Structure

Traditionally, organizational theory deals with two types of relationships: 1) responsibility (who is responsible for what) and 2) authority (who reports to whom).

Structure, so conceived, can be represented by a two-dimensional chart in which boxes represent responsibilities and levels and lines represent the loci and flow of authority. (Fig. 11)
The criteria used for dividing the whole into areas of responsibility, and for determining their relative importance (line of authority), represent the major differences among organization theories. These criteria, not surprisingly, have evolved primarily around three components of a system: input (technology), output (products), and environment (markets).

Depending on the nature of the competitive game at any given time a priorities scheme is used to designate one component as primary and the other two as subordinates. For example, when the ability to produce was the defining factor of competition, input became the primary concern rendering market and product subordinate to manufacturing. The marketing era saw the shift of emphasis from production to market and thus subordination of manufacturing to marketing.

IT SEEMS THAT A SELF-IMPOSED UNI-DIMENSIONAL CONCEPT OF ORGANIZATION HAS PREVENTED REALIZATION OF A MULTI-DIMENSIONAL ALTERNATIVE.

For a majority of designers, the uni-dimensional mode of organization based on structurally defined tasks, segmentation, and hierarchical coordination of functions seems the only acceptable way of organizing work. A predominant management culture continues to value command and control very dearly and considers any form of variety in the organizational structure unacceptable, wasteful, and at best, impractical.

The multi-dimensional structure assumes that the three common criteria—input (technology), output (products), and environment (markets)—are complements. Treating them as interdependent dimensions and managing their interactions eliminates the need for periodic reorganization when a change in competitive environment necessitates a change of emphasis from one orientation to another—for example, from products to markets or vice versa.

Accelerating change and the periodic shift of emphasis from one concern to another force large organizations into constant disruptive reorganizations. The cost of reorganizations, as well as the frustrations and tensions associated with them, generate a desire for stability and a resistance to change.

The viability of any organization depends on its ability to adapt actively to the changing requirements of the emerging competitive game. The ability to adapt requires some form of flexibility and responsiveness, which in turn demands that some degree of redundancy be built into the system. A modular structure embedded in a multi-dimensional scheme can achieve the required level of flexibility and redundancy to create an adaptive, learning system by shift its attention from micro-managing the parts (power over) to macro-managing the interactions (power to do).
Power-to-do is what organization is all about. It should not be confused with power-over. Power-to-do is the foundation of organizational potency and duplication of power while power-over is about domination. Potent organizations are not built on impotent principles. Power-to-do multiplies when it is duplicated in special purpose modules. These modules enjoy considerable freedom as long as they meet the interface and functional requirements of the larger system of which they are a part. In any system it is differentiation that keeps the system alive and potent. Organizations that differentiate and integrate create real value for themselves and others.

Multi-dimensional, modular design, in my experience, is the most practical means of handling complexity and uncertainty. It makes it feasible to implement a complex design without getting lost in the process.
Multi-dimensional modular structure consists of a set of distinct, but interrelated, platforms. Each platform represents a dimension of the system signifying an

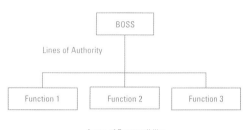

Lines of Authority

Areas of Responsibility

11‹ Authority and Responsibility

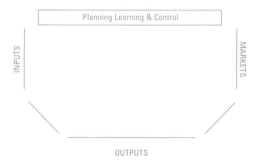

12‹ Multidimensional Modular Design

unique context, mode of operation, and predefined set of performance criteria and measures. Each platform hosts a set of special purpose modules with the same set of behavioral characteristics. Relationships and the interfaces among platforms are explicitly defined integrating them into a concept of the whole. Parts operate as independent systems with the ability to be relatively self-controlling and act as responsible members of a coherent whole with the ability to respond effectively to the requirements of the containing system.

For example, a technology platform provides a friendly environment for "component builders". Component builders are modules that usually host a core technology and therefore require a different mode of management and performance criteria and measures than those which are necessary for managing and controlling the marketing modules.

The organization, so conceived, then becomes capable of expanding or contracting by the addition or deletion of replaceable modules that have the means of vertical and horizontal interactions. The resulting mode of organization is capable of redesigning its structure and redefining its functions, allowing it to exhibit different behavior and produce different outcomes in the same or different environments. This means work can be organized in a variety of ways, and indeed an organizational choice does exist. Figure 12 is an outline of the Multi-dimensional Modular Design.

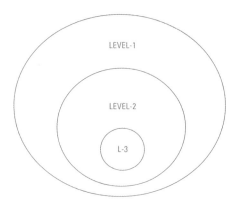

13◀ Multilevel purposeful systems

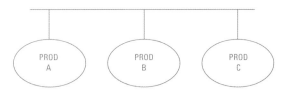

GENERAL PURPOSE OUTPUT MODULES

14◀ Output Dimension

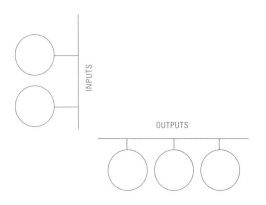

15◀ Input Dimensions

4.1 Outputs Dimension

Responsibility for achieving an organization's end is vested in the output dimension. The output dimension or platform consists of a series of *general purpose*, semi-autonomous, and ideally self-sufficient units charged with all the activities ultimately responsible for achieving an organization's mission and production of its outputs. Note that the semi-autonomous, self-sufficient, and purposeful units, for simplicity, are referred to as modules. Modules are self-sufficient and autonomous to the degree that the integrity of the whole system is not compromised.

EACH OUTPUT MODULE REPRESENTS A SPECIFIC LEVEL IN THE HIERARCHY OF MULTI-LEVEL PURPOSEFUL SYSTEMS (FIG. 13). IT IS A MINIATURE OF THE WHOLE—THE LARGER SYSTEM OF WHICH IT IS A PART.

Since each module may consume scarce resources of its environment, its outputs should be responsive to the needs of the environment. The lowest-level output module is the smallest unit that can be accountable for producing a tangible, measurable output.

Performance of an output module preferably should be as independent to the behavior of other peer output modules as possible; it should have enough authority over its resources—money and people—to be responsible and accountable for its success or failure. It should also be able to retain a percentage of its contributions above a minimum level for incentive and internal development.

Each output module is responsible for making those decisions that affect only its operations. Decisions that impact on the other units will be made at higher levels with the participation of all affected modules. An output module is usually conceived as a unit hosting a product, a project, or a program. An effective product module has an entrepreneurial role. It has the responsibility for the development, design, marketing, and profitability of

the final product. Although they should not be burdened
by responsibilities for fixed production facilities, output
managers should have the financial authority to select the
production facilities and distribution system

Including high-capital-intensive production and distribution
facilities in a product development module will tie the fates
of an organization's major divisions into a single product.
The facility-oriented division unwilling to develop any
product requiring the use of different facilities will, like
the product, experience the cycle of growth, maturity, and
inevitable decline.
Ideally, the output platform, will be a virtual entity,
would have up to date information about environmental
opportunities and internal competencies. It would have a
distinct capability to consider new set of alternatives and
choices that might be available to the organization. Finally
modules of output platform should have the ability and the
authority to re-engage inputs in a new order.

4.2 Inputs Dimension

To create a system that is more than the sum of its parts,
the organization needs to use its synergy fully. Economies of
scale, the need for specialization, technological imperative,
and development of core technologies are among the
reasons why some functions and technologies required by
output modules ought to be shared.

These shared services and specialized functions can be
provided by groups of special-purpose modules, which together
constitute the input dimension of the organization. (Fig. 15)

For example, designating the manufacturing unit as a profit
center in the input dimension not only results in more
competitive and flexible facility management, but also
provides the product managers with the freedom to buy
their manufacturing requirements from within or outside the
organization without constraint from fixed facilities.

The input modules, in general, are provided with working
capital and are expected to earn their operating expenses
plus a return on the investment by charging the market price
for their services.

If insufficiency or unpredictability of demand makes
it necessary to provide additional support for an input
function, then the general rule is to subsidize the demand
instead of the supply. In the early stages of the conversion,
the operating budget of an input unit may be given to it by
means of a purchase contract for its total services.

HOWEVER, IN GENERAL, CENTRALIZATION SHOULD BE AVOIDED UNLESS ONE OR ALL OF THE FOLLOWING SITUATIONS WEIGH OVERWHELMINGLY AGAINST DECENTRALIZATION OF A PARTICULAR SERVICE.

Uniformity. Some aspects of the system will be centralized
when they are common to all or some parts and cannot
be decentralized without rendering serious damage to the
system's proper functioning. For example, in areas such
as measurement systems, where common language and
coordination are major concerns, uniformity will serve as
criterion for centralization. Meanwhile, certain activities that,
because of their nature are deemed indivisible and so require
a holistic design, can also be centralized. For example, the
effectiveness of a comprehensive information system lies
in its holism, consistency, real-time access, and proper
networking to transfer information as needed to different
users. Developing such a system requires cooperation and
coordination among all actors in the system.

Economy of Scale. Although economy of scale is generally
considered an important factor in creating Shared Service,
the trade-off between centralization and decentralization
of each function should be made explicit to prove that the
benefits significantly outweigh the disadvantages before
the function is moved to Shared Services. In this case, it
is expected that a service, once centralized, will either
generate significant savings for the system as a whole or
help those units that otherwise would be unable to afford
them on their own.

Core Technologies. Feeling that a certain level of mastery
in a given technology will be critical for the enterprise's

future success, management may decide to centralize, develop, and make the technology available for all units. Sometimes a technology developed by an output unit has a much greater potential in the marketplace than as a competitive advantage to the product division. In this case it is management's responsibility to identify it as a core technology and centralize it for full-scale development.

WHATEVER THE JUSTIFICATION FOR CENTRALIZATION, THE INPUT UNITS WILL HAVE TO BECOME STATE-OF-THE-ART AND COST-EFFECTIVE PROVIDERS OF CHOICE.

However, a sure way to obstruct the functioning of an input unit is to mix its function with that of control.

THIS PRACTICE UNDERMINES BOTH THE EFFECTIVENESS OF THE SERVICE FUNCTION AND THE LEGITIMACY OF THE CONTROLS.

To protect themselves against the creeping hegemony of service providers and the obvious risks involved in relying on control-driven services, the output units resort to duplicating the support services that could otherwise be easily shared and effectively used. Rampant, excessive duplications of services are symptomatic of the natural reaction of operating units to service functions assuming the additional function of control.

On the other hand, disguising a legitimate and necessary control function as a service function transforms the nature of control from learning to a defensive and apologetic act. Extra care should be taken to ensure that none of the functions of Shared Services undergo a character change and assume control properties. Under the pretext of a need for consistency and uniformity, there is a natural tendency to let the service provider perform the necessary monitoring and auditing function. This practice has always proved misguided. The providers cannot avoid the slippery slope of wanting, increasingly, to assume a control function.

THIS OBVIOUSLY WOULD SCARE AWAY USERS WHO DIDN'T EXPECT TO FIND A NEW BOSS IN THE GUISE OF A SERVER.

While Shared Services will provide the customers with requested services (such as information, benefits, payroll, and billing) it will be the planning and control system that will be setting the policies and the criteria governing these services as well as conducting the necessary monitoring and enforcing functions to ensure proper implementation of those policies.

4.3 Markets Dimension

Market, the third dimension of the organization, is defined as the access mechanism to a class of customers having sufficient purchasing power and an explicitly known need or desire for a given service or product. (Fig. 16)

The markets dimension is the interface with the customers. In most cases, this is the where organization actually happens. Depending on the diversity of the customer base, there might be a need to create a number of costly distribution channels.

IT THEN BECOMES IMPERATIVE TO SHARE THESE CHANNELS WITH OTHER OUTPUT UNITS.

Two major functions of markets dimension are distribution and advocacy. Distribution represents the organization to the outside. Advocacy is responsible for sensing environmental conditions and exploring the expectations of the customers. Advocacy serves all those affected by the activities of the organization. Especially important is its role in advocating the consumers' point of view inside the organization

Distribution and advocacy units may be organized geographically or by market segmentation. However, if one is organized geographically, the other should be based on market segmentation.

Input, Output and Market platforms form an interactive whole engaged in an ongoing process of redesign to create new orders spontaneously as deem necessary.
Since interactions among purposeful actors take many forms (actors may cooperate on one pair of tendencies, compete over others, and be in conflict over a different set, all at the same time) we are dealing with a dynamic structure. In addition members learn, mature and change over time. The result is an interactive network of varying members with multiple relationships, recreating itself continuously.

4.4. Internal Market Economy

Defining the relationships between input, output, and marketing modules is the most critical task of this conception. Extreme difficulties are encountered when several output units share the vital services of an input or a market unit set up as an overhead center.

The key problem of matrix organizations also has been management of the implicit, ambiguous, and conflicting relationships between the network of input and output units. The "two-boss system" not only has failed to understand the problem, but has also resulted in confusion and frustration.

The answer for this inherent complexity is to create an internal-market environment, which converts the relationships between input, output, and market units into the same type of relationships that exist between a supplier, a producer, and a distributor.

While superior-subordinate relationships have traditionally been the only building block for exercising organizational authority, the supplier-customer relationship introduces a new source of influence into the organizational equation. With the supplier-customer relationship emerging only in an internal market environment, the helpless recipient becomes a real customer. Armed with purchasing power, the customer becomes an empowered actor with the ability to influence and interact with his or her supplier in such a way that both parties together can now define the type, cost, time, and quality of the services rendered.

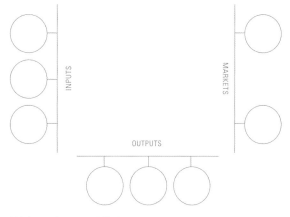

16‹ Inputs, Outputs and Markets

Creation of the internal-market mechanism, and thus a supplier-customer relationship, is contingent upon transforming the Shared Services into a performance center. Unlike overhead centers, performance centers do not receive a fixed budget allocated from the top. They have working capital with a variable operating budget. In this model, expenses are proportional to the income generated by the level of services rendered and the revenues received in their exchange.

TREATING ALL UNITS AS PERFORMANCE CENTERS MAKES IT POSSIBLE TO EVALUATE EVERY UNIT AT EVERY LEVEL IN EXACTLY THE SAME WAY.

These two pairs of horizontal (supplier-customer) and vertical (superior-subordinate) relationships are complementary and reinforce one another. While superior-subordinate defines the formal authority dealing with hiring, firing, and promotion, the supplier-customer relationship creates a new source of influence that tries to rationalize demand.
In the absence of an internal-market environment, there is no built-in mechanism to rationalize demand. An agreeable service provider with a third-party payer creates and fuels an insatiable demand. A disagreeable service provider, on the other hand, triggers prolific duplications of the same services by the potential users. This results in an explosion of overhead expenses in the context of an essentially cost-plus operation. The trend is irrational, and the corrective interventions prove to be ad hoc and ineffective at best.

Creating an internal market not only eliminates growing problems of bureaucratization, but also provides an effective means for dealing with allocation and evaluation problems. Meanwhile, it gives an organization a market orientation by forcing each part to consider the marketing consequences of its actions.

In the internal-market environment, modules ought to have a choice with respect to selling or buying their required services from inside or outside the organization; otherwise, internal buyers or sellers will have a monopolistic

advantage. Higher level authority can always over-ride outsourcing by agreeing to pay the cost incurred or the profit lost.

The following provides a real-life example of converting traditional organization to multidimensional design. During a design session, a group of executives produced the following organizational chart as the initial structure of their business. (Fig. 17)

When I asked them whether they would mind if I changed their design into the following format (Fig. 18), they had no objection: "If you like colors [patterns] use as many as you like," one of them said jokingly.

HOWEVER, DESPITE THE APPARENT SIMILARITIES IN THE TWO DESIGNS, SIGNIFICANT DIFFERENCES EXIST BETWEEN THEM.

Version one represents a design concept concerned only with defining responsibilities and the line of authority. The case at hand is a mix of functional and divisional units all reporting to the CEO. The relationships among peer groups are conveniently ignored, as though the organization is an aggregate of unrelated parts. This is a linear conception of structure in which a single pair of a superior-subordinate relation is used as the building block of the organization. But to produce the structure that fits our purpose here—that is, to design a business architecture—parts not only have to be differentiated and their roles clearly defined, but the relationships among all peer units must be explicitly known and understood.

This is why version two used color to differentiate the parts and group according to the role they would play in the organization. In this context, a part can assume the function of input, output, market access, or control. So, in this particular case, green was used to identify the output units (product-market divisions); yellow was chosen to identify the input (Manufacturing and Engineering); red was used for control (Finance and Human Resources); and blue for market access (sales units).

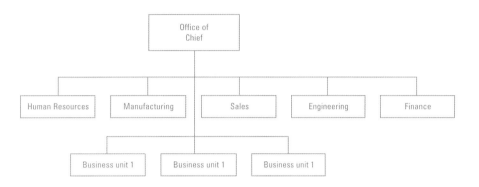

17❬ Traditional Divisional structure

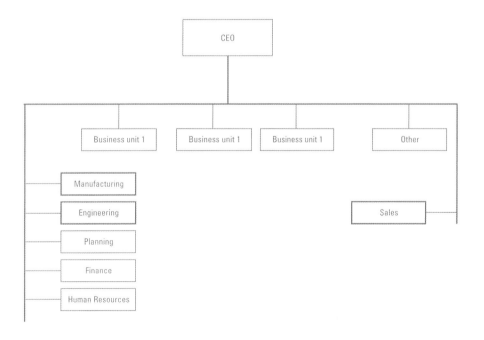

18❬ Multidimensional Representation of the Same Design

To demonstrate the flow and the relationship in the value chain, the following format was adopted to underline three basic relationships among peer units:

Figure 19 Value Chain Relationship

Output units are in competition with one another. So much so that animosity among sister organizations is much higher than it is with outside competitors. To avoid structural conflict, output units should operate virtually independently of one another, with a modular structure and adequate levels of autonomy and self-sufficiency.

1)   Relationships between each output unit with the input and market access units are complementary. It is the same relationship that exists between a producer and its suppliers or between a producer and its distributors. An effective interface with all-out cooperation between them is a must to generate a competitive throughput. If the output unit is to be held accountable for the ultimate outcome and proper integration of the operation, it must have some kind of leverage on both input and market access units to influence their behavior. We will revisit this notion when we discuss organizational processes and measurement systems.

2)   The relationships between control units and all the input, output, and market access units are one-way, usually bureaucratic and more or less autocratic in nature. This is why combining a service function with a control function in a single unit, which is usually done under the pretext of coordination, is a design for failure. For example, when any one of the service functions like HR, Legal, or even Information Services becomes provider and controller at the same time, both the control and service functions will be undermined.

Finally, the linear framework of version one lends itself to a unidimensional concept of system architecture where product, market, and technology are arranged in sequential order based on their relative importance. The criteria used for determining the order of subordination defines the major differences between alternative designs. The second version tries to create an interactive relationship among technology (input), product (output), and market (access). This requires a multi-dimensional structure.

To create a multi-dimensional structure we need at least two distinct types of relationships. A single superior/subordinate pair can produce only a uni-dimensional structure; despite claims to the contrary, a matrix organization is not a multi-dimensional design. Two-boss systems fail because they create confusion in the power system.

USING THE SUPERIOR/ SUBORDINATE PAIR IN TWO CONTEXTS CREATES FRUSTRATION, NOT INTERACTION.

For interaction among peer units, interactive paradigm uses two distinct pairs of relationships: 1) superior/subordinate and 2) customer/provider. This becomes real and meaningful when, and only when, the user of the service has the power of the money and controls the payment to the provider. This requires that providers function with a variable budget paid by the customer in exchange for their services. If a provider of a service has a fixed budget, which is directly paid by the boss, then the boss becomes the customer as well. In this case user of the service has no power and customer/ provider relations is meaningless.

Customerprovider relationships can be forged between input, output, and marketing units in the context of an internal market mechanism. If properly operationalized, the customerprovider relationship will effectively supplement the superior-subordinate pair and provide the organization with a much desired market orientation. This means each part of the organization not only understands but also lives with the marketing consequences of its actions.

The unit of organization, in this context, is a performance center, a value-adding link in a well-defined value chain. Although each unit has only a single boss (the superior/ subordinate relation with its containing system), it can have several customers and suppliers. Customers are the sole source of its operating income. The measure of each unit's performance includes not only its own operations but also the contribution it makes to the success of its internal suppliers. All units have working capital and operate on a variable budget dependent on the throughput of the system.

5 Processes

Recall that throughput processes are those directly concerned with the actual output of the organization. Organizational processes, on the other hand, are concerned with creating integration, alignment, and synergy among the organization's parts. In this context, Planning, Learning and Control system is an integral part of designing architecture.

5.1 Planning, Learning and Control System

An organization's decision-making process is reflected in its mode of planning. Planning as traditionally practiced is either one or a combination of two dominant types: reactive and proactive.

Reactive planning is concerned with identifying deficiencies and designing projects and strategies to remove or suppress them. It deals with parts of an organization independently of each other.

An organization is a system whose major deficiencies arise from the way its parts interact, not from the actions of its parts taken separately. Therefore, it is possible, and even likely, that improving the performance of each part of an organization separately will bring down the organization's performance as a whole.

Proactive planning consists of two major activities: prediction and preparation. The objective is to forecast the future and then prepare the organization as well as possible. Unfortunately, such forecasts are chronically in error, since the social, economic, and political conditions, as well as the behavior of supplier, consumer, and competitor, are affected by what the planned-for organization, and others like it, do. Therefore, it is precisely such plans taken together that shape the future.

Systems methodology rests on the *interactive* type of planning, which assumes that the future is created by what others and we do between now and then. Therefore, the objective is to design a desirable future (idealization) to invent or select ways of bringing it about (realization).

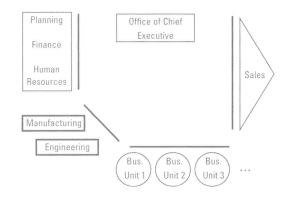

19◄ Value Chain Relationship

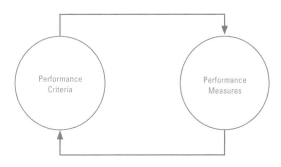

20◄ Relation between Performance Criteria and Performance Measures

Planning and control system is the executive function of the organization. It oversees the operation of the whole system by managing the *interaction* between the dimensions. The executive function also has responsibility for creating a vision, generating a shared image of a desired future, and providing the leadership for achieving the organizational mission. It has final responsibility for financial viability, technological ability, and human effectiveness of the organization as a whole.

Our design must be viable in the existing environment. To assess the viability of a business enterprise requires a measurement system. As a matter of fact, defining the characteristics of the measurement system is the last connecting piece in the design of an architecture.

5.2 Measurement System

To develop an effective measurement system we need to deal iteratively with two elements: performance criteria and performance measures

Performance Criteria

Performance criteria are the expression of what is to be measured and why (for example, how success is defined). The selection process involves identifying dimensions and/or variables relevant to an enterprise's successful operation.

Relevancy is the most important concern in selecting performance variables. Traditionally, the overriding concern has been with the accuracy of measures. Since we find it difficult to accurately measure what we want, we have chosen to want what we can accurately measure. Unfortunately, the more accurate the measure of the wrong criteria, the faster the road to disaster. We are much better off with an approximation of relevant variables than with precise measurement of the wrong ones.

In the case of emergent properties such as success or development, when a direct measure is not possible, look for measuring a manifestation of the phenomenon that is co produced by multiple variables. For example, although growth may be an important manifestation of development,

it measures only a single dimension (wealth), whereas real measures of development would include four other complementary dimensions: freedom (power), justice (values), competence (knowledge), and ambition (beauty).

Viability of a business enterprise is an emergent property. It is the product of the interactions of various entities. It cannot be measured directly (i.e., by using any of the five senses). We can measure only its manifestation. Growth is the most popular one, but some prefer return on investment while others like net present value of future cash flows.

Unfortunately, using the single manifestation of a phenomenon as the measure of an emergent property has proved misleading and very costly. For example, if a business is successful, chances are it will grow; however, growth alone does not mean that the business is successful. The same outcome (manifestation) could be produced by different means.

LOUSY ACQUISITIONS CAN PRODUCE HIGH RATES OF GROWTH BUT AT THE SAME TIME DESTROY THE COMPANY.

Therefore, when we measure an emergent property by means of its manifestation we have to do it along several dimensions. For example, concern for people, when combined with the concern for production, has a quite different manifestation from the one without it. Dr. Blake (1968) in his famous work, *The Managerial Grid*, demonstrated how the nature of a variable in a "1.9 orientation" is different from the nature of the same variable in a "9.9 orientation." Freedom without justice leads to chaos, while justice without freedom leads to tyranny.

Performance Measures

Performance measures are the operational definition of each variable—that is, how each variable is to be measured specifically. For example, if we have identified capacity utilization as performance criteria, then turnover ratio might be designated as its measure. Now we would need a procedure for calculating turnover ratio (e.g., divide sales by assets, divide revenues by assets, or divide output by input).

An important consideration in selecting any measure is its simplicity. The cost of producing a measurement should not exceed the value of the information it generates. Although objective measures are preferable, if the cost of obtaining an objective measure is prohibitive, then use a subjective one. Remember that collective subjectivity is objectivity (provided that collectivity represents a variety of value systems). For example, in evaluating the performance of a gymnast we rely on the collective judgment of a number of different judges.

Development of effective performance measures is easier said than done. More often than not, the operational definitions are left vague and ambiguous, even when the underlying concepts are relatively simple, such as minimizing the cost.

THE USUAL PRACTICE OF ALLOCATING OVERHEAD TO VARIOUS OPERATING UNITS DEMONSTRATES HOW AN INNOCENT MATTER OF A CONVENIENCE PRODUCES UNINTENDED CONSEQUENCES.

The criteria for allocation of overhead are usually based on conventional wisdom. Factors such as space occupied by a unit, or the labor content of a production process, are among the most popular ones. Since overhead usually constitutes more than 40% of the total cost, then we should not be surprised to see that these variables (space and direct labor) are the ones targeted for cost reductions. The fact that allocation rules were only a convention doesn't matter anymore. Once the allocation criteria become a rule, their relation with generation of cost, by default, is assumed to be causal, as demonstrated by the following case. A large supermarket chain decided to close down 10 of its stores because the accounting system showed they were not covering their allocated overheads. Since the shutdown had no effect in reducing overhead, the remaining stores now had to carry a larger share of the overhead. This in turn put a few more of the stores in the red, and they too were subsequently closed. The company was gradually withdrawing from the market. Then a new design was developed. Each store became responsible for its own operation without having to worry about any artificial overhead allocated to it. The surplus generated by each store was then passed on to the corporation as the income of the executive office. This made the executive office a profit center responsible for managing its operation, or so-called overhead, within the bounds of its income and the profit it needed to generate to meet the cost of its capital.

THIS SITUATION IS BY NO MEANS ATYPICAL.

With the prevalence of allocation rules based on labor, pressure is unduly shifted to direct labor. The default reaction is to lay off productive manpower. If the police department is facing deficits, policemen are the first to be fired. If schools are in financial trouble, the number of teachers is reduced. Reduction of operating units does not automatically reduce overhead, as management seems to assume. On the contrary, it will increase the burden of the remaining units until the whole system comes to a halt. In the mid-1970s, when per capita income was the conventional measure of development, sudden increases in oil prices produced instantly developed nations. Since this was not acceptable, a new set of indicators had to be developed. We now have a whole series of indicators that substitute for development, such as per capita steel production, per capita consumption of fuel, etc. It is not surprising, then, to find national development policies aimed at improving these measures, usually at an incredible cost to the society at large. Yes, winning is fun. But to win, one has to keep score. And the way one keeps score defines the game.

TABLE 1: VIABILITY MATRIX: Identifying Dimensions and Variables

	Structure (Inputs)	Function (Outputs)	Environment (Markets)	Process (Know-how)
Throughput	Capacity Utilization Profitability	Attributes of the Outputs • Cost • Quality • Availability	Access Mechanism Reliability of demand	Throughput Capability • Waste • Cycle-time • Safety • Control
Synergy	Default values of the culture	Compatibility of Performance criteria	Credibility in the market place: Relations with: • Suppliers, • Creditors, • Customers	Value chain analysis Reward systems Value-added ratio
Latency	Bench strength Core knowledge	Product potency	Market potential Intensity of competition	Early-warning system Planning process

6 Viability Matrix

The viability matrix developed below (Table 1) is a framework for identifying the relevant dimensions—the performance variables—for measuring a business's viability or the different aspects of an operation.

The first dimension of this matrix identifies the variables that define the organization as a whole:
- Structure (inputs)
- Function (outputs)
- Environment (markets)
- Process (technology)

The second dimension of the viability matrix identifies the processes that define the totality of the management system:
- Throughput (production of the outputs)
- Synergy (management of interactions, adding value)
- Latency (defining problems and designing solutions)

THE FOLLOWING DEFINITIONS CLARIFY SOME OF THE VARIABLES I HAVE USED IN DEVELOPING THE ABOVE SCHEME.

Capacity Utilization: Turnover ratio is a good indicator of capacity utilization. Compared to industry standards and best in class, it can signal the existence of an excess capacity that can be the major source of malfunctioning and fluctuation in the system.

Profitability: A dynamic and interrelated model of operating income, operating expense, investment (hard and soft), cash flow, and cost of capital.

Attributes of the Outputs: The outputs are defined in terms of a quantifiable delivery of goods or services in time and space. It is measured on three dimensions: price, quality, and availability (time).

Reliability of Demand: Demand for a product is reliable if the amount to be purchased can be predicted reasonably and if actors beyond a firm's influence do not create unexpected fluctuations.

Throughput Capability: The level of integration and effectiveness of activities required for the delivery of goods and services to satisfied customers is measured by cycle time, waste reduction, safety, and competency of critical processes.

Default Value of the Culture: The degree to which members accept responsibility and act with authority; duplication of power, assumptions regarding the source of value, nature of competition, and relationship between equality and competence.

Credibility in the Marketplace: A firm is credible when it can take actions its stakeholders will initially accept on good faith alone, i.e., relationships with customers This is the reflection of the firm and its sound relationships with customers, suppliers, and creditors.

Value Chain Transaction Index: A model for explicitly measuring the total contributions that a business unit makes to the profitability of the whole organization. The model recognizes not only the unit's own profitability, but also its contribution to the profitability and/or success of other units within the context of a value-chain architecture.

Value-added Ratio: A calculation of the value a unit produces in comparison to the value it consumes. The value a unit consumes is adjusted to reflect the cost of the resources, the amount and kind of inputs (scarce or excess resources) the unit consumes, and whether they are obtained internally or externally. The value a unit produces is also modified to recognize the contribution of each line in its product/market mix. For example, to encourage new product/new market introductions, one might multiply revenues generated by selling a new product in a new market by 120%.

Reward System: A priority scheme superimposed on the measurement system, which will allow the organization to assign priorities to particular variables (activities) and thus influence the behavior of the actors toward achieving organizational goals.

Product Potency: Defines the degree to which the product meets a variety of customer needs and desires, in absolute terms as well as relative to competitors' and substitute products.

Market Potential: A market has potential when there is a real and sustainable need and sufficient (size) or growing purchasing power to satisfy those needs.

Intensity of Competition: Competition is intense when the supply of a product is greater than the demand, and it is easy to enter but difficult to exit the market.

7 Realization Successive Approximation

Idealized design evolves on the assumption that the system has been destroyed overnight and that the designers have been given the opportunity to recreate the system from a clean slate. The only condition is that the outcome be technologically feasible and operationally viable.

THE REALIZATION OF THE DESIGN HAS TO TAKE PLACE IN A REAL-WORLD ENVIRONMENT. THEREFORE, WE MUST IDENTIFY ALL THE CONSTRAINTS THAT MIGHT INTERFERE WITH PROPER IMPLEMENTATION.

It is crucial to the success of the whole redesign effort that all involved demonstrate the highest degree of candor in identifying any reservations they may have, subjective or otherwise, about the successful realization of the design at this time. If there is one juncture in the entire process of idealized design where nothing, not even an imaginary hang-up or second guessing, should be spared, this is it. Anything likely to inhibit the implementation is strongly encouraged to be put on table, shared, and dealt with right then and there.

The constraints to realization usually fall into the following three distinct categories (Fig. 21).

Type I Constraints

Type I constraints cannot be removed within the existing framework. Such constraints would require revisions and improvisations of the design in order to create a target design capable of being implemented. Target I would be the first approximation of the idealized design. If necessary, subsequent approximations will identify Target II and Target III generations of the idealized design.

It is critical that Type I constraints be continuously monitored so that the target design can further approximate the idealized design as soon as these constraints are removed.

The realization effort, therefore, will not be a one-time proposition. Successive approximations of the idealized state make up the evolutionary process by which the transformation effort is conducted. It may take a number of attempts before the idealized design is reached.

Type II Constraints

Type II constraints are those whose removal will require extensive preparation. They consist of activities that consume considerable time and resources, as well as knowledge and management talent.

THESE ACTIVITIES USUALLY INVOLVE REDESIGN OF THE PRODUCTS (IF NECESSARY), REDESIGN OF THROUGHPUT, AND REDESIGN OF ORGANIZATIONAL PROCESSES.

Design of the measurement and reward system with variable budgeting and target costing seems to be an integral part of all successful realization efforts. This usually is the most resource-intensive part of the change effort. For control purposes, all critical assumptions and expectations about the selected course of actions must be explicitly recorded and continuously monitored.

REALIZATION: SUCCESSIVE APPROXIMATION

Identify constraints which prevent achievement of the ideal design:

Behavioral	**Type I**	**Type II**	**Type III**
rational • measurement & reward system • those responsible for change benefit from existing order emotional • fear of unknown/uncertainty • mistrust/lack of cooperation • apathy (hopelessness) cultural • self-imposed constraint (default value)	Constraints that cannot be removed under existing conditions	Constraints whose removal requires extensive preparation	Constraints that can be removed now if the designers so desire
Functional technical • inadequate know-how product • deficiency in product mix market • limited market access operations • critical process not under control leadership • insufficient influence with critical actors **Structural** legal • legal constraints components • missing critical components	Create successive approximations of the ideal design, producing a constrained design which improvises for the elements of the ideal design that could not be realized.	Identify preparatory activities which will remove the constraints to achieving the "constrained" design.	Identify all of the immediate decisions and changes to the existing system so the realization process can start.

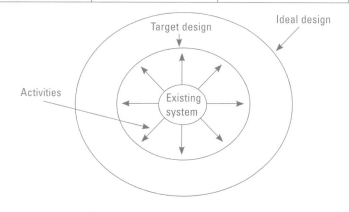

Type III Constraints

Type III deals essentially with behavioral constraints. These are the constraints that can be removed if designers so desire. Selling the idea, removing resistance to change, ensuring acceptance, cultivating support, and providing training are among the efforts targeted at constraints that are basically self-imposed. These constraints, taken together, act as the cultural default of the organization, and their function is to reinforce the status quo. Without a prior foundation of trust and commitment, the system would simply refuse to undergo the planned transformation irreversibly. And in this context, removal of the "second-order machine" is the most critical phase of realizing the idealized design.

Dissolving the Second-Order Machine

Dissolution of the second-order machine consists of two separate yet interrelated processes of self-discovery and self-improvement. They involve, first, identifying what is relevant and supportive to our *shared vision of a desirable future* and, second, diagnosing what turns out to be part of the "*mess*" and therefore obstructive to our renewal and progress.

Accordingly, successful cultural transformation will involve 1) making the underlying assumptions about corporate life explicit through public discourse and dialogue, and 2) gaining, after critical examination, a shared understanding of what can happen when defaults that are outmoded, misguided, and/ or downright fallacious are left unchanged. The process is a high-level social learning and unlearning. Only by the very act of discovering and interpreting our deep-seated assumptions can we see ourselves in a new way. The experience is liberating because it empowers us to reassess the purpose and the course of our lives and, through that, be able to exercise informed choice over our preferred future.

For example, in a design experience with a health-care system, I found that a dominant set of simple organizing assumptions (such as nurses report only to nurses, doctors report only to doctors, or integration is synonymous with uniformity) was at the core of the system's "mess."

A CANDID, OPEN, AND IN-DEPTH GROUP DISCUSSION OF THE RELEVANCE AND THE CONSEQUENCES OF THESE ASSUMPTIONS FOR THE BEHAVIOR OF THE HEATH-CARE SYSTEM WAS THE FIRST STEP TOWARD DISMANTLING THE SECOND-ORDER MACHINE AND IMPLEMENTING THE TARGET DESIGN.

Recap

- Idealized design is a process for operationalizing the most exciting vision of the future that the designers are capable of producing. It is the design of the next generation of their system to replace the existing order.
- Although idealizing, we are not dealing with science fiction; our ideal system is designed to be self-sustaining in the current environment. We are not forecasting the future. The ideal design will have sufficient sources of variety to learn and adapt to possible environments.
- Design of a throughput process is essentially technology driven, whereas design of organizational processes depends on paradigm in use.
- Winning is fun. But to win, one has to keep score. And the way one keeps score defines the game.
- The realization effort is not a one-time proposition. Successive approximations of the idealized state make up the evolutionary process by which the transformation effort is conducted.

CORPORATE INNOVATION AND DESIGN ‹

MICHAEL SHAMIYEH ❮

The simultaneous persistence of focus and flexibility in the management and governance of business innovation remains one of the central aspects of strategic management today.

THE DESIGN OF BUSINESS INNOVATION, IF VIEWED AS AN ONGOING PROCESS OF LEARNING AND EXPERIMENTATION, MUST BE OPEN TO EMERGENT OPPORTUNITY.

Attempts towards planning innovations in the sense of strict control and procedural foresight then become misleading and impediments. Flexibility can and must be designed into systems. In fact, it must be designed into systems in order to be achieved.

This section is concerned with the role of design and the role of planning in governing innovation projects.
Sonja Zillner illustrates how design thinking supports the generation of a common vision and understanding, and suggests how to reframe innovation planning as the management of contexts and settings that support the emergence of innovation.

Gerald Fliegel, in highlighting the differential innovativeness of larger and smaller companies, points out strategic elements to foster innovation that are more easily accessible by larger companies. Numerous examples are given as best practices, which show how the different elements of the innovation system are implemented at Siemens.

Thomas Duschlbauer suggests directing attention to corporate strengths by connecting them in the right way or using them for the building of alliances instead of setting concrete and binding targets. The existing resources are defining our desired future instead of a predicted future that determines which resources an organization desires.

Markus Miessen questions existing models of organizational participation and the need of revision, both in terms of the culture of consensus and the ethos of compromise. He identifies potentials in actors operating from outside existing networks of expertise, leaving behind circles of common proficiency attempting to overlap with other post-disciplinary realities.

The management and governance of innovation is a complex
task that cannot be addressed with short term and oversimplified
solutions. Moreover, the planning of innovation seems to be
impossible, as it provokes a paradox situation. In this article, we
are concerned about the role of design and the role of planning in
governing innovation projects. Along a case study of a large scale
innovation project, we will illustrate how design thinking supports
the generation of a common vision and understanding. Moreover,
we follow the idea of reframing innovation planning as the
management of contexts and settings that support the emergence
of innovation.

1. Introduction

Organisations and firms see themselves confronted with an increasing dynamic in the commercial dealings and international markets. An increasing rate of innovation is the cause and the consequence; remote competitors are likely to become threat to previously local businesses. Companies need to systematically identify new business opportunities and to develop, prioritize and implement new ideas for products and processes. The competitive advantage of an organisation rises and falls with its capability of innovation. Nevertheless, the majority of companies struggle with the successful realization of innovative solutions. Although the importance of innovation is common understanding, the implementation and successful realization of innovation still remains an unanswered question (Drucker, 1998).

THE MANAGEMENT AND GOVERNANCE OF INNOVATION IS A COMPLEX TASK THAT CANNOT BE ADDRESSED WITH SHORT TERM AND OVERSIMPLIFIED SOLUTIONS.

Our experience in the management and implementation of large scale and technology-based innovation projects shows that, due to their complexity, planning is necessary. At the same time, we experience that due to their uncertainty and innovativeness, it is not possible to implement the project outline in accordance to a formal specified plan. Too many things are unknown and uncertain, it is unclear what the final result will be, external influences are likely but yet unrecognized, and environmental changes need to continuously be reflected. In a nutshell, large scale innovation projects require planning, but it seems to be impossible to set up an explicit planning process.

Being struggled by those contradicting observations, our aim is to investigate the governance of innovations. In particular, we are searching for mindsets (as frames of reference and actions) beside the planning paradigm—mindsets that could provide guidance in implementing large scale innovation projects. This paper summarises the outcomes of our investigations and is structured as follows:

First, we will argue that the *planning of innovation is a paradox phenomenon:* Innovation—and here we are concerned about discontinuous and non-incremental innovation—create something new and unknown. If we define planning as the formalized procedure to produce articulated results (Mintzberg, 1994), it becomes obvious that any act of planning requires a clear target. Thus, innovation that is planned is either no innovation or the plan is not implemented as formalized procedure.

Secondly, we are interested in mindsets and approaches that are different or complementary to planning and provide support in handling the complex setting of large scale innovation projects. We identified *Design Thinking* as promising approach.

DESIGN THINKING IS CENTRED ON THE EMERGENCE AND CREATION OF NEW THINGS, THE CREATION OF A DESIRABLE FUTURE, AND THE BACKTRACKING TO THE PRESENT FROM KNOWLEDGE DERIVED FROM FUTURE SCENARIOS.

Thirdly, we will discuss a *practical case*: The MEDICO project is a large scale innovation project that aims for the next generation of medical image search engine. We will discuss the *role of design and the role of planning* in implementing the MEDICO project: Valuable input was derived from the design method "Pictures of the Future" that helps to identify technologies with major growth potential, to recognize technology break-throughs, and to anticipate future customer needs and new business opportunities. By generating illustrative future scenarios that could be related to concrete technology challenges, the method helped to describe an attractive project vision. Its convincing vision made the decision for MEDICO straightforward and helps in the ongoing process of implementing the project to continuously keep an eye on the big picture. Innovations cannot be planned, but usually pretend to follow a specified plan. Beside the very basic structuring and controlling tasks, a project plan provides the basis for establishing and governing settings and situations that should make the emergence of innovation more likely.

2. The Paradox of Innovation Planning

As we already mentioned, the term innovation in general is used for any kind of new product and process development. Being concerned about the question whether innovations should be design or planned, it is helpful to distinguish two different types of innovations:

The first type of innovation deals with the incremental development of new and improved products or services. It is the most frequent type of innovation activity and usually lies in the responsibility of the R&D departments (Deschamp, 2008). Incremental product and process improvements are aiming to make better products that can be produced in a more efficient manner.

THE OBJECTIVE IS TO IMPROVE THE EXISTING STATUS-QUO BY DEFINING GOALS THAT DESCRIBE THE EXPECTED PERFORMANCE GAP OR POTENTIAL FOR IMPROVEMENT.

By using benchmarks that relate to the capabilities of existing technologies, quantified goals can be defined. For instance, a project for the development of new magnet resonance technology might define the ambitious goal to create the next generation of MRI scanner that make examinations in less than 15 minutes with a resolution of less than 1 mm possible. For achieving such improvement, structured approaches that allow carrying out all tasks according to precisely conceived plans are necessary (Eberl and Puma, 2007: 263). There exists a variety of innovation methods, such as the Qualified Function Deployment Method or TRIZ, that provide valuable support in achieving the ambitious goals in a systematic way. If the goal of the innovation or improvement effort is clearly stated, then planning helps to elaborate and operationalize the goal and its consequences.

Secondly, there are non-incremental or discontinuous innovations. Those innovations often are the foundation for a company's ongoing renewal and growth. They do not fit into the current structure and product portfolio of the company,

their purpose is to bring a different value proposition to the market (O'Connor, Leifer, Paulson, and Peters, 2008). Discontinuous innovations are less frequently envisioned in the company's innovation strategy (Deschamp, 2008). And in cases they are addressed within the company's strategy, the activities are usually labelled as visionary and there is only a long-term expectation in terms of return of investment.

In this article, we are concerned about the governance of the second type of innovations. What are the driving forces behind the success or failure of pioneering and groundbreaking innovations? The retrospective analysis of successful innovations yields a number of success factors. The list of factors is long: highly motivated inventors and scientists with an entrepreneurial attitude, innovation culture, good cooperation between marketing, production and sales, innovation leadership and strategy, good communication inside and outside the company, etc. (Eberl and Puma, 2007: 263). The variety and large number of success factors demonstrates the ambiguity of any answer.

IN OTHER WORDS, THE SUCCESS FACTORS OF ONE PROJECT CANNOT BE TAKEN AS SUCCESS CRITERIA OF A SECOND PROJECT.

But this leads us to the second questions: What are good management practices and approaches in the context of governing innovations? And, due to the paradoxical nature of discontinuous innovations: how is it possible to develop something that cannot be planned?

As planning is a quite common procedure, "plan" and "planning" are defined in various ways. We follow the definition of Mintzberg who defines planning as a formalized procedure to produce an articulated result, in form of an integrated system of decisions (Mintzberg, 1994). The role and benefit of planning is well recognized: They provide the basis for increased efficiency (Weick, 1995a: 411) and they help to translate business decisions into specific action patterns for implementation (Ansoff and Brandenburg, 1967). If we view planning as formalized process to achieve well-defined goals, then it becomes obvious that the paradigm of planning is not suitable for innovations. In other words, the planning of discontinuous innovation is a *paradox phenomenon:* Non-incremental and non-linear innovations aim to create something new and unknown in terms that we do not know where and how to find it, how much effort is required and what type of result can be expected (Ortmann, 1999). On the other side, the planning of innovation is based on the assumption that there is a clear goal to be achieved. But as soon as it becomes possible to formally specify the precise goal of any "innovation", we are no longer dealing with something that is new and unknown. Assuming we knew what we want to achieve, the envisioned result would not be innovative. Thus, planning and innovating do not fit together and the planning of innovations is neither possible nor appropriate. Taking this into account, the formalization of a process that seems overly simplified and sterile when compared to the complexity of innovations is not able to explain how this kind of approach will produce results that by definition are unforeseeable. That leads us directly to our third questions: Are there schools of thoughts that provide orientation in governing complex settings without planning them?

3. Design and Design Thinking

Design and "design thinking" is gaining recognition as an important integrative concept in management practice. Our interest is to explore the extent to which design and design thinking can address the problems and challenges in managing discontinuous innovations. Let's start with some basic definitions, usage of terms and related discussions: *Design* is often used to describe an object or an end result but it also can be seen as process or as action. Although the techniques and tools differ, their core processes aim for solving problems and discovering new opportunities.

DESIGNERS ARE USUALLY PROUD TO BREAK RULES, EASILY UNDERMINE ESTABLISHED AND ACCEPTED NORMS AND OPPOSE TO FOLLOW EXISTING SOLUTIONS AND ROUTINES.

But there exists no definition that captures THE design approach and the various professions have developed

their own appreciation of "design". Is there a common design mindset and attitude? Michlewski (Michlewski, 2008) empirically analyzed the nature of the design mindset espoused by professional designers. He approved that designer focus on future solutions where they perceive reality and culture as something pliable. Designers connect to work on emotional, rational, and aesthetic levels, and their attitude towards workable solutions is assertion-based rather than evidence-based. They act on assumptions that they need to coherently consolidate and align. Relying on a limited extent on predetermined, cumulatively created framework, designers prefer proposing novel, original forms that challenge the status quo and embrace change.

Due to their strengths in finding and solving non-routine problems, in constructing and shaping new realities, design approaches, techniques and methods are analyzed and discussed in the context of organisations, management, strategy and innovation. For instance, Farson emphasizes the importance of leadership and design joining forces (Farson, 2003). The challenge of organisations and management is to cope with today's extremely complex problems and to handle bewildering dilemmas. This requires not only to follow the present path, but to design a better future world. Liedtka (Liedtka, 2004) discusses the "wicked" nature of problem solving in the context of business strategies. Being concerned about creating new futures that are aligned with the present, strategy problems call for elements of design as well as scientific methods; the discipline of design deals with what does not exist yet, while the discipline of science deals with explaining what is. Thus, Liedtka concludes that scientists can help to discover the laws that govern today's reality, while designers can help to invent different futures.

"Design thinking" is actively discussed in the communities of managers that are interested in design and vice versa. The basic idea here is that managers start to approach business problems in a way designers approach design problems (Dunne and Martin, 2006). Boland and Collopy (Boland and Collopy, 2004a) analyze the consequences of the premise that managers should act not only as decision makers but also as designers. Their book provides a comprehensive overview of the existing approaches

and ongoing discussions in the context of designing and managing organizations. It encompasses the contribution of several authors from the field of design and management that comment on the parallels between the two domains and explore the intellectual foundation for approaching managing as design. The authors developed a conceptual framework that distinguishes between the *design and the decision attitude* (Boland and Collopy, 2004b):

- The *decision attitude* is the dominant attitude in management practice and solves problems by making rational choices among alternatives. The underling assumption is that it is easy to come up with considerable alternatives but difficult to choose among them. The decision attitude as well as the many decision making tools are suitable for clearly defined and stable situation when feasible alternatives are well-known.
- In contrast, the *design attitude* assumes that it is difficult to come up with a very good alternative but due to the outstanding quality and originality of the solution its selection becomes trivial. It strives to construct a more satisfying solution than what has been proposed. Each project is the opportunity for new inventions and a chance to go back to those assumptions that have become invisible and unnoticed. The designer aims to change an existing state of affairs into a more preferred one by not being trapped in organisational habits and routines. Within this approach, there is no predefined final goal, but a clear momentum to enhance the *variety* of alternatives and possibilities.

IN THE CONTEXT OF INNOVATION ACTIVITIES, THE DIFFERENTIATION BETWEEN DECISION AND DESIGN ATTITUDE ESTABLISHES A USEFUL MINDSET.

Assuming stable and well-defined situations, the decision attitude is not appropriate in uncertain settings such as innovations. On the other hand, the design attitude brings valuable awareness towards the governance of innovation. In particular, in situations when the tendency towards suboptimal routines and compromises due to missing

alternatives and options becomes too strong, shifting to the design attitude can be promising. However, the cognitive framing is only the first steps, concrete actions have to follow.

In this context, we are concerned about the question how to trigger design attitude within an innovation project team. How to enable the flexible shift between attitudes in accordance to the requirements of the situation? Following this argument, we have to take another question into consideration: how to support a team in effectively shifting between those different attitudes? To answer this question, we will turn to some practical observations and conclusions.

4. Case Study: MEDICO Project / Siemens AG

The MEDICO project exemplifies an ongoing innovation activity at Siemens AG. The project envisions the implementation of the next generation of medical search. Due to its inherent complexity, uncertainty and innovativeness, classical planning approaches are not appropriate for governing the project. Other approaches are needed. Thus, we need to investigate the role of design and the function of practiced planning procedures in governing the MEDICO project.

The MEDICO Project

Due to vast progress of medical image devices, clinicians today deeply rely on images for screening, diagnosis, treatment planning and follow up. However, these medical images are still indexed by keywords and can not be searched and retrieved for their content.

THE INNOVATION PROJECT MEDICO STRIVES TO IMPLEMENT INTELLIGENT MEDICAL IMAGE SEARCH BY MEANS OF MACHINE LEARNING ALGORITHMS AND SEMANTIC TECHNOLOGIES.

The vision of MEDICO is to automatically extract the meaning of the medical images and to seamlessly integrate the extracted knowledge into medical processes, such as clinical descision making. In other words, the computer and medical devices should learn to interpret images, catalogue them, find them in databases and detect similarities. By investigating similar cases of patients, clinicians can learn about the disease progress and effectiveness of treatments. Moreover, the semantic labels of medical images provide the basis to automatically provide relevant context and patient related information for the clinician, such as medical literature to the particular patient's symptoms, statistical reports summarizing the success and risk rate of a particular treatment, or a list of recommended treatments.

SIEMENS AG, AS A LEADING INTERNATIONAL HEALTHCARE PROVIDER, IS THE INITIATING AND LEADING PROJECT PARTNER OF THIS JOINT, PUBLIC-FUNDED PROJECT.

With five years of duration, and two and half years already past the project is an ongoing endeavour. The technological focus and conceptual underpinnings of the project are semantic technologies. Semantic technologies are seen as a still emerging, but promising technology with an estimated break through success in the next ten years.
But let's imagine ourselves three years in the past and posing the question: For what reasons was the MEDICO project originally initiated? Why was it convincing for the management to decide for this alternative? The answer here is: this management decision was based on the outcomes of the design method "Pictures of the Future". By establishing illustrative stories of future scenarios, the future technological requirements could be mapped to concrete and convincing project visions.

The "Picture of the Future" Design Method

For ensuring the competitive advantage of business products with long-lasting development and engineering periods, such as medical imaging devices, power plants, building technologies, and industrial automation systems, one needs to reflect the potential future scenarios in terms of changes in society, environment and technology. In close cooperation with it's operational Groups, Siemens Corporate

Technology Department have compiled and adapted a collection of foresight methods to optimize the company's R&D activities in a systematic and sustainable manner.

The result, the so-called "Picture of the Future" design method (Eberl and Puma, 2007), (Pillkahn, 2007: 460) integrates two complementary viewpoints: "Extrapolation" focuses on the known facts of the world today and "Retropolation" focuses on the unknown aspects of the world of tomorrow. The first perspective—extrapolation or road-mapping—is based on the assumption that the future will be similar to the present. It simply projects the technologies and products of today into the future. The goal here is to predict the point in time at which certain things, such as known technologies or product families, will be available or when a (market) need for them will arise.

THE STRENGTH OF THIS METHOD IS ITS RELIABLE INITIAL DATA BASIS AND THE LINEAR PREDICTION OF THE FUTURE.

This advantage makes the method at the same time blind towards possible future disruptions and susceptible to false estimation. Due to it's nature, the method fails in predicting discontinuities and so called "quantum leaps" forward. To overcome this shortcoming, a second perspective was developed, that allows to reflect the complementary information. Retropolation or scenario planning (Schwartz, 1995) involves imaginatively placing yourself some 10, 20, 30 years into the future and then to think about the present. Depending on the life cycles of the technology involved, different time-scales are recommended. For the selected time frame and a set of relevant influencing factors, such as the development of social and political structures, environmental considerations, globalization, technology trends, or customer needs, alternative future scenarios are developed. Each scenario is telling an illustrative story detailing the interaction and interplay of the different influencing factors and economic conditions. In addition, possible alternative ways of action and solution strategies are analysed. The goal is to develop decision criteria for the early diagnosis of incisive environmental changes, such as drastic changes in the market. Opposing to classical and

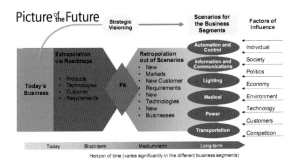

Picture of the Future

1< Siemens Picture of the Future Method (Eberl, 2004)

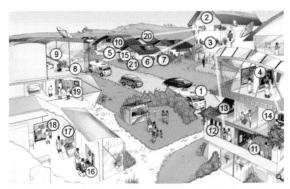

2< PoF Healthcare (http://w1.siemens.com/innovation/de/ueber_funde/ergebnisse/health.htm)

linear road-mapping methods that are restricted on the past experience and data, retropolation establishes a form of convergent thinking about divergent futures.

From Future Design to the MEDICO Vision

Innovation activities—such as the MEDICO project—need to be aligned with the company's strategic direction. The future healthcare scenarios are used to communicate and illustrate the possible envisioned future directions. The development of future scenarios starts with an initial question, for instance: "How will the application of medical imaging devices in clinical diagnose develop?"

THE INITIAL QUESTION USUALLY REFERS TO SOME FUTURE DECISION THAT WILL HAVE IMPACT ON THE SUSTAINABLE COMPETITIVENESS OF THE COMPANY.

Although many future developments, such as the megatrend "demographic change", are already known, the precise timing of the development remains an open issue. In addition to the comprehensive field research, expert and stakeholder interviews, the statistical data of the megatrends serves as important input for developing the future scenario. The demographic change, for instance, predicts an increase of the average life expectancy worldwide (from 46 years in 1959 to 72 years in 2025) and the growth of the world population (from 6 billion now to 8 billion by 2025). It highlights that 95% of the global population growth is taking place in developing countries and that the 65+ generation will nearly double worldwide by 2030. By mapping the statistical data of the megatrends to future healthcare scenario, the relevance and timing of future challenges and problems becomes transparent. All the data is used to develop comprehensive stories integrating the different variations and types of the future healthcare market, such as home-based care (i.e., medical care of patients in their own homes), new processes for diagnosis and therapy, and the vision of personalized healthcare. The different stories (indicated by the numbers in Fig. 2) have different main and minor players, different settings and requisites. The comprehensive stories allow drawing conclusions for the particular technology domain conclusions are drawn. For instance in the context of imaging methods, the following summary is provided: "This market will undergo dramatic changes in the coming years. While the focus today is on providing faster and more efficient imaging methods, future systems will be so advanced that doctors will use them to detect and analyze the various processes that are precursors to illness. Molecular imaging, for example, combines conventional imaging with special contrast media to detect signs of disease at a very early stage. Because this system's examinations are at the molecular level, it will be able to detect illnesses such as cancer years earlier than is now possible" (Siemens AG, 2004)

The established healthcare scenarios and technological conclusions were clustered into three challenging and promising technological areas: Firstly, the early detection of diseases by combining state-of-art laboratory diagnosis (in-vitro) and imaging technologies (in-vivo), secondly, outstanding quality of healthcare IT solutions, and thirdly, efficient processes in hospitals paving the way for reduced healthcare costs (Siemens AG, 2009). The three main directions and area of the company's technology vision are well communicated. Technical experts and scientists use this strategic information when aligning technologies with (future) user requirements by continuously reflecting to which extent user cases fit to the company's technology direction and future scenarios. Envisioning a universal search engine for medical images that supports individualized diagnoses and therapy plans, MEDICO addresses the first two technology directions.

THUS, IT IS SEEN AS PROMISING AND A GOOD FIT TO THE COMPANY'S VISION.

The Role of Design

As we have seen, the method "Picture of the Future" provides comprehensive material for illustrating and clarifying the project vision. The depicted future scenarios are stories that exemplify future alternatives. By backtracking to the present from knowledge derived

from the future scenarios, people can understand the big picture of the project. Images and related thoughts might come up. In a sense, this activity might have the same qualities as the process of "Sensemaking" described by Weick (1995b: 231)—an activity that basically describes the process people use to retrospectively make sense of their actions. Due to the well-communicated big picture of the project and the companies' vision, the project team is able to take responsibility for their assigned work-packages and accomplish them independently, self-responsibly and with an entrepreneurial attitude. The future scenarios underline that the status quo is not the envisioned solution and serve as invitation for the development of alternatives.

BASICALLY, THE SCENARIOS TRIGGER AND INSPIRE THE DESIGN ATTITUDE OF THE PEOPLE INVOLVED AND THE DEVELOPMENT OF VISIONARY SOLUTIONS BECOMES POSSIBLE.

38

Moreover, there is a strong focus to realize technological prototypes and demos that implement first building blocks of the project vision. Often still struggling with technical shortcomings, demonstrators—as a way of prototyping first project results—aim to communicate future stories from the "bottom-up" perspective. The main focus is to demonstrate the technological capabilities in the context of future scenarios and use cases to support the discussion with clinicians and product developers. Playing around and trying different functionalities helps both of them to develop further ideas in proceeding and detailing the story of the use case. The clinicians might provide further details about the clinical workflow, and the product manager might brainstorm how selected functionalities can be implemented in already existing products.

In a nutshell, the design method "Pictures of the Futures" helps to formulate a vision. The more convincing and illustrative the accompanying future scenarios and stories are, the easier it becomes to align the project activities with the project vision.

The Role of Planning

We follow the assumption that the planning of innovations in terms of formalized procedures yields contradicting incidents. However, we are facing the situation that innovation activities rely on some kind of "planning" that is specified as project proposal, project roadmap, project plan, etc. Knowing that the planning of innovation is paradox and therefore not possible, we are interested in the function of project plans. What are the effective functionalities of plans and the activity of planning? Here we can identify three relevant aspects and functions that are addressed by project plans, i.e. high-level structuring, controlling, and the governing of opportunities and contexts.

In joint projects, the proposal specifies the involved partners, indicates relevant interfaces between partners, and details the expected contributions. Thus, the proposal provides a first orientation and communicates the *high-level structuring* in terms of roles and contributions of each partner but at the same time keeps the situation flexible for changes.

PLANNING HELPS TO COORDINATE THE ONGOING ACTIVITIES, ENSURES THEIR COHERENCE AND HELPS TO GUARANTEE THAT EACH PROJECT MEMBER PULLS IN THE SAME DIRECTION.

For *controlling* purposes, the continuous reporting along predefined milestones is requested by the sponsors, management, and stakeholders. Plans specify what behavior and contribution is expected of particular units and individuals in order to accomplish the innovation vision by structuring project activities into tasks, milestones, and deliverables. The task definitions leave enough room for interpretation but detail the type (report, prototype, analysis, etc.) and time needed. In addition, interrelations between tasks, and thus between project partners, are specified. The project process is monitored on the basis of written reports and review meetings.

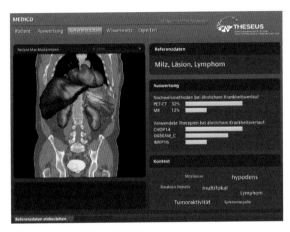

3 Screenshot of the first MEDICO Demonstrator

THE WRITTEN REPORTS PROVIDE SHORT SUMMARIES LISTING THE WORK ACCOMPLISHED AS WELL AS QUANTITATIVE DATA, SUCH AS NUMBER OF PUBLICATIONS, INVENTIONS DISCLOSURES, PATENTS, OR CONFERENCE VISITS.

Such key figures help to evaluate the success of the project in terms of predefined expectations, but do not measure the success of the innovation itself which is determined by its market response and is unknown when the innovation is still under development. If the project controlling gets too strong, there is the danger that the project member put too much focus on the analytic and quantitative guidelines and loose track of the future vision and scenarios. However, we view the regular control as important and required steps for aligning the project activities with the project vision and vice versa. The written reports force each single partner to retrospectively position the accomplished project activities and contributions in relation to the envisioned scenarios. In addition, the regular review meetings bring the team together and "force" them to think about the joint story in terms of the complementary interplay of single components in accordance with the overall project vision. This process is accomplished in iterations. The intermediate results are related to the big picture of the project, and, thus, make the re-usage, enhancement, and complementary combination with other intermediate results more likely. This process of "bottom-up sense-making" enhances the transparency and capabilities of single project results and provides the basis for the emergence of a new technology that constitutes a "Gestalt" that is more than the sum of its single components.

In summary, the project plan establishes a flow of meetings, interfaces, individual and joint reflection times, as well as unrestricted exploration time. By establishing *settings* and *contexts* that make the emergence of innovation more likely, the project proposal supports and guides the communication and collaboration patterns. The aim here is to enable a constant flow of iterations between the present and the future focus, in other words: between

project vision and project achievements. The individual work gets inspired by joint discussion or by concurrent ideas in collaborative work sessions, and provides further input for the next group meeting. Because of their spontaneous nature, the content of those initiatives cannot be planned beforehand. But due to the structured process they are able to guide and give direction for the research activities of the project team on the basis of the future scenarios. In the end, the regular reporting and reflection in terms of project progress helps to iterate between project vision and project achievements.

Conclusion

As we have seen, innovations cannot be planned but contexts can be established that make the emergence and development of innovations more likely. In any case structuring and controlling of innovations is required. But if the planning process takes control over the flow of ideas and inspirations within the project work, any leeway or slack allowing new combinations of routine will disappear. In the end, planning eliminates any notion of improvisation and variation—both important ingredients for fostering discontinuous innovation (Weick, 1995a: 411).

INSTEAD OF PUTTING TOO MUCH ATTENTION TOWARDS A FORMAL PLANNING PROCESS, WE RECOMMEND ESTABLISHING A "CONTAINER" IN ORDER TO GOVERN INNOVATION.

The containment of innovating activities (in terms of managing contexts and settings that support and convey the emergence of new ideas) is one of the most critical success factors in breakthrough innovations and thus should be integrated into any managerial approach for these kinds of projects. Design attitude helps to generate a common understanding of the future vision that support people to think and act in alternative options. Here innovation often follows the same logic as improvisation—as every good musician or actor knows, improvisation cannot be planned, but need a structured framework in order to happen.

References

Ansoff, H. I., and Brandenburg, R. C. 1967. A program of research in business planning. Management Science, 13(6). (http://www.jstor.org/stable/2627702).

Boland, R., and Collopy, F. 2004. Managing as designing. Stanford, Calif: Stanford Business Books.

Boland, R. and Collopy, F. 2004. Design matters for management. In R. Boland and F. Collopy, Managing as designing. Stanford, Calif: Stanford Business Books.

Deschamp, J. 2008. Innovation leaders—how senior executives stimulate, steer and sustain innovation: XXII, 433. Chichester: Wiley.

Drucker, P. F. 1998. The discipline of innovation (HBR Classic). Harvard Business Review.

Dunne, D. and Martin, R. 2006. Design thinking and how it will change management education: An interview and discussion. Academy of Management Learning and Education, 5(4): 512–523.

Eberl, U. and Puma, J. 2007. Innovatoren und Innovationen—Einblicke in die Ideenwerkstatt eines Weltkonzerns: 263. Erlangen: Publicis Corp. Publ.

Farson, R. 2003. Management by design. Design Intelligence.

Liedtka, J. 2004. Design thinking: The role of hypotheses generation and testing. In R. Boland and F. Collopy, Managing as designing. Stanford: Stanford Business Books.

Michlewski, K. 2008. Uncovering design attitude: Inside the culture of designers. Organisation Studies, 29(373).

Mintzberg, H. 1994. The rise and fall of strategic planning—reconceiving roles for planning, plans, planners: XIX, 458. New York: Free Press.

O'Connor, G. C., Leifer, R., Paulson, A. S., and Peters, L. S. 2008. Grabbing Lightning: Building a capability for breakthrough innovation. San Francisco, Calif: Jossey-Bass.

Ortmann, G. 1999. Innovation als Paradoxieentfaltung. In D. Sauer and C. Lang, Paradoxien der Innovation. München: Campus-Verlag.

Pillkahn, U. 2007. Trends und Szenarien als Werkzeuge zur Strategieentwicklung – wie Sie die unternehmerische und gesellschaftliche Zukunft planen und gestalten. Siemens: 460. Erlangen: Publicis Corp. Publ.

Schwartz, P. 1995. The art of the long view—paths to strategic insight for yourself and your company: XVI, 272. New York: Currency Doubleday.

Siemens AG, C. C. 2004. Pictures of the future healthcare. (http://w1.siemens.com/innovation/de/ueber_funde/ergebnisse/health.htm).

Siemens AG, C. C. 2009. Innovation@Siemens 2009.

Weick, K. E. 1995a. Der Prozess des Organisierens. Suhrkamp-Taschenbuch Wissenschaft, 1. Ed., Vol. 1194: 411. Frankfurt am Main: Suhrkamp.

Weick, K. E. 1995b. Sensemaking in organizations. Foundations for organizational science, 2. [pr.]: 231. Thousand Oaks: Sage.

393

Often larger companies are said to be less innovative than their smaller competitors, and the situation really is a different and not easy one. It is shown that there are a lot of important levers for large companies they can work on to keep their competitiveness. As a prerequisite a corporate infrastructure for innovation—communication, process, tools and strategy—must be established, and an innovation friendly corporate culture has to be built on it to motivate people to generate enough ideas. As an advantage for large companies there are strategic elements to foster innovation which are more easily accessible for larger companies than smaller ones. A lot of examples are given as best practices which show how the different elements of the innovation system are implemented at Siemens.

Innovation nowadays is considered to be a key factor for business success. In particular this is valid for technology driven companies, regardless of the size of the company. Many small and young ones, often venture capital financed start-ups, only live on their excellence in innovation and the trust of their investors to keep this status. But also large companies, if they want to stay successful enduringly, have to be a leader in innovation in its fields of business, though they often have to cope with a corporate environment adverse to innovation: a highly structured organization, complex corporate processes and many decision levels. This article intends to give an answer how large companies can meet innovation requirements despite these difficult circumstances.

MANY GENERAL STATEMENTS WILL BE GIVEN BASED ON THE EXPERIENCE OF THE AUTHOR OF MORE THAN 10 YEARS IN CORPORATE INNOVATION MANAGEMENT.

These statements will be illustrated by examples from within Siemens, but many statements will reflect the situation of other larger companies too. This knowledge results from external benchmarkings, discussions with R&D and innovation leaders of other companies and the exchange of experiences in conferences on innovation management. There will be no comprehensive answers on the question how a complete innovation process could be designed successfully in large companies. The article will focus clearly on the first phases of the process, the front end part, where creativity and a high voluntary engagement of employees are playing a major role: The first chapter gives an overview on the innovation hurdles for large companies and shows in a lot of examples how a technology driven company like Siemens is anchoring innovation in its corporate values, its strategy and processes. The second chapter focuses on the topic of the implementation of a corporate innovation system and how employees can become part of it. The final chapter gives general recommendations on how large companies can meet the innovation requirements.

Innovation as an Important Part of Corporate Strategy

What makes innovation so difficult for larger companies? In most large companies there are clear descriptions and models for all important corporate processes, and innovation will be no exception. But there are three characteristics of the innovation process which distinguish it strongly from other ones and make it so difficult to implement it successfully:

Creativity. Each innovation needs, to make it different from existing solutions, a creative act as a starting point. But creativity often lacks space in large companies because it is, as a process parameter, difficult to control and its output, efficiency and effectiveness are difficult to measure. So this first step in the innovation process, where creative freedom is essential, often is not developed very well or even avoided, although it is by far the cheapest part of the process. The later stages, when the importance of creativity decreases and a more structured procedure is required, when more money has to be invested to develop a marketable product, are usually implemented better (see Fig. 1).

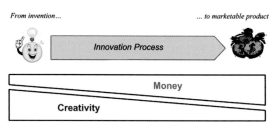

1◖ A generic innovation process

Complexity. As the innovation process covers all steps from generating first ideas for new business to successful commercializing, it is probably the most complex of all corporate processes. It involves or at least has interfaces to many functions within a company, like Research and Development, Marketing, Sales, Human Resources, Logistics, etc. For larger companies this means not only the involvement of many people, but also the involvement of many corporate departments, each with its own tasks, objectives and interests. Furthermore, the innovation process has special attributes which normally are not welcome in a structured and process oriented environment: It is future oriented, based on assumptions and often long-lasting without short-termed results.

Emotions. As mentioned before, involvement of—the right—people is crucial for an innovation idea to become real business. You need people to have the ideas, you need people to market these ideas internally, you need at least one sponsor in upper management—and you will always meet people who doubt the potential. So, you have to cope with emotions as part of the innovation process, and this makes handling and controlling of this process so difficult.

How can Innovation be Incorporated by Larger Companies?

In the following chapter, the examples given are taken from publications of Siemens AG, Berlin and Munich.

Communication. To really show that innovation is a main part of the corporate strategy, the topic has to play an important role in all internal and external publications and presentations. Siemens underlines its commitment to innovation by a direct link from its global homepage (http://www.siemens.com) to "Innovations", where a lot of information is given about actual innovation highlights from the Siemens sectors, there are links to innovation-related publications, some figures about R&D resources and so on. In the same way the topic innovation should also be frequently mentioned in internal presentations. All this intends to establish a clear connection between innovation and the company's corporate identity—externally as well as internally. It is important that a consistent picture is given in all publications—and innovation must be a part of it.

THE SAME COMPANY PRESENTATION AS MENTIONED ABOVE ENDS WITH A SLIDE SHOWING "*OUR VISION AND OUR VALUES*".

Siemens again documents the outstanding importance of innovation: "Being innovative to create sustainable value" is one of only three corporate values (beside being responsible and being excellent). To create sustainable economic value for the company, innovation has to create a unique value and competitive advantages for the customers. Therefore it must become a part of business planning within a company, and methods have to be implemented to make innovation "not happen by chance", but repeat it systematically.

Innovation Framework. Siemens has developed a whole innovation framework for internal use with different elements to keep its position as a technological leader in its fields of business. Elements within this framework are:

- In-depth knowledge of its customers' businesses and processes: As only the business value for the customers decide long-term about the success of an innovation, you have to understand the business model of the customer to provide the right solution.
- A strong strategic oriented patent portfolio: While a large patent portfolio is a positive indicator for leading edge Research and Development activities, it is a cost factor too. By aligning the business strategy to the patent strategy, the optimal patent portfolio in terms of protection and costs can be found.
- A worldwide partnership with leading experts and international cooperation with research institutes: Companies need access to the latest technological findings in basic and applied research and therefore Siemens cares for a global scientific network with more than 1000 partners.
- Optimized innovation processes which are challenged regularly by a special innovation benchmarking: The so called "Innovation radar" as a result of a benchmarking projects determines how well developed the skills of an organizational unit are for successfully implementing the innovation strategy.
- R&D presence in leading markets: It is a clear strategic goal of Siemens to take advantage of its global presence and to establish R&D hubs near to the customers. R&D as part of a local supply chain will help to better design customers' solutions.

Defined processes with clear goals behind these elements give the innovation framework a strong strategic position among the organization of the company.

Corporate Strategy. An important tool to support this strategic innovation planning was developed by Strategic Marketing of the central technology department of Siemens, Corporate Technology. The goal of this tool is to provide a consistent vision of the technological future for a specific business field by extrapolating from today's business and technological status on one side and "retropolating" from a long-term view on the other side, taking technological as well as socio-economical trends into account (see Figure 1 Zillner, p. 392).

The result of this approach is where the extrapolated and the retropolated perspectives meet. This point, called Picture of the Future, is expected to be the most likely scenario and gives the starting point for quantifying future markets, identifying upcoming technologies or predicting customer requirements.

Motivation of Innovative People

A question of culture

The main elements of an innovation system in a company are organization, strategy and culture (see Figure 2), whereas large companies often prefer to cope with organization and strategy. These latter components of the corporate innovation system are based on formal relationships, clear interfaces, defined processes and methodologies and therefore can be handled more easily in a well-structured environment.

FOR EXAMPLE, KEY PERFORMANCE INDICATORS TO JUDGE THE EFFECTIVENESS OR EFFICIENCY OF AN ORGANIZATION CAN BE GIVEN, AND THERE ARE WAYS TO MEASURE THE DEGREE OF IMPLEMENTATION WHEN A NEW ORGANIZATION OR AN IMPROVED STRATEGY PROCESS IS TO BE INTRODUCED.

2⟨ Three crucial elements for a successful innovation system

On the other hand, corporate culture is much more difficult to cope with: It is very much based on the behavior of individuals, it cannot be ordered via guidelines or working instructions and any change in the culture needs a long time to come into effect—if at all.
Corporate culture strongly influences the attitude of people towards the company and their willingness to make their creativity, experience and implicit knowledge available to the corporate innovation system.

THUS IT IS CRUCIAL, ESPECIALLY FOR THE FIRST PHASES OF THE INNOVATION SYSTEM, TO ESTABLISH A SUPPORTING CORPORATE CULTURE.

Probably the most supporting attitude for an innovation friendly culture is that of being failure-tolerant. That is often difficult to promote and to understand in an environment where "Zero Defect" or similar concepts are part of a corporate strategy. But for innovation it is absolute essential to understand that failures are part of the process and necessary for a creative start and a continuous improvement. Not to hide errors allows them to be detected early before becoming expensive or even critical. An honest analysis of the reasons for failures, which must be compulsory, enables to progress towards a learning organization where the same failures do not happen repeatedly because the system is continuously improving. A supporting innovation culture accepts or even stipulates failures to encourage innovative approaches in an organization.

VIP Concept of Siemens Austria

Design of the Concept. With the introduction of the VIP concept in 2004, Siemens Austria made an important contribution to build on an innovation-friendly culture. The starting point when designing the concept were three independent processes which all dealt with ideas submitted by employees: An innovation process for new businesses, one for suggestions of improvement for existing products and internal processes, and a patent process. Though these processes were quite different regarding the kind

of ideas, the incentives for the submitters, the objectives and the success criteria, the source was always the same: An employee, having an idea which he thinks can produce a value add to the company. So the employees, as the common and connecting element of the processes, were the target for establishing the brand for the new initiative: VIP. VIP in this context is an abbreviation used in an ambiguous way: it stands for the initial letter of the focus of the three processes in German: Verbesserungen (*engl.*: improvements), Innovations, Patents, but it also means the common Very Important Person. The basic idea of the concept now was that every employee can gather so-called VIP-points by submitting a successful idea in one of the processes. The amount of VIP points given for an idea depends on the evaluation of the economic potential of the idea. If an employee gathers more than 100 points with his ideas within twelve months he becomes a VIP for one fiscal year, officially and personally nominated by the board of directors during a specific VIP event. Beside the reputation of being awarded a VIP, including a certificate and an intranet promotion film about the VIP event, there were some additional advantages of being a VIP:

- An individual present, the value of which was depending on the sum of VIP points gathered.
- The preference for minor internal incentives.
- A birthday present which was delivered directly to the office desk of the VIP on his/her birthday; this should remind and motivate the colleagues that they could become a VIP too by submitting good ideas.

Starting and Promoting the Initiative. An important step before starting any initiative to change or at least influence the corporate culture is to ensure the absolute commitment of the board of directors. In the best case the board not only stands without reservation behind the campaign but starts and pushes it itself.
The whole concept was developed together with the Corporate Communication department so that all activities for the promotion of the initiative were in line with other measures of internal communication.
Any change within the corporate culture of a large company has to be broadly communicated to reach all employees. So during the first year there was a lot of advertising to

make the VIP brand really known all over the company which meant for several thousand people: There was "Cool ice for hot ideas", a VIP welcome doormat for the main sites, posters, peanuts as brain food, VIP napkins and tray covers in the canteens, and so on. All employees should be familiar with the VIP initiative and its message behind, namely: Everybody has the potential for an idea to make the company more competitive! This is valid regardless of the function or value somebody has within the company. A value add can be generated with a suggestion of improvement for an internal procedure which has to be followed, by passing on new requirements for a product after a customer's visit, or by submitting an invention disclosure which could be the first step to file a patent.

IN PARALLEL AN APPROPRIATE ELECTRONIC INFRASTRUCTURE, USING THE NEARLY OMNIPRESENT INTRANET ACCESS, WAS BUILT UP TO GIVE EVERYBODY THE OPPORTUNITY TO SUBMIT AN IDEA.

All information showed at the end a link to the central VIP homepage in the intranet, and a direct link from the Siemens Austria intranet homepage was introduced. On the VIP homepage an idea could be submitted via forms for one of the three specific processes, or an unstructured email with an idea could be sent to a team which then decided to which process the idea fits best.

Generating a Steady "Dealflow"

Many studies exist which give an impression how many ideas are necessary to get one real breakthrough innovation (Stevens and Burley). Regardless of the different figures in detail there is one common clear message for all the studies: A lot of ideas is needed at the beginning of an innovation process for one commercially successful new business. The reason for that is the complexity of the innovation process: A real market success depends on so many parameters, which cannot—and should not—all be taken into account when generating new ideas. In this early phase there should be no restriction, no discussion, no objection because this would degrade creativity.

Furthermore, the more innovative an idea the more difficult it is to evaluate it correctly because there is no experience regarding technology, customer requirements or market potential. So you have to give many ideas and concepts a chance and decrease the number step-by-step when more and more knowledge is gathered and an evaluation becomes more reliable. Although there will still be enough cases where the business plan was simply misjudged up to the end.

THIS IS WHY A STEADY DEAL FLOW IS REQUIRED.

In the next step, after setting up a very open and creative front end for the innovation process, it is important to make it very transparent in respect to evaluation criteria and success rate. No unrealistic expectations regarding the hit rate may be produced, neither for the employees submitting ideas nor for the management awaiting successful new businesses. A very important message always was, referring to Linus Pauling who is said to be the origin of the sentence: *"The best way to have a good idea is to have a lot of ideas".*

As you have to skip far more than 90% of the ideas at the end, which is very frustrating for the employees, the following points have to be taken into account if you want to keep up a steady dealflow into your innovation process:

- It is not possible to get only the few successful ideas. The innovation process has to be open for all ideas, as this is part of an innovation-friendly corporate culture and a prerequisite to find real new business opportunities by means of an innovation process.
- The implementation of a highly efficient evaluation procedure is crucial. It must be fast to give the submitter of the idea a feedback in an appropriate time, and it must be honest. If the idea is refused, the decision has to be communicated clearly, and the reasons should be disclosed. This is of interest for the submitter to learn which ideas are assumed to have the potential to be followed up and which not. And, even more importantly, this is the minimum of appreciation which can be given to an employee whose idea is declined to keep up his/her motivation.

- Concentrate your resources on the most valuable ideas. The implementation of an innovation idea can be extremely expensive and resources normally are very limited. So it is crucial to allocate your resources to the most promising opportunities. Though it is sometimes difficult to decide about the potential in an early stage of an idea due to many imponderabilities, this decision has to be done fast and resolutely. But also in positive cases it is essential that later, when the knowledge about the potential future business impact is increasing steadily during realization, this first rating of an idea is questioned from time to time. It is not easy but essential that is it possible to stop implementation of an idea also in later stages of the process when probably a lot of money was already invested. It must be said at this point that, based on the author's personal experience, the rate of cancelled innovation projects can be a very meaningful indicator of the quality of a company's innovation process.

What Drives People to be Innovative?

As already discussed earlier an appropriate corporate culture is a prerequisite for an efficient innovation process. Employees must have the feeling that all ideas are welcome and that innovation has a very high management attention. To keep the dealflow of innovation ideas on a high level, additional measures have to be taken to directly motivate people to contribute and support innovation ideas.

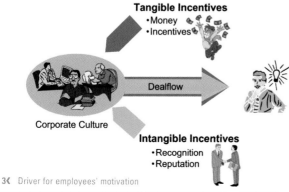

3⟨ Driver for employees' motivation

40

Tangible Incentive Systems. There are contradictory statements on the impact of a monetary bonus system on the quantity and quality of submitted ideas. At Siemens for example there is a long tradition of getting a bonus for an idea if it is not within the own area of responsibility and an economic benefit for the company can be identified. It is argued that submitting an idea is an act of creativity and an additional personal effort outside the work assignment of an individual and therefore a kind of incentive as also given to the management for high performance. Of course the bonus has to correlate directly with the generated profit or the productivity increase for the company so that a bonus can be seen like an employees' participation in the additional profit a company gets by successfully realizing ideas.
If top management really believes in long-term positive impact of internally generated innovation ideas it can be helpful to define corporate wide top-down goals for the innovation system. Derived from these quantitative and partly qualitative objectives a clear set of targets can be defined department wise as part of a management incentive system. Typical targets can be the participation rate, the number of submitted or implemented ideas, generated economic benefit etc.

BY SETTING THESE TARGETS ASIDE OF TYPICAL PERFORMANCE GOALS LIKE SALE- AND EBIT-FIGURES, THE TOP MANAGEMENT UNDERLINES THE IMPORTANCE OF AN EFFICIENT INNOVATION SYSTEM AND SUPPORTS THE ESTABLISHMENT OF AN INNOVATION CULTURE TOP-DOWN.

In context with the VIP concept of Siemens Austria, there were tangible as well as intangible incentives, and the experience with this kind of incentive system was a very good one. In addition innovation competitions were conducted on special topics which were identified to have a high demand on new products or solutions. Though the prizes were mere tangible ones (laptops, journeys, vouchers, etc) the experience with this focused way to generate ideas was a very positive one, and often a very high number of ideas was submitted. So probably an idea competition, though only presenting very tangible prizes, has a highly motivating intangible component additionally.

Intangible Incentive Systems. Without doubt intangible assets have a very high effect on motivation when it comes to fostering creativity in a large company bottom-up and gathering ideas from employees. Broad internal communication about the importance of innovation for the success of the company as the base for any further measure to establish an intangible asset system was already discussed in the previous chapter. Everyone in the company should know that there is top management attention on innovation and an internal contribution via employees' ideas is highly appreciated.
Internal reputation as positive differentiation to others is a great motivator. Therefore people who have contributed with their ideas to a successfully realized innovation with a positive impact on the company's profit should be honored personally by the executive board and made visible within the company.

INTERNALLY PUBLISHED SUCCESS STORIES HELP TO INCREASE THE REPUTATION OF THESE "CORPORATE INNOVATORS" AND HELP OTHERS TO LEARN HOW THEY CAN BECOME JUST AS SUCCESSFUL WITH THEIR IDEAS.

Looking at examples within Siemens it can be noted that Siemens pays high attention to the personal reputation of their bright minds. For example every year about 10 "Inventors of the Year" are awarded for their extraordinary scientific work which is expressed in a high number of valuable invention disclosures and patents. And in 2007 Siemens even published a book with the story of 30 inventions and the people behind them: The book (Eberl and Puma, 2007) *"…looks behind the scenes and introduces some of the people who are helping Siemens to continue its tradition of successful innovations".* People want to feel appreciated for their voluntarily submitted ideas—finding themselves as protagonist in a book they surely do. Siemens Austria expresses the high attention it pays to innovative people with the very brand of the VIP initiative

itself. Beyond that it uses the whole bandwidth of corporate communication tools to give the innovators the credit for their creativity and engagement: VIP's names and pictures are published internally, they get a picture while handshaking with the CEO, success stories are published, etc.

Strategic Levers for a Corporate Innovation System

As shown in the statements above and documented by examples from within Siemens, large companies have possibilities to meet the innovation requirements if they decide to announce innovation a top-ranking corporate value and align organization, strategy and culture to this value. It will need a steady effort and a steady renewal of the commitment to innovation to stay in an innovation-friendly state and not to be overcome by too much structure and bureaucracy.

THERE ARE ADDITIONAL STRATEGIC LEVERS FOR INNOVATION WHICH LARGE COMPANIES CAN APPLY EVEN MORE EASILY THAN THEIR SMALLER COMPETITORS.

Hire the Right People. Especially for the research and development department, where inventors and innovators usually come from, the first, but very important step is to hire the right people—to hire innovators. Though there is no guarantee that during a recruiting process potential innovators can be identified without a doubt, it could be part of a Human Resource strategy to explicitly look for characteristics of people who tend to be innovative. Another way to find the right young people which is done by large companies is to sponsor student programs on universities and finance diploma theses and dissertations regularly to stay in close contact with potential new employees and get to know them over some months of collaboration. This gives more information about people's traits to identify those who fit best to the company's expectation.

Diversity. As shown before, innovation means among other things that you have to have a lot of different ideas and that you must be prepared for problems you did not anticipate in advance. Both requirements—many good ideas and finding the best solution—are met the best way by diverse thinking—done by a diverse team, which is usually more creative by higher flexibility and a broader base of approaches.

Diversity can become an important element to foster innovation and can be another advantage for the innovation system of a large company with hundreds and thousands of employees as it is more easily to realize than in small ones. In the context of corporate teams diversity means different gender, nationality, cultural background, and in this context also diversified age and professional skills. Though very homogenous groups are smoother to lead from a mere management point of view, the internal discussion and an exchange of different opinions can cross-fertilize team members to generate optimized solutions. So if you succeed in providing a culture where diversity is seen as high value you can take the advantage off, diversity can make the essential difference and should be preferred as attribute of the organizational setup of an innovation driven corporate environment.

ANOTHER POSITIVE THING ABOUT DIVERSITY IS THAT IT MAKES A COMPANY AN ATTRACTIVE EMPLOYER.

In times of a global war for talents no company can afford to miss out on the best and brightest people, and diversity can have the positive side-effect that it additionally attracts creative people if clearly communicated as a corporate value.

Ideas Outside Business Focus. Creativity plays a major role at the front end of the innovation process and should be systematically unleashed. This sometimes leads to promising ideas which lie outside the company's core business and offer no other strategic advantage. Normally, especially in small companies, where there is no clear strategy how to deal with these ideas, they are suffocated. But there are also ways to exploit innovation ideas outside the existing business focus if they offer an attractive business. For example they can be spun off as a new separated business, sold completely or licensed out.

Larger companies have the advantage that they can provide resources to support this innovation strategy. Thus no innovative development with high business potential will be wasted regardless of whether it is within the company's core business areas or not. For example Siemens has, aside from all its innovation departments in the business units, set up the Siemens Technology Accelerator (STA). This subsidiary has the goal to market inventions which, though often patented, cannot be turned into products within Siemens by an external start-up. STA refines the business model, supports to find external investors and keeps a minority share in the start-up until an IPO is possible or the business can be sold completely to an external partner.

Open Innovation. During the last years open innovation not only has a trend started in the innovation community worldwide but is also a major paradigm shift in the mindset of corporate innovation departments. While the former "The lab is my world"—mentality assumes that any innovation ideas should be kept as secret as possible so that it cannot be stolen, the new "The world is my lab" approach is based on the convictions that an innovation network, which includes external resources like research partners, suppliers and customers can offer a value add. As these external parties represent different stages of the supply chain, a company gets much additional input directly from the market for its innovation process. Therefore a wrong evaluation of an innovation regarding its chances to be commercialized successfully becomes more unlikely and a shorter time-to-market, higher flexibility on changes in the market and an improved hit-rate for innovations are expected.

THOUGH NORMALLY USED FOR A NETWORK EXCEEDING THE COMPANY'S BOUNDARIES, THE SIMILAR CONCEPT IS APPLIED INTERNALLY WITHIN SIEMENS.

The goal is to link the experts of different sectors or divisions to share their knowledge on application fields of interest—though working in different organizational units all over the world. So recently a new, highly interactive Web 2.0 platform was started to create an open expert network to globally link technology workers. Additionally

first so-called innovation jams were experienced, which are web-based, expert-moderated discussion forums to share knowledge in a cross-sector community.
Open innovation is a comparatively young trend in innovation, and there still are some questions and critics out there—in any case issues to be observed. But in a global world, linked closely by high-speed multimedia communication, open innovation can bring a completely new pattern and culture to corporate innovation management systems. It leverages internal innovation processes by integrating external input.

AND MORE AND MORE LARGE COMPANIES HAVE STARTED TO WORK WITH OPEN INNOVATION, AT LEAST AS AN ADDITIONAL APPROACH TO THE CONVENTIONAL ONE.

Conclusion

Large companies depend on the success of their innovations as much as smaller ones do. Based on an appropriate corporate culture, the difference is clearly shown in the way the components of the innovation system are implemented: the large companies have to explicitly define all these elements via guidelines, process descriptions, etc, while the smaller ones do many of these things implicitly, driven by a common innovation spirit. Depending on the specific situation a company is in (product portfolio, market, competitive situation, consumer or infrastructure business), at the end each company must find its own way to be and stay an innovation leader: Different tools, different levers, different strategy and a different culture will form the company's own, specific approach to innovation. Surely the size of the company influences the way the innovation system has to be set up strongly, offering both disadvantages and advantages. But with a clear commitment, including the willingness to permanently work on the innovation capabilities, large companies can succeed to meet the innovation requirements.

References:

Eberl, U. and Puma, J. 2007. Innovative minds: A look inside siemens' idea machine. Erlangen: Publicis Corporate Publishing.

Siemens 2010. (http://w1.siemens.com/press/pool/de/ homepage/the_company_2010.pdf, accessed December 2009).

Stevens, G. and Burley J. 3,00 Raw Ideas = 1 Commercial Success, Research Technology Management, 40 (3): 16–27.

THOMAS DUSCHLBAUER ❮ From Dogma to Style
On Wittgenstein and Redesign

The digital camera was not invented at Kodak due to the fact that one did some optimization or redesign on the already existing analogue camera but because Steven J. Sasson was a tinkerer, who dreamt of a pocket calculator with a lens. In an Interview with the *Süddeutsche Zeitung* he said that he invented the camera without a plan—just according to the following assumptions: It should be a portable device but without a reel and it should be able to record pictures but without a film. Sasson wanted to see an image but on a screen like in television. (Winkler 2008)

Although there have been no clear targets, no masterplan etc. one of the most revolutionary inventions of the second half of the 20th Century was born. One may say that this could have been achieved by pure accident—but we know that at the beginning there was a vision. And in this interview for the *Süddeutsche Zeitung*, Sasson said that the digital camera was invented while it was developed and the main reasons why he was able to do that were the possibility to ask colleagues or experts from different disciplines and that there were plenty of components at hand. Therefore, Kodak had nearly no investment concerning this innovation because everything was already there. The first camera without any moveable part was at its beginning a low budget project.

This example shows that not everything that can become successful must be in accordance to a plan or to a causal chain of actions. It also demonstrates that we have to put in question common approaches on organizational theory which are based on a mechanistic or Newtonian view—just as Mr. Sasson did with his camera.

IT IS TIME TO GIVE UP THE OPTIMIZATION OF THIS KIND OF PRACTICE BECAUSE ITS OBJECTIVE IS NOT ABLE TO HANDLE THE IMMENSE VOLUME OF INFORMATION AND ITS COMPLEXITY ANY MORE.

The Kodak example also makes evident that it is worth just to direct the focus on the given strengths by connecting them in the right way or using them for the building of alliances—instead of setting concrete and binding targets. The existing resources are defining our desired future—instead of a predicted future that determines which resources an organization desires.

To do that we even have to challenge the notion that organizations can be described in terms of system theory or as a set of formal rules. Organizations are the place of social interaction and discursive practices that can not be framed in a universal way. This would suggest that identity means total self-conformity, but as the simple formula 1 = 1 shows, this tautological assertion earns no additional information or rather epistemological surplus although it is absolutely right (Flusser 2000: 171). The more organizations are not totally identical with themselves and the more they are open for ambivalent interpretations of themselves the more they have the ability to create additional meaning and to develop new chances. Constantly working on its own definition can be seen as a major key for innovative solutions.

This also implies that the only realistic constant of our time has to be truthfulness instead of truth which also marks the difference between a discourse of style and a dogmatic discourse. Because the dogma claims a truth without any critique on the foundations of this kind of "knowledge" and refers to something universal as well as creating clarity and unambiguousness. The dogma as a conviction determines cognition.

Style is an important part of different aesthetic conceptions and in general, style refers to something individual and authentic. Insofar, Umberto Eco (1989: 165) e.g. describes Style as a very personal, unrepeatable and characteristic "way of forming"—the recognizable trace that an artist leaves in his/her work and which coincides with the way a work is formed.

In the further remarks I will discuss the conception of style by Ludwig Wittgenstein because it leads to insightful conclusions on the *speakable* and the *unspeakable* as well as on the *fragment*. These assertions, that have their roots at authors like Goethe or thinkers of romantic philosophy, can be regarded as a key to understanding the complex problems within organizations of our time. There it is not possible to verbalize all kinds of information (Tsoukas 2005: 133) and we have to handle the gaps between fragments.

BY READING THESE CONCEPTS OF WITTGENSTEIN WE HAVE TO TAKE INTO ACCOUNT THAT HE NEVER WROTE A REALLY COHERENT TEXT AS IS COMMON PRACTICE IN ACADEMIC SOCIETY.

All we know about Wittgenstein's philosophical reflections is mediated to us via fragments like in the *Tractatus*, in his *Vermischte Bemerkungen* as well as in his dictionary for elementary schools. If we agree with McLuhan's opinion that *"the medium is the message"* this means that we can assume an interrelation between the text and the style in which it is mediated to us. Wittgenstein's style of philosophy represents exactly this interrelation and permanent play between form and content, silence and voice. Consequently, I will not only focus on the content of Wittgenstein's rather isolated texts but also on the context or the gaps between these fragments. Wittgenstein himself once said that only in the stream of life had words their meaning.

Seedless: The "Fruits" from the Tree of Knowledge

"THAT FRUITFULNESS ALONE IS TRUE." JOHANN WOLFGANG VON GOETHE (TESTAMENT, 1829)

The statement above seems to be a daring one of Goethe's and was written during his last years—in the context of a poem about a life devoted to truth (Goethe 1994: 220–221). It maybe seems so bold because it tempts us to daring interpretations and conclusions. One interpretation of this kind would be to say that true is only what is useful, practicable, and what gives us gratification. This rather utilitarian interpretation sees the fruit, because of their seeds, mostly from a perspective of production and further reproduction. The problem caused by this view is that the purpose of reproduction is likely to become an end in itself. The fruit, or in correlation with this metaphor, the *"truth"* has not got the purpose to be nutritious and tasty any longer but to grow more fruits and by this fact we can also see an approach for a critique of science which is maybe part of the motif in Goethe's Faust—especially in the second part.

For a better understanding of what Goethe means with fruitfulness and truth we also have to look at the context in which Goethe uses the word *"truth"*. In the afterword of the Hamburger Goethe-edition, Carl Friedrich von Weizsäcker observes that Goethe does not use the word

"truth" (Wahrheit) as a predicate belonging to judgments and that this *"truth"* is also something other than *"truthfulness" (Wahrhaftigkeit)*, which is *inter alia* expressed in religious confessions. What is true, for Goethe, is equal to what is *"natural"*; and what he calls the *"healthy"* or the *"capable"* is often implied in this concept of truth. Truth is the presence of the appearance's essence. In this sense, Goethe judges for example a man as a "true man" (Weizäcker 1955: 549–550).

Insofar, as the essence is at work in the entirety of the appearances—even in myself as a part of this entirety—I have the ability to contemplate parts or fragments of this entirety and in one of his epigrams of the *Alterswerke* Goethe (1981: 304) writes: *"Willst du dich am Ganzen erquicken,/So mußt du das Ganze im Kleinsten erblicken"* meaning that: If you want to enjoy the whole you have to see the whole in the smallest. If my judgment, my way of thinking, my attitude, or my actions are *"true"* they are necessarily *"fruitful"* too because from the fragment—wherein the essence of the whole is present—the richness of the whole can be seen as a predicate for proving the truth. What one regards as truth depends on what one has confidence in. To have confidence in something or someone is not so much a matter of opinion or decision but of an individual way of life or style (Weizsäcker 1955: 550) and in this we can recognize some interesting parallels with Wittgenstein's concept of style.

Dogma and Style

Wittgenstein also demands constant attention to change in details instead of summarizing the whole in so-called universal propositions or formulae, which has great relevance for decision making in organizations within a context of permanent change and unpredictable or rather ambivalent situations.

This similarity between Goethe's *Morphology of Plants* (1817)—which stands in the centre of this comparison—and Wittgenstein's works (e.g. *Philosophical Investigations*) is mentioned by Garver (1994: 199) who writes about the latter one: "He points out, for example: 'Natur hat weder Kern noch Schale' (Nature has neither seed nor peel). The idea is that nature cannot be described or understood by the words that are perfectly in order once nature and natural phenomena are accepted as a given. Nuts and fruits have kernels (seeds) and peels (shells), but this familiar truth makes no sense unless we have already taken for granted something that itself has neither a seed nor a skin, namely, the natural world of plants and trees."

FURTHERMORE, GOETHE'S AND ESPECIALLY WITTGENSTEIN'S NOTION OF TRUTH IMPLIES ANOTHER IMPORTANT ELEMENT, NAMELY, THAT IT ALSO DEPENDS ON EACH OF US IN WHAT WE CAN HAVE CONFIDENCE.

Truth is nothing universal but often something quite individual and in some cases even something which is impossible to share with other individuals—that also means that for complex organizations we have to assume that there is knowledge that cannot be verbalized with common instruments of knowledge management.
Therefore, style is an individual way to approach, experience, and define truth. Both ideas of truth are extremely vivid in comparison to a positivist approach of searching for universal propositions and formulas; we can realize this vividness, for example, again in Goethe's *Morphology of Plants* when he claims that a really educated person has to submit to a permanent process of re-education because if we want to achieve a lively notion of nature we have to become as flexible and agile as our object of study, as nature itself (1981: 56).

Continuing this metaphor of nature and epistemology, we have to ask what a fruit which has neither seed nor peel really means. Although there are seedless *"fruits"* (e.g. grapes and oranges) available in supermarkets, from a logical point of view, they are contradictions in themselves because they can no longer be fruits if they are not *"fruitful"* in the reproductive sense of the word. The seedless fruit is reduced to only one purpose or one clip of reality, to our everyday *"practice"* of eating fruits because of their healthy nutrition and their good taste; but due to the fact that it is possible to produce for example vitamins in the form of pills

we can say that in our time the seedless fruit is more or less a pure matter of taste. If a fruit has no seeds and therefore no longer represents what we regard as a fruit it would also have nothing to protect and it would consequently need no peel anymore. The seedless *"fruit"* does not exist for reproduction but for pleasure and consumption. Although— or because—it is not fruitful, for us as consumers, it is especially fruity and therefore more and more determines our picture of a fruit.

For Wittgenstein, the individual is also purely constituted by the power of the image or by style. *"Wrong"* behavior is equal to *"faults"* in one's *"own style"* which have to be accepted *"almost like the blemishes"* in one's face (Wittgenstein 1988: 86e). In this sense, Wittgenstein agrees with Buffon's dictum of style when he writes: *"Le style c'est l'homme"*, *"Le style c'est l'homme meme"*. The first expression has cheap epigrammatic brevity. The second, correct version opens up quite a different perspective. It says that a (wo-)man's style is a picture of him/her (1988: 78e)

Consequently, style is not only a decorating, fashionable and outwardly directed course of actions but it also corresponds with the person himself/herself. Exactly in this point of view Joachim Schulte sees the concurrence between Goethe and Wittgenstein: Both lay the particular emphasis on the individual achievement: The great works of art are exceptions, not comparable with other works. If we look, for example, at a symphony by Beethoven, Wittgenstein is of the opinion that it is no longer possible to judge it according to the categories of "right" and "wrong". Such great works exclude themselves from a critical judgment because they do not fit into a framework like this.

THEY ARE NOT AN EXEMPLARY MODEL FOR IMITATION BUT FOR AN EXTRAORDINARY ACHIEVEMENT—A QUALITY BEYOND ARTISTIC CRAFTSMANSHIP (SCHULTE 1990: 63–64).

Insofar, we also can see an affinity to Roland Barthes's notion of style. For Barthes, style is something biological or

biographical, which means that it cannot be separated from the person creating it: *"Style is never anything but metaphor"* and, according to Barthes, these metaphors are expressed in a certain language:
"[...] which has its roots only in the depths of the author's personal and secret mythology, that subnature of expression where the first coition of words and things takes place, where once and for all the great verbal themes of his existence come to be installed. Whatever its sophistication, style has always something crude about it: it is a form with no clear destination, the product of a thrust, not an intention, and, as it were, a vertical and lonely dimension of thought. Its frame of reference is biological or biographical, not historical: it is the writer's 'thing', his glory and his prison, it is his solitude. Indifferent to society and transparent to it, a closed personal process, it is in no way the product of a choice or of a reflection on Literature. It is the private portion of the ritual, it rises up from the writer's myth-laden depths and unfolds beyond his area of control. It is the decorative voice of hidden, secret flesh, it works as does Necessity, as if, in this kind of floral growth, style were no more than the outcome of a blind and stubborn metamorphosis starting from a sub-language elaborated where flesh and external reality come together." (1977: 11)

FOR BARTHES AS WELL AS FOR WITTGENSTEIN STYLE CAN BE REGARDED AS A PERMANENT PRACTICE OR THE ENDLESS WORKING ON ONESELF.

Style is the shaping of the picture of an individual (Wiesing 1992: 120) in which this picture can be considered as an allegory. In contrast to a portrait—in which the spectrum of an interpretation is limited to the signified object and to at least one of its characteristics up to its complete identity with the model—the picture as an allegory can in every imaginable way be connected with what it is derived from (Haller 1990: 10–11). This notion of style and picture is also expressed in one of Wittgenstein's reflections:
The effect of making men think in accordance with dogmas, perhaps in the form of certain graphic propositions, will be very peculiar: I am not thinking of these dogmas as

determining men's opinions but rather as completely controlling the expression of all opinions. People will live under an absolute, palpable tyranny, though without being able to say they are not free. I think the Catholic Church does something rather like this. For dogma is expressed in the form of an assertion, and is unshakeable, but at the same time any practical opinion can be made to harmonize with it; admittedly more easily in some cases than in others. It is not a wall setting limits to what can be believed, but more like a brake which, however, practically serves the same purpose; it's almost as though someone were to attach a weight to your foot to restrict your freedom of movement. This is how dogma becomes irrefutable and beyond reach of attack. (198: 28e)

The process of giving meaning to a dogma does not happen through its content but through its form or the pictoriality and vividness of a proposition. For Wittgenstein, pictures or respectively their diverse possibilities for imagination dominate humankind in a more subtle and radical way than dogmatism. Pictures do not demand concrete rules or commandments but form the basis of the regulations of the human possibilities of expression. The content of a dogma leaves open such a wide room for interpretation that virtually every opinion can be brought into accord with it, and this would also mean that virtually no opinion can be brought into accord with the dogma—as it was, for example, the case in the history of the Inquisition. In contrast to the form, the content of a dogma does not constitute the individual attitude (Wiesing 1992: 120).

With such radicality which is implied in this observation we approach the heart of the discussion about rules in the *Philosophical Investigations* or respectively the paradox of the concept of rules: 201. This was our paradox: no course of action could be determined by a rule, because every course of action can be made out to accord with the rule. The answer was: if everything can be made out to accord with the rule, then it can also be made out to conflict with it. And so there would be neither accord nor conflict here. It can be seen that there is a misunderstanding here from the mere fact that in the course of our argument we give one interpretation after another; as if each one contented us at least for a moment, until we thought of yet another standing behind it. What this shows is that there is a way of grasping a rule which is not an interpretation, but which is exhibited in what we call "obeying the rule" and "going against it" in actual cases. Hence there is an inclination to say: every action according to the rule is an interpretation. But we ought to restrict the term "interpretation" to the substitution of one expression of the rule for another. (Wittgenstein 1953, § 201)

In this paragraph Wittgenstein asks how it is possible that we are following rules if they do not *"automatically"* imply that they are obeyed in the sense of a causal determination or a law of nature? If a rule exists to regulate something then it simultaneously assumes the possibility of a contradictory behavior. Therefore, the rule exists because of its contradiction, and exceptions to the rule are only the consequence of another interpretation.

WITHOUT THIS INTERPRETATION WE WOULD NOT BE ABLE TO UNDERSTAND THE NOTION OF REGULARITY AND WITHIN A SYSTEM WITHOUT DIFFERENT AND ALSO CONTRADICTORY KINDS OF BEHAVIOR WE DO NOT HAVE THE OCCASION OF REFLECTING THE SENSE OF A RULE AND CONSEQUENTLY THE RULE ITSELF.

This paradox can be seen as the outcome of the attempt to save the explanation as a useful methodological instrument and to bring the rule and its obedience into a certain relation through interpretation. But this implies that it becomes impossible to gain precisely the definite relation which was acknowledged in its existence before. Apparently, this special relation has to be denied as long as the presence of one interpretation refers to the absence of other interpretations (Ohler 1990: 30). In this context, Bouveresse presents a helpful distinction between a cause (as in the case of strict natural laws) and motives (as in the nature of an interpretation). The motive is a kind of interpretation that we assign to our actions. This interpretation is surely not completely arbitrary but it strongly depends on the— individual way (or style) of *"seeing"*. The motive makes our actions intelligible and endows them with meaning and

the diversity of motives is in essence nothing else than the diversity of possible interpretations that come to our mind (also and especially through the presence of rules) when we attempt to understand our actions. Bouveresse concludes that "[. ..] in the language of Wittgenstein, the exploration of motives on the whole invokes the 'aesthetic' explanation in the larger sense than the causal explanation properly speaking." (1995: 78–81).

According to this notion, style cannot be derived from a knowledge of rules *(Regelkenntnis)* in a deductive way and therefore it cannot be imitated by simply obeying a particular set of rules. What is regulated by rules belongs to a universal sphere and style, which cannot be grasped by rules, belongs to the sphere of the individual. Again, we can see Goethe's influence. In this respect, it is impossible to gain individuality out of the knowledge of rules, it is as such not universal and it is justified to argue that an individual style can be subsumed under the non-grammatical and paralinguistic means of expression (Frank 1989: 30).

Humankind mutates from a rational being to an imaginative being that is no longer in search of truth but style. This approach makes the aesthetizising of truth possible in order to defend the plurality of different opinions and therein we maybe can see the formulation of Wittgenstein's basic idea: there are forms of representation which are independent of the content, as Wittgenstein says, and they determine the expression of opinions. These forms of representation are the pictorial proposition of a person and therefore he agrees with Buffon's comment that style is the picture of a person. Due to this perspective, the identity of an individual is based on his/her style and with this Wittgenstein implements a concept of style into anthropology which has originally been developed in the history of art (e.g. Wölfflin, Freyer): constraints of expression determine the human being or, in other words, style instead of truth becomes important for imaginative beings like us.

This idea of style instead of truth sounds familiar when we think of Nietzsche who regarded absolute truth as something impossible and acknowledged the arts as its substitute too. For him, the only truth humankind is faced with is that it has to live without it. We can see in the following quotation from

Heller that Nietzsche's rejection of truth, and therefore of representation through language, is the consequence of the assumed *"death of God"*; and I imagine that in Wittgenstein's case things were the other way round, namely, that he increasingly began to doubt all certainties because of his investigations of language.

"In Nietzsche's thought, the persistent misgiving that the established conventions of philosophical language did not cater for our 'real' intellectual needs was only one fact of his central thesis: With the death of God, with the silencing of that Word which was in the beginning, all certainties of faith, belief, metaphysics, morality, and knowledge had come to an end, and henceforward man was under the terrible compulsion of absolute freedom from thought, the threat of unlimited intellectual license. His choice was that of either creating, with surpassing creativity of the Creator, his own world, or of spiritually perishing. For the world as it is has neither meaning nor value, meaning and value must be given to it: by God or by man himself. If God is dead and man fails, then nothing in this world has any value and our own language deceives us with all its ancient intimidations of higher meanings." (Heller 1990: 153)

Beyond Logic and Explanation

In general, Wittgenstein does not only describe human behavior but also thinking as a phenomenon of style and his questioning of propositions becomes transformed into a question of form through his style-instead-of-truth-thinking. One of the most evident examples for this shift can be found in his *Tractatus*. In its foreword we can read the following: "Its whole meaning could be summed up somewhat as follows: What can be said at all can be said clearly; and whereof one cannot speak thereof one must be silent." (1951: 27)

Obviously, the main problem with which Wittgenstein faced in this book was the problem of drawing *"a limit to thinking"*, a line between the meaningfully expressible and the inexpressible. The area of the expressible should be separated from the inexpressible. Therefore, it is necessary that both sides of the limit are accessible to thinking: "[...] for, in order to draw a limit to thinking we should have to be able to think both sides of this limits (we should therefore have to be able to think what cannot be

thought)." (1951: 27) Accordingly, it seems that Wittgenstein saw his task in finding a medium functioning as an alternative to all kinds of terminology *(Begrifflichkeit)*. His suggestion for the solution of this problem can be seen in the following: "There is indeed the inexpressible. This shows itself [...]" (1951: 6.522) because there is, as Manfred Frank points out explicitly, a phenomenon exactly at the borderline between the expressible and the inexpressible; and this *"third"* is style. Style is able to offer a medium for the inexpressible because it pictures or illustrates its sense in a subtle and sensitive way (Frank 1989: 28); even in senseless propositions:

"My propositions are elucidatory in this way: he who understands me finally recognizes them as senseless, when he has climbed out through them, on them, over them. (He must so to speak throw away the ladder, after he has climbed up on it.)" (1951: 6.54)

FOR THIS REASON IT IS NOT POSSIBLE TO USE LANGUAGE ONLY IN AN INSTRUMENTAL WAY.

Language neither descends from a causal nexus nor does it follow a unified telos. It does not serve exclusively as a means of representation and therefore it does not automatically lead to understanding or to a compromise. (Mersch 1991: 35). Consequently, Wittgenstein compares our use of language and signs with playing a game:
"I shall in the future again and again draw your attention to what I shall call language games. These are ways of using signs simpler that those in which we use signs of our highly complicated everyday language. Language games are the forms of language with which a child begins to make use of words. The study of language games is the study of primitive forms of language or primitive languages. If we want to study the problems of truth and falsehood, of the agreement and disagreement of propositions with reality, of the nature of assertion, assumption, and question, we shall with great advantage look at primitive forms of language in which these forms of thinking appear without the confusing background of highly complicated processes of thought." (1969: 17)

Wittgenstein uses the concept of a game as a means of comparison. Language games regulate our talking about the world through semantic and syntactic preconditions in their grammar. In this context, the idea of rules enables an authentic practical contemplation independently from causality and teleology. Moreover, it opens a perspective beyond logic and explanation which is why we follow rules "blindly". Susan Brill writes that our "rules for language games (such as the underlying critical theories upon which actual critical work is based) are like signposts. The rules (or theories) determine the general direction and define the language games themselves" without either completely fixing or wholly determining the play or applications (1995: 56)

To make this clear, Brill (1995: 118) makes use of the comparison between a language game and a chess game: "[...] within the bounds of a particular language game, only the fundamental defining rules of the game (its essential grammar) are immutable. (Of course, those rules may change, but then we would have a different game.) However, the way in which those rules are applied is not completely restricted or predetermined (as in the case of chess moves)."

"Therefore, Wittgenstein describes the language game as the 'Hinzunehmende' which means that it is something that we have to accept or to take for granted (Wittgenstein 1953: §§ 217–219) and he regards language 'as a practice involving various skills and forms of knowledge rather than language as a deep structure of rules which could be reduced to theoretical knowledge (episteme)' (Steuermann 1992: 114), that has an enormous impact on how we look at an organization."

Language seems to have lost its two main functions, namely, representation and legitimation, or respectively both have collapsed into each other. We can now choose between the following "alternatives": Either we live with contradictions or with tautologies.

Conclusion

"YOU SEE, THE WORLD IS IN FRAGMENTS, SIR. NOT ONLY HAVE WE LOST OUR SENSE OF PURPOSE, WE HAVE LOST THE LANGUAGE WHEREBY WE CAN SPEAK OF IT. THESE ARE NO DOUBT SPIRITUAL MATTERS, BUT THEY HAVE THEIR ANALOGUE IN THE MATERIAL WORLD." PAUL AUSTER (CITY OF GLASS, IN THE NEW YORK TRILOGY)

Central for a conclusion of this paper is Wittgenstein's fragmentary style of writing because it corresponds to many important aspects of his philosophy (e.g. questions of plurality, his aesthetic judgments, the idea of language games etc.). As we have seen in the chapter about Goethe's influence on Wittgenstein, style functions as a connection between the speakable and the unspeakable, and the fragmentary style—as Wittgenstein makes use of it—can be regarded as something which ironically tries to represent the unrepresentable. In this respect, Wittgenstein shares a long tradition, which I finally want to discuss in the context of this essay:

According to Manfred Frank, Wittgenstein's texts are fragments failing to belong to a wholeness which actually cannot be represented in the field of logical and calculated propositions because of the grammar of its language games. Therefore, these fragments are related—presumably unwillingly—to the tradition of early Romantic philosophy (Frank 1989: 34).

For Schlegel, it is the most important task of philosophy to express the infinite although he is aware that it is only possible to say something limited. If one simultaneously has to respect the limits of the speakable but nevertheless wants to transgress them, one has to make perceptible what is said as something which was not actually meant. This is the case in irony which is no pragmatic-syntactic means but a stylistic one. One says something special but in such a way that it suggests one could mean something different. One has to sacrifice the appearance of the ultimate in order to say something infinite (Frank 1989: 31–32). In general, irony is the difference between saying and meaning, and philosophy becomes ironic insofar as on the one hand it is fixed to certain ideals and on the other hand it is in doubt of their existence and content but unable to replace the old ideals by new ones. We can find such irony, for example, in the *Tractatus* when Wittgenstein at first claims that he has solved the essential problems of philosophy and then calls philosophy as such in question and tells us that none of our problems are solved (Schulz 1979: 11). This ironic strategy consists in preprogramming a misunderstanding which is exactly the reason why we become aware of the real problems, why we begin to ask different questions, and finally, why philosophy is still able to teach us something.

SCHLEGEL DOES NOT ONLY TRY TO COMPENSATE THE IMPOSSIBILITY OF REPRESENTING THE INFINITE IN THE FINITENESS OF ALL DISCOURSE THROUGH THE STYLISTIC PRINCIPLE OF IRONY BUT ALSO THROUGH CHOOSING THE FRAGMENTARY GAME.

Due to this, it was essential for him not to mistake the fragment for an aphorism because aphorisms are self-sufficient messages which are insulated towards the outside. In contrast, fragments are not self-sufficient and the plurality in which they appear reflects what Schlegel would call the impossibility and necessity of a sufficient message. As mentioned before, Schlegel postulates that it is necessary to say everything—or even better—the Absolute. This is doomed to fail especially because of the finiteness of our means of representation. However, the plurality of fragments can in terms of Schlegel indicate *(an-deuten)* the unrepresentable wholeness by relativizing itself through contradiction and exclusion. Paradoxically, the unrepresentable becomes represented in an indirect way by the mutual—and ironical—negation of the fragments. This process of indication *(An-Deutung)* also happens through the implementation of poetry into the philosophical

discourse. Philosophy turns into poetry and its fragmentary character represents *ex negativo* what cannot be achieved systematically. We can approach this paradox—which has a similar structure to Wittgenstein's paradox of rules—from the following points of view: it is equally impossible to have a system (because the system presupposes a principle which is unrepresentable) and to have no system (because without the orientation according to such a system the propositions we gain about it would not have the character of fragments and cannot cancel each other out). Due to this paradox, we can only say that what in terms of philosophy has failed (to express the infinite) can possibly and indirectly succeed in aesthetic terms (Frank 1989: 34–35). In this concept one can see the influence of Kant who postulates that it lies in the character of reason to struggle for a systematic wholeness although he doubts if a complete and systematic understanding is actually possible. In his *Kritik der Urteilskraft* the Sublime functions as the example for such an impossibility. To have *the feeling* of the Sublime *(das Gefühl des Erhabenen)* means to be confronted with a complete wholeness or with something Absolutely-Great but due to our limited cognitive faculties we are unable to understand it as such. Therefore, our minds are moved by the imagination of the Sublime in nature and our aesthetic judgments about its beauty are in a state of silent contemplation (Kant 1989: 34–35).

Moreover, Manfred Frank remarks in relation to Schlegel's fragments that the fragment establishes unity and chaos and it is the expression of our consciousness. The fragment's inherent spirit of contradiction *(Widerspruchsgeist)* is a necessary effect of detotalization or de-composition of the highest unity, which is no more a unity of a whole (or of a system) but only a unity of a particular thing and without systematic links to other particular things: out of the fragmentary universe results no system but asystasy, inconstancy, and incoherence (Frank 1989, Einführung in die frühromantische Ästhetik, 297).

If we agree that there are actually parallels between Romantic irony and Wittgenstein's style, we consequently have to admit that Wittgenstein cannot be seen as apolitical or ahistorical anymore. Romanticism propagated the autonomy of the Self and considered the historical development as the reconciliation between nature and freedom. Due to this, thinkers like Schiller (whose aesthetic concept became very influential for philosophical Romanticism) or Fichte were often in conflict with the church (e.g. Fichte's *Atheismusstreit)* or the Absolutist regime.

IN ITS OWN INEXPLICIT AND IRONICAL WAY THE FRAGMENTED CHARACTER OF WITTGENSTEIN'S TEXTS ALSO REFERS TO A POLITICAL AND HISTORICAL DIMENSION.

For Wittgenstein, fragmentation is not only connected with the object of his thinking; it also reveals an intuitive understanding of the time when he made use of this style (Stern 1990: 28).

The social inclination towards fragmentation *inter alia* caused by the industrial standardization of cultural products, by the growing importance of advertising, and by economic processes of diversification—was already evident during his lifetime and in our times this tendency has reached its provisional climax due to the possibilities for the excessive use of the electronic media (channel hopping, network surfing, e-mail, clip aesthetics, twittering etc.).

Wittgenstein was quite skeptical towards new socio-cultural shifts in his later life. What concerns these shifts, his typically fragmented style is maybe a—parodistic or ironic reflexion of contemporary transitions of the culture industry. Whereas the fragments of our culture industry have the character of calculation because they are part of a system of industrial s(t)imulated diversity, Wittgenstein's fragmented texts have a contemplative character because of their immense abundance of metaphors. What is artistic in the context of Wittgenstein can be regarded as artificial in the context of our culture industry.

Wittgenstein's texts are the cause for further speculation in contrast to the *"cool"* products of our culture industry which are the effect of (commercial) speculation. In this respect,

we can again see an affinity with Heidegger and especially with Heidegger's critique of the processes of concretization *(Verdinglichung)*.

The consequence of this critical attitude, as Richard Rorty emphasizes in his *Philosophy and the Mirror of Nature*, was that Heidegger tried to discover new philosophical categories, which should have nothing to do with science, epistemology, or the Cartesian search for certainty, and that Wittgenstein elaborated a new theory of representation which should not have anything to do with our traditional mentalism (Rorty 1987: 15). In order to discover new philosophical categories or to elaborate a new theory of representation, Wittgenstein—and e.g. also Heidegger—had to investigate the relation between language and existence. Whereas Wittgenstein's emphasis lay maybe more on language (e.g. on the analysis of language games), Heidegger's lay more on existence (e.g. existential hermeneutics).

It is maybe a fruitful approach, as Thomas Rentsch suggests, to analyze the Wittgensteinian work within this context of a critique of the processes of concretization (1985: 178–179). In the foreword of his *Philosophical Remarks (Philosophische Bemerkungen)* Wittgenstein, for example, sets two different existential attitudes, namely technology and contemplation, against each other (1964: 4) and the techno-civilization represents the *Zeitgeist* which is confronted with his spirit of contradiction *(Widerspruchsgeist)*. It is also quite evident throughout Culture and Value that Wittgenstein was critical of cultural transitions and a style of thinking determined by the belief in the progress of the technological—scientific civilization which goes along with the loss of artistic sense. Although this style was unappealing and even disgusting for him he did not want to condemn it as immoral because from his point of view the disappearance of a certain culture is not equal to the disappearance of human values (Schulte 1990: 60).

Apart from Wittgenstein, there are some similar attempts to propagate and use a fragmented style of writing as a means for the critique of our culture industry. In this respect, I first think of Adorno (1973: 36) who follows the Kantian tradition by claiming that: "Only a philosophy in fragment form would give their proper place to the monads, those illusory idealistic drafts. They would be conceptions, in the particular, of the totality that is inconceivable as such".

Moreover, one can think of the fragmented style of *The Medium is the Massage* by Marshall McLuhan and Quentin Fiore which critically parodies the permanent manipulation (or the massage of our brains through messages) by the media; and appropriate as an example for fragmentation is also Roland Barthes's *Roland Barthes*. In her introduction to *A Barthes Reader,* Susan Sontag (1982: xvi) writes the following about Barthes and his use of a fragmented style: "Much of his writing proceeds by techniques of interruption, sometimes in the form of an excerpt alternating with a disjunctive commentary, as in Michelet and S/Z. To write in fragments or sequences or 'notes' entails new, serial (rather than linear) forms of arrangements. These sequences may be staged in some arbitrary way. For example, they may be numbered—a method practiced with great refinement by Wittgenstein. Or they may be given headings, sometimes ironic or overemphatic—Barthes's strategy in Roland Barthes. Headings allow an additional possibility: for the elements to be arranged alphabetically, to emphasize further the arbitrary character of their sequence—the method of A Lover's Discourse (1977), whose real title evokes the notion of the fragment; it is Fragments d'un discours amoureux."

To choose *"serial forms"* for writing philosophical texts has the advantage that it is easier to demarcate the bounds of the speakable and the unspeakable; and according to Garry Hagberg, exactly this "strict demarcation of the bounds of the intelligible is of course the objective of the Tractatus" (Hagberg 1994: 21). In this respect, style becomes a means to communicate the sense of the unintelligible because style is able *to show* meaning without postulating compulsory and universal rules for its understanding. This approach of an extreme aesthetic thinking which is central to this essay would consequently lead to the abolition of the traditional limits between scientific discourse and artistic practice.

If we agree with Haridimos Tsoukas who postulates that within organization we also have to deal with knowledge

that cannot be verbalized and that *"it is precisely the interdependence of chaos and cosmos that makes organizational life patterned yet indeterminate"* (Tsoukas 2003: 619) this concept of style and fragmentation can be regarded as very fruitful—especially when our means of verbalization are generally regarded as the capital of the future. Aesthetic approaches like that of Wittgenstein open up new ways to get access to this hidden kind of knowledge via metaphors or e.g. in particular through mood charts produced by designers.

In the context of the paradox of the concept of rules we can see that a huge potential for organizations lies in an approach that negates the idea of a fixed identity and a certain "inner logic" (Tsoukas 2003: 619) in favor of a notion of an organization that is permanently changing and re-defining itself and therefore is also able to actively form its future.

An impressive example for this kind of practice that is combined with a learning process is given by the new layout of the Oxford Circus in London. Before, the crossing with its conventional settlement was not able to handle the huge frequency of people. More than 200 million of visitors a year are using this area with peaks of around 40,000 an hour.

THAT WAS THE REASON WHY THE CITY OF LONDON DECIDED TO MAKE A REDESIGN BASED ON THE SO-CALLED CONCEPT OF "ANT CROSSINGS" IN TOKYO.

The new design, which was presented in November 2009, stops all traffic in all directions and allows people to cross straight ahead as well as diagonally. Consequently, for a very short time there are no strict rules for the pedestrians why they have to adopt and find the best solution for themselves using their common sense and acting responsible. The effect of that self-organizing process is that it became possible to remove barriers and to widen the pavement, giving 70 percent more space for the people and also reducing the risk of becoming a victim of pick-pockets (Walker 2009).

References

Auster, P. 1987. *City of glass, in The New York Trilogy.* London & Boston: Faber and Faber.

Barthes, R. 1977. *Writing degree zero, selected and trans.* Annette Lavers and Colin Smith. New York: Hill and Wang.

Bouveresse, J. 1995. *Wittgenstein reads Freud: The myth of the unconscious, trans.* Princeton: Princeton University press.

Flusser, V. 2000. *Ins Universum der technischen Bilder.* Göttingen: European Photography.

Eco, U. 1989. *The role of the reader. Explorations in the semiotics of texts.* London: Hutchinson.

Frank, M. 1989. *Wittgensteins Gang in die Dichtung.* In M. Frank and G. Soldati, *Wittgenstein. Literat und Philosoph.* Pfullingen: Neske.

Frank, M. 1989. *Einführung in die frühromantische Ästhetik: Vorlesungen.* Frankfurt a. M.: Suhrkamp.

Garver, N. and Seung-Chong L. 1994. *Derrida and Wittgenstein.* Philadelphia: Temple University Press.

Goethe, J. W. von. 1981. *Goethes Werke. Erich Trunz (Eds.), Vol. I, Gedichte und Epen.* München: Ch. Beck.

Goethe, J. W. von. 1994. *Vermächtnis. In Gedichte.* Stuttgart: Reclam.

Hagberg, G. 1994. *Meaning and interpretation: Wittgenstein, Henry James, and literary knowledge.* New York: Cornell University Press.

Haller, R. 1990. *Wie man nicht mit dem Hammer philosophiert.* In W. Schmidt-Dengler, M. Huber, and M. Huter (Eds.), *Wittgenstein und.* Wien: Edition S.

Kant, I. 1963. *Analytik des Erhabenen. In: Kritik der Urteilskraft.* Stuttgart: Reclam.

Mersch, D. (Ed). 1991. *Gespräche über Wittgenstein.* Wien: Passagen Verlag.

Ohler, M. 1990. *Sprachphilosophie oder Sprachwissenschaft? In F. Wallner and A. Haselbach (Eds.), Wittgensteins Einfluß auf die Kultur der Gegenwart,*

Philosophica 9. Wien: Wilhelm Braumüller.

Rorty, R. 1987. *Der Spiegel der Natur: Eine Kritik der Philosophie.* Frankfurt a. M.: Suhrkamp.

Schulte, J. 1990. *Chor und Gesetz: Wittgenstein im Kontext.* Frankfurt a. M.: Suhrkamp.

Schulz, W. 1979. *Wittgenstein: Die Negation der Philosophie.* Pfullingen: Neske.

Sontag, S. 1982. *Writing itself: On Roland Barthes, introduction to a Barthes reader, S. Sontag (Ed.).* London: Jonathan Cape.

Stern, J. P. 1990. *Literarische Aspekte der Schriften Ludwig Wittgensteins. in: W. Schmidt-Dengler, M. Huber, and M. Huter (Eds.), Wittgenstein und.* Wien: Edition S.

Steuerman, E. 1992. *Habermas vs. Lyotard: Modernity vs. Postmodernity. In A. Benjamin (Ed.), Judging Lyotard.* London and New York: Routledge.

Tsoukas, H. 2003. *New Times, Fresh Challenges. In H. Tsoukas and C. Knudsen (Eds.), The Oxford handbook of organization theory.* New York: Oxford University Press.

Tsoukas, H. 2005. *Complex knowledge: studies in organizational epistemology.* New York: Oxford University Press.

Weizsäcker, C. F. von. 1955. *Nachwort. In Goethes Werke, Vol. XIII, Naturwissenschaftliche Schriften.* Hamburg: Christian Wegner Verlag.

Walker, P. 2009. *X marks the spot: new Oxford Circus crossing opens. In: Guardian, Nov. 2nd.* http://www.guardian.co.uk/uk/2009/nov/02/x-oxford-circus-crossing

Winkler, W. 2008. *Der Mann, der das Pixel erfand. Interview with Steven J. Sasson. In: Süddeutsche Zeitung. Nov. 25th,* http://www.sueddeutsche.de/computer/581/331440/text/

Wittgenstein, L. 1953. *Philosophical investigations, trans. G. E. M. Anscombe.* Oxford: Basil Blackwell, 1953.

Wittgenstein, L. 1964. *Philosophische Bemerkungen.* Frankfurt a. M.: Suhrkamp.

Wittgenstein, L. 1969. *The blue and the brown books.* Oxford: Basil Blackwell.

Sometimes, one could argue, in order for democracy to emerge, democracy itself has to be avoided at all cost. In order to make decisions within any given collaborative structure, network or institution, conflicts can ultimately only be overcome if someone assumes responsibility.

Gustav Metzger once said: "I relate my approach to homeopathy, which puts poison in the system in order to generate energy to defeat the weakness." In this context, let us imagine a post-consensual practice, one that is no longer reliant on the often ill-defined modes of operating within politically complex and consensus-driven parties or given political constructs, but instead formulate a necessity to undo the innocence of participation.

We are currently experiencing a point of transition within participatory practices: within politics, within the Left, within spatial practices and—foremost—within architecture as its visible and most clearly defined product. Participation, both historically and in terms of political agency, is often being read through romantic notions of negotiation, inclusion and democratic decision-making. However, it is precisely this often-unquestioned mode of inclusion being used by populist politicians as a mode of campaigning for retail politics. Hence, it does not produce critical results as criticality is being challenged by the conception of majority. Let us instead imagine a conflictual reading of participation as a mode of practice, one that opposes the brainwave of the democratic facilitator: one that has to assume, at times, non-physical violence and singular decision-making in order to produce frameworks for change.

AS A NEXT STEP, LET US CHALLENGE THE IDEA THAT—IN GENERAL—PEOPLE HAVE GOOD INTENTIONS. CONVENTIONAL MODELS OF PARTICIPATION ARE BASED ON INCLUSION.

They assume that inclusion goes hand in hand with a standard that is the democratic principle of everyone's voice having an equal weight within egalitarian society. Usually, the simple fact that one proposes a structure or situation in which this bottom-up inclusion is being promoted, the political actor or agency proposing it will be most likely be understood as a "do-gooder", social actor or even philanthropist. Interestingly, the model of the "curator", for example, is essentially based on the practice of making decisions and therefore eliminating choice rather than boosting plurality by inclusion. In the face of permanent crisis, both the Left and the Right have celebrated participation as the savior from all evil, an unquestioned form of soft politics. But can we employ the idea of crisis to question our deepest assumptions? Should we rethink our values and devise new principles for action?

Let us imagine a conception of participation as a way to enter politics—proactively and consciously forcing us

into existing power-relations by intent—as opposed to a politically motivated model of participation, which tends to propose to let others contribute to the decision-making process. The latter, we might think, is habitually stirred by the craving for political legitimization. The former may be of interest not out of disbelief of democratic principles per se, but out of sheer interest in critical and productive change.

ONE COULD ARGUE THAT THIS MODEL INHABITS A CERTAIN OPPORTUNISM.

Yes and no. It challenges the widespread default that majority equals judiciousness, while arguing for a pro-active citizenship in which the individual outsider to a given inbred political structure can become a driving force for change: forcefully entering an existing discourse rather than opening it up to the floor. Remaining within the arena of "the democratic", let us instead bastardize participation into a form of non-democratic practice, an opportunistic model of interventionism, in which interference is made possible due to the fact that one is no longer following existing protocols of internalized political struggle. Such model, we could then argue, is that of Crossbench Practice.

Let us imagine this as an ongoing project. Let us begin now. As a first step, let us attempt to open up a new language of practice, a field of operation rather than confronting an existing one. Within this frame, let us unleash a series of experiments that shall be conducted over time. Each of those experiments shall be directed towards the undoing of the innocence of participation. Some of them may be text-based, others set up as projects, yet again others as urban interventions or institutional models—small-scale local test-grounds for change.

Each one of those projects to come shall be understood as particles within a galactic model, in which planets are circulating around an empty void. This void may be loaded with a model for practice by the end of the experiment. The model may present and open questions neither hierarchically organized nor in a field, but in form of a galaxy: a relational model that challenges political romanticism in order to open up the potentiality for a more diffused form of work.

Within a series of case studies conducted over the past years, this pamphlet is the third component within a tripartheid structure that attempts to question existing notions of participatory practice, resulting from increasing gradients of political disillusionment: the first one simply